Strangers in the Wild Place

Strangers in the Wild Place

REFUGEES, AMERICANS, AND A GERMAN TOWN, 1945–1952

Adam R. Seipp

INDIANA UNIVERSITY PRESS   *Bloomington & Indianapolis*

This book is a publication of

INDIANA UNIVERSITY PRESS
601 North Morton Street
Bloomington, Indiana 47404-3797 USA

iupress.indiana.edu

Telephone orders 800-842-6796
Fax orders 812-855-7931

© 2013 by Adam R. Seipp

All rights reserved

No part of this book may be reproduced or utilized in any form or by any means, electronic or mechanical, including photocopying and recording, or by any information storage and retrieval system, without permission in writing from the publisher. The Association of American University Presses' Resolution on Permissions constitutes the only exception to this prohibition.

⊖ The paper used in this publication meets the minimum requirements of the American National Standard for Information Sciences – Permanence of Paper for Printed Library Materials, ANSI Z39.48-1992.

*Manufactured in the
United States of America*

Cataloging information is available from the Library of Congress.

ISBN 978-0-253-00677-6 (cloth)
ISBN 978-0-253-00707-0 (eb)

1 2 3 4 5   18 17 16 15 14 13

FOR LESLIE, ROWAN, AND CORA

Contents

Acknowledgments   ix

Introduction   *1*

1 The Wild Place, 1933–1945   20

2 The Seigneurs of Wildflecken, 1945–1947   55

3 Keeping Refugees Occupied, 1945–1948   97

4 These People, 1947–1949   142

5 A Victory for Democracy, 1949–1952   181

Conclusion   223

Notes   233

Bibliography   259

Index   271

Acknowledgments

This book would not exist without the help, guidance, and support of a great many people. For several years, friends, family, and colleagues have had to endure my decidedly Wildflecken-centric view of modern German history. Mostly, they made it possible for me to research, write, and publish a book about a subject that I still find fresh, compelling, and fascinating.

The influence of Konrad H. Jarausch looms large over my efforts to understand German history. His comments at an early stage, along with encouragment by Gerhard Weinberg and Norman Goda, helped to move the project forward. Laura Hilton and Kathy Nawyn were indispendible and patient guides to, respectively, the complexities of the DP camp system and the vagaries of the National Archives. Michael Meng has been a great friend and an intellectual sparring partner who forced me to refine many of my arguments long before they got to print.

Funding for this project came from the German Academic Exchange Service, German Historical Institute – Washington, College of Liberal Arts at Texas A&M, Office of the Vice President for Research, Scowcroft Institute of International Affairs, and the Race and Ethnic Studies Institute. The Center for Advanced Holocaust Studies at the United States Holocaust Memorial Museum both funded part of my research and gave me a congenial spot to work. My thanks especially to Dieter Kuntz, Nicole Frechette, Vincent Slatt, and Eric Steinhart.

Research travel for this project took me to lots of interesting places and gave me the chance to work with some really fascinating people. In Würzburg, Ingrid Heeg-Engelhart at the *Staatsarchiv Würzburg* was a great help making my way through a mass of documentation. Jochen Achilles and Birgit Daewes made my time in the city both productive and a lot of fun. Klaus and Rosemarie Zepke were wonderfully hospitable and generous guides to the place and its history. Andrea Sinn's friendship helped to make Munich an even more terrific place to work. Susanne Urban and Dieter Steinert were immensely helpful in Bad Arolsen, while Panikos Panayi was an amiable companion at the *Bundesarchiv* in Freiburg. Michael Brodhead helped me during my trip to the US Army Corps of Engineers Archive.

The day I arrived on my first visit to Wildflecken, I missed a bus connection, was offered a ride by strangers, and soon found myself invited to a family reunion. What started as a research trip turned into an unforgettable experience with wonderful people. Heinz Leitsch has helped this project along in countless ways. Peter Heil and Bürgermeister Alfred Schrenk were terrific hosts in the local archive. Walter Koempel and Norbert Rueckel offered their time and expertise. Werner and Evelyn Kirchner made me welcome (and kept me well fed) at the Hotel Würzburger Hof. Volker and Maria Zinn of the Kreuzberg-Apotheke opened their home for me and the rest of the NordicTreff Wildflecken, who welcomed me as a temporary teammate and treated me to a *Kulturabend*. I also have to thank the many people around the world who inhabit a virtual community of Wildflecken. Whether as former residents of the DP camp, locals who later emigrated, or American soldiers who came after the story I tell here came to an end, these people have given their time to tell me their stories. Special thanks to Janie Michelli, Andrew Zdanowicz, Chester Wolkonowski, and Dale Pluciennik.

The Department of History at Texas A&M continues to be great place to teach and write history. This has much to do with the successive leadership of Walter Buenger and David Vaught, as well as that of Deans Charles Johnson and José Luis Bermúdez. R. J. Q. Adams, Chip Dawson, Sylvia Hoffert, Walter Kamphoefner, Hoi-eun Kim, Arnold Krammer, Brian Linn, and the members of the Faculty Colloquium series have all been greatly helpful in this process. Chuck Grear did a terrific job with the map. Graduate and undergraduate students have consistently challenged me to find ways to explain the dark heart of Europe's twentieth century in all its complexities. Special thanks to Jared Donnelly, who came through with some last-minute help in locating a photo. Muldoon's Coffee Shop in College Station kept me caffeinated and didn't object as I wrote much of the first draft of this book at a table in the back.

Leslie, Rowan, and Cora have been the center of my world throughout this process. This book would not exist without their love, support, and patience. Good friends have helped to see this project through, hosted me on various trips, and been there for my family while I was away. Special thanks to Matt Woods, Tasha Dubriwny, and Zariana Woods; Dario Vittori; Jonathan L'Hommedieu; Bruce Baker; Norm Leung; Jason, Meg, and Nathan Savage; and Mike, Anna, and Oscar Anderson. My extended family has been a source of support and comfort through all the moves and changes of the past decade.

My grandmother, Virginia Ramsey, died as I finished work on this book. My mother, Catherine Kane, has battled illness with extraordinary courage and strength through much of the time I have been writing. Finally, I want to honor the memory of Officer Stephen Tyrone Johns, who lost his life on June 10, 2009, while protecting hundreds of people, myself included, from a gunman at the United States Holocaust Memorial Museum.

Strangers in the Wild Place

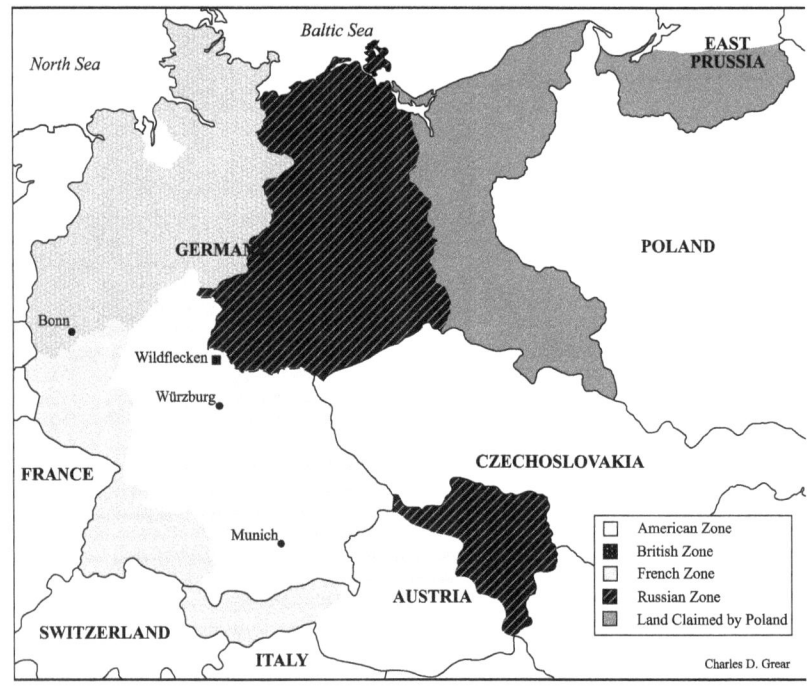

Occupied Germany, 1945–1949. *Prepared by Charles Grear.*

Introduction

This book is an international history of a very small place. Over the course of less than two decades, Wildflecken, a tiny town in northern Bavaria, went through a series of extraordinary and wrenching transformations that mirrored the profound shattering and reformation of political, social, and economic life in mid-twentieth century Germany. An obscure farm town in 1935, Wildflecken became a base community for the rapidly growing German military machine of the late 1930s. In the aftermath of Hitler's disastrous war, American-occupied Wildflecken became a catchment area for several distinct groups of refugees. Just as the refugee crisis began to ebb in the late 1940s, the nascent Cold War escalated, and the American presence, previously declining, dramatically reversed course. For the next forty years, Wildflecken became an American base town, one of many to dot the region as a guarantor of West German security in the midst of a global conflict.

This is a book about land and the strangers who lived there, in close proximity to each other, during the years after the war. The land was a hilly, forested 18,000-acre tract just north of Wildflecken stretching out between the town and the border between Bavaria and the state of Hesse. Over twenty years, different groups and institutions laid claim to that land and asserted their right to make use of it as they saw fit. Military and civilian officials passed countless maps back and forth. They outlined in vivid and contrasting colors the shifting boundaries of a piece of property shaped and re-shaped by events taking place far beyond the valley of the Sinn River.

Strangers came to Sinn Valley by the thousands, beginning with the construction of a Germany military base in 1936. At the end of the war, the pace only quickened as streams of refugees flooded the valley to escape devastated cities, flee the oncoming Red Army, or because they had no way of returning home. To understand Wildflecken is to understand something important about the transformation of West Germany from defeat to stability. In postwar Germany, local and regional politics were dominated by questions of what to do with millions of people made refugees by the war. Debates over their fate had much to do with land and property, which became an issue of sovereignty as West Germany moved toward self-government but continued to play host to hundreds of thousands of occupation troops. To understand this nexus of competing groups, interests, and ideas, one must try to see it from a multitude of perspectives. This book examines the experiences of ethnic German expellees fleeing Eastern Europe, homeless German civilians from heavily bombed urban areas, non-Germans who came from liberated concentration camps, compulsory labor facilities, or from Soviet-dominated Eastern Europe (Displaced Persons or DPs), refugee administrators from both German and United Nations bureaucracies, American soldiers, and the community itself.

Many of these people were strangers to the country, foreigners who found themselves in the Sinn Valley because of the tides of war and the tumult of the postwar period. But all of them were strangers to each other, thrown together by choice and circumstance. While tension and conflict suffused the relationships within and between these groups, there were also opportunities for compromise and coexistence. In the debates over the future of a tract of land in northern Bavaria, the outlines of a plural and democratic Cold War state began to emerge. Out of this experience developed a distinct, stable, and self-consciously West German society from the ruins of dictatorship and defeat.

The creation of civic and governmental institutions in West Germany, and with it the Cold War political and military order in Central Europe, was closely linked to problem of refugees. Refugee policy was a crucial test of German self-government from the beginning of the occupation period. Debates over refugees shaped the creation of German institutions at all levels, from local to federal. Refugees also provided the backdrop for tensions between the West German state, its constituent parts, and the occupying powers. Refugees of all kinds were themselves often actors in these debates. If we are going to understand the central role of refugees in shaping postwar reconstruction and the history of the American military presence in Cold War West Germany, we have to foreground their voices and the voices of those responsible for managing and caring for them. As Paul Steege notes in his study of postwar Berlin, "everyday life" had a great deal to do with how the Cold War came to be and how it became part of the daily experience of those living on its front lines.[1]

There have been a number of excellent local histories of German communities published during the first half of the twentieth century, driven by a new interest in studies that bridge the Nazi and postwar years.[2] Some of the most interesting local studies, like Neil Gregor's work on Nürnberg or Helmut Walser Smith's work on the Prussian town of Konitz, seek to use the local to elucidate themes that connect events at the community level to national and global levels of analysis. Atina Grossmann, in her excellent work in Jewish DPs in postwar Germany, has proposed "entangling" histories of DPs, Germans, and Americans. Drawing upon the insights of Frank Stern, Grossmann describes a triadic relationship through which these groups came to understand themselves and each other in the aftermath of the war.[3] While Grossmann acknowledges the diversity within each of these groups, I would argue that the category of "Germans" was simply too broad, particularly in the immediate aftermath of the war. German refugees, particularly expellees from Eastern Europe, had a very different self-conception and were initially perceived as alien by their unwilling German hosts. This was especially true in small rural communities like Wildflecken where most expellees found themselves. Ethnic German expellees were able to integrate into these communities in part because of the presence of other groups of outsiders, notably DPs and occupation forces.

Wildflecken's story is best told in the manner that Saul Friedländer calls "integrated history," an effort to write the history of a place in a way that reflects the multivariant and multifaceted interactions that took place in and around it.[4] It is possible to write a history of the town of Wildflecken that mentions the DP camp in passing and mostly as a dangerous nuisance, or a study of the American base that stood there for forty years with little mention of the expellee settlements that base construction uprooted.[5] What is missing from these approaches is a sense of the vital interaction between and within each of these units, or the immersion of one small town's tumultuous story within the context of local, regional, national, and international dynamics.

There is also a considerable need to reappraise the periodization of the postwar refugee crisis. DPs, expellees, and occupation troops feature prominently in studies of the postwar "rubble time" (*Trümmerzeit*), a period of about three years dominated by recovery from the physical and emotional destruction of the war.[6] However, the refugee crisis was actually far more pervasive and enduring. The Jewish DP camp at Föhrenwald near the Munich suburb of Wolfratshausen did not close until 1957. Two years later, there were still forty-four camps with about 9,600 refugees from Eastern Europe in Bavaria alone.[7] Expellees and DPs were not just a feature of the immediate postwar period; they were an integral component of the early history of West Germany. Because that history is entangled with the story of the American military presence, these narratives have to be viewed in an integrative, complicated, and fundamentally convergent way.

The integrated history of Wildflecken can only be written from the perspectives of institutions that left their records in Germany, the United States, France, and from personal memories of individuals who have since dispersed around the world. For a few years, events taking place in Wildflecken had implications in Washington, Bonn, Munich, and the district capital of Würzburg. Decisions taken in each of those places not infrequently clashed with those made in the others. Each had a dramatic impact on the day-to-day lives of ordinary people in and around Wildflecken. These interactions at times were quotidian and left few tangible records, as when a young expellee woman married a Polish DP and started a family. They were sometimes broader and more regional, as in the case of networks of black market traders that included DPs, expellees, and locals, along with police sent to break them up. Finally, these interactions played out across a grand stage of international events, as when conservative members of the Bavarian parliament denounced the West German government for giving precedence to the United States

Army over a few hundred farmers in a rural valley in northern Franconia. Such an approach calls for shifts in perspective from the intimate and local to the national and global and for telling stories in a way that is firmly rooted in the discrete chronology of the seven years during which these interactions took place, while embracing the parallel structure of many of the meta-histories examined within.

This book makes two principal arguments. First, during the half-decade following the Second World War, the United States Army found itself deeply engaged with an enormous and unprecedented refugee crisis across occupied and semi-sovereign Germany. Directly and indirectly, American decisions and influence proved decisive in both the successes and failures of refugee management and integration. Second, the presence of non-German "foreigners," notably DPs and American troops, sometimes had the entirely unintended but very important effect of catalyzing the integration of expellee populations into pre-existing communities. In a world filled with foreigners, in which the dynamics of power clearly favored those outsiders, the community of insiders could grow to encompass ethnic Germans who fled their homes in Eastern Europe.

As American attention shifted from the occupation of defeated Germany to the rebuilding of a new Cold War ally, so too did refugee policy. The management of the multiple refugee crises in postwar Germany was a significant component of and challenge to the American occupation and its efforts to set up sustainable institutions in the ruins of Central Europe. Despite the centrality of refugee issues in the day-to-day management of the American occupation, very little attention has been paid to the relationship between occupation troops and the multiple categories of refugees in postwar Germany.[8] Much of what has been written has emphasized the troubled efforts of American Constabulary troops to keep order in the DP camps and the halting, initially uncomprehending American response to the problems of Jewish DPs.[9] Local histories of American occupation often mention the problem of expellees and conflicts over the need for temporary accommodation for them but do not identify the important continuities between American basing needs during the occupation period and the post-1950 creation of permanent bases for Cold War defense.[10] Given that expellees comprised roughly one in five of those Germans living under American occupation, the American military government at all levels had to dedicate a considerable amount of energy to expellee issues. Sylvia Schraut, one of the relatively few scholars to explore this connection directly, concludes that expellees "could not have gained the rights they enjoyed in post-war Germany without the intervention of the American military government."[11]

There has been a great deal of work on the Displaced Persons camp system and on the wider issue of DPs in the postwar years. Historians have examined the creation of DP communities within and outside the camps, the interaction between different groups of DPs and equally diverse German civilians in the wake of the war, the experience of emigration, the subsequent creation of diasporic communities, and the important role that the DP problem played in helping to create the framework for an international humanitarian regime in the second half of the twentieth century.[12] There has been a particular focus on Jewish DPs (the *She'erit Hapletah,* or "surviving remnant"), an important group within the DP universe but by no means the largest.[13] The majority of DPs, Jewish and non-Jewish, came from Eastern Europe and endured some part of the terrible double occupation of Nazi Germany and Stalin's Soviet Union. This not only made many of them hesitant to return home, but also created what Daniel Cohen has recently termed "estrange(ment) from the national body" in the wake of the war that could only be rectified after the end of the Cold War.[14] For most of the Wildflecken DP camp's history, its inhabitants were non-Jewish Poles. The transformation of Eastern Europe during the early Cold War framed discussions within the camp about inhabitants returning home and international debates about what to do with the DP camp system.

The past decade has also seen a tremendous interest in the story of Germans made homeless by the war (*Evakuierte*), the ethnic German expellees who fled or were expelled from East-Central Europe in its wake, and the German communities in which they found themselves.[15] Rainer Schulze's extensive work on Celle, Doris von der Brelie-Lewien's research on Fallingbostel, and Schraut's study of Württemberg-Baden, among others, remind us of the centrality of expellees in the everyday social and political life of occupied and post-sovereign West Germany.[16] Both German and non-German historians free of the Cold War association between expellees and revanchist politics have taken a new look at the East European milieu that produced the expellees, the murderous ethnic politics of the war years, and the experiences of defeat and expulsion. The historian Andreas Kossert's 2008 study *Kalte Heimat,* which attacked many of the comfortable myths of the speedy integration of expellees into their host society, was a commercial and critical success in Germany. Remarkably, the first synthetic study of the expellee crisis did not appear in English until 2007. At the same time, a growing literature on both sides of the Atlantic has questioned the notion that West Germans in the postwar period "forgot" the Nazi and wartime past. As Robert Moeller has argued, "a selective past, a past of German suffering, was in fact ubiquitous in the 1950s."[17] At the core of this narrative of suffering lay the expellees, civilians forced from their homes during or after the war and now reconceptualized innocent victims of Communism.

The problem is that most studies of DPs and expellees treat the two groups in isolation In reality, DP and expellee camps were often in close proximity, and efforts to ameliorate the plight of one group could have a profound effect on the other. Contemporary observers certainly saw these two categories as linked, both through the challenges of refugee management and in their origins in the broader postwar crisis. West German observers in the 1950s tried very hard to place the experience of expulsion within the wider narrative of refugees after the war. The sociologist Elisabeth Pfeil wrote in her 1950 study *Five Years Later* that "the problem appears not just in Germany. If we have 12 million expellees to cope with, Europe has 30 million who had to leave their homes by force or who cannot go back to them."[18] Malcolm Proudfoot, who worked with the DP camp system and became one of its first chroniclers, took a similar line in his posthumously published 1956 study of people made homeless by "policies adopted by Germany and the Soviet Union."[19]

Over the next few decades, the stories of the DPs and the German expellees effectively decoupled. In the wake of the disastrous collapse of Yugoslavia, historians of Europe have focused attention on the European and global phenomena of "ethnic cleansing" and "forced population removal" in the modern world.[20] Timothy Snyder, in his study of Eastern Europe's "bloodlands" has revived this older argument by situating the source of these refugee flows in the geographic zone in which German and Soviet occupation overlapped during the period surrounding the Second World War.²¹ The experience of the expelled ethnic Germans now appears more prominently, but it is difficult to integrate their story with the multifaceted forced and compulsory labor program of the Third Reich, which produced the DP problem. An ambitious and multinational effort to write a history of forced population movements during and after the Second World War, for example, has an awkwardly placed chapter on forced laborers at the very end, with little to tie it to the rest of the book.²² Jessica Reinisch recently noted that there is "no consistent historiography that looks at the many different kinds of refugees and dislocated people in the same context."²³ On the surface, there is good reason for this. DPs were managed by the UN and received considerable assistance from the international community. Expellees, on the other hand, were the responsibility of German authorities. As West German state and local governments grew, so did their capacity to deal with expellee issues. Because neither the UN nor the American occupiers had any mandate to manage expellees, they generally did not play any active role in doing so.

This distinction was far less meaningful in practice than it now appears. These two groups, part of what Wolfram Wette has called "experiences of uprootedness," occupied the same limited space and often had to draw from the same pool of locally available resources.²⁴ Both interacted with each other, with pre-existing communities and, just as crucially, with a new group of strangers in postwar Germany, the Allied troops who transitioned from conquerors to occupiers. Without examining the interactions within and between these very different groups, we cannot understand the uneven, contested, and above all, highly contingent rebuilding of postwar German society. Negotiations between Americans, German administrators, DPs, and ethnic German refugees shaped the physical, political, and cultural landscape of West Germany within the broader framework of the new Cold War world.

For many living in occupied and semi-sovereign West Germany, the DP and expellee issues were not at all distinct. Local communities, many of which faced their own material deprivation, often concluded that neither group had a legitimate claim to material assistance. Certainly, DPs were often regarded as foreigners and subjected to a variety of stereotypes and anxieties about violent crime. Germans perceived the

DPs as a threat and the specter of revenge hung over interactions between locals and those who had recently been the subsumed into Hitler's racial empire. As Richard Bessel has vividly evoked the problem, DPs represented "evidence of a world turned upside down. . . . the victims of the Nazi regime now could victimize their former masters."[25] Similarly, expellees often found themselves unwelcomed guests in a country with its own monumental problems. Expellees were, as a pastor in Lower Saxony described them, "like potato beetles" that devoured more than their fair share of resources in his already suffering region.[26] This pervasive sense of insecurity in the face of refugees was particularly acute in rural and small-town Germany, in large part spared the worst of Allied bombing. There, expellees, DPs, local communities, and occupation troops lived cheek-to-jowl, with important consequences.

The German refugee crisis was primarily a rural and small-town phenomenon. Particularly in the early years, badly damaged cities could not support their own reduced populations, much less encampments of refugees. In Bavaria, which absorbed by far the largest number of expellees, this meant a profound transformation of rural life that Paul Erker has called "de-provincialization."[27] In Bavaria in 1948, sixty percent of expellees lived in communities with less than 2,000 inhabitants. In Lower Franconia, forty-six percent of the 174,000 expellees lived in communities with less than 3,000 people and sixteen percent lived in towns of fewer than five hundred.[28] The question of what do with this new and materially deprived population was also a question of how to transform small towns in rural Germany. Wildflecken is an excellent example of this broader process at work. Part of a region known for terrible rural poverty, the area had seen a number of rural development plans come and go before it became a base community shortly before the outbreak of war. Wildflecken after 1945, like many parts of rural West Germany, found itself torn between competing visions of its postwar future, largely driven by the question of what was to be done with the expellees.[29]

At the same time, DPs had priority in the assignment of potential accommodation space. DP camps, intended to be temporary, ended up proving far more durable than anyone could have anticipated or wanted. In March 1948, Bavaria alone contained 242 DP facilities, the majority in rural or suburban settings. In the Munich area only one of the nine camps operating in 1946 sat near the heart of the city. The others lay either in the suburbs near the industrial facilities or in small towns not far away. The smallest of the camps in Germany held about five hundred DPs. The biggest, with a standing population of around 15,000, was Wildflecken.[30] Some DP facilities comprised just a few buildings. Larger camps, typically outside of devastated cities, were effectively small towns.

Land and infrastructure lay at the heart of an evolving political struggle over the future of the camps and their inhabitants. Initially, officials from the United Nations Relief and Rehabilitation Administration (UNRRA) and their American sponsors sought out standing structures like disused German military barracks and industrial facilities to house DPs. At the same time, German authorities tasked with managing the expellee problem coveted exactly the same buildings. Before either the DP problem or the expellee crisis could be resolved, the changing strategic calculus in Central Europe brought the U.S. Army into the contest directly in its effort to secure basing facilities for its troops. For individuals, communities, and policy makers, the problems of DP management, expellee integration, and the future of the American military presence in Germany were not only indistinct, they were inseparable. Contests over property had significant policy implications. The initial postwar crisis, in which standing and usable housing was at a premium, created a zero-sum game between competing German, American, and UN officials. In the midst of all of this were the refugees themselves and the populations of rural communities. For them and for their leaders, the contest over property was a proxy for a larger debate over sovereignty, victim status, and national identity. In practical terms, the property issue could and did drag on interminably, causing acute frustration on all sides and causing many observers and participants to question the decision-making process in an emerging Cold War democracy.

Wildflecken was not a typical German town after World War II, but neither was it particularly untypical. Refugees of various categories were nearly ubiquitous in the immediate aftermath of the war. Wildflecken reveals particularly well the multi-sided nature of the refugee problem because all of the actors involved occupied a relatively small physical space and interacted with each other intensively across a period of several years. Not only was the Wildflecken DP camp one of the best documented in Germany, but the area was later part of a very public political debate in the early Federal Republic. This rich documentary record reveals a complex interplay of forces over a finite piece of territory and its inhabitants. The problems of refugee management, economic reconstruction, and occupation politics required compromises from all sides. These compromises, sometimes after bitter and hard-fought competition, ultimately helped to forge a more functional and democratic society in postwar western Germany.

The large and populous DP camp at Wildflecken lay at the geographic and symbolic center of the story. Initially, it housed both Christian and Jewish Poles, though Jews soon had the option to move to their own camps. For DPs, many of whom had no desire to return to Poland, it became a home that they were prepared to defend. By imagining it as a Polish town *in absentia,* they built a durable community with its own politics. Particularly in the years before the Currency Reform of 1948, the DP camp also acted as the center of the local economy, a fact that generated enormous resentment from area residents. For local elites, the facilities on which the camp stood held the key to the economic reconstruction of the area, and what they saw as intransigence on the part of Polish DPs kept them from achieving their aims. For expellees, the grounds of the disused base offered opportunities to build new communities. However, the wretched state of the local economy made such endeavors difficult. The American mission in Germany added a further layer of complexity. Present initially to provide local governance and basic security, the U.S. Army's interest in the Wildflecken area rose and fell over the course of the occupation period. By the time the Americans decided to build a permanent base at Wildflecken, they had been in the district for six years. When the Americans finally made up their minds about the fate of the Wildflecken facility, they suddenly and profoundly altered the postwar spatial and social order in the Sinn Valley. Over the next four decades, they accomplished the kind of transformation that many locals had previously sought, but in a way that no one could have imagined a few years before.

This project began as a study of the interactions between German communities and the new American military mission along the inter-German border in the 1950s. The story of the American military presence in West Germany ties many of the strands of this history together. For concrete and practical reasons, the history of American basing was fundamentally and inextricably tied to the refugee problem. Many of the most important American facilities in West Germany were built on sites previously used as camps for refugees. When I got to the archives, I found that the problem of refugees intruded into plans by West Germans and Americans alike to develop infrastructure in the border region. These refugees, both UN-supported DPs and ethnic German expellees, proved to be both a logistical nightmare and a vivid reminder of the human costs of Hitler's disastrous bid for a racial empire in Europe. In nearby cities like Würzburg, Aschaffenburg, and Schweinfurt, the building of American base communities in the late 1940s and early 1950s collided head-on with material needs of different refugee groups. Examples of this relationship abound. Construction of the Skyline Barracks facility at Würzburg, home to a Cold War–era division headquarters, forced the sudden removal of more than 1,000 expellees from the Galgenberg camp. At Wiesbaden, the first European headquarters of the newly created United States Air Force was built atop a former DP camp. Significantly for this story, the creation of all three of the training areas used by the U.S. Army during the Cold War – Grafenwöhr/Vilseck, Hohenfels, and Wildflecken – forced the removal of DPs and expellees who had been living on these sites since the end of the war. These stories, particularly that of Hohenfels, intersected with the events in Wildflecken. While locals proved quite happy to see DPs moved out, the problem of expellees was much more difficult. These refugees lived under the care of German authorities and any move to displace them meant that the local and state governments had to find someplace for them to go.

My project shifted, as tends to happen, because of a compelling source that was quite literally gathering dust on the shelf of my university's library. While there were hundreds of DP camps, only Wildflecken had a chronicler like Kathryn Hulme. The peripatetic Hulme spent six years in Germany working in the DP camp system. From 1945–1947 she was the Assistant Director of the Wildflecken camp. Her 1953 memoir *The Wild Place* is an affectionate but open-ended account of those years, capturing the excitement, stasis, and muddle that marked efforts to find homes for some of the war's civilian victims.[31] As the noted ethnographer

Bryce Ryan wrote at the time, "Had she been in any one of the scores of camps her story could have been essentially the same."[32] While *The Wild Place* is a magnificently entertaining book, it is all the more interesting for what Hulme failed to describe. While she dealt with the messy reality of a polyglot staff, fractious camp politics, and a complex relationship with distant authorities, for much of the book the camp is described as if it were on an island. Visitors come to camp occasionally, often to herald some new and onerous bureaucratic innovation. There is almost no mention of the German town just below the camp or any indication that the area just outside the DP camp perimeter was at that moment in the geographic center of one of the largest population movements in human history.

It struck me that this was precisely the problem with the history of refugees after the war. The people on the ground who dealt with refugee issues – soldiers, German officials, or UNRRA administrators – were responsible for a very narrow patch of bureaucratic turf. At a time of material scarcity and a domestic economy strained past the breaking point by war and defeat, these individuals had no time, no resources, and no desire to deal with problems outside of their sphere of responsibility. Another UNRRA officer in Bavaria summed up the problem succinctly, writing that "it was not that we were callous, but our work was with the freed slaves – the Germans were a background."[33] Hulme's book, certainly the most widely read memoir from the DP camp system, looms large over the literature on the subject. Wildflecken has been used as a case study in several very good books on postwar reconstruction and the refugee crisis, but I would argue that these tend to replicate some of the blind spots in Hulme's official correspondence and published work.[34]

Hulme, in her diary and private writings, had a considerably broader perspective on how the larger refugee crisis affected her surroundings in rural Germany. However, when she wrote reports to her UNRRA supervisors, or when she later worked on her memoirs, she defined her camp experience in terms of her area of responsibility and little else. When I read documents produced by German refugee officials, they often referenced the DP camp because it was an inescapable reality, but they had no reason to have any real interest in what was going on inside. When DPs crossed outside of the perimeter of the camp, local authorities had to deal with them but often tried as hard as they could to shift jurisdiction on to someone else. The Americans, partially responsible for the welfare of the DPs, grew increasingly frustrated with UNRRA and the DPs themselves. This later manifested itself in a growing sympathy toward other refugee groups and a willingness to informally support them in ways that sometimes ran counter to policy.

During the half-decade following the Second World War, the United States Army found itself deeply engaged with an enormous and unprecedented refugee crisis across Central Europe. Directly and indirectly, American decisions and influence proved decisive in both the successes and failures of refugee management and integration. While relations between expellees and locals initially proved tense, as they often did in rural West Germany, the presence of DPs and the American military in Wildflecken and other garrison towns like it along the border ultimately helped to forge a new corporate identity within and among these communities. Initially, locals saw the expellees as victims of the war but also as foreigners. Expellees, many of whom found themselves in considerably reduced circumstances, complained of marginalization and of feeling unwelcome. Neil Gregor has recently argued that stories of victimhood helped to "re-forge . . . a minimum degree of civic consensus" in the wake of the war.[35] In the case of Wildflecken, expellees and locals had different wartime experiences but came to see themselves as victims of changing postwar circumstances. These disparate communities drew closer, both physically and emotionally, in the face of the efforts of the U.S. Army to militarize the border region.[36]

The structure of this book reflects its focus on the multiplicity of stories that intersected in this small geographic area. I employ evidence from a variety of sources and organizations, from the policies of states and international non-governmental organizations to the personal stories of individual refugees. Chapters, like the lives of the people and groups I describe, are often overlapping and entangled. Perspective sometimes changes within chapters, largely to emphasize the important two-way interactions between policy-making at various levels and the individual and small-group behavior and attitudes on the ground in rural Franconia. The first chapter briefly outlines the principle participants in the Wildflecken story. The town's history during the early twentieth century was critical in what came next. Prior to the 1930s, the region was overwhelmingly rural and poor, with most inhabitants earning a living from small farms or the timber industry. Ambitious attempts at economic reform during the Nazi era largely failed and the district earned a designation as an economic "disaster zone." The arrival of the German army in the late 1930s began to change the structure of the local economy, but the war pre-empted any chance of real transformation. This chapter goes on to discuss the broader issue of forced labor in wartime Germany, the creation of the DP camp system, and the arrival of ethnic German refugees and evacuees in rural Franconia.

Chapter 2 explores the history of the DP camp at Wildflecken between 1945 and 1947. Far from being an isolated island in the middle of the Franconian hills, the DP camp integrated into local society. The camps were in many ways the engine of the area's postwar economy. While locals remember the very real problem of DP "banditry," this mode of interaction paled in importance next to the central place that the camp played in the restoration of commerce in the Sinn Valley. While commercial ties between the DPs and the local community were often in violation of the law, in a rural economy where cash had little or no value, the camp functioned as a large and reasonably efficient grey market zone. This chapter also explores the complex political life within the camp. Camp politics, while largely opaque to UNRRA officials, played an important part in the future of the facility. Because it was widely assumed that DPs wanted to go home, many observers were surprised by the growing strength of anti-repatriation sentiment. This culminated in a riot in 1947 that helped to change the practice of DP management more broadly.

The third chapter follows the story of the district around Wildflecken under American occupation. Expellees poured in the western zones of occupation. In the district around Wildflecken, expellees made up about a third of the population. This became a staggering challenge for the local economy and government. Since the American presence on the ground was tiny, the Americans searched for local elites through whom they could work. In the meantime, Americans, Germans, and expellees all had to deal with the DP camp on the hill above town, which remained the center of the local economy. Despite real security worries, the camp became a vital part of local social and economic relations. With the DPs confined to part of the old German military facility, expellees and locals began to reoccupy parts of the base abandoned when the facility was built in the 1930s. In the shadow of the DP camp and with limited support from the new Bavarian government, expellees began to construct "refugee towns" on the base grounds. This initiative quickly catalyzed a sense of community between expellees and locals, albeit one that was largely directed against the continued presence of DPs.

The fourth chapter carries this story further, focusing on the growing frustration felt by locals and American occupation officials in the late 1940s over the apparent stasis in the DP crisis. As UNRRA ceded control of the camps to the International Refugee Organization (IRO), the focus turned from repatriation to emigration. At the same time, local political and business leaders began creating extensive plans for the industrial development of the region. Proponents of industrialization explicitly cited the importance of industry to provide jobs for expellees. Development advocates grew increasingly critical of the persistence of the DP camp, which they blamed for occupying land necessary for industrial facilities. As American priorities shifted toward the creation of a stable West Germany in the waning days of the occupation, the occupiers became increasingly receptive to the idea that the integration of expellees should be a priority, but were unable to effectively resolve the DP problem.

Chapter 5 carries the story of Wildflecken to its conclusion. After years of sporadic discussion, the U.S. Army formally moved to take control of the Wildflecken facility in 1950 as part of the massive military build-up in Germany following the outbreak of war in Korea. By this time, the DP camp population was dwindling, but closing the camp meant turning the remaining inhabitants over to the care of the West German government. The decision to use Wildflecken was a complicated and highly political affair. Wildflecken was not the first choice of the Americans, but efforts to requisition another nearby facility met with stiff resistance in West Germany, largely because this plan would require the displacement of a significant number of expellees. The expellees acted in their own interests to protest American plans, but also worked in concert with local communities to make the claim that they deserved to be treated as victims of the war and allowed to resume their lives without fear of losing their new homes. In the end, the expellees and other locals lost their battle to head off the requisitioning process and a crash program of home building began in an effort to resettle the displaced population.

As befitting a place with an outsized history, my search for Wildflecken has taken me to a number of archives, including regional and local archival collections in Munich, Würzburg, and Wildflecken, the National Archives and Records Administration in Suitland, Maryland, the Archives Nationales in Paris, the United Nations Archives and Records Management Section in New York, the International Tracing Service Archive in Bad Arolsen, and the United States Holocaust Memorial Museum in Washington, D.C. The project has also benefitted from a number of oral history interviews. There is a large and thriving online community of individuals and families whose histories crossed paths with Wildflecken. Many people have graciously provided me with their memories and the mementoes that they accumulated along the way. The result, I hope, is a book that tells the story of a town, its people, and the events that surrounded and transformed it from a variety of perspectives, from the deeply personal to the relationship between nations and governments. The story of Wildflecken and its strangers requires as much.

There is also a personal and generational element to this story. I, like much of the cohort of early-career historians in the United States, was a child at the end of the Cold War. I grew up in northern Maryland, in an area dominated by the presence of several U.S. Army installations with large pools of civilian workers. Many of my friends and classmates spent time living in West Germany with their families. They were a small part of the fifteen million Americans who lived and worked in West Germany over the course of the Cold War.[37] By the time I finished high school, much of the American story in Germany was as much history as the idea of a divided Germany itself. In 1994, the German-American encounter ended in Wildflecken, with results still very much felt in the Sinn Valley. On any number of occasions, after a conference presentation or in the course of a conversation when I mentioned my work on this book, someone in the room wanted to talk about time spent in the Rhön hills as a soldier or dependent. In Wildflecken, the Americans are deeply missed. My grandparents' generation encountered Germany as a broken and defeated enemy. My parents' generation saw a peaceful and prosperous West German state and forged cultural and personal ties with America's Cold War ally. These bonds are now fraying with the passage of time. For a historian trying to understand the transformative effect of that German-American encounter, it is well worth considering the shattered and deformed world in which both sides forged that relationship. Wildflecken, with its extraordinary story of strangers living next to and among each other, offers a window into this larger process.

A few notes on terminology are warranted here. The vocabulary of flight and exile in postwar Europe remains inexact and politically charged. I use the word "refugee" generically, to refer to individuals or groups compelled to leave their place of residence and take up temporary or permanent residence elsewhere. In the text, groups of refugees will be individually distinguished to avoid confusion. The technical name for Germans forced to leave their homes because of wartime damage was *Evakuierte* (evacuee). During the war, state and national governments established bureaucracies to deal specifically with the needs of this category of refugee. When referring to DPs, Germans generally used the English term, until and even after their legal status changed in the early 1950s and they became *Heimatlose Ausländer* (stateless foreigners). The German word *"Verschleppte"* was also used. It literally means "displaced" but generally had a pejorative connotation. I will note its use in my translations.

The terminology used to describe ethnic Germans is far more confusing. Those who fled or were forced from their homes east of the boundary between the western and Soviet occupation zones during the last stages of the war or in its immediate aftermath were initially typically called *Flüchtlinge*, or "refugees." Soon the terms *"Vertriebene," "Heimatvertriebene,"* and *"Ausgewiesene"* (expellees) came into common use as well. Making matters more confusing, authorities in the Soviet Zone/East Germany cynically referred to their refugee populations as *"Umsiedler"* (resettlers), effectively denying that they had been forced from their homes. By the early 1950s, the term *"Neubürger"* (new citizen) was also in common use in West Germany. Since its use represented a linguistically important shift, I will note its use as well. However, to minimize confusion, I have generally used the English word "expellee" when referring to ethnic German refugees. I have made some exceptions, particularly in the early part of the story when the word "refugee" was clearly intended (as in *Bayerische Flüchtlingsverwaltung* – "Bavarian Refugee Administration"). Also I typically use the term "Federal Republic" or "West Germany" instead of FRG or BRD when discussing the post-1949 semi-sovereign and sovereign state that emerged from the occupation period.

As with any book where much of the research touches on contemporary German history, I have tried to respect both the letter and the spirit of Germany's strict archival privacy laws. Because Wildflecken is a small town and many of the individuals being discussed are either still alive or have descendants living in the area, I have employed pseudonyms for most German and Polish characters in the manuscript. In some cases, particularly with regard to files from the International Tracing Service Archive that are organized only by name, this practice will make it impossible for anyone to locate the identical files. This is regrettable but necessary to protect personal information. Following scholarly practice, pseudonyms will use a first name and last initial (e.g., Helmut S.). The only exceptions are public officials, those whose role in this story would be known from widely available contemporary media, and oral history subjects who have given me or the agency responsible for collecting the testimony explicit permission to use their name.

ONE

The Wild Place, 1933–1945

On a summer day in 1937, a hunter pauses at the edge of a meadow halfway up to the summit of the Löserhag and looks behind him into the valley of the Sinn River. Yellow and blue flowers dapple the clearing in the bright sun. A few feet away, a narrow footpath plunges into the gloomy darkness of the great beech forests of the Franconian Rhön. The hunter looks down the slope to the valley floor toward the village of Wildflecken. With its tidy red roofs, the town of a few hundred souls nests in between two ranges of hills along a single railroad track that connects it to the world beyond.

But the hunter's home is changing as he watches. He can see the red brick bridge over the Brückenau road and the new square in the middle of town. Across the valley and up a hill, hundreds of workers put the last touches on rows of squat, narrow buildings. Soon there would be horses in the newly built stables and hundreds, then thousands, of soldiers living in the barracks. A new street connects the town and the base, paved with heavy white stones to accommodate the vast bulk of military vehicles that will soon rumble through the valley. Turning to the west, our hunter shakes his head when he sees farmhouses and villages sitting abandoned in neat clearings a few kilometers away. A year ago, those villages had been his neighbors. Then the German state ordered them abandoned to build the new troop training facility. As he shoulders his rifle and walks into the woods, he wonders to himself what all of this change will mean for his family and his town. Perhaps he suspects that Germany is on the road to another war, but he cannot know what that struggle will mean for this quiet valley.

Like so many places in Europe, the titanic conflicts of the 1940s transformed Wildflecken and the Sinn Valley. This rural area typified many of the ruptures and upheavals experienced across defeated Germany during and following the Third Reich. In the wake of the war, four groups lived in close proximity in and around the town. Local residents, DPs and the UNRRA field workers sent to supervise them, American troops, and ethnic German refugees created a dense network of associations, compromises, and conflicts in the postwar period. Each group was a product of the war, its status determined or changed by the preparation for, initial successes of, and ultimate catastrophic failure of Hitler's war of conquest and racial imperialism in Europe.

This chapter will consider the paths that each of these groups followed to Wildflecken. In each case, the history and geography of the region played decisive roles in shaping the demography and the fate of the town and its people. Wildflecken spent much of its history in isolation and obscurity, tendencies that perversely helped to project it into the arena of international politics during the early Cold War. Its local history is not unlike thousands of other communities in rural Central Europe, for whom the tides of war and the boundary changes that followed meant new masters, new populations, and a precarious existence as border communities.[1] If we are to understand the transformation of Wildflecken, we have to examine the history of the place itself, its role in the German war machine of the 1930s and 40s, events taking place in war-torn Central and Eastern Europe, and the politics of the victorious wartime alliance. While the history of Wildflecken is the history of a very small place, there is no question that this tiny community played an important part in the wider history of Germany, Europe, and the world.

The "unweaving" of multiethnic Europe reached its terrible zenith in dark years of the 1940s.[2] In the shatter zone of Central and East Central Europe, Nazi and Soviet population policy, coupled with the violence of the war, produced an enormous wave of refugees, probably totaling about thirty million individuals.[3] The experience of displacement, whether by act of war or state policy, was one of the central narratives of postwar period in Europe. However, accounts of forced population removal have tended to privilege the power of the state and to draw broad and undifferentiated groups of victims.[4] Local history allows us to disaggregate categories of refugees, locals, and occupation troops and to move beyond contemporary legal categories to examine the interaction between refugee groups and between refugees and other participants in Germany's postwar history.

The postwar refugee crisis in Germany was a primarily a rural one, in that smaller communities that suffered less wartime damage were best able to accommodate vast numbers of the dispossessed. Three characteristics of Wildflecken and its war contributed to the dramatic transformation of the town and its people: its strategic location near the boundary of the American and Soviet occupation zones, the relative lack of wartime damage, and its role in the Nazi forced labor program.

Wildflecken is located in an isolated corner of the Bavarian district of Lower Franconia (*Unterfranken*). Lower Franconia is culturally very distinct from the other two districts that comprise Franconia (*Franken*), Upper and Middle Franconia. Franconia as a whole is dominated by Protestants, while Lower Franconia was, and remains, largely Catholic. In 1934, Catholics made up eighty-one percent of a population of about 800,000. Lower Franconia was also considerably less industrialized than its neighbors, particularly the large urban conglomeration around Nürnberg in Middle Franconia. The district capital at Würzburg was the only significant population center, with a population of around 100,000. Schweinfurt and Aschaffenburg were both about half that size. Nearly fifty-four percent of the population worked either in agriculture or forestry, about eight percent higher than the figure for Bavaria as a whole.[5] In the north, Lower Franconia's land rises into the hills of the Rhön and Spessart. While lovely, these hills were unproductive country for agriculture and housed pockets of intransigent and desperate rural poverty well into the twentieth century.

The Rhön region around Wildflecken has been isolated and remote for much of its history. Despite various government-sponsored development plans during the first half of the twentieth century, life in the area remained difficult and the population largely impoverished. A few miles to the north lies the border between Bavaria and the neighboring German state of Hesse. To the northeast, visible from the heights of the Kreuzberg, is Thuringia and the pre-1990 border between East and West Germany. This region has long been a border zone, dating back to the rabbit warren of competing polities during the time of the Holy Roman Empire. The town and surrounding communities date from the early sixteenth century, when farmers from the Archbishopric of Würzburg settled the hilly frontier region near the boundary with the Prince-Bishop of Fulda. They did not secure permission to build these settlements, and early maps noted their presence with the descriptor "*ein Wilder Flecken*" or "unauthorized settlement."[6] From its early history, the community was tied to its more famous neighbors Bad Brückenau and Bad Kissingen, both of which benefitted from their mineral baths and emerged as resort destinations in the eighteenth and nineteenth centuries. Wildflecken's immediate neighbors were other tiny farm towns like Reussendorf, Dalherda, and Werberg. A lovely pilgrimage church sat in the middle of this nexus of towns, and narrow paths connected them between the fields and dense woods. In the seventeenth century, the Franciscans built an impressive monastery on the nearby Kreuzberg with spectacular views of the surrounding countryside.

Life in Wildflecken and neighboring towns proved difficult for the descendants of the first settlers. The weather in the Rhön is legendarily bad. In 1952, as the events described in this book threatened to displace these communities, a valedictory article in a nearby newspaper described local towns "frequently wrapped in weeklong fog. The first snows frequently fall before the harvest. Winter imposes its own strict discipline. Nevertheless, and perhaps because of it, the people of the Rhön love their *Heimat*."[7] Somewhat more prosaically, several generations of German soldiers have passed along the doggerel "Lieber den Arsch voller Zecken als ein Tag in Wildflecken," which favorably compares the experience of ticks biting one's most sensitive areas to spending time in the Rhön. The area had few roads, terrible soil, and most farmers tried to scratch what they could from fields cut from deep forests that yielded little but more generations of poverty.

The nineteenth century changed the geopolitical order in Wildflecken. At the end of the Napoleonic Wars, many of the diffuse political entities in Franconia passed to Bavaria. Wildflecken now lay near the border between the Wittelsbach domains and Ducal Saxony. The consolidation of the Prusso-German Empire later in the century temporarily ended Wildflecken's long history as a border town. After 1871, it lay at the center of the German Reich. As the spa towns nearby prospered, the farm communities of the Sinn Valley declined. At the beginning of the twentieth century, Wildflecken had fewer than five hundred inhabitants. Werberg was slightly more than half as large, but its population declined by thirty percent in the decades before the Second World War. Most of those who left Werberg moved to urban centers in Germany, but thirty Werberger made their way to the United States. Part of the problem lay in the system of land tenancy in Lower Franconia, which was dominated by very small landholdings further reduced by a tradition of partible inheritance. In the early 1930s, almost twenty-five percent of farms in the region totaled five acres or less, more than double the Bavarian average. As a result, local farmers had a great deal of trouble competing with producers from outside the area.[8]

Tourism brought a few non-locals to the region. A train line connected the town with Brückenau, now the administrative seat of the local rural county (*Landkreis*). This single track allowed a few hardy nature-enthusiasts to travel up the Sinn Valley. In winter, some came to ski in the rugged country around the Dammersfeld. Later this line brought a generation of soldiers and refugees into the Sinntal. Wildflecken merited a small mention in an 1883 Baedeker's handbook to southern Germany, which suggested that visitors hire a local guide to take them up to the monastery on the Kreuzberg.[9]

The politics of this region reflected its religious and economic circumstances. Lower Franconian politics were dominated by the Bavarian People's Party (BVP), a center-right Catholic party with a tenacious hold on voters during the political turbulence of Weimar Germany. Until the two elections of 1932, the BVP polled around fifty percent of Lower Franconian votes in every election. While the electoral power of BVP was inescapable, it was also notable that the second most important group of voters came from the political left. Beginning in 1919, the Communists and Social Democrats taken as a block won the second highest number of votes across the district. The best numbers for the Communists came from the urban areas and from the desperately poor countryside of the Rhön and Spessart. Even in the relatively stable years at the end of the 1920s, when the republic's shifting politics produced something resembling a workable government, the Left did very well in northern Lower Franconia. In the state parliamentary elections in May 1928, the Communists won 5.3 percent of the vote in Landkreis Brückenau, the highest of any county in the district and well above the average in Bavaria (3.8 percent). Between them, the Communists and the Social Democrats consistently captured about twenty percent of the vote in the Rhön. The BVP was still the dominant party in the area, but the Rhön region clearly produced significant numbers of deeply disaffected voters who found Communism attractive.[10] This electoral constellation was important for several reasons. First, both the region's political Catholicism and its support for the Left proved to be a significant impediment to the growth of new parties like the Nazis. Second, many rural voters who abandoned Communism during the Nazi period returned to it after the war, presenting a challenge to American and West German plans for the region. Finally, Catholicism later helped to bridge some of the divides between locals, foreign workers from Eastern Europe, and Catholic ethnic German expellees.

Nazism developed along very different lines in Lower Franconia than in the rest of the Franconian region. If Protestant Franconia was one of the great success stories of the party, Nazism faced an uphill battle in Lower Franconia. This was due in large part to the party's poor organization in the area, the durability of older political allegiances, and skepticism about particular aspects of the Nazi program. The local party boss (*Gauleiter*) and later district leader (*Regierungspräsident*) was Otto Hellmuth, a dentist from the Würzburg. Hellmuth was thirty-three when he became Gauleiter in 1928. He cut an eccentric figure as the face of Nazism in the district. He despised the Catholic Church, which put him at odds with much of the population. He famously named his daughter Gailana after the pagan princess responsible for the martyrdom of St. Kilian, the seventh-century "Apostle to the Franconians." Hellmuth was abrasive, pushy, and had trouble hiding his disdain for the religion of his constituents. He was also notably lazy and had little patience for the day-to-day operations of either the party or the district. Hellmuth initially did little to inspire confidence in his party bosses, one of whom suggested that the district had "one of the poorest organizations in the country."[11] Hellmuth ascribed his misfortunes to the continued presence of church power. He described Lower Franconia, using the color associated with Catholic politics, as "the blackest district in Germany."[12]

In the Bavarian parliamentary elections in 1928, the NSDAP received less than four percent of the vote and 1.7 percent in the county around Wildflecken.[13] Even this does not accurately reflect the totality of Nazi electoral misfortune, since at least some of the voters in the county were vacationers from other parts of Germany where Nazi votes were stronger. Across the district, the party was disorganized and morale was low. In 1929, the party began a campaign to send speakers to rural areas to give speeches like "The Young Plan and the Farm Crisis." The scheme, and Nazi propaganda more generally, failed for four reasons. Nazi agrarian thinking focused on mid-sized family farms of ten to one hundred acres (*Erbhofen*), an ideal that clashed with the tiny and frequently divided agricultural properties of Lower Franconia.[14] Second, there were simply not enough Nazis to run the campaign. Of 113 registered party speakers in Bavaria, only four lived in Lower Franconia. Third, the continued strength of the Communists in rural areas limited the Nazi appeal. Finally, the church mobilized against Nazism in the area. In September 1930, a Capuchin friar named Benedict Johannes told his rural congregation near Schweinfurt that the church would deny sacraments to members of the party. The resulting furor eventually brought in Munich's Cardinal Michael Faulhaber, who worked out a compromise.[15] The party only began to make real inroads in the early 1930s after the failure of several agricultural banks and the deepening depression. One of the few subjects that did arouse popular passions, the Jewish issue, demonstrates some of the tensions at play in the district and its rural communities.

Jews maintained a presence throughout the region. At the time of Franconia's accession to Bavaria after the Napoleonic Wars, Lower Franconia had the highest percentage of Jews in Bavaria. While the Jewish population declined during the nineteenth century, Jews were relatively well integrated into local communities. The population of nearby Bad Brückenau (2,462 in 1933) included more than 120 Jews. The Jewish community there completed a new synagogue in 1913. In addition, a number of local rural communities had substantial Jewish populations, including towns near Brückenau like Zeitlofs and Unterriedenberg. Jews were a linchpin in the rural economy, functioning as middlemen and merchants who mediated between non-Jewish farmers and cattle-dealers. For this reason, many rural communities in Franconia resisted or tried to ignore anti-Jewish measures.

During the Weimar period, Jews sat regularly on the city council in Brückenau, but there were also growing signs of vigorous anti-Semitism. There were clashes in rural areas between local members of the nationalist German League for Defense and Defiance (*Deutschvölkische Schutz- und Trutzbund*) and Jewish self-defense groups. Elise Schapira, born in 1920, remembers a series of anti-Semitic incidents after 1933. Her parents, who owned a hardware store, let her leave at fifteen for Würzburg. "Life was a little better there, because they had a large Jewish community." She eventually made her way to Britain, but her parents did not survive the Holocaust.[16] During the 1938 *Kristallnacht* riots, locals destroyed Brückenau's synagogue, Jewish school, and several Jewish-owned hotels in the city. The town then purchased the synagogue and religious school for far below their market value and took steps to convert them into a vocational school. Those plans fell through when a fire destroyed both buildings in 1941.[17] In other parts of rural Franconia, Jewish life vanished and never returned. Villages that once had substantial Jewish populations forced them out with violence. In tiny Adelsberg near Gemünden, with sixteen Jews among a population of 370, attacks by local Nazis and SA Brownshirts from nearby towns drove Jews out of town for good. But even in the area of Jewish policy, Lower Franconians remained deeply skeptical of the Nazi message. Gestapo files from the region suggest that, despite local anti-Semitism, many Lower Franconians found the violence and destruction of Kristallnacht deeply troubling.[18]

Lower Franconians proved intransigent in the face of Nazi electoral gains nationwide until late 1932. Lower Franconia had the lowest percentage of pre-1933 "Old Fighters" of any district in Germany. Some locals rushed to join the party after Hitler's ascension in January 1933. Lower Franconia had the third highest percentage of "March Violets," or those who joined the party in the heady days after the Nazis gained the Chancellery. For reasons of conviction or self-interest, the people of the Sinn Valley joined the national tide toward Nazism in the subsequent years. The Nazis polled about thirty-four percent in Landkreis Brückenau in the April 1934 election, with the BVP still receiving about fifty percent of the vote. However, the fact that the election was in April meant that a significant number of those votes were cast by tourists. Simply put, the Nazi message never really resonated with many ordinary voters in Lower Franconia.[19]

Even after locals joined the party, not many became ideological enthusiasts. Few farmers took the opportunity to convert their land to Erbhofen. By the outbreak of war, only twelve percent of the districts farms had that designation, compared to around thirty percent in Middle and Upper Franconia.[20] In 1938, party officials in rural Kitzingen candidly admitted that they could not compete with priests for the affections of the population. The party even looked shabby. In 1937, the district leadership appealed to Munich for financial support to buy five hundred uniform jackets for party members in the Rhön, Spessart, Odenwald, and Steigerwald who otherwise had to appear at public events in civilian clothes. Not long before the war broke out, an inspection of the district party drum and bugle corps revealed an array of mismatched instruments, bent trumpets, and uniforms that the inspector believed might have been secretly used for field work by the band members.[21]

If Wildfleckeners did not migrate to Nazism, the Nazi state certainly came to Wildflecken. Hellmuth and the Gau leadership became convinced that they could both tackle the endemic poverty of northern Lower Franconia while also attaching themselves to the kind of showcase project that tended to attract the attention of Berlin. The result was the Rhön, or Hellmuth, Plan, an ambitious but incoherent effort that drew both from Nazi ideology and from earlier efforts at reform in the Rhön.[22]

Plans for economic development in the region did not start with the Nazis. Rural poverty in the Rhön bedeviled generations of Bavarian governments. In the early 1920s, local citizens groups successfully petitioned for the construction of more than twenty kilometers of new roads in the Rhön in the hopes of both easing transportation problems and encouraging industry. These projects collapsed for lack of funds, but the ideas lingered. In 1933, the government declared the Rhön and Spessart to be economic disaster areas (*Notstandsgebiet*). Hellmuth welcomed outside assistance for these areas, particularly the provision of food assistance and improved access to medical care. Hellmuth emphasized the deplorable housing conditions in the rural region. "If political prisoners were housed in such pits," he commented acidly, "foreign governments would protest through the League of Nations." Residents of the zone, which included thirteen of the twenty-five counties in Lower Franconia, now received aid from Nazi charitable programs like the Winter Assistance (*Winterhilfswerk*).[23]

For the Gauleiter, there were obvious advantages to this new government attention to the Rhön. Hellmuth began to portray himself as a modernizer, drawing on previous visions of rural economic development but aligning them with Nazi ideology. He began to articulate an ambitious development strategy intended to improve the area's transportation infrastructure, to clear forests for additional farmland, and to encourage farm consolidation to reverse the effects of partible inheritance.

The road-building program was the only part of the plan that yielded any significant dividends. Hellmuth managed to win support for a new road, the *Rhönstrasse*, from Fladungen to Bischofsheim. When the road opened in 1937, it encouraged Siemens to open a plant in Neustadt and resulted in about two hundred new homes. The road built in the 1920s was now renamed "Dr-Hellmuth-Plan-Strasse." Forest clearing proved to be less successful. Hundreds of laborers toiled in the Rhön hills and lived in ten forest camps built by the Reich Labor Service (*Reichsarbeitsdienst*). Unemployed young men from the rest of Germany now came to the area, interacting with the local population and working among them. Remains of the camps they built still dot the area's landscape, but the work they performed did little good for anyone. Despite Hellmuth's hopes, the newly cleared land was of limited use for either farming or animal husbandry and much of it went unused. Existing farms began to suffer because forest clearing displaced wild animals, particularly deer and boar, which then descended on settled land. Berlin finally had to intervene and send state foresters to cull the wild game before it did more damage. In Landkreis Brückenau, the timber industry benefitted most of all. By the outbreak of war, there were nine lumber mills, two cardboard plants, and a flooring mill in the district.

At least in public, Berlin praised the plan effusively. A senior official from the Propaganda Ministry praised the region as "an outstanding example of National Socialist development policy" and "an exemplar for the Reich." However, there was precious little support for it either in the capital or on the ground. Farmers rejected Hellmuth's vision of tidy, consolidated, ideologically sound Erbhofen. Despite Hellmuth's efforts to promote his efforts as congruent with the official ideology of "blood and soil," he lacked many of the important political connections that helped other regional development efforts like Gauleiter Erich Koch's program in East Prussia. Planning remained haphazard. Officials connected to the plan seldom met and never seemed to grasp the legal complexities they needed to overcome. The plan crossed legal and jurisdictional boundaries into Thuringia and Hesse. A bitter dispute between Hellmuth and the Gauleiter of those neighboring states over the scope of the plan ended up in the party court system.

In the end, not much came of the Rhön Plan. One historian's summary of its accomplishments enumerated only "178 chicken breeding stations and the promotion of rabbit, silkworm, and honey-bee breeding."[24] This is somewhat uncharitable. The Siemens factory proved to be an important and durable addition to the region. More fundamentally, the five-year effort had three important consequences. First, it established the principle of the Rhön as an economic crisis zone. Second, it effectively normalized the use of semi-voluntary outside labor in an isolated rural district. Finally, and most tangibly, the Hellmuth initiative brought the Rhön to the attention of Reich authorities, albeit in ways that the Gauleiter never intended. If the region could not be the centerpiece of an economic development initiative or job creation program, it could serve the military needs of the Nazi state.

As the *Reichswehr* of the interwar period transformed into the massive conscript *Wehrmacht,* the need for training facilities increased dramatically. In 1936, the first mass maneuvers since before World War I took place in nearby Hesse. While the large maneuvers of the prewar period mostly took place on the plains of north Germany, an army that faced the prospect of fighting in the forested hills of places like western Czechoslovakia needed to be able to work out tactical problems in rough terrain.[25] The Army identified a number of promising spots to construct or expand training areas. Several of these had major implications later when the Americans sought similar facilities. The former Bavarian Army training area at Grafenwöhr/Vilseck in the Upper Palatinate (*Oberpfalz*) nearly tripled in size to ninety square miles. A new facility was built at nearby Hohenfels that covered sixty-three square miles. Both required the expropriation of agricultural property and the compulsory movement of significant numbers of farmers.[26]

The Rhön, with its open spaces, minimal population, and paucity of industry, offered another ideal spot. In 1936, surveying began to demarcate a training area near the Dammersfeld mountain above Wildflecken. The decision transformed the area quickly and dramatically. The 18,000 acres claimed by the Army for the new *Truppenübungsplatz Hohe Rhön* (Maneuver Area – Upper Rhön) included eight settled towns, including Werberg, Reussendorf, and Dalherda. Wildflecken itself sat just outside the boundaries of the base and would serve as the transportation hub for the facility. The Wehrmacht made funds available to resettle inhabitants of communities included in the base boundaries. The enormous bureaucratic effort closely tied town government to the base. Peter M., a forty-year-old Wehrmacht civilian administrator from Salmünster, helped to manage the resettlement effort, then remained in the community through the war and later played an entirely unintended role in the town's postwar history.[27] For many of the evacuated families, this resettlement was an opportunity to start anew somewhere else. The Hüfner family from Werberg, for example, resettled near Offenbach with the funds they received from the government. As farmers who had been in Werberg for generations, they never reconciled fully with the loss of their house and town.[28]

With the opening of the maneuver area, Wildflecken became a base town, closely tied economically to the particular needs of a military facility. In the near term, this meant jobs and a flourishing service industry. It also normalized the presence of military units and the inconveniences of living near military training. A decade later, when the facility hosted a different army, locals were accustomed to the problems of tank tracks in their fields, artillery thundering at night, and roads clogged with traffic. While enormously disruptive, village clearance actions like the ones around Wildflecken took place across Germany in the late 1930s as the Wehrmacht built new bases and expanded old ones. At Grafenwöhr, for example, an almost identical process took place when the expansion of the training area necessitated the evacuation of Pappenberg.[29]

The influx of jobs and cash-flush soldiers changed the character of the town. While some locals displaced by the bases' construction took the opportunity to leave for other parts of Germany, most stayed. For the first time, workers poured into the region as the hill above Wildflecken hummed with construction activity. For the town, investment in new infrastructure included the distinctive red bridge across the main road to Brückenau. Workers building the base lived in some of the partially abandoned towns, in Wildflecken, and on the post. Space was cleared in Wildflecken for a bus depot (today it is the *Rathausplatz*). By summer 1937, construction finished on a facility that could house 9,000 soldiers with space for 1,500 horses. Nazi labor boss Robert Ley and SS Chief Heinrich Himmler attended the opening ceremonies. Shortly thereafter, the sounds of artillery thundered through the Sinntal for the first time. Already transformed from a sleepy agricultural community into a base town, Wildflecken soon found itself drawn into the war effort.

The arrival of soldiers at the training base in the upper Rhön brought more strangers into the region. From the beginning of the war, Wildflecken served as an important maneuver ground and as a site for organizing Wehrmacht formations. Three divisions, the 82nd, 95th, and 232nd, formed there – the last of these as the war reached its final crisis in the spring of 1944. A number of *Waffen-SS* formations trained at Wildflecken, including the French and Belgian Charlemagne and Wallonia Divisions. Soviet civilian and military personnel who volunteered to fight on the German side also came to Wildflecken to train. Many local residents later recalled the curious sight of Central Asian volunteers coming to town for training in 1943. Some of these brought with them their families, creating colorful scenes at the train station as rural Franconians encountered these caravans from the east.[30]

Even as residents saw the tangible benefits of militarization, older forms of allegiance continued to exert a considerable pull in the region. While the military helped to bring much needed economic development to the region, many in rural Franconia continued to doubt the benefits of Nazi rule. For small farmers, government interference in rural matters, particularly price caps and changes in inheritance law, looked like outside "Prussian" intrusion. A 1941 party report from the Landkreis suggested that "people frequently question the necessity of this war. They are not clear about the magnitude of the struggle and its far-reaching significance for the future of the German people."[31] While some in the area undoubtedly became committed Nazis, many more retained notions of Bavarian or Franconian particularism. Growth came at a considerable cost; not least was the intrusion of increasing numbers of foreigners who came to work and live among the people of the Sinn Valley.

The transformation of Wildflecken accelerated when it became part of the Third Reich's attempt to develop its industrial capacity while engaged in an increasingly desperate conflict. On a hill near the main base, the Army built a small *Heeresverpflegungsamt* (HVA) that manufactured uniforms and other necessities. As the German economy belatedly adjusted to wartime production, the base further expanded with the addition of a munitions plant (*Munitionsanstalt* or *Muna*) in 1940. More than 260 Munitionanstalten were built during the course of the war, of which 180 served the needs of the army. Unskilled or semi-skilled laborers at the Muna assembled and stored ammunition, the components of which had been produced elsewhere.[32] The Munitionanstalten tended to be in out-of-the-way places, making them hard for potential enemy bombers to find and presumably reducing the risk that accidental explosions might endanger larger production facilities. To protect the Muna, the Wehrmacht built a network of bunkers in the hills around Wildflecken.

The construction of the Muna was part of the transformation of the local labor force that accompanied the beginning of the war. A war for economic self-sufficiency had to be fought with a labor market undercut by the large-scale conscription of German manpower. Early labor mobilization efforts brought thousands of Polish workers to farms in Germany in order to stave off agricultural collapse, but this did little to resolve the problems of manning the military and industrial needs of a modern society at war. In early 1942, Hitler appointed Fritz Sauckel as General Plenipotentiary for Labor Mobilization. Sauckel, born not far from Wildflecken in Haßfurt, embarked on what a recent economic historian of the Third Reich has characterized as "one of the largest coercive labour programmes the world has ever seen."[33]

The *Ausländereinsatz* ("foreign labor deployment") of the war years stemmed from a mix of traditional labor migrancy from Eastern Europe, the crisis of the German war economy, and the ideology of Nazism. Polish military and civilian personnel, followed by waves of French and Soviet POWs in 1940 and 1941 and recruits from the Protectorate of Bohemia and Moravia, kept German industry going. Like so many of the Nazi state's programs, this conscription of labor divided the leadership between racial ideologues who demanded harsh treatment and those who recognized that leniency might improve production.[34]

The most comprehensive attempt to estimate the number of foreign laborers in Nazi Germany and its occupied territories has counted 13.48 million total workers throughout the course of the war, of whom almost ten million could be categorized as either "forced" or "slave" labor. This included 8.4 million civilian workers, 4.6 million POWs, and 1.7 million concentration camp inmates. The largest national grouping came from the Soviet Union (4.75 million), followed by 2.3 million from France and two million Poles. By the end of the war, foreign labor made up about twenty-six percent of the total labor force in Germany.[35] Because much of the best research on forced labor has focused on industrial work, historians know considerably less about the experiences of foreign workers in rural areas. Of all sectors of the German economy, none was more dependent on foreign labor than agriculture. In August 1944, 46.6 percent of farm laborers were foreign. Other sectors, including mining, building, and metalwork, were more than thirty percent foreign by that point.[36] In Wildflecken and rural Franconia, predominantly agrarian but with industrial facilities as well, foreign labor became a critical source of manpower and a part of everyday life.

Wildflecken and places like it across rural Germany saw the results of these programs quickly and comprehensively. It is doubtful that anyone living in the region did not interact with foreign laborers at some point. Much of what we know about rural labor in Lower Franconia has been unearthed in recent years by local historians and students under the direction of Herbert May. Their work has been part of a growing effort in Germany and Eastern Europe to tell the stories of foreign laborers and to help resolve some of the outstanding financial claims remaining from the war years.[37]

One of the challenges in writing about forced labor has been the unevenness of records from the Third Reich, particularly with regard to rural areas. There are reasonably robust files for Upper and Middle Franconia but far fewer covering Lower Franconia. In September 1944, there were likely around 150,000 foreign forced laborers in Franconia, of which 60–70,000 were working in Lower Franconia.[38] A considerable number of these probably worked in the large industrial plants in Schweinfurt. Thanks to another amateur local historian, we know that the capital and largest city, Würzburg, had at the end of 1943 only 3,615 foreign workers, most of whom worked in service industries.[39] The vast majority of foreign laborers in Lower Franconia worked on the land or in rural communities.

Germany's labor needs were virtually bottomless. Foreign laborers in rural Franconia performed a range of functions. In the Rhön, foreign workers labored in clearing forests, construction, and water management. The files of the International Tracing Service in Bad Arolsen include a comprehensive overview of the deployment of foreign labor in Landkreis Brückenau. The majority of compulsory laborers came from the POW camp in nearby Hammelburg. During the course of the war, nearly one hundred specific levies of foreign civilian or military labor worked in the Landkreis. Some operated for a few weeks or months, others over the course of virtually the entire war. While the largest groups of laborers worked in the Muna and HVA, most levies came to labor in the district's farms, forests, and roadways. Perhaps the most labor-intensive project in the district involved cleaning and regularizing the banks of the Sinn River at Brückenau, a project that involved large numbers of Soviet, French, Italian, and American POWs.[40]

While most of these laborers lived and worked in the Muna, many others circulated in local communities, bound to their work by the full force of German law. Of the 1,107 workers at the Muna in June of 1944, 217 were male or female laborers from the Soviet Union (*Ostarbeiter*), 127 French men, and 264 Czech men and women.[41] While many of these forced laborers lived in the production facility, the town itself contained a significant number of foreign workers. By one postwar estimate, a community with a population of little more than three hundred employed sixty-two foreign workers, almost half of them Ukrainian with a number of Czechs, French, and Balts. While most worked in the fields, they also kept local laundries, bars, and shops running during the hard years of war. As the war dragged on, some foreign laborers found themselves living in the common rooms of rural inns as a way to keep them close to their workplaces.[42] While Nazi racial ideology played a role in the fate of foreign laborers, day-to-day life varied widely and often depended on the kind of work assigned and the nature of a worker's supervision. Concentration camp labor experiences were typically brutal and dangerous. Factory work grew progressively more hazardous, not least because of the encroaching bombing campaign and deteriorating material conditions. Farm labor, however, could be different. Stephan W., arrested in 1941 near Krakow, remembers his mother urging him to tell the Germans that he was a farmer so at least he would have something to eat. Despite lacking any experience in farming, he found himself in a tiny village near Absberg. After the war, he remained there and spent the rest of his working life in the village. As historians who have worked with oral history testimonies have concluded, relations between foreign laborers and farmers depended in large part on the attitude of the farmers themselves. "Good farmers broke the rules and gamed the system; employing forced laborers proved to be a test of humanity."[43]

This program of placing foreign workers in rural communities could have unintended consequences. In rural, deeply Catholic northern Bavaria, local farmers sometimes responded to laborers, particularly fellow Catholics, in ways that defied Nazi attempts to enforce racial hierarchies. As early as November 1939, the Reich Security Service (SD) issued orders forbidding Poles to attend mass with Germans. In rural areas, farmers routinely ignored this directive. Hellmuth complained in 1939 about complicity between the church, farmers, Polish POWs, and even guards sent to enforce labor rules. "The attitude of the population leaves much to be desired. Apparently, rural districts have been offering Sunday clothes for church going. One priest even gave out three marks to the guard to pick up cigarettes for the prisoners." Bettina Kahn of Römershag was arrested in September 1940 for bringing a Polish domestic worker with her to mass.[44] As foreign labor became normalized in rural Franconia, relations between farmers, workers, and others in the community took on a veneer of conviviality. Local archives are full of accounts of Poles eating, drinking, and openly socializing with their hosts. In Wildflecken, the presence of Soviet volunteers compounded the problem. In June 1944, the Gestapo in Nürnberg wrote to local authorities demanding that they put an end to fraternization between Russian volunteers and Ostarbeiter at the *Gasthaus* Wittman in Brückenau.[45] While local officials promised to put a stop to such behavior, the temptations for both sides must have remained considerable.

Sometimes this familiarity led to romantic or sexual relationships. These relationships were strictly forbidden by law. In late 1939, the Gau government urged women and girls to keep "a racially-aware attitude" when dealing with foreign labor. The following September, the Reich Security Main Office (RSHA) issued guidelines concerning relations between Germans and Poles. Polish men convicted of having sexual relations with German women faced death, often euphemized as "special handling," unless they could prove that they were "fit for Germanization." German women could be sent to concentration camps for the same offense, after being publically humiliated and potentially forced to have an abortion if pregnancy resulted. There were also penalties for German men, but these were considerably less harsh than those for women. In September 1940, Reich Security Main Office chief Reinhard Heydrich informed local Gestapo offices that Polish women faced coercion by German men to have sex. "For this reason, sexual relations between German men and women workers of Polish nationality are not to be dealt with by special handling."[46]

The legally established double standard for men and women derived both from prevailing notions of racial pollution and sexual purity and from the reality of a war that drew men away from their homes in large numbers. Across Franconia in early 1944, 21.5 percent of farms were run by women. This was five percent higher than the Bavarian average. As Robert L., child of a German woman and a French POW laborer, later told an interviewer: "My mother was a servant girl on a farm. My father was a rural laborer, a farmhand [*Knecht*]. They were together doing timbering work and clearing a road and, my God, when young people are together, you know how that goes."[47] While German authorities wrestled from the beginning of the war with how to regulate sexual contact between Germans and foreigners, they were never able to figure out a way to strike a balance between banning sex and allowing social contact with "western" workers like Robert's father.[48]

For Poles and other East European laborers, penalties for unauthorized relationships could be swift and very brutal. The Gestapo across Germany worked hard to root out any hint of contact. Public hangings by roving courts often took place in front of assembled foreign workers. For the Gestapo, the biggest challenge was that people in small rural communities, particularly in places like Lower Franconia where affection for the Nazis was never high, often proved unwilling to turn in their neighbors. "Crimes" like taking foreign workers to mass or having lunch with them afterward were to some extent communal offenses, requiring the complicity of several community members including the priest. This was a significant disincentive to inform on one's neighbors. The lack of compliance in rural Lower Franconia infuriated the Gestapo. In 1944 and 1945, prosecutions for unauthorized contact dropped off to nothing in Lower Franconia. The Gestapo office in Nürnberg concluded that investigators in the field were simply taking the law into their own hands and punishing offenders on the spot. Grim photos of kangaroo courts and their aftermath in the countryside seem to bear this out.[49]

A great many farmers and town residents in rural Lower Franconia never embraced Nazism and held complicated but profound sympathies for some of the foreign workers who lived among them during the war years. As true as this might have been, it should not distract from the overriding brutality and callousness of a system designed to compel and exploit human labor. On farms and construction sites, foreign workers needed to be kept alive and productive, which meant certain minimum standards and often little more. Food could be minimal, and winter clothing, essential in the brutal cold of the Rhön, often arrived late in the season if at all. Irene W., a young woman from Łódź, worked in series of rural inns, where she remembers being beaten and essentially held prisoner by the proprietors. Sexual relations between Germans and foreign laborers certainly included non-consensual sex in which the foreign worker had relatively little recourse under the law. A limitation of oral history sources is that forced labor survivors are unlikely to discuss issues of rape and sexual coercion openly. Many died in Germany, victims of illness, starvation, Allied bombing, or harsh German justice. Small towns across the region are dotted with cemeteries like the *Russengrab* in Obermässig and the *Russenfriedhof* in Langenzenn. In Reussendorf, where many forced laborers on the Muna lived, authorities recorded dozens of deaths. All too often, the cause listed was simply "exhaustion."[50]

As the end of the war drew closer, some took the opportunity to flee. The local Gestapo spent a great deal of time and resources tracking down fugitive foreign workers, who could now after all take advantage of a dense and increasingly minimally-supervised network of their countrymen across rural Bavaria. In January 1943, authorities classified 20,353 foreign laborers across Germany as having fled their workplaces. In rural Franconia, the security officials were concerned enough that they organized watch groups, primarily composed of over-aged World War I veterans, to patrol the countryside in search of escapees. The local Gestapo dedicated considerable time and resources breaking up real and imagined networks of forced laborers like the "Revolutionary Committee" among Soviet POWs in Ebelsbach. These anxieties deepened toward the end of war. In September 1944, the Gestapo in Würzburg issued a warning over the radio that the Allies were planning to use foreign laborers to sabotage the German war effort.[51] This paranoia had important consequences in the postwar period. Regardless of how well they might have gotten along with local foreign laborers, rural Lower Franconians knew at the end of the war that they had participated in and benefitted from a brutal and exploitative system. Because they carried their own prejudices, inflamed by years of state propaganda and exacerbated by anxieties about the war, many came to fear the revenge that might come after defeat. When millions of forced laborers remained in Germany after the war as Displaced Persons, local reactions to their presence reflected this sense of guilt and fear.

The development of war industries in the region did little to alleviate the long-term structural problems in the local economy. With the Muna drawing most of the foreign labor, the few existing industrial plants slowed production. Several lumber mills sat idle for the bulk of the war, allowing their equipment to rust past the point of repair. By the end of the war, the district's most productive industrial sector ran at about forty percent capacity.[52] The local economy was largely spared the devastation of Allied bombing. It appears that Allied planners did not know of the existence of the Wildflecken facility, which had been built partly for concealment, until near the end of the war. When a single bomber dropped its payload near Schondra on the night of November 19, 1943, damaging several farm properties, local police assumed that the pilot intended to hit the Muna.[53] The fact that this did not happen had profound consequences for Wildflecken and the region. By 1945, relatively few such facilities existed untouched and ready to be occupied anew. There were a few small air raids in the closing days of the war, but they did little damage. The deadliest killed seven Wehrmacht personnel, including a woman, on March 28.

The town and the base above it knew well in advance that the war would soon be over. As happened in so many places across the collapsing Reich, the military turned on itself in a murderous and morbid spasm of violence. A twenty-four-year-old non-commissioned officer was "shot while trying to escape" on March 23. He became one of the more than 20,000 Wehrmacht personnel executed during the war, a disproportionate number of which took place during "end-phase excesses" of 1945.[54] For Waffen-SS *Oberscharführer* Robert Gavaud, the impending end of the war brought the prospect of a likely return to his native France and little mercy for those who served in the Charlemagne Division. He took a fatal overdose of atropine on March 18.[55]

For the town, the end of the war came as something of an anti-climax. As the U.S. Seventh Army pushed hard through northern Bavaria toward Nürnberg, towns along the way fell in succession. American progress slowed in the hilly terrain north of the Main Valley, where steep slopes and poor roads hindered progress. The Americans reached Wildflecken on April 6, 1945. After a short exchange of fire outside of town, a single jeep nosed its way slowly down the main street. Two local women who had lived in the United States came out to greet the Americans. In the hill country of the Bavarian Rhön, an uneasy period of occupation began that would transform the region in ways that the inhabitants could scarcely imagine that spring day.

After occupying the town, the invaders discovered the massive cache of arms and munitions at the Muna above. They also found hundreds of laborers understandably ready to end their time in the Rhön. The Americans left a small guard to protect the military supplies before pushing on into Thuringia. When the war ended a month later, occupation borders regularized and Thuringia became part of the Soviet zone.

Once again, Wildflecken became a border town, living along a frontier shaped by the circumstances of the war's end and the already growing tension between the victorious Allies. Wildfleckeners could only watch as the consequences of the Soviet domination arrived at their doorstep.

While the Americans found forced laborers already in place at Wildflecken, another group was just beginning to arrive. Ethnic Germans living across vast swaths of Eastern Europe, along with Germans living in the path of the Soviet counter-offensive, trickled and then poured westward. When Germany's empire crumbled, the revenge of the Red Army and those who suffered under occupation began in earnest. German refugees from the East began to arrive as the war turned permanently against Germany. Their story, much like that of the forced laborers, stemmed from the messianic vision of Hitler's racial empire.[56]

The war conceived by the German leadership in the late 1930s was fundamentally different from past conflicts in Europe. Hitler had no patience for revisionists who wanted to see adjustments to Germany's borders that harkened back to the German Empire of 1871–1918. He saw himself as a *Raumpolitiker,* a "politician of space," who understood that Germany's destiny lay not in moving boundaries but in achieving an unprecedented demographic revolution. The ethnic diversity of Eastern Europe, Hitler and the senior Nazi leadership believed, needed to be rationalized, controlled, and ultimately homogenized by a biologically determined master race of Germans.[57] This attempt at a fundamental reordering of the continent necessarily fell disproportionately to the East of the Reich, a land upon which several generations of German extreme nationalists projected their fantasies. Hitler's SS chief Heinrich Himmler admired both the crusading Teutonic Knights and the pseudoscience of "blood and soil." Hitler himself famously remarked that "what India is for England, the eastern territory will be for us."[58] The Nazi war effort in the East therefore included a vast reorganization of the population and an effort to put into practice the dream of racial domination.

That eastern territory, which in Hitler's imagination sprawled to the Ural Mountains, owed its political shape to the rise and collapse of the great multiethnic empires of the Hapsburgs, Hohenzollerns, and Romanovs. In the wake of the First World War, when each of these empires collapsed, the peacemakers tried to reconstruct the region in a way that satisfied the political demands of some of the many ethnic groups living in the region while building buffers between Germany and Russia. The result was the creation of a network of states that drew their legitimacy as representatives of an ethnic group but faced the significant challenges of integrating large national minorities and coping with irredentist claims by their neighbors. The results tended to polarize ethnic identities and to weaken the democratic institutions in these new states. The presence of national minorities in a nationalizing age set up what the sociologist Rogers Brubaker has called a "dynamic interdependence" between minorities, the states in which they found themselves, and sometimes distant national homelands.[59]

Language, religion, and a web of associational life sustained an extraordinary and long-lasting pluralism across the region. Ethnic Germans, if more widespread than most, were just one of the groups dispersed across the region at the turn of the twentieth century. While most densely concentrated in the German and Austro-Hungarian Empires, the forty-two million ethnic Germans living in settlements spread eastward into the Balkans and the western Russian Empire. Germans lived in Volhynia, Bessarabia, Banat, Transylvania, Dobruja on the Black Sea, and in communities on the Volga descended from the Saxon farmers invited by Catherine the Great in 1763. These communities, later called *"Volksdeutsche"* (ethnic Germans), lived in close proximity to their neighbors, speaking a variety of languages and subject to a host of governments.[60] The national question came to the fore in the tumult of the nineteenth century. Nationalist ideals began to create alternative models of loyalty, but institutions like the Hapsburg monarchy and the bonds of religious faith helped to diffuse the force of nationalization.[61] These pressures could not be blunted forever, however, and the combination of the zero-sum ethnic nationalisms of the late nineteenth century and the political transformations that followed World War I sharpened the minority problems in Eastern Europe keenly enough that a network of treaties was designed to protect minority rights in the imperial successor states.[62]

The issue of nationalities proved to be among the most intractable problems facing the new states of East-Central Europe. Poland, for example, was less than seventy percent Polish, with significant numbers of Ukrainians, Jews, Byelorussians, and Germans.[63] Combined with the territorial irredentism stemming from the post-1918 boundary demarcations, these controversies significantly weakened states in this critical buffer zone between Germany and the Soviet Union. Efforts by states to "modernize" and homogenize populations only highlighted ethnic divisions and fostered the growth of ethnic parties.[64] In Czechoslovakia, Konrad Henlein's aggressive Sudeten German Party worked through much of the 1930s to undermine state control of the strategic border region where many of the country's three million ethnic Germans lived.

Hitler's war, with its explicitly racial objectives, drastically radicalized these already dangerous dynamics. The Volksdeutsche were, in Nazi ideology, co-ethnics separated from their natural home by the vicissitudes of history. They were supposed to be readily identifiable, conscious of their racial identity, and above all delighted to be reunited with their kinsmen. In reality, German administrators found themselves trying to find mythical purity in regions where people regularly intermarried and sometimes proved maddeningly reticent to join the master race. Massive social engineering programs like the *Heim ins Reich* (Home to the Reich) plan envisioned hundreds of thousands of sturdy ethnic Germans from southeast Europe settling land in Poland that had been cleared of Poles, Jews, and anyone else who already lived there. In reality, many of those selected for resettlement had no desire to do so and had to be coaxed or forced to realize their racial destiny. These "resettlers" often found themselves idling in camps as the demographic revolution sputtered and its planners increasingly turned to the murder of subject populations to realize their vision.[65]

Those who actively sided with Germany often did so by participating in the atrocities and institutionalized violence that marked the German effort in the East. In areas like Ukraine, where the Germans undermined their rule through the brutality of the occupation, ethnic Germans were over-represented both in the killing squads and in the occupation administration.[66] In doing so, identities once marked by "ambiguity and fluidity" became death sentences in the killing grounds of Eastern Europe. The Volksdeutsche, whether they liked it or not, became "German" in the eyes of their neighbors.[67]

As the conflict wound down, it became clear that the ethnic Germans would not be allowed to remain in Eastern Europe. The Czechoslovak government-in-exile in London issued a series of decrees earlier in the war, depriving Germans (as well as Hungarians) of their citizenship. Poland lost territory in the east to the Soviet Union, but gained in the west as large chunks of prewar Germany came under Polish control. Ethnic Germans, both in prewar Poland and in the euphemistically titled "Recovered Territories" now faced the loss of rights and property. The massive ethnic cleansing of Eastern Europe was sanctioned, if not encouraged, by the major Allied leaders. Citing the examples of the Greco-Turkish exchanges of the 1920s and the perennial trouble spot of Alsace-Lorraine, Churchill and Roosevelt acceded at the Potsdam Conference to formal expulsion of Germans. Stalin, an experienced practitioner of ethnic redistribution, needed no encouragement. The Allies asserted that the burden of expelled Germans should be shared evenly throughout the zones of occupation and that "any transfers that take place should be effected in an orderly and humane manner."[68]

Nothing of the sort happened. Forced population movements at the end of the war lasted for years and were marked by brutality, terror, and death. This massive flight effectively began the summer of 1944, when the Red Army began to sweep through Romania, and panicked civilians, both German and Hungarian, headed west by any possible conveyance to escape the Soviets and their own vengeful neighbors. By the end of that year, the Red Army stood on Germany's pre-1939 territory, setting off successive waves of flight from Silesia, East Prussia, and other eastern parts of the Reich. Across the ethnic borderlands of Central Europe, a reckoning began for the crimes of the German empire. In Czechoslovakia and Poland, militias detained, tortured, and sometimes murdered Germans before sending others, by foot, wagon, and train, into a defeated Germany that many had never even visited. Between 1945 and 1948, more than twelve million ethnic Germans fled or were formally expelled from their homes in Eastern Europe.[69]

As the great Soviet offensive crossed into pre-1939 Germany at the end of 1944, a trickle of ethnic Germans from the East began to appear in distant Lower Franconia. Within months, the streets of Würzburg, Aschaffenburg, and Schweinfurt filled with Prussians, Memellanders, Transnistrians, Bessarabians, Sudetenlanders, and Silesians. Horse and ox drawn carts loaded with baggage and harrowed-faced farmers navigated the bombed-out streets of once modern cities. Local authorities had few resources and little will to deal with this new population. A Sudeten woman who later became active in expellee politics in the region remembered that "most expellees were simply registered into a camp, given some soup and a blanket, and then sent on. One could only stay two days, then be moved out to the rural districts."[70]

This practice, which continued after the arrival of the Americans, meant that rural areas like Wildflecken, which suffered minimal physical damage from the war, now received the lion's share of those fleeing its aftermath. While these rural communities lacked the infrastructure to receive or care for refugees, they were generally in a considerably better position to do so than were the devastated cities. This last point is critical to the story that follows. The story of the arrival of the expellees in Germany was fundamentally a rural one. Because of the lack of housing or economic activity in cities, most expellees found themselves in small communities. About seventy-three percent of expellees in Bavaria lived in towns with fewer than 5,000 inhabitants and sixty percent lived in communities with populations of less than 2,000.[71]

Given the confusion that dominated at the end of the war, it is unsurprising that record keeping proved inadequate to the task at hand. During February, five hundred refugees entered the Landkreis, bringing the total to 5,889, of which 380 stopped in Wildflecken.[72] In Landkreis Brückenau, the situation only got worse. While expulsions included other ethnic groups (Hungarians, Slovakians, and Italians prominently among them), the Germans bore the brunt. Slovakia officially deported about 25,000 Germans. Hungary deported 110,000 during the first half of 1946. Poland and Czechoslovakia, homes of the largest German communities, now began regular transports of expellees into Germany's eastern and western zones. Roughly four million expellees from Poland and Czechoslovakia settled in the Soviet Zone, while 6.5 million ended up in the western zones.[73] Towns untouched by the physical damage of war now watched the arrival of refugees in strange clothes with odd accents.

For rural communities across the defeated Reich, the arrival of expellees signified another group of outsiders thrust into their midst by the exigencies of war. As Germany's cities burned under Allied bombing, thirty-five percent of available housing stock suffered enough damage to make it uninhabitable. This ushered in a wave of evacuations, beginning in 1942, to the countryside. Now, as the war moved toward its conclusion, the expellees arrived with virtually no material possessions and progressively less support from the collapsing German government.[74]

The soon-to-be victorious Allies faced the task of coping with the massive humanitarian needs of the continent. To manage this immense challenge, the Allies established a series of organizations and agencies charged with locating, sorting, and eventually finding homes for the masses of people victimized by the war. While the list of eligible victims notably excluded Germans, the Allied effort nevertheless endeavored to find solutions for some of the most seemingly intractable consequences of six years of war. Before Allied troops landed in Western Europe in force, the Allies were aware of the scale of the human tragedy unfolding in occupied and contested Europe. While information often proved incorrect or exaggerated, Allied planners and observers at home discussed the possibility that the liberation of Europe likely meant taking an active role in reconstructing a shattered continent and putting its human components back together again.

In late 1943, the Allies announced the formation of the United Nations Relief and Rehabilitation Administration (UNRRA). As Roosevelt said at the White House meeting that produced UNRRA's charter:

> When victory comes there can certainly be no secure peace until there is a return of law and order in the oppressed countries.... This means that the more quickly and effectually we apply measures of relief and rehabilitation, the more quickly will our own boys overseas be able to come home.[75]

From China to France, millions lost their homes and livelihoods to the physical destruction of war while others found themselves far from home working for occupying powers. While the League of Nations had experience dealing with refugee problems stemming from the First World War and the rise of Fascism, the challenges that faced the Allies in the future looked far more daunting.[76]

Of particular concern were those left outside of their country of citizenship or made stateless by the war. The Supreme Headquarters, Allied Expeditionary Force (SHAEF) drew up a quick, catch-all definition of so-called "Displaced Persons," which included but was not strictly limited to "evacuees, war or political fugitives, political prisoners, forced or voluntary workers, *Todt* workers, and former members of forces under German command, deportees, intruded persons, extruded persons, civilian internees, ex-prisoners of war, and stateless persons."[77] In principle, DPs had to be either stateless because of the war or citizens of an Allied nation who found themselves outside of their natal borders. This definition covered an enormous range of wartime experiences, including both victims of and participants in the policies of the Third Reich. Any apparatus established to help these people faced considerable challenges in determining who would be eligible for assistance. More critically, SHAEF believed that DPs posed a real threat to military operations, both by clogging the roads and through epidemic diseases like typhus. In May 1944, the Civil Affairs Division (G-5) created a Displaced Persons Branch, tasked with identifying and fixing in place DP populations on the continent so that care could be provided *in situ*.

At its founding, UNRRA's responsibilities in Europe were limited by the fact that the Allies controlled very little territory on the continent. In 1944, this changed dramatically as the Allies pushed further into Italy and invaded France. Almost exactly one year after UNRRA came into existence, General Eisenhower formally recognized its role in the care of the displaced in the European theater. As the Allied armies moved into Germany, UNRRA teams fanned out behind the lines. The problems were legion. UNRRA was almost entirely dependent on American supplies for its personnel; training and vetting of volunteers proved overly hasty; and the November 1945 agreement with SHAEF did not explicitly delineate roles and responsibilities. UNRRA proved unable to bridge the vast and growing gulf between available facilities and the number of people in need. SHAEF requested 450 UNRRA teams, but training proceeded slowly and only fifteen proved ready for deployment a month before the war in Europe ended. By August, more than 4,500 UNRRA staffers and subordinate agency employees worked in Europe. While the agency remained understaffed, by the fall it had enough personnel in the field to begin taking over refugee facilities from the occupying armies.

Across Germany, initial responsibility for DPs fell to the advancing Allied armies. As factories and other facilities fell to the invaders, foreign laborers took to the roads. Hamburg alone had more than four hundred sites where foreign workers clustered at the time of liberation. The solution was to concentrate these disparate groups in holding camps. As one GI later explained, "We herded them into camps to clear the roads." By the fall, there were 277 centers in western Germany and twenty-five in Austria. This number only increased in the coming months, reaching 762 by 1947, 416 of which were in U.S. zone in Germany.[78] For the Americans, desperate to find intact buildings in which to house DPs, disused German military facilities were a tempting target. The problems facing German bureaucrats with regard to expellees were equally valid in the case of DPs. Germany's cities lay in ruins, barely able to support the remnants of urban populations. While DP camps became part of the urban landscape in the postwar period, the vast majority of camps were built in and near suburbs, small towns, and rural communities, generally on the site of disused military bases or industrial sites. As with the expellees, Germany's smaller communities faced the task of hosting the bulk of the DPs. The former Wehrmacht training areas at Hohenfels and Grafenwöhr/Vilseck, just to name two, now housed large concentrations of DPs and continued to do so for years. These early choices unwittingly set up significant problems a few years later.

For Bavaria's American occupiers, the DP problem became a fundamental one in the day-to-day life of the occupation. The Army had neither the institutional expertise nor the desire to be in the refugee management business and clearly looked forward to the day that the task might be passed off to UNRRA. The scope of the problem was simply beyond the linguistic, cultural, and administrative capacity of units still engaged in wrapping up the war in Europe. The great Polish writer Tadeusz Borowski, an Auschwitz survivor who ended up a DP in Munich, later wrote: "At the time West Germany was swarming with starved, frightened, suspicious, stupefied hordes of people who did not know where to turn and who were driven from town to town, from camp to camp, from barracks to barracks by young American boys, equally stupefied and equally shocked by what they had found in Europe."[79]

UNRRA came behind, prepared to take over control when the military situation stabilized. While UNRRA depended on the Army for virtually all of its material and logistical needs, it was outside of the command structure and could only appeal to the goodwill of local personnel. Neither UNRRA nor the Army had enough trained linguists or civil affairs specialists to get a handle on the DP problem. This situation bred chaos. Francesca Wilson, a British refugee specialist with extensive experience working with the displaced in Spain, arrived with an UNRRA team near Starnberg outside Munich. She found the town administered by an American captain named Paisly:

> He was a pleasant young man, fair-haired and good-looking, with the amused, rather caressing manner of the well-bred, kindly American. He received us with great urbanity, though he had no idea that we were coming and had never heard of UNRRA.[80]

During summer 1945, the Allied command structure changed considerably. SHAEF dissolved as a joint command and was replaced by United States Forces, European Theater (USFET). Care of DPs now rested with zonal commanders. In the American zone, commanders emphasized repatriation, an effort that initially met with considerable success. More than two million DPs left the American zone during the summer. However, most of those who repatriated during those months came from Western Europe and very much wanted to return home. Matters proved very different for those from the East.[81]

Contemporaries knew that they faced a considerably steeper challenge convincing DPs from Eastern Europe to return home. In September 1939, the Red Army occupied a vast swatch of Poland, in temporary partnership with the Germans. The thirteen million inhabitants of this multiethnic border zone suffered violence, sovietization, mass deportation, and other hardships for nearly two years. After June 1941, German rule replaced Soviet domination, starting another round of hideous violence directed against Jews, non-Jewish Poles, Ukrainians, and other ethnic minorities.[82] At the end of this miasma of bloodletting, the Soviet Union annexed the territory it took in 1939. As a result, districts in eastern Poland now endured fearsome ethnic cleansing as the postwar Polish government pushed Ukrainians eastward and faced the prospect of Poles coming west across the new boundary. The security situation in Poland worsened as competing armed groups fought for control of what Daniel Blatman has described as a "torn apart, wounded, demographically unbalanced, and economically devastated" country.[83]

The Yalta Agreement in February included provisions that pointed to the loss of Polish territory in the East to the Soviet Union and that made Soviet citizens liable for forcible repatriation after the war. Many Poles resident in Germany now found that their homes fell inside the new boundaries of the Soviet Union. Since many of those Poles had lived under Soviet occupation between 1939 and the German invasion of 1941, they were all too aware of the consequences of Soviet policy.[84] Even those Poles whose homes fell west of the new Soviet border were often leery of returning to a devastated country under Soviet occupation.

Many Soviet citizens in the West welcomed the chance to return home after captivity and slave labor. For others, like the significant number who willingly served the German war effort, repatriation loomed ominously. Scenes of sometimes bloody forced repatriation followed and an unknown but considerable number of those who returned vanished into the Soviet prison system. One recent scholarly estimate suggests that almost forty percent of the more than 5.2 million Soviet repatriates found themselves engaged in compulsory service or turned over to state security organs.[85] The U.S. Army, heavily involved in identifying repatriates, found the task of forced repatriation enormously distasteful, particularly in cases where people became Soviet citizens against their will thanks to Soviet wartime conquests. This was particularly true for Balts and Poles. Diplomatically, this was tricky, since the Soviets remained a member of the Allies. Gradually, the western Allies lost interest in forced repatriation, save those clearly identified as having fought for Germany. Forced repatriation incidents, particularly concerning Soviet citizens who joined the German military during the war, took place as late as 1947. However, by mid-summer 1945, Baltic DPs and Poles "coming from East of the Curzon Line [were] not to be considered Soviet citizens unless they affirmatively claim Soviet citizenship."[86] Ironically, many Poles who remained in the West benefitted from Soviet efforts to get some of their countrymen forcibly repatriated. As American annoyance with Soviet intransigence grew, so too did the will to definitively protect all Polish DPs. In September, Seventh Army passed the word that "No Polish National will be returned against his will."[87]

Definitive numbers for DP population flows in the immediate postwar period are elusive, in large part because of the near constant movement of people into and out of the camps and the continued entry of Eastern Europeans into Germany after the war. Nonetheless, a few patterns are worth noting. In the months after the war, massive repatriation took place, largely self-motivated with the notable exception of those Soviet citizens who balked at returning. More than 5.8 million people returned to their homes in the five months following the war's termination. These included almost all of the 2.1 million Western European DPs. Numerically, these were dwarfed by the huge number of DPs from Eastern and East-Central Europe. Large-scale repatriation continued through 1946, as will be discussed in the next chapter. Of the 500,000 who returned home in 1946, more than seventy percent returned to Poland. Nonetheless, more than a year after the Army turned over control of the camps to UNRRA, the DP problem in the western zones crystallized around a "hard core" of DPs unwilling to repatriate. A staggering 914,997 DPs remained in the West, of whom the largest segment were 293,086 Poles. More than sixty percent of these DPs lived in the American zone, by far the largest number of the three western zones.[88] As the DP population stabilized, their care became a necessary and important component of occupation government and daily life in parts of occupied Western Germany. Their continued presence posed a significant challenge to a military government then struggling to deal with a host of other problems, not least the continued influx of other types of refugees.

The American zone included the largest number of DPs and by far the largest concentration of ethnic German expellees. The former were eligible for American and Allied assistance, while the latter were not. That task fell to the reconstituted German civil authorities. The Americans were eager to establish a functional German-led government that could help with the enormous administrative tasks of rebuilding the country while relieving the administrative burden on the Americans. By the end of May, in consultation with non-Nazi Bavarian politicians, a state (*Land*) government formed in Munich.

The new government faced any number of serious challenges. Perhaps the most pressing was the continuing influx of expellees into the western zones from Eastern Europe. In the tumultuous postwar period, it proved difficult to even establish a reliable count of the population of Bavaria, much less the number of expellees.

In December, the Bavarian government created the position of State Commissioner for Refugee Affairs (*Staatskommissar für das Flüchtlingswesen*), an extraordinary position under the Ministry of the Interior. In turn, each region and district got its own commissioner with a staff. The new administration was headed by Wolfgang Jaenicke, an inspired choice. Born in 1881 in Breslau, Jaenicke had a long and distinguished career as an administrator and diplomat before being forced into retirement by the Nazis. He spent the war living quietly near Munich and was nearly murdered by vengeful SS men in the last days of the conflict. A Silesian, Jaenicke found himself unable to return home like so many of the refugees with whose care he now found himself charged. He threw himself into the task of organizing part of one of the largest population movements in human history. His methods were not always popular. Many in the new Bavarian government complained that Refugee Affairs workers acted like petty dictators in their districts. There may have been some truth to this, but since much of the crisis took place out in the countryside, Jaenicke found himself relying on deputies who could operate effectively from well beyond Munich's supervision.[89]

Jaenicke's fledgling organization, built mostly from the ground up, depended on the competence and skill of its regional and local officials. Wildflecken and Lower Franconia were fortunate. Jaenicke's deputy in Lower Franconia was Dr. Josef Winter, a lawyer and another expellee from the Sudetenland. Relatively young at forty-six, he proved energetic and able.[90] Winter dispatched Anton Beck, a capable local bureaucrat, to Landkreis Brückenau. While Beck later found himself overwhelmed by events, his actions during the first days of the postwar period demonstrated a great deal of cleverness, resourcefulness, and, perhaps most critically for an administrator in a crisis, a marked willingness to allow and encourage initiative from below. Events soon put these skills to the test.

It is difficult to overstate the demographic transformation engendered by the war. Numbers changed constantly as new refugee flows arrived and populations shifted. In the months after the conflict's end, the population of Bavaria stood at 8.2 million, up from a prewar population of seven million. This estimate reflected the enormous numbers of refugees and evacuees then resident in the area.[91] In October 1946, Bavaria held 1,657,765 expellees, about twenty-one percent of the state's total population, of whom 1,110,940 came from outside Germany's pre-1937 borders. For geographic reasons, the largest group of expellees in Bavaria came from the nearby Sudetenland (871,863). The second-largest group came from Silesia, east of the new Polish border (431,808). Proximity to the Sudetenland had significant consequences for Bavaria, since a plurality of expellees was skilled or semi-skilled workers, many with education and experience that they tried to put to work in their new surroundings.

Later this gave Bavaria a comparative advantage in rebuilding compared to other regions that absorbed greater numbers of farmers and rural laborers. Of all of the German states in the western zones, Bavaria took in the largest number of expellees, but both Lower Saxony (twenty-seven percent) and Schleswig-Holstein (thirty-three percent) in the British Zone had higher percentages of expellees. The French had little interest in dealing with German victims of the war and managed to keep most expellees out of their zone.[92]

Within Bavaria, refugee populations dispersed widely but unevenly. Expellees concentrated in districts close to the eastern border. Lower Bavaria (*Niederbayern*) had the highest concentration of any district. Almost a quarter of residents had fled from elsewhere. As a whole, Lower Franconia absorbed relatively few expellees (142,121 or fourteen percent of the total population). In keeping with the general trend, 83,212 came from the Sudetenland. These statistics, however, conceal the disproportionate impact of the refugee crisis on the countryside. The region's three cities, Würzburg, Aschaffenburg, and Schweinfurt, were devastated and could not absorb many new residents. This pushed expellees into rural districts like Landkreis Brückenau, where expellees made up twenty percent of the population. Since many of the skilled Sudeten workers concentrated to the southeast, the expellee population in Landkreis Brückenau was more heavily weighted toward farmers. This had significant implications for the region in the years to come.[93]

Even in defeated Germany, few places witnessed the kind of demographic transformation encountered in Landkreis Brückenau at the end of the war. A poor rural district with barely 20,000 inhabitants concentrated in a mid-sized spa town more than doubled in population within a few months. As expellees streamed in from Eastern Europe and DPs arrived by the truck and trainload, rural northern Franconia faced an extraordinary challenge. With the expellees and DPs came bureaucrats, both military and civilian, who endeavored to manage a chaotic and potentially dangerous situation. No one knew how to accomplish such a mission, in no small part because such a thing had never been done before. The encounter between soldiers, civilians, and refugees endured long after the first dangerous days of peace. It left in its wake, a region, its people, and a way of life forever altered. The center of this transformation was the massive DP camp on the hill above Wildflecken. The camp, where DPs, locals, American soldiers, and facility administrators interacted for the next six years, coalesced in a way that typified the improvised, uncertain, and chaotic situation facing all of these groups at the end of the war.

On July 20, 1945, a truck set out from the UNRRA training facility at Jullouville in Normandy. Twelve team members, speaking at least five languages, spent ten days bouncing across the highways and secondary roads of the shattered continent. One of them was Kathryn Hulme, a forty-five-year-old American who became the most famous chronicler of the DP camp experience. Hulme was a remarkable woman. Born in San Francisco, she left the University of California after her junior year and, along with another student, moved to Connecticut to raise chickens and write. She later worked in advertising for a travel agency in New York. After the war broke out, she returned to California to work in the Richmond Shipyard #2 as a journeyman welder and filed an application to work for the newly formed UNRRA. In her memoir, she wrote that her shipyard experience "was a compelling reason for my acceptance into UNRRA, since it proved I was flexible."[94]

Hulme's easy and gracious humor nearly reached its limits as the truckload of UNRRA staffers wound through the back country of northern Bavaria. All they knew was that they had been tasked with finding a town called Wildflecken, where 2,000 Poles supposedly lived under the control of the U.S. Army. The town is difficult enough to find with good roads and clear signage. In the aftermath of the war, the task proved almost impossible. It was nighttime when the truck with its eager, cramped, and half-trained cargo arrived "by guess and by God," at their destination.[95] Instead of 2,000 DPs, they found nearly 20,000, just a small foretaste of the vastness of the task awaiting them. "This is absolutely the most beautiful spot on God's green earth," Hulme wrote in her diary, "It is also a volcano of frightful human portent on which we sit, our team, trying to learn how to hold hands, if not to pray together." A new era in the four-hundred-year history of the Wild Place, its surroundings, and the divided nation whose new borders lay just a few miles away, began.

TWO

THE SEIGNEURS OF WILDFLECKEN, 1945–1947

On the morning of May 16, 1945, news reached Wildflecken that a villager had been injured in a fight at the camp. Mayor Bruno Kleinhenz grabbed local physician Erich L., Wehrmacht civil administrator Peter M., and the town's sole law enforcement officer, the young Wilhelm Henties. Together they jumped in a car and headed up the hill. Henties knew the camp's erstwhile commander, a Russian major named Pavlov, and hoped to find him. By American orders, none of the Germans were armed, and Henties did not have the right to wear a uniform. In the midst of thousands of angry former forced laborers, this was a dangerous situation. Things went wrong quickly. The crowd turned on the delegation, dragging them from the truck and beating and stabbing all four. A Frenchman among the laborers ran to the American military post nearby and summoned help, which arrived and dispersed the mob. The bodies of Kleinhenz, L., and M. lay in the street, while Henties, grievously wounded, survived to recover in the hospital in Brückenau.[1]

This chapter begins and ends with riots. In between can be found the story of a curious hybrid society that grew up inside, and outside, of the perimeter of the giant DP camp at Wildflecken. The postwar relationship between Wildflecken and the camp on the hill began with a multiple homicide. This single tragedy, when merged with the chronic instability and violence of the place and time, quickly vanished from view. Yet it colored relations between the town and the camp dwellers for years to come, setting a pattern of mistrust and anxiety that hardened as time went on. The multiple murders of May 16 were never solved or even investigated. Within weeks, those responsible likely left Wildflecken as the army began the process of sorting DPs into national groups to prepare them for repatriation. This made little difference to the people in Wildflecken, who understandably did not and often could not distinguish between the incoming and outgoing camp populations.

The Wildflecken DP camp and its relationship with the surrounding community between 1945 and 1947 reflected the uncertainties of that fluid era. Locals, administrators, and governments far from the Sinn Valley shared the fundamental belief that the camp, and hundreds like it across Central Europe, was a temporary housing facility that would be closed as soon as its residents went home. Observers based these plans on the idea that camp residents badly wanted to go back to Eastern Europe. By the time it became clear that this was not the case, it was too late.

The DP camp in its early years was both an integral part of and a world apart from the surrounding community. The needs of the camp, combined with the remote location of the facility, meant that its administration had to compete with other local interests for scarce resources. This had the effect of integrating the economic affairs of local communities, the DP camp, and the occupation authorities. These relationships were further complicated by two factors. First, power relations between these groups were manifestly unequal. Foreign laborers, who had lived in the Sinn Valley through the war years, now held economic power and had the support of the occupation authorities. Second, local communities were themselves dealing with an influx of refugees who were largely their responsibility. This will be discussed in more detail in the next chapter.

The DP camp was the center of the local economy during the first years after the war. Because of the sheer amount of goods moving through the camp, and because many of these goods came directly from the occupation authority, the camp served as a clearing house for both scarce luxury and staple items. Economic activity in and around the camp included both black market (trade in illegal goods like controlled food and clothing) and gray market (the unauthorized distribution of legal goods) elements.[2] In occupied Germany, where currency had little if any worth, the barter economy clustered around those with access to rationed or otherwise unobtainable commodities. Some DPs used their ambiguous legal status to develop far-reaching and sophisticated trade networks that entangled DPs, locals, and even UNRRA staffers and

American troops. While only shadowy traces of these networks remain, they were obviously a critical nexus point of economic life in the region and connected the camp with other parts of the DP archipelago and with the surrounding community.

At the same time, the camp had its own public and subterranean identity that marked it as separate from local communities. It was a legally incorporated Polish town with its own government that paralleled the apparatus of UNRRA. Relief workers, both by design and because they had difficulty finding interlocutors, failed to realize the extent to which camp life became politicized. The political community in the camp divided along prewar political lines, wartime fractures, and the needs of a growing and dynamic community in exile. Much of the internal debate, which can only be partially reconstructed, concerned repatriation to Poland. When residents rioted against repatriation in January 1947, UNRRA was caught flat-footed.

Along with the development of formal and informal political structures came a rise in unrest and violence among camp residents. In the legal limbo of the camp, the lines between politics and criminality blurred. Weapons became an inescapable part of camp life, a danger repeatedly brought home by assaults, accidental shootings, and a prolonged period of insecurity in the nearby countryside. It is unnecessary to resort to the hoary stereotypes of "DP criminality" to conclude that bored young men with grievances against Germans, access to weapons, and little fear of serious repercussions proved likely to try their luck as practitioners of economic violence.

Many of the later problems, however persistent, resulted from the initial conditions under which the camp formed and grew. From a core of local laborers, the facility exerted a centripetal force on a quickly growing population of former laborers already on the move. At the same time, American efforts to manage the process only exacerbated the confusion by moving large numbers of the displaced without a long- or medium-term plan for their disposition. At the same time, UNRRA waited in the wings. This, in turn, relieved American tactical commanders of anything other than a temporary responsibility for the DPs.

The first wave of DPs to arrive in Wildflecken differed greatly from the camp's eventual composition. First, they were ethnically mixed, with significant numbers of Catholic Poles, Ukrainians, Yugoslavs, and Jews.

Second, they came both in organized transports and on their own, a process that the U.S. Army eventually reversed in the late summer when camps were reorganized along ethnic lines. Finally, the camp during the period of Army administration saw very little contact between administrators and residents, which had the unfortunate side effect of abetting chaos in the camp and in its relations with the town. Food supplies remained irregular, Army officers in charge of the facility had little idea how many people were in their charge, and they gave little thought to perimeter security. Civil Affairs officers visited the camps and offered limited training, but they were understaffed and bounced frequently between constituent parts of the ever-growing network of camps.

Morris Krakowsky, from Łódź, arrived on one of the early transports to Wildflecken from Buchenwald. Fifty years later, he was still angry at the way the Americans administered the camp. "We ended up in a DP camp called Wildflecken, which was a miserable place, almost as bad as a prison. [There] was an idiot commandant of the camp, a Major Adams who was – I don't know – an anti-Semite or a martinet or just miserable."[3] With very few troops on the ground in the area and little experience with running a growing camp, the Americans struggled to manage events.

In the meantime, DPs continued to arrive at Wildflecken, often in ways completely beyond the control of the Americans. There is no single story of how people came to Wildflecken in the immediate aftermath of the war. However, a few broad generalizations can be made that can be applied to the larger issue of DPs in the wake of the war. The initial wave of DPs largely self-organized as more freed laborers and refugees either encountered allied liberators or simply left their workplaces as the war ended. A significant number of Jewish DPs who came in the early days of the camp arrived, like Krakowsky, from Buchenwald in nearby Thuringia after they learned that the area around Buchenwald would be turned over to the Red Army. DPs tended to cluster near the occupation zonal borders, in no small part out of anxiety over the presence of the Soviets. Jan Dudzinski, a young Pole from Warsaw who escaped from a prisoner train in Prague, walked across the Czechoslovak border into the American zone. Having fought briefly in the Prague Uprising in early May, Dudzinski found himself living between the Red Army, which he feared, and the Americans, who disappointed him by not pushing further into

Czechoslovakia. Years later, he recalled: "I didn't like Russians. I didn't want to go back to them because I knew what happened – anyway, they invaded Poland."[4]

Another Pole who came to Wildflecken to escape the Soviets was Andrezj (Andrew) Zdanowicz. Born in 1938 near Bialystok, Zdanowicz fled westward from Soviet-occupied Poland with his mother in 1940 after the arrest and disappearance of his father and uncle. In 1945, the family fled again in the face of a great Soviet offensive early in the year. As the war ended, they found themselves pinned between the Soviet Army, the Americans, and the last German defenders of Thuringia. After being caught in a savage artillery duel near the village of Bilzingsleben, the family managed to push south far enough to end the war behind American lines.[5]

Wildflecken became a camp for Christian Poles, but a significant number of Jews lived there during the initial months of the camp's existence. In August, there were 552 Jews living in the facility, though the number was probably somewhat higher.[6] Polish Jews had good reason to fear revealing their identity to their one-time neighbors. In some cases, Jews moved into the DP camps using the same subterfuge that allowed them to survive the war. Maria Friedland, a twenty-three-year-old Ukrainian Jew who acquired false papers identifying her as a Christian, ended the war in the Thuringian town of Wahlwinkel, where she lived on a farm and enjoyed generally good relations with the family for whom she worked. When an American unit arrived in early May, she became an informal translator despite her admittedly limited English skills. Friedland and a small group of Polish laborers left Wahlwinkel shortly thereafter, moving slowly south and connecting with other foreign workers on the road. The group swelled as word-of-mouth connected disparate groups, until all of them eventually got word of a large camp where the Americans provided food for foreigners trapped in Germany.

Still concealing her identity, Friedland and her fellow ex-laborers settled in the Wildflecken camp. They had little choice. Allied refugee policy initially rested on the notion that DPs should be classified by their country of origin, leaving Jews in a precarious position alongside co-nationals who had little regard for them. In August, a report on Jewish life in the DP camps by the American Earl Harrison shocked President Truman. Harrison bluntly suggested that "we appear to be treating the Jews as the Nazis treated them except that we do not exterminate them." He urged, among other reforms, the creation of specifically Jewish camps. Within a few months, the U.S. Zone alone had twelve camps for Jewish DPs, including the large facilities at Landsberg and Wolfratshausen.[7] Among those who rejoiced at the chance to move was Maria Friedland. She recalls being at Wildflecken for "weeks," though it was likely a matter of months. When she learned of the new Jewish camps, Friedland confessed her Jewish identity to a friend, who promptly revealed that she too was a Jew with false papers. Friedland left the camp by the end of summer, eventually making her way to Canada.[8] By early 1946, there were no Jews left in the Wildflecken camp.

When the UNRRA team designated to administer the Wildflecken facility arrived at the end of July, they were, if anything, just as diverse a group as the refugees resident there. They came from a variety of backgrounds, with a range of wartime experience and competencies. The American UNRRA officer Ephraim Chase worked at the DP camp at Dillingen in Swabia. In November 1945, as he left the camp, he filed a report filled with trenchant and often mordantly funny observations. His account captured the enormous frustrations of dealing with a population that the UNRRA staff did not understand well and with whom they often lacked the linguistic capability to even communicate.

> In light of actual experience in DP field operations, I do not hesitate to define the qualifications of a successful DP field worker as "a degree of intelligence, a human sympathetic approach to the problem and a good knowledge of the language the people you deal with speak." Anything more than that is much to the good, anything less is tragic.[9]

Chase, like many UNRRA officers in the year after the war, had to learn all of this from a standing start. The staffers at Wildflecken perhaps could have guessed, but did not fully understand, just how difficult their task would be and how unprepared they or anyone else was for the job. Aside from Hulme, the camp staff represented a cross-section of Allied states and a wide range of backgrounds and experiences. Turnover was a significant if not crippling problem, but a brief snapshot of the staff at Wildflecken suggests some of the key characteristics in the essential makeup of the UNRRA effort in Germany. Staffers tended to be either old enough to have had significant prewar careers or at least to have acquired specialist training. They spoke a range of languages, though few claimed to speak German and, most significantly, only one claimed to speak "some" Polish.

The camp's first director was George Masset, a forty-five-year-old Frenchman who joined UNRRA in June after working as an interpreter for the U.S. Army in Paris. He was a World War I veteran and spent much of the interwar period working in international commerce. His work took him to India, the U.S., and Europe, and UNRRA authorities initially believed him to be highly skilled and capable. Both the second deputy director, Gaston Rouwens, and the supply officer, Paul Goosens, were Belgian. Rouwens had a long career as an accountant, working mostly with the railroad industry and representing a variety of international firms. Goosens (forty-four) was also a World War I veteran and spent most of the intervening years as a salesman and hotel manager. Most of the other staffers were French and in their mid-twenties. The camp's medical officer, Dr. Rene Muracciole, was technically still on active duty in the French Army. Also on the team was a Belgian nurse named Marie Louise Habets, a former nun with nursing experience in the Congo and war-torn Europe. Habets and Hulme, who met at the UNRRA training facility, became romantically involved at some point and remained together for the rest of their lives. Hulme later wrote about Habets in her book *The Nun's Story*, which subsequently became a 1959 movie starring Audrey Hepburn.

In total, about twenty UNRRA staffers worked in the camp at any given time. This was a larger-than-average UNRRA team, but small proportionate to the sizable camp population.[10] This team now faced the task of organizing and establishing some sort of control over a vast and fractious cluster of humanity in the woods of Lower Franconia. Personnel problems bedeviled the Wildflecken mission. More than sixty UNRRA workers passed through the camp during its first eighteen months. Of these, according to the official history compiled by Hulme, "5 ran away from the team without orders, 6 were taken by the district, 5 were transferred, 10 resigned, 9 were terminated, and 2 were arrested by the military authorities."[11]

As UNRRA prepared to take over management of the camp, relations between the army and the Poles deteriorated. The DPs, many of whom spent considerable time living under the eye of armed guards,

Kathryn Hulme and a DP wait for a repatriation train, April 1946. *Yale Collection of American Literature, Beinecke Rare Book and Manuscript Library.*

resented the presence of soldiers assigned to keep them from going too far from the camp boundary. In August and early September alone there were three fatal shooting incidents. Two of them involved Poles trying to sneak out of the camp. The last followed an argument between an African-American soldier and a Pole inside the camp. The camp committee described these shootings as "infamous, without argument and contradictory with [democratic] principles, therefore we demand to open the limits of the Polish camp."[12]

The army had good reason to remain in the area. Just up the hill from the camp remained much of the ammunition left in the Muna "which, if accidently set off by the Germans or the DPs would, according to our local military government, have killed every living thing in three counties including the grasshoppers." The army did not go far when they ceded control of the camp to UNRRA, though they comprehensively abandoned their administrative mission more or less overnight. Hulme recalled that:

> When we entered the camp, Army was in control in the form of a Captain, but he took off at the end of the first week, leaving us a handsome large office equipped with mahogany desks empty of all documents, reports or even carbon copies of letters which might have given us a clue to what had gone on in the camp prior to our arrival.[13]

If Hulme's book and reports to UNRRA superiors reflected her frustration with the U.S. Army, her private diary was far more caustic and angry. She was particularly vituperative toward American military personnel and what she described as their "phony militarism." An American colonel with his "swagger cane and pimp perfection" exemplified the very different approaches that UNRRA and the military took toward camp management. "It sickens me to my soul to think of it . . . but this is the Army. This is the stunted mentality of West Point dealing with a human problem. Prod them with a Lugers gun . . . that's all they know about how to get action from the Poles."[14]

The DP camps in Lower Franconia, and all over Germany, occupied the same space and had the same needs as the foreign military occupation of the country. While the U.S. Third Army turned control of the camps over to UNRRA, it retained the right to inspect the camps, provide external security for the facilities, and to requisition the same supplies that the camps needed for maintenance and, particularly in the fall and winter, survival. The Americans consistently demanded that UNRRA crack down on black marketeering, increase the cleanliness of the camps and their inhabitants, and better maintain internal security. UNRRA similarly demanded a share of precious local resources appropriate for the mass of people under their charge. Ephraim Chase summed up the resulting problems:

> often when our trucks arrived at the saw-mill to gather the products of the previous two or three days we would find that someone beat us to it. The XYZ Engineers, we would learn, appeared on the scene a day or an hour ago and removed every splinter of wood on the premises leaving a tell-tale notice behind to the effect that from now on everyone else is to keep out of here. At first we felt frustrated, but gradually we became inured and mastered the game of matching wits. Compromise and gentlemens' agreements were effected, and the supply

of lumber resumed its steady flow so that we shall have a quantity of lumber left over to meet emergency repairs during the winter months and for the camp shop to make simple furniture.[15]

The facility that UNRRA inherited was about twelve square miles in area. From town, it was a steep walk up a densely forested hill to the northeast or a drive along Florian-Geyer-Strasse, a road paved to accommodate the tanks that operated there when it served as a training facility. The camp was laid out in an arc, with the open end facing east. The buildings on the grounds were in various stages of repair, with about eighty inhabitable buildings including blockhouses, single-family homes, administrative buildings, stables, seven kitchens with dining areas, and workshop facilities. UNRRA estimated that they could salvage about 1,700 rooms for DPs.[16] None of the buildings were properly winterized, rooms were large and more suitable for men in bunks than for families seeking a modicum of privacy, and a number of buildings fell into disrepair, becoming a constant fire danger and a "trysting place for amorous Poles."[17] The central formation ground, renamed Eisenhower Platz (formerly Adolf-Hitler-Platz), sat at the center of the facility and formed the focal point of camp life.

Along with housing, food was probably the most pressing problem in the camp. The UNRRA staff blanched at the enormity of the camp's supply needs. Kitchens could produce nine tons of bread a day, but that required a massive influx of raw materials. These included a weekly supply of fifty-two tons of potatoes, six tons of vegetables, eight tons of meat, and four tons of fat. American policy was to provide 2,500 calories per day for each DP, about 1,000 more than the calories designated for German civilians. Most of this had to come from UNRRA supplies or from the army, represented in Wildflecken by a single American lieutenant who remained behind to help coordinate military aid to the camp.[18] Food and other supplies had to come in along a few narrow roads and a single train track up from Brückenau. In September 1945, the army abandoned the policy of requisitioning German crops, with the exception of potatoes, in anticipation of widespread food insecurity among the civilian population. In any case, the farming communities of the Rhön had little to contribute. At the same time, the district faced an influx of

German expellees who further diminished food stocks. UNRRA had its mandate to care for DPs but relied on the army for much of its supplies. The Military Government, on the other hand, faced the real problem of keeping order in an area that became a catchment for refugees of all kinds, including many for whom UNRRA had no responsibility.

This tension is very clear in the most remarkable passage of Hulme's diary, dated October 3, 1945. On that day, she had an unwelcome visit from an American lieutenant named Kelso who came from the Military Government detachment in Neustadt. He accused Hulme of allowing "her" Poles to steal from local farmers with abandon. Tempers flared, at which point Kelso added that he "hated" the Poles. "I would perhaps have been able to do something but I went into one of those states . . . wanting to shout at him 'Then if you hate them, why the hell are you IN Military Govt???' but decided to act the lady." Hulme asked Kelso whether the Poles or the Germans had been liberated, a question that flustered the young lieutenant. "MG [Military Government] acts always as if the Germans were liberated. They have to handle the civil complaints . . . every German who loses a sheep runs to MG and complains of Poles, Poles, Poles. The German looks neat, sound, intelligent. MG unconsciously sides with the military-looking gent; the poor Pole in rags with wild blue eyes looks evil besides the bowing paragon of a German."

At that point, Kelso turned the argument around on Hulme. He began to tell her about the growing tide of German expellees, expected to reach two million before long. He described caravans of sick, hungry refugees adding to the human toll of the war while DPs received allied assistance. "'Hungry, cold Germans,' he said, 'all out here (waiving [sic] window-ward) and in here, tons of food.'" Later that day, Hulme wrote that she was "haunted by the story of the typhus-ridden German refugees being kicked across borders back into their own land, which is mainly occupied by DPs who do not wish to return to their own country. He said there is bound to be trouble. Raiding Poles will mix with returning Germans. The Poles have everything on their side now . . . "[19] These stories and these concerns did not appear in Hulme's book, nor did they merit mention in the dispatches she wrote to her UNRRA supervisors. While her diary reveals the mix of sympathy and fear that she felt when confronted with the growing refugee crisis in the district and in occupied Germany, Hulme and her colleagues faced tremendous near-term challenges in their own camp.

The DP camp's population fluctuated dramatically during the period of transition between the army and UNRRA. Solid numbers are difficult to ascertain for the early period as new convoys arrived and others went on to other camps in the DP system. The population likely reached its height a few months before the handover. A camp resident charged with preparing a report for the UNRRA staff claimed a total population of 17,011 people, of whom more than ninety percent were agricultural workers and 1,063 were veterans of the Polish military. These were probably POWs taken during the 1939 campaign and sent west as laborers. For most of the next several years, the population of the camp hovered around 15,000.

The Wildflecken Poles eagerly assumed a kind of limited self-government within the camp perimeter. During the summer the residents held elections under Polish law for a committee to run the camp. The camp's sixty-five blockhouses elected a Municipal Council, which then chose a seven-person Municipal Commission to serve as the town's co-ordinating body. The commission then elected Zygmunt Rusinek, an economist, as the first committee chairman. Rusinek, who left the camp to return to Poland that fall, played an important part in Hulme's book. She called him *"Tak-Tak Schön"* after his habit of answering requests with "yes, yes" in Polish or "great" in German, regardless of whether or not he understood the question or intended to comply. Legally, the camp considered itself a town in Poland, even renaming itself Durzyń after a tribe of Slavs who supposedly inhabited northern Bavaria during late antiquity. In her book, Hulme praised the Polish leadership as "serious people, the real leaders of our troubled flock, our intelligentsia." In her diary, however, she described them as "blue-eyed gangsters," the most effective among the 2,000 or so "ruffians who control the camp by fear."[20]

The composition of the Municipal Council, which alternately assisted and bedeviled the UNRRA team, was of great importance to the operations of the Wildflecken camp. While members were elected by the barracks, they also fractured along ideological lines drawn in large part around the issue of repatriation. They are also virtually invisible in the extant camp records. Any intense political activity, particularly which touched on repatriation, could get a DP thrown out of the camp. Because of this, there were relatively few printed political materials and much of what can be reconstructed comes from intelligence sources or from denunciations. Oral histories, which are useful in reconstructing much of camp life, are less so when it comes to camp politics. Most of the camp's leaders were older, did not have the opportunity to emigrate, and died in Germany long before various oral history projects began to record the experiences of DPs.

Camp politics revolved around a small leadership cohort with strong ideological ties to the London-based government-in-exile. These leaders in turn linked to other Polish DP camps through organizations like the Polish Union in Germany (*Zjednoczenie Polskie w Neimczech*) and the Union of Polish Centers in Northern Bavaria, which had its first meeting at Wildflecken in December 1945. These welfare organizations had a strongly political element as well. Combined with a strong Catholic presence among the generally lower-class Polish camp population, these organizations spread "directives aimed at the patriotic and anti-communist upbringing of the Polish youth." As DPs moved through the camp system, representatives of various political entities in the Polish diaspora came and went in Wildflecken. At various times, army and UNRRA intelligence identified members of the nationalist AK (Home Army or *Armia Krajowa*), a shadowy nationalist group called the NSZ (Polish Underground Movement or *Narodowe Siły Zbrojne*), and even members of the Anders Army, which fought in the Soviet Union, Europe, and the Middle East during the war. Several of General Anders's relatives lived in the camp at various times and his photo hung on the wall in the offices of the Municipal Council.[21] The political imperative to create a Little Poland in the Franconian woods hardly attracted the notice of UNRRA or army personnel, who considered the Council a useful if noisy partner in administering the camp. However, the growing assertiveness of this political community in exile proved to be a serious impediment to later efforts to encourage Poles to go home.[22]

Piotr L. was probably the most consistently and obstreperously troublesome DP in the eyes of UNRRA officials. The forty-four-year-old lawyer from Warsaw followed a circuitous track to Wildflecken. During the last stages of the war, he worked as a waiter in Breslau, then in Karlsbad in the Sudetenland. After the end of the war, he took up residence in the DP camp in Fulda. In October 1946, he transferred to Wildflecken with his wife Marja, a journalist. Both were highly educated, spoke French and English well, and had extensive contacts among prewar Polish elites. Now that many non-communist elites found themselves living in exile, networks began forming in the camps.[23] It is difficult to reconstruct exactly how extensive L.'s contacts in underground DP politics were, but it is clear that he played both a public and subterranean role. Later there was at least some suggestion that his transfer to Wildflecken was the result of a coordinated effort to disrupt UNRRA's repatriation mission. Shortly after arriving at Wildflecken, he travelled to Brussels to participate in a meeting with the London government-in-exile. Polish intelligence, admittedly a biased source, told UNRRA that L. was also part of a shadowy network involved in "terroristic underground organizations" in Poland and funded by the Anders organization.[24] Regardless of the truth of this claim, L. was clearly one of the principle organizers of a nationalist, anti-communist group within the Wildflecken camp that called itself the Red and White Civic Militia. This group, which wore armbands in the colors of the Polish flag, quickly became a *bête noire* of the UNRRA team at Wildflecken. As one frustrated repatriation official complained later, the group existed as part of an organized effort to "resist repatriation, eviction, and camp movement."[25]

The only option open to UNRRA was to remove anti-repatriation activists from the camps. This was the case with a legendary character named J. who headed the Polish Committee at Coburg. UNRRA staffers there tried to engineer his removal, only to find themselves outmaneuvered at the election. Frustrated, they called in the American Military Government to remove J. from the camp by force. When UNRRA arranged an election to replace him, he showed up in the camp to prevent the election and continued to operate his organization outside the camp. In frustration, UNRRA shipped him to Wildflecken where he allied himself with Piotr L.'s militia. J. was blustery, garrulous, and entirely unafraid to tell UNRRA staff that it was "the duty of all Poles abroad" to fight against repatriation. He bluntly told them that he would not work with anyone, Polish or otherwise, who promoted return to Poland. The Wildflecken Poles who disagreed were, according to J., "wartime collaborators." At one point, he requested Masset's assistance in removing one from the Municipal Council. In a conversation laced with irony given J.'s Coburg experience, Masset told him that such a move would not be democratic.[26]

Most of the Wildflecken Poles had little interest in the nationalist exile politics playing out among their leadership. There were children to raise, supplies to gather, and increasingly dense networks of familial and social relationships both within and outside the camp. Healthy men could get work in labor service units, which often took them far from the camp but paid reasonable wages and even allowed limited access to coveted Post Exchange stores. Anna Hamadyk's husband went to Mannheim in such a unit, leaving her in Wildflecken with a child and another on the way. More than 60,000 Poles also joined DP police units, which guarded both camp facilities and other installations across Germany and gave members a chance to serve under Polish officers. As one official historian wrote, the labor and police programs "improved the morale of those employed and lightened the expense of caring for them."[27]

Within a very short time, the Polish DPs in the Wildflecken camp created a workable refugee society in their new, temporary home. In many ways, the Wildflecken camp functioned as a place apart. Security, initially the responsibility of American troops, became a shared duty after Americans mistakenly shot a Polish woman in late summer. By November, the Americans turned over the camp perimeter to the DPs. The Municipal Council, now able to keep order with its own law enforcement arm, grew bolder in its negotiations with UNRRA, promising labor in exchange for favors targeted to its political supporters in the camp. Hulme described it as a "Tammany-like octopus with tentacles touching every aspect of camp life." Still, the cooperation between UNRRA and the DP leadership began to yield results. More than a quarter of the camp's adult population worked for the camp administration. As the number of trained Poles increased, this reduced the need for German labor in the camp.

Much of the community's infrastructure had to be improvised. UNRRA, with American backing, travelled the surrounding countryside acquiring tools and machinery that they believed might have been taken illegally from the camp. Uninhabited buildings were torn down and stripped of plumbing fixtures and salvageable wood. Power had to come from distant Würzburg, necessitating the construction of jerry-rigged transformers and acquisition of thousands of light bulbs and switches. The camp's fire department had one truck, a German vehicle acquired through uncertain means and painted red using equally mysteriously acquired paint.

Many of those who lived in the camp were young and had been separated from home and family for years. Driven by loneliness, the experience of relative freedom, and in a hurry to pick up lives interrupted by the war, many chose to get married early in their camp life. For some, this was a religious recognition of relationships that began in forced labor facilities. Mass weddings took place across the DP camp system. They were also social occasions, accompanied by music, feasting, and copious amounts of drinking. In this way, DPs could reproduce something like the Poland they left behind. Ephraim Chase recalled that "the life of a member of an UNRRA Team is never dull, and there are times when it is positively exciting. Weddings, christenings and confirmations are some of the functions he is invited to attend. And if he does, a good time is assured. . . . And the price of admission, at least for the Director, is a toast or a speech couched in general terms and containing a reference to the hope that better days are coming. The collations are rather good and the drinks vary from ersatz coffee to wine and that indigenous beverage known in native parlance as 'samogon.'"[28]

With this extraordinary surge of marriages came a baby boom. The rise in births actually predated the marriage mania. UNRRA staffers expressed amazement at the number of women who arrived in the camp heavily pregnant and that children not infrequently attended their parents' wedding. By September 1945 the camp averaged two births a day. When Hulme asked Dr. Murraciole about the spike in births, "He looked at me astonished at my ignorance. Then he said 'Les fêtes du Nouvel An, naturellement' . . . and I had to think back to last New Years . . . and remember that day is more to the European than is Christmas to us. So I looked at these results of a brief fete last year before liberation."[29] Many of the DPs experienced liberation during the end of 1944 and the first days of 1945, and with it an end to the restrictions on human relationships that marked the camp and forced labor experiences.

The rash of births precipitated a serious crisis of medical care in the camp. The hospital began as a decidedly improvised facility, staffed by the remains of the Wehrmacht medical team responsible for the base medical compound. The staff pharmacist, who was allowed to leave after two months to return to Berlin following the death of his father, was in fact a Nazi "Old Fighter" who arrived in the area after being released from French captivity at the end of the war. By early 1946, DP medical staff took over the hospital, which expanded to four facilities, school health programs, and newborn health clinics in the blockhouses.[30] There was a special maternity hospital, staffed by three DP physicians, ten nurses, an assistant, and three midwives. During 1946, Catholic priests alone performed 465 baptisms, bringing the number of camp residents under the age of twelve to more than 1,400.[31] Hulme later recalled with some bitterness the rise of illegitimate children "unwanted and flourishing in ever-mounting statistics in our camp." Some of these infants did not survive to be registered or baptized. UNRRA staff tracked down the mother of an infant found suffocated in a trashcan. The young DP woman admitted that she killed the infant, who was conceived in a relationship with a long-gone American soldier.[32]

Camp cultural life thrived quickly as bored DPs sought something to do and displaced professionals yearned to practice their trades again. By the end of 1945, seven hundred schoolchildren received an education from sixty teachers. Three theater companies competed for customers, led by a successful husband-and-wife team from Warsaw who revived the famous "*Stara Banda*" (Old Gang) vaudeville troupe in the camp. There were weekly athletic competitions and a wide range of vocational training for youth and adults. Largely thanks to efforts of a priest, Wildflecken even had a thriving Boy Scout program with more than five hundred members. Generally, American and UNRRA observers reacted enthusiastically to the presence of Scouts, an impression not dulled when the

Scoutmaster returned to Poland and one of his deputies was caught using the small printing press in the "Scout Room" to print anti-communist and anti-repatriation literature.[33]

Hulme's published account and the voluminous records of UNRRA give the impression of Wildflecken as a closed system in which personnel and residents changed but little or no contact developed with the town outside the edge of camp. Town residents appear sparingly and as an undifferentiated mass. In reality, the situation was much more complicated. From the beginning, the camp and the people living around it developed a mutually dependent, unequal, and often antagonistic set of relationships. At the heart of this development lay the permeability of the camp itself.

The camp functioned as an unsanctioned open-air marketplace in which virtually anything could be purchased at the right price. When the war ended, the camp became a hub of commercial activity as liberated workers turned the kitchens into a profitable enterprise. Locals went to the camp to buy food and other supplies, but did so at great risk. Just days after the Americans arrived, a group of workers waylaid a woman who ventured into the camp in search of bread. She was raped by several men before American troops arrived. On this occasion, rescuers found the men responsible and arrested them. Days later, the mayor's office petitioned the Americans to protect a woman who lived and worked near the camp perimeter with a teenage daughter who "frequently was home alone."[34]

As American supplies filled the camp's larders, opportunities for commercial activity expanded dramatically. Quickly, the market developed into a regular if at best quasi-legal institution. Locals carried what they could into camp and bartered for scarce goods, which, thanks to access to American stores, existed in relative profusion among the DPs. At the top of the barter system were cigarettes. One of the few things upon which former camp residents and locals who lived through this period can agree upon is the bargaining power of the American tobacco, which one young DP recalled was the "main currency" among traders.[35] One of the few truly black-market staples (in that the good themselves were illegal) was the ubiquitous supply of home-distilled *samogon*. While ingredients varied, DPs generally depended on outsiders to trade for the fruit and yeast needed to keep stills running. The hill on which the camp sat turned, in Kathryn Hulme's words, into "a magic mountain made of sugar and Spam, of margarine and jam." For the Poles, it was "a sort of New Year sport that broke the monotony of just sitting around waiting for something to happen." Of course, the power inversion represented by forced laborers now lording consumer goods over their one-time masters was lost on no one. The Poles became "the seigneurs of Wildflecken."[36]

Hulme, the UNRRA team, and local authorities were much more concerned about what came out of the camp than what went in. If tobacco was the primary currency of the market, this put DPs in a position of unassailable advantage. In a society effectively without legal tender, a cigarette-based system of exchange made a certain amount of sense. But what could locals use to buy in to this network? The answer seems to have been virtually anything of value. Furniture, jewelry, and, crucially, livestock and fresh produce found their way into the world of the camp. Locals not infrequently then reported the goods stolen. Periodic raids could do little to redress these complaints. The camp became, unassailably, the nodal point of a far-reaching network of barter and exchange.

Such a commercial opportunity attracted more than just local villagers. On February 16, 1946, Bernd M. stopped his truck in Brückenau to get a bite to eat before getting back on the road heading west. Nearly sixty, Bernd lost everything he owned in the bombing of Düsseldorf and now made his living in the vast underground economy. When he returned to his vehicle, he found two policemen pulling the tarps off his cargo. His heart must have sank when it became clear that he was caught. The contents of the truck included four geese (two of them still alive), 302 eggs, three pounds of cheese, eight pounds of coffee, one hundred cigars, and several thousand American cigarettes. "The last of these items," wrote the arresting officer, "we can say with great certainty were taken from the storerooms of the Polish camp at Wildflecken."[37] Since the Americans did not supply the camp with live geese, it is likely that the camp traders themselves acquired their poultry on the wing from local farmers in exchange for goods from the camp. Despite efforts by friends in Düsseldorf, he received a stiff fine for his troubles. Perhaps Bernd was not yet a veteran in the underground economy, as his unfortunate decision to stop with a truck full of goods might suggest. However, he was not alone in his activities. We can safely presume that he was not the only entrepreneur taking advantage of the warehouse at Wildflecken or the network of DPs inside the camp who serviced the underground economy.

American forces posted flyers that called such sales "a menace to law and order, to the security of U.S. Forces, to the value of German money, and the price control and rationing measures."[38] This was particularly true for the sale of items like gasoline and even American uniforms. DPs, who could legally possess such items, had to dye uniforms a different color. German civilians had no right to any American items. In theory, marked goods like cigarettes were easy to identify, while gasoline or raw tobacco posed greater challenges. In reality, such items were in such short supply in rural Franconia in early 1946 that any supply of them must have come from American stores.

UNRRA staff proved susceptible to all of these blandishments. In February 1946, MPs stopped two vehicles coming from the camp, travelling separately near Gersfeld and Brückenau. They uncovered seven hundred packs of cigarettes and a variety of delicacies not normally found along those rural roads. The drivers were the camp's Supply Officer, Paul Goosens, and another UNRRA staffer named George Aime. The staffers, arrested along with several female DPs, confessed separately to working together on the smuggling operation. Goosens claimed ignorance as to the origins of most of the goods, but Aime freely admitted that he stole them from the warehouse. Each had requested leave, then headed for Brussels where they planned to sell their ill-gotten gains.[39] Both were dismissed from UNRRA service.

While she only touched on the subject in her book, Hulme privately chafed at the corruption of her fellow UNRRA staffers. Months before, she wrote in her diary that members of the team, divided along national lines, were engaging in illegal trade. "Our Dutch group is thick as thieves, and thieving heavily – sugar, goods by the yard, chocolate." In *The Wild Place,* she praises Director George Masset as a decisive and caring leader who "gave orders like a General and looked like one too." In private, she appears to have loathed him. In a letter to an UNRRA supervisor, she accused Masset of being the brains behind the Goosens and Aime smuggling operation and of covertly providing UNRRA supplies to the Municipal Council "for entertainment purposes." "I believe," she wrote, "that I have been consistently tricked, bluffed, and lied to by my Director since December 1945."[40]

UNRRA staffers were not the only foreigners engaged in the local black market. American Military Government and Constabulary reports on illegal commerce are full of suggestions, often maddeningly difficult to prove, that American soldiers played a significant role in the trade.[41] Given the amount and variety of goods available, this conclusion was inescapable. The black market was a highly integrated and adaptive network, determined in large part by the availability of goods and the complicity of individuals willing to take the risks to acquire them. The 12th Constabulary Squadron, charged with patrolling the area around Aschaffenburg, spent a great deal of time and energy trying to break the supply lines running between Polish DP communities in Aschaffenburg and Wildflecken. The unit's reports claimed that DPs had assistance from American troops eager to profit from illegal commerce. The "negro troops of the 4355 Quartermaster Baking Company" acted as the primary conduit for goods vanishing from American depots.[42]

While Americans, locals, and Germans from beyond the Sinn Valley came to the camp to do business, DPs moved regularly in and out of the facility. Whether to take advantage of employment possibilities in the limited local economy or simply to escape from the boredom of camp life, a steady stream of DPs formally joined the local community. After the initial postwar chaos settled and the regular registration of inhabitants resumed, an average of nearly three DPs per week registered to live in Wildflecken. In a community of a few hundred, even this limited influx must have made a considerable impact on the demographics of the town.[43] Many of these DPs promptly returned to the camp, while others diffused out into the countryside. It was not uncommon for Wildflecken Poles to develop important and lasting ties with locals that allowed both to more easily navigate the limits of town and camp life.

Legally, DPs could choose to be "free-livers," dependent partially or fully on the German economy. By 1948, about 140,000 DPs (almost twenty-five percent of all DPs) lived outside of camps.[44] Wicenty M. was one of those who moved back and forth across the camp boundaries. A clerk from Radom, Wicenty met a woman from nearby Frankenheim in 1945. They married and had a daughter the next year. The family lived in the camp until 1950, when they emigrated to the United States. Stanislaw Z. arrived at Wildflecken as a teenage DP. There he met Maria, an ethnic German expellee from Beuthen (Bytom) in Upper Silesia. He may have spoken some German, while she no doubt learned Polish growing up in linguistic borderland. They married, started a family, and tried to make a life for themselves in the new postwar world.[45] These stories reinforce the idea that the camp and its surroundings were not mutually exclusive or purely antagonistic toward each other. DPs, locals, and the new group of expellees were all too often cut off from the world they knew before the war, lonely, and in need of support and companionship. Sometimes, across seemingly rigid lines of legal categorization, they found each other.

Theoretically, free-livers were supposed to receive German ration cards and live like local residents. However, DPs living outside had little trouble entering the camp and claiming supplies which enabled them to live considerably better than their German neighbors. For UNRRA administrators trying to manage over-crowded camps, it must have been very tempting to continue to feed free-livers if they would simply go and live somewhere else. Free-livers also could claim German rations, which subtracted from the amount available to Germans and refugees living on the outside economy. On top of that, many locals assumed (not without cause) that those living outside the camps acted in conjunction with traders inside the camp, fencing various sorts of goods both inside and outside the camp boundaries. "A resident is complaining that these Poles are breaking in to homes and conducting a lively trade [in stolen goods] with those in the camp" wrote the mayor to the office of the *Landrat* (County Commissioner) in early 1946. Apparently not satisfied, he wrote to UNRRA several days later, arguing that the presence of free-livers only increased black market activity. Could the town force DPs back into the camp?[46]

This process became even more confused when DPs lost their camp privileges for some reason. Natalya N., a forty-six-year-old mother of two reunited with her husband at Wildflecken after separation during wartime. For some reason possibly having to do with the fact that she had a German surname, UNRRA officials did not accept her identification and removed her from the camp. Now a registered resident of Wildflecken, she found an unlikely partner in the local government, which campaigned to get her reinstated to the camp and, not coincidentally, off their rolls.[47] Eventually, Natalya's petitions succeeded in gaining re-entry for her into the camp and a reunion with her family.

This sort of conflict appears to have been endemic to the region during this period. The Military Government in Brückenau issued a memo the following month to all responsible officials endeavoring to clarify the legal position of DPs. Clearly frustrated, an American officer in the town reiterated the special rights of DPs while acknowledging the potential for serious abuse. "If those in camp wish to live outside, they must give up their camp connection. If those outside wish to enter the camp, they may do so by registering there."[48] For the Wildflecken Poles, there were clear economic and material advantages to continuing the practice of living on both sides of the divide. For the town and for American military authorities, such ambiguities seemed to invite chaos and threaten the fragile postwar economy.

The American Constabulary found this ambiguity very difficult to manage. The Constabulary spent much of its time keeping order and fighting black marketeering, which in Landkreis Brückenau meant keeping DPs and locals as separate as possible. In practice, there were two ways to accomplish this: going into the camps in force or trying to interdict illegal goods as they moved through networks outside the camps. Both tactics were crude and neither was particularly effective, but they highlighted the integrated and complex network of trading that involved actors inside and outside the camp.

On July 18, 1946, a Constabulary squadron set up roadblocks near Bad Kissingen and searched cars. The action netted, among other things, a car carrying twenty-five gallons of "American gasoline," a DP with nine pairs of black-market shoes, and "numerous Displaced Persons" driving cattle for which they could not prove ownership.[49] It is useful to consider the range of transactions and interactions represented here. The gasoline, taken from a car belonging to a local German, likely emerged from American military property, sold into the black market by American troops. Gasoline pilferage seems to have been something of an open secret among Americans stationed in the region. After another raid near Aschaffenburg, in which American soldiers found 133 cans of gasoline, the investigator concluded that "sufficient evidence could not be determined against American soldiers believed to have been involved to bring charges against these men."⁵⁰ The shoes, since they belonged to a DP and were readily identified as "black market," likely were matching pairs taken from the stores at Wildflecken.

As historians of the period have noted, DP criminality was a common trope of news reporting and popular opinion during this period. "History," writes an American historian of the camps, "has not been kind to the DPs."⁵¹ The American geographer Malcolm Proudfoot, both a participant in international aid efforts and later one of its first historians, wrote that "many of the displaced persons developed the attitude that any German's possessions that might be useful, or have barter value, or that just struck their fancy, was theirs to take."⁵² British aid worker Francesca Wilson left a vivid description of her time in southern Bavaria, during which she noted the impotence of local administrators and the studied disinterest of the Americans. "We were often awakened at night by a faint siren like a fog horn. It was some peasant in the hills, whose home and stables were being ransacked, calling wistfully to the Americans to come to his protection."⁵³ Occupation authorities granted German police permission to carry small arms in October 1945, but this concession meant little in places with few police and well-armed criminals. Wildflecken's official history records that "robbery and theft reached alarming proportions. Those living around the base were thoroughly terrorized by those within."⁵⁴

There was a spike in violence throughout the region during this period and DPs feature prominently in contemporary police reports. Across Bavaria, American military courts conducted 2,700 trials involving DPs between June and November 1945 alone. While most offenses concerned food and luxury goods smuggling, there were also significant numbers of violent crimes often involving weapons. Generally speaking, DP crimes may have garnered more attention because of the violence associated with them rather than the number of incidents.⁵⁵ The oft-told tales of DP criminality had at least some basis in reality, the seriousness of which needs to be emphasized. Wildflecken could be a violent place. Arms proved distressingly easy to acquire. Some no doubt served as hunting weapons, but it is hard to escape the idea that a significant number of camp residents believed that they needed weapons for offensive or defensive purposes within the camp. More disturbing, weapons tended to concentrate in the hands of emerging political interests. The results could be very dangerous. In the early days of the camp, UNRRA officials regularly found the bodies of murdered "collaborators" as political scores from occupied Poland or the years of slave labor resolved themselves in the camp.

Only the police had the right to carry weapons, and the control of the police became a significant political conflict within the camp. The Polish police armed themselves with a hodge-podge of German weapons and American-supplied arms. However, it is abundantly clear that the officially mandated weapons made up just part of a much more complicated network of arms flows within and outside the camp. Many of the police carried Polish weapons of unknown origin. Third Army HQ repeatedly expressed concern about the presence of armed police and the "security problem" at Wildflecken. Zone Director J. H. Whiting countered that without armed Polish police, the army would have to return to provide security.[56]

While the police notionally had permission to carry weapons, many of them abused this privilege, adding to the dangers of camp life. In March 1946, an army raid on the camp arrested five men, including Police Chief Krzysztof D. and his brother, on charges of possessing and distributing illegal weapons.[57] Those arrested suffered no more than a token punishment. This frustrated both UNRRA and army officials, since the latter believed that the former was not doing enough to crack down on illegal guns while the former believed that the latter's drive to disarm the camp only increased the level of disorder within. The arrest of the D. brothers did nothing to alleviate the trade in illegal arms. The problem of guns within the camp could have very serious consequences, both for those within and outside of its perimeter.

It was an open secret that guns were readily available in the camp and often fell into the hands of those who wanted self-protection, advantage in the fractious world of camp politics, or opportunities to commit robbery outside the perimeter. When murder victims were found in the camp, the rumor mill generally made it clear that the victim was guilty of some unspecified transgression or of "collaboration" during the war. The gun problem became all too clear on Easter Sunday, 1947, when DPs holding a procession fired in the air "according to old Polish tradition." A bullet ricocheted off some paving stones by the Grain Mill, wounding three women. DP police arrested one of their own, Aleksy L., who claimed that his licensed pistol misfired as he worked to clear a jam. While L. readily acknowledged responsibility, his confession rings somewhat hollow since the women's statements clearly indicated that a number of bystanders fired at the same time and "how we were wounded we cannot say."[58] L. conveniently took the blame, likely because he had the only authorized firearm.

Hulme acknowledged that Poles often went beyond the wire and stole to supplement their rations and to give them something to sell. She recounted these stories – like the tale of an industrious group of rustlers who dressed two pig carcasses as old women to avoid detection – in an amused, boys-will-be-boys tone. She also expressed regret that UNRRA's lack of seriousness about the problem of theft "was the beginning of the legend that would cling to the DPs for the rest of their days, that they were nothing more than a looting horde sitting pretty under the protection of UNRRA."[59]

In truth, the number of active bandits who emerged from the DP camp was small, probably no more than a few dozen out of a population of nearly 15,000. However, they made a sizable impression on the local population. Incontrovertibly, some DPs had access to weapons and incentives to use them. As incidents like the accidental shooting during Easter festivities proved, a number of DPs were armed and had relatively little trouble procuring ammunition. In a disarmed country where even the police had little access to weapons, this made organized theft particularly brazen and dangerous.

Property crimes generally involved either animal rustling or home robbery. During the week ending October 12, 1946, six homes in the Wildflecken area suffered burglary. A frustrated bureaucrat reported to the office of the Landrat that catching the thieves proved almost impossible. Local police had no right to go onto the grounds of the camp, so robbers simply had to cross the boundary and could feel safe from interception. "Despite an increased police presence, this rash of theft is getting completely out of hand."[60]

Animal rustling was a different, and considerably more dangerous, activity. Small bands of DPs regularly went out into the countryside to bring back livestock. There were several reasons for this. The camp diet did not include a lot of fresh meat, and certainly not the beef or mutton that lay temptingly close in the barns and fields of the Rhön. Second, it was something for bored DPs to do. The American constabulary in the area believed that the Poles stole cows to sell, estimating that each cow fetched 2–3,000 marks.[61] This seems less likely, if only because devalued marks played a relatively small role in the local economy. If DPs ever sold cattle for cash, they likely did so for American dollars. Finally, the importance of getting some measure of revenge on German farmers who had freely used Polish labor must have played a part. These answers must remain speculative, as oral histories of camp residents certainly do not mention participation in such raids. Rustling tended to involve breaking into barns often guarded by farmers, creating the potential for violence. Recognizing this, the Americans took an active role in trying to stop rustling. Periodic raids into the camp in search of stolen animals offered some deterrent, but could not stop the regular nighttime arrival of stolen sheep, pigs, and cows. On July 5, 1946, a local man employed by the Americans as a translator arrived at the Rathaus with a cow following behind. The cow, recovered in a raid that morning, had markings indicating ownership. After some searching, it turned out to belong to a farmer in Oberbach, who later arrived to pick up his animal.[62] The regular theft of livestock linked local farmers, American troops, and DPs in a sometimes brutal and always frustrating cycle of suspicion and hostility.

Americans stationed in the area became all too aware of this growing problem. "The Wildflecken Poles are again becoming more active and more bold," wrote an American officer in a 1946 report shared with UNRRA. Another officer, attached to the 1st Batt, 15th Infantry brandished a pistol to frighten off two Poles outside of town. American actions in the area, the report points out, were primarily "in connection with the Russian border," and suggests that if ten percent of DPs were criminals, a whole regiment would be needed to keep order in the region.[63] For American troops in the area, keeping the peace between

German farmers and DP sheep rustlers was low priority, irritating, and contravened the expressed American policy of favoring DPs over Germans and other refugee categories.

A raid during the closing days of 1946 gives some hint as to complicated relationship between Germans, Americans, and DPs. On the night of December 16, more than 2,400 American troops pushed into the camp and searched it for thirteen hours. Masset clearly did not know about the raid, an omission he politely termed "regrettable" in his report on the incident. Happily for the UNRRA district office, the Americans found relatively little in the way of illegal property. The report's concluding paragraph is remarkable enough to quote at length:

> It was inferred by the [UNRRA] officers that to some extent, aside from black market consideration, this raid was designed to give practice to troops who are badly in need of this sort of exercise. This is fully appreciated. However, it would be regrettable if the DPs were to be too frequently made the unwilling participants of such maneuvers. *There are still the German population which might serve as well for the purpose.*[64]

In truth, neither the UNRRA team nor the Americans particularly trusted each other. By the end of 1946, each side had considerable reason to believe that the other acted contrary to their interests. Raids, in addition to finding pilfered livestock and illegal uniforms, served as a salutary reminder of just who controlled the landscape in the Sinn Valley. Increasingly, American forces in the area came to the same conclusion that many locals did: the DPs had to go. Matters only got worse before they got better.

The apex of bandit activity appears to have been the heart of the legendarily brutal winter of 1946–47. "The thieves are armed," wrote the Landrat to the Military Government, "and now Germans are active among them." The town government requested armed police, but limited resources would not allow the dispatch of any more *Landespolizisten*. After the shooting of two town police members in Frankenheim in January, the mayor concluded that he could no longer risk the lives of unarmed volunteers in the hills at night. By this time, even the Americans conceded that the threat to farmers was too great. From then on, local police in the Landkreis could carry weapons, provided they filled out paperwork attesting to a "non-Nazi" past.[65] Occupation authorities slowly came to the realization that the violence in the Franconian hills undercut efforts to provide security and stability along the crucial border area. The decision to allow German police to carry arms demonstrates two important developments in American occupation policy toward DPs and other civilians. First, official policy favoring DPs over Germans and other refugees increasingly ran into complications on the ground when it clashed with the need for security. Second, the Military Government proved flexible enough to allow this kind of decision making at the local level.

The rate of attacks decreased markedly in the months to come. While other factors, like economic recovery and the end of a terrible winter, may have played a role, the addition of armed law enforcement in the area helped to stem a rising and dangerous tide of lawlessness. Like the black market, the outbreak of banditry in the Rhön hills indelibly marked relations between locals and DPs. Not least, the small but violent crime wave helped to emphasize increasingly vocal calls for speedy repatriation from a variety of directions. Frustrated Americans, UNRRA officials, and locals joined in arguing for the accelerated removal of camp residents. Many in the camp had very different ideas. The struggle over repatriation shaped the history of the Wildflecken camp, the DP system, and the broader effort to find a solution to Europe's postwar refugee crisis.

In late July 1945, photographers from *Life* magazine visited Wildflecken. The photos of camp residents playing soccer in German prison uniforms and staring listlessly at the camera over plates of food reminded American audiences that while war raged in the Pacific, a new and terrible crisis had emerged on what had recently been the battlegrounds of Europe. Fortunately, this problem seemed well on its way toward resolution. "The March of the Displaced Persons," the article suggested, "the biggest and quickest mass migration in world history, was last week drawing to a close." Many of those who wanted to return home to France, the Low Countries, or the Soviet Union were already en route. A few "hard cores" might perhaps wish to remain, unwilling to go home as intended.[66] Still, it seemed that Europe might rid itself of the problem of mass population displacement quickly and efficiently. American optimism lasted a year after the establishment of the camp system. On the first anniversary of the end of the war in Europe, American soldiers participated in a celebration in camp, during which Polish police and American troops marched side by side. An American military newspaper suggested that "these men were not just acting out the part of relieved guards at the parade. They were turning over to the American troops the trust of controlling the German nation while they returned to Poland to rebuild their devastated land."[67]

Initially, there was good reason for optimism. If anything, the first challenge facing UNRRA's repatriation mission was an excess of willing repatriates. Poles were so eager to go back to Poland that they posed a security challenge. Between August 19 and 21, 1945, four trainloads of Poles arrived at the camp from Eichstätt, Ansbach, Ingolstadt, and Freising, bringing the camp population briefly over 16,000. Passengers appear to have believed that they were going to Poland and were nonplussed when the train stopped in rural Franconia. An American lieutenant reported that these passengers and about 6,000 of the camp's residents were "vehemently and urgently desirous of going to Poland."

The period of unrestrained repatriation did not last long. UNRRA's official history archly suggests that "it was, perhaps, unfortunate that the limited transport facilities then available did not permit the mass return of Poles . . . for, with the first flush of enthusiasm on liberation, practically all would have gone, thus eliminating one of the dire problems of 1946 and 1947." By September, the numbers of willing repatriates slowed. Unsurprisingly, numbers vary widely, but something like 1.8 million DPs passed into UNRRA supervision across Europe. In Germany, Poles made up the largest contingent by far with more than 425,000 by the end of the year.[68]

The repatriation crisis grew from the decision in summer 1945 to divide the DP population along ethnic lines. In the case of Polish DPs, the particular constellation of the postwar settlement created a large group of DPs with very good reasons to fear repatriation. This in turn made it all the more difficult to convince others to go. The mass of DPs looked undifferentiated to camp administrators who often lacked the cultural knowledge to understand the ethnic and religious tensions in Eastern European areas like Poland. Not long after the U.S. took the lead in abandoning forced repatriation, the Military Government began a process of screening to try to weed out camp residents who might not be eligible for DP status. Many camp administrators harbored real doubts about the victim status of some of their charges:

> Who are these people? The vast majority of them are, no doubt, victims of the Nazis. Some of them were former inmates of Nazi concentration camps. Some however, I suspect, are slick individuals, who, having bet on the wrong horse and lost, have developed overnight such a fondness for democracy that they refuse to be repatriated.[69]

In a confusing and fluid environment, the Allies and UNRRA invented a system of ethnic classification that all but insured that a large group of DPs would have no interest in doing what they were supposed to do – namely to go home as soon as possible. Efforts to distinguish between Poles and Ukrainians, who often lived in close proximity in Eastern Europe, proved to be hopelessly complicated and badly damaged repatriation efforts. The war had significantly worsened ethnic tensions in the East European borderlands, and the postwar border adjustments created tremendous anxiety about forced repatriation and ethnic classification.

Many Poles had little interest in returning to homes no longer in Poland and feared being reclassified as Ukrainians because of their place of birth. Hulme later recalled posting a map of the peace terms before an anxious crowd of DPs. "You could tell from their faces which ones came from East of the river Bug. Some of the women wept quietly while the men stared in disbelief too keen for comment, uttering only the names of home towns in the lost litany of sorrowful sounds ... Lwow ... Rovno ... Stanislav."[70] For these DPs, return seemed like an impossibility, or at least a very bad bet.

For ethnic Ukrainians from Poland, fears of either living as an ethnic minority in Poland or ending up in the Soviet Union made many resistant to repatriation. The question of what to do with ethnic Ukrainian DPs bedeviled UNRRA administrators and Allied occupation authorities in Wildflecken and beyond. The Allies did not recognize the Ukraine as a state or Ukrainians as a nationality, so many Ukrainians from within the 1939 borders of the Soviet Union faced compulsory repatriation in the months after the end of the war. Ukrainians from Poland or the Baltic states, on the other hand, could not be forcibly repatriated. This caused considerable confusion and resulted in a brisk trade in forged Polish ID cards as Ukrainians tried to avoid the possibility of repatriation. In December 1945, the Americans ended compulsory repatriation for Soviet citizens and reaffirmed the protection of Polish and Baltic Ukrainians. Despite Allied promises, Poles from eastern Poland still feared repatriation to what was now the Soviet Union. At the same time Ukrainians began claiming Polish citizenship in ever-larger numbers. The Polish government made this even more complicated when it issued a statement in November 1946 claiming, in part, that "persons of Polish citizenship in 1939 but of Ukrainian nationality, formerly domiciled in the territories east of the Curzon line ceded to the Ukrainian Republic, have lost their Polish citizenship. Those of Polish nationality retain their Polish citizenship." For UNRRA staffers, the task before them included finding a way to determine both the putative citizenship and the ethno-cultural "nationality" of their charges.[71]

Despite the efforts of the Americans to isolate ethnic groups, the Wildflecken camp reflected the diversity of the East-Central European homelands of its inhabitants. The majority of inhabitants were clearly Polish-speaking Catholics. However, a significant number of Lutherans lived in the camp as well, and several oral history sources recount sometimes violent confrontations with Polish Lutherans whom their Catholic countrymen frequently accused of being "Volksdeutsche."[72] Certainly, no one would identify themselves as such to authorities, since ethnic Germans fell outside the jurisdiction of UNRRA and doing so would likely lead to forfeiture of assistance. A Committee for Protestant Displaced Persons and Refugees from Poland, meeting in Ansbach in November, urged American authorities to speed the process of emigration for their constituents. "A return of the displaced Protestants to Poland which had been their home since the 17th century is impossible because [we] are considered Reich Germans."[73]

In some cases, the identity of DPs proved impossible to determine. Whether by intentional obfuscation or simple lack of verifiable identification, some tested the boundaries of UNRRAs willingness to be flexible. Pablo D., who also called himself Pawel or Paulo, claimed to be a Barcelona-born veteran of the Spanish Civil War. According to his own biography, he was one of the thousands of Republican veterans living in camps in France who became a prisoner after the German invasion in 1940. When the war ended, he was at Mauthausen, which he fled in the company of some Polish prisoners and thus ended up at Wildflecken. There he married a Polish woman and had a child. It is clear from his file that UNRRA officials had doubts about many portions of his story, but had no way to prove anything about the man except that he was living in the camp and had an undeniably Polish wife. Through a long and very circuitous path, the family ended up in the United States.[74]

Frustration followed as repatriates dwindled along with options. By the middle of 1946, the relationship between DPs, UNRRA, and the U.S. Army began to suffer because of the halting progress in repatriation. Successive efforts by the authorities to entice, cajole, or strong-arm potential repatriates only made things worse. After a DP made the decision to repatriate, he or she became subject to considerable pressure from their more resistant campmates, making it all the more important for UNRRA to develop speedy and streamlined procedures for incentivizing, identifying, and moving repatriates through the series of steps that would eventually lead to their return to Poland.

The procedure for repatriation was relatively simple. Once a DP indicated that they were willing to go back, the Municipal Council took the lead in organizing biographical information, drawing up rolls of repatriates, and conveying all of this to UNRRA. Before leaving, each repatriate received a ration card entitling them to draw supplies when they reached Poland. This step was crucial and carefully monitored, since ration cards also functioned as tickets to be provided when leaving Wildflecken by truck or by train. While UNRRA staffers feared a black market in ration cards, they were more anxious about efforts to influence would-be-repatriates. "It is recalled once again," wrote Masset to the Municipal Council, "that all propaganda to influence the people against repatriation will be severely dealt with. Any persons attempting by rumors, lies or fantasies to influence the people against repatriation *will be immediately arrested and handed over to the military authorities.*"[75]

A number of repatriates felt a kind of buyers' remorse as soon as they agreed to go back. A considerable number of Poles, having repatriated, now returned. Camp administrators noticed a significant number of repatriates returning clandestinely to the camp, having made the arduous journey from Poland. These included the legendary *Tak-Tak Schön*, whose own return to Poland ended not long after it began. Stefan Czyzewski, a DP police officer who served in the Home Army during the war, later told an interviewer that he used his training in forged documents to help such people get into the camp.[76] Until things improved at home, perhaps Wildflecken would suffice.

The practicalities of getting would-be repatriates out of Wildflecken and in transit could be interrupted by hearsay and innuendo. Some of this was no doubt intentional on the part of those opposed to repatriation. In July 1946, a rumor spread that one trainload departed from town guarded by Soviet soldiers. UNRRA staffers made sure that the next departing train left the station festooned with American flags.[77] This must have been small comfort to the returnees, who knew full well that they would travel through Soviet-occupied territory and arrive in a Poland dominated by the Red Army. Still, it is hard to overstate the totemic value of American symbolic power. Provided that repatriates believed that they were protected by the Americans, many proved willing to take that crucial step into the unknown.

Organized opposition to repatriation formed and formalized during the cold winter of 1946. Administrators grew frustrated but could do little. From the shadows, a new politics emerged in the camp that helped turn it from a temporary facility into a problem with no end in sight. The camp received a steady stream of visitors representing the Polish exile community in London. While these delegates were ostensibly there to encourage repatriation, they passed along warnings of what was going on in the home country. At the same time, the Soviets threw up a series of administrative roadblocks, including refusing to provide transportation through their zone for repatriates or to provide assurances that Poles resident east of the new Polish-Soviet border could keep their Polish citizenship.[78] When an UNRRA-affiliated consultant on Polish repatriation named Nowicki visited the camp in August 1946, he came away with the impression that the Municipal Council worked regularly against repatriation. Nowicki recommended "censoring" the camp's "anti-Russian" newspapers, distributing candy to willing repatriates, and transferring a Polish-American aid worker "to a place where he will not be able to meet with meet big groups of Polish DPs."[79]

UNRRA's extensive and integrated network of camps now worked against it. Poles moved back and forth between Wildflecken and other Polish camps in the region, spreading the message of resistance. The network established by anti-repatriation advocates like Piotr L. and J., having themselves transferred into the camp, now extended across the Polish DP universe in Germany. At the same time, repatriated Poles who then returned to Germany disseminated news and, lacking DP identification, moved in secret between camps.[80] Those engaged in political organizing travelled easily between Wildflecken and the much larger city of Aschaffenburg, frustrating UNRRA efforts to contain the spread of rumors that undermined their efforts. At times, politics merged with criminality as increasingly desperate and unauthorized Poles ran protection rackets and extorted cash from their fellow DPs.[81] This phenomenon, combined with the relatively widespread access to weapons in the camp, created a potentially dangerous situation. UNRRA, even with support from the army, left a tiny footprint in the camps. Inside the perimeter, increasingly contentious debates over repatriation seriously threatened UNRRA's ability to fulfill its mandate. As the repatriation crisis deepened, the Military Government grew increasingly irritated at the slow pace of movement by Poles. While the U.S. Army made it clear that they would not compel repatriation, the military administration had other ways of strongly encouraging Poles to consider leaving the camps.

The solution, in the eyes of an increasingly frustrated U.S. Third Army, was to step up a program of camp inspections designed largely to make life as difficult as possible for DPs and their UNRRA supervisors in the hope of encouraging Poles to repatriate. Nothing caused more friction between the army and UNRRA than these intrusive and intentionally provocative visits. One American officer, General Watson, became a local legend for his whirlwind appearances and extraordinarily brusque manner. Masset could not stand Watson. In exasperation, he wrote to the UNRRA offices in Bad Kissingen unofficially to protest what he saw as outrageous behavior. Emphasizing the connections between DP camps and concentration camps, Masset angrily noted that the general

> [gave] hell to a DP worker who was dressed in the striped coat of Buchenwald! None of Gen. Watson's commands and orders were made privately; at all times he was surrounded by a crowd of 200 to 300 Poles, many of whom understand English. You cannot imagine the state of this camp today.[82]

For Watson's part, he was entirely consistent in his demand that the pace of repatriation speed up immediately, ideally to about 1,500 per week. In the meantime, he insisted that the Municipal Council and UNRRA tighten regulations on sanitation, compel residents to bathe more frequently, and crack down on what he believed to be "Soviet" tendencies among the camp's Polish leadership. Masset told his superiors that the Wildflecken Poles now believed that the camp "is occupied more rigorously than were concentration camps during the war or German cities since the peace." How, asked Masset, did the army expect sanitation to improve with limited resources and a hygiene situation that already was "more clean and healthy than many European cities of 15,000 inhabitants?"[83]

For UNRRA, too, repatriation remained the cornerstone of DP policy. In fall 1946, the UNRRA Council ordered its staff to encourage "the speedy return of the greatest possible number of displaced persons to their homeland as soon as possible." Meyer Cohen, a senior UNRRA official, wrote in an open letter:

> There is work for all. There is a livelihood for all. There is dignity for all. Make no mistake about this, do not be misled by false rumors. And remember too, that UNRRA now, as before, will not be a party to any forcible repatriation. But to remain behind is to face the most dark and doubtful of futures. And the opportunity to go home – to be sent home, at no expense to you and with every opportunity and every necessary care for your well-being and comfort – is again being offered you.[84]

By the winter of 1946, UNRRA officials closer to the daily life of the camps had doubts about the wisdom of continuing to push for repatriation. After all, they were the ones on the ground dealing with fearful and discontented DPs. As an agency, UNRRA remained committed to repatriation, and this growing gap between policy and practice began to alarm supervisory staff. In December, District Director A. C. Dunn responded to a report by a subordinate that cast doubt on the wisdom of advocating repatriation:

> This [report] seems to run counter to the policy of the Organization by which we are employed. Moreover, the question of whether we as individual UNRRA employees feel that Displaced Persons will be happy in their homes or elsewhere seems beside the point. The Displaced Person himself must make this decision; we are merely asked to do everything we can to help him arrive at a decision by putting before him all the available facts.[85]

This was hardly an unqualified endorsement of a policy that many in the organization found distasteful or, more important, impossible to carry out. In the camps, UNRRA officials faced episodic pressure from above, American pressure from outside, and a potentially perilous situation within. Repatriation numbers, which had been steady, began to suffer. An UNRRA report in April 1946 offered a gloomy assessment of the future. While 57,000 Poles repatriated during that month, more than 450,000 remained in Germany. Easter brought repatriation to a standstill and it grew increasingly difficult to convince Poles to return on their own. The reasons seemed clear. Reports flowed steadily westward of large-scale inter-ethnic violence along the Polish-Soviet border and there was little confidence in the integrity of upcoming elections in Poland. "There is every indication that we are rapidly approaching a point where the number of Poles willing to be repatriated will be at a minimum."[86]

The result of this soul searching was Operation Carrot, a massive effort in the summer of 1946 to encourage voluntary repatriation. UNRRA offered repatriates a sixty-day supply of essentials if they returned to their homes. Kathryn Hulme recalled setting up a large display in a kitchen showing the rations for a family of four. This display, which comprised 376 pounds of food, included enough lard for one of her DP assistants to carve the Polish eagle on its surface. When "Ignatz" suggested that this was enough food to trade for a house in Poland, it reminded Hulme that Ignatz and many like him lost their homes in the postwar border transfer. "But not I, said his face of habitual renunciation, not I in my expropriated village on the Russian side of the River Bug; I cannot be bought with food."[87]

Many others, however, took the rations. Almost 80,000 Poles repatriated during August and September. These included Bruno S., brought to Germany in 1943 as a farm laborer and sentenced to hard labor for unspecified crimes a year later. Dawid L. spent five years working on farms across the south of the country. Reunited with his wife and two children (eighteen and six years old), they now made the choice to take their chances on a return to Poland. Some combination of material incentive, frustration with camp life, and a sense that there were no other viable options compelled them to take the offer and get on the train.

But countervailing forces were at work as well. News from Poland did not improve, nor did the weather, as another fall turned to winter.

The winter of 1946–47, remembered in Germany as the *"Hungerwinter,"* was one of the most brutal in Europe's modern history. DPs and their UNRRA minders, just like so many across the continent, huddled in their barracks for warmth. By January, monthly repatriation of Poles across Germany fell to just over 1,000. With Operation Carrot running out of steam, a new phase in the history of Wildflecken, and the DP camp system, began.[88] Those who remained in the camps were unlikely to repatriate and had lived for eighteen months in camps dominated by anti-repatriation activists. Skepticism about repatriation turned to hostility. Those who advocated return to Eastern Europe found themselves under suspicion, which readily turned to anger.

UNRRA continued to press voluntary repatriation. By this time, those who chose to stay in the camps were even less likely to be persuaded by delegates from Warsaw than they were by UNRRA's blandishments. Late 1946 and early 1947 were the most dangerous days in the confrontations over repatriation. While many camps reported that repatriation efforts met with sullen silence or even small acts of violence, a new spirit of resistance grew in the facilities. In Naples, a camp for royalist Serb *Chetniks* erupted over a visit by a Yugoslav official. A crowd beat the diplomat to death in front of his erstwhile British protectors, who then did nothing to punish the offenders.[89] Cold weather and hardening attitudes on all sides combined to radicalize an already dangerous situation. At Wildflecken, with camp elections looming and the tedium of winter spent inside, matters came to a head in the early days of the new year.

In November, two delegates from the Polish Repatriation Mission in Berlin, accompanied by an American lieutenant-colonel, visited the camp. The Poles and their American colleague found aggressive anti-repatriation sentiment among many in the camp, "at least 40% [of whom] might be regarded as from the Ukrainian territory." This sort of language, which UNRRA worked hard to suppress, was very dangerous because it brought to mind the early forced repatriations. The delegation argued once again that the Wildflecken Poles lived under the influence of Anders Army veterans, which UNRRA believed controlled the school, the Boy Scouts, and many of the functions of government. As evidence they pointed to the portrait of General Anders in the Municipal Committee office. As a remedy they suggested "segregation" of the camp to remove those "whom Polish liaison officers will consider Ukrainian" and "anti-repatriation Poles."[90] As if in response to this apparent coordination of interests between the Americans and Communist Poles, flyers appeared throughout the camp proclaiming that "The Americans have lied to us! They are no better than the Germans!" In a more direct effort to impede repatriation, unknown parties broke into the file room at UNRRA's local headquarters and ransacked the facility.[91] As rumors of screenings at Wildflecken spread through the DP camp system, UNRRA began to encounter resistance at other camps. A group of Poles ordered to be transferred from Aschaffenburg to Wildflecken refused to do so. "This incident is very important in our estimation, since it is the first large-scale refusal of DPs to obey Army and UNRRA orders," wrote a concerned UNRRA official a few months later. "A few more successful resistances of this nature could have grave consequences for both Army and UNRRA."[92]

Later in November, Major Maliszewski visited senior UNRRA officials in Heidelberg to discuss Wildflecken. He blamed slow repatriation efforts on Ukrainians who, having lost Polish citizenship, intended to keep others from returning to Poland. He rather blithely noted that "this is the law of suggestion that usually accompanies masses."[93] He suggested a screening, based on the utterly unscientific criteria of names that were "not Polish sounding" and the adherence to Orthodox or Uniate Christianity that supposedly distinguished Ukrainians from Poles. With the cooperation of UNRRA, teams of Polish army officers stationed in Berlin fanned out among Polish DP camps. During the second week of January, they came to Wildflecken.

At first, the Polish Committee cooperated with the screening efforts. On the morning of January 13, 125 people reported, of whom 114 satisfactorily proved themselves Poles while ten proved to be White Ruthenians and one Greek. By afternoon, the mood turned ugly. A crowd of several dozen DPs came into the hall and demanded an explanation of the procedure. "The DP group did not seem to be very impressed by the explanation," wrote the attached UNRRA observer phlegmatically. The Polish officers made for the door, with shouts of "Moscow agent!" and "Stalin!" behind them. "My personal opinion," wrote the observer, "is that this demonstration may have been an organized movement started by elements who may find for various reasons such a screening very embarrassing."[94] Even with considerable evidence that such screenings were massively unpopular and potential lightning rods, they would continue. Staff posted orders around the camp, promising punishments that included expulsion from the camp for anyone who did not show up for screenings on January 22. Given the atmosphere in the camp, it seems unlikely that UNRRA's promise that "this screening has no connection with repatriation and politics" mollified anyone.[95] UNRRA's inattention to the camp's internal politics now turned against them as events moved swiftly beyond their control.

"Everyone knows that Poland is ruled by Bolsheviks, and not by the Polish government," read a flyer passed around between camp residents. "We shall not allow this screening to be done because the moment our documents are stamped we submit to administration by Warsaw and they will force us to repatriate!"[96] Cooperation with the Polish government cost UNRRA precious credibility with camp residents. For some residents, UNRRA was now as much the enemy as the Polish liaison officers with their stamps and maps of a truncated Polish state.

The Mess Hall of Kitchen 7 was quiet and very cold on the morning of January 27, 1947. Resplendent in dress uniforms and gold braid that seemed utterly incongruous in the morning chill, four Polish Army officers stamped their feet and surveyed the ominously empty room before them. Two UNRRA workers stood sheepishly by, unable to provide any information about the camp residents who were supposed to be lining up to fill out the stacks of forms carefully laid out on long tables in the Mess Hall. This was going to be a long day for the officers and their commander, Captain Mikalajczyk.

The officers heard the crowd long before they could see it. The streets of the camp filled with DPs, many wearing red and white armbands that were the symbol of Piotr L.'s Civic Militia. The camp's subterranean politics now took a very public center stage. Above the crowd flew banners: "Away with the Polish Mission," "Abolish the Screenings, "We Want Elections." As the crowd shouted insults into the hall, a few DPs pushed their way in. When the Polish officers, badly outnumbered, confronted the leaders, matters began to escalate. When Hulme arrived, the harassed and frightened Poles at least began to believe that they might escape with their lives. "Are you staying?," one panicked officer asked Hulme, under the assumption that he might survive if the Assistant Director stayed close by. The officers traded shouts and threats with the masses outside as the UNRRA workers furiously tried to defuse the situation. From headquarters, Masset took the unprecedented step of calling the U.S. Army post and requesting the immediate dispatch of American Constabulary troops. For the Polish officers in the Mess Hall, help was coming, but not nearly fast enough.

When an UNRRA worker managed to close one of the hall's windows, a DP outside pulled a wool hat over his own face and used his head to shatter the glass. The crowd now surged, completely beyond the control of anyone. Hands grabbed uniforms and fists connected with flesh. As jeeps full of American troops raced into the camp, the officers fled to their waiting car. Bleeding and absent much of their braid and ornamentation, they made it to the vehicle only to find its exit blocked by hundreds of angry bodies. As the car pulled away, the jubilant crowd thronged through the streets of the camp. A delegate from the Committee made a hurried speech above the noise of the crowd. "If they arrest one of us," the speaker pledged, "the entire camp will stage a revolution." The camps' informal network of underground politics, a product of bifurcated structure of authority, had just produced its first international incident. A few days later, the *New York Times* ran an article about the Wildflecken riot, emphasizing to its readers the strong sentiment in the camps against "Soviet" efforts to encourage repatriation.[97]

The Polish officers and their supervisors were quick to place blame for the events on the camp's leaders, including Piotr L. and J. They repeated charges that Wildflecken Poles had ties to armed underground movements in Poland and asserted the "Ukrainians calling themselves Poles" were behind the majority of anti-repatriation activity.[98] In reality, the anti-communist Poles simply proved better at conveying their message within the camp than did either UNRRA or the representatives of the postwar Polish government. The events at K7 did not reflect a dramatic turn of events, but rather confirmed what should have been known by the camp's UNRRA overseers; repatriation at Wildflecken was moribund. A local Military Government officer wrote an open letter to the camp, calling the riot "discourteous" and emphasizing that the screenings did "not mean 'Forced Repatriation' but is to determine who are Polish and who are not." During any future screenings, "U.S. Army troops will be present to maintain order, and whole-hearted cooperation of the camp population is desired in eliminating further disturbances, continuation of which could only result in hardships for all people of the Wildflecken Assembly Center."[99]

The four Polish repatriation officers survived their encounter with an angry crowd at K7, but the hope of finding an expedient solution to the problem of the Wildflecken Poles suffered a mortal wound. While the resistance of camp residents did not come as a complete surprise to the camp administration, the riot marked a clear turning point in the history of the camp and in the broader UNRRA effort to deal with the problem of DPs. The Wildflecken Poles responded both to pressures from outside the camp and from the internal dynamics of the hybrid society in which they lived. As the Cold War order emerged in Central and Eastern Europe, the inhabitants of Wildflecken turned against repatriation and, more important, began to organize against it. The radicalization of politics within the camp helped to shape its future, that of its increasingly impatient residents, and of the wider structures of refugee life in the post-1945 world.

For those who operated in and on the margins of the DP camp at Wildflecken, the riots were a sobering dose of reality. Within a few months of the riots, Masset was dismissed from UNRRA service. Hulme became a supervisor responsible for a large swath of northern Bavaria, including Wildflecken, and left the camp along with Habets. The Wildflecken Poles faced a much less certain path forward. Thousands of DPs clearly would not willingly return to Eastern Europe and, lacking other options, seemed likely to remain in the Sinn Valley for the indefinite future. The DPs were just one facet of a complex postwar crisis across Central Europe. In Wildflecken, as in so many other places like it in the remains of Hitler's Reich, there were others who fled their homes and faced an uncertain future. Living cheek to jowl with the DPs, another set of refugees tried to make a new life in the Franconian Rhön. Their story will occupy the next chapter.

THREE

Keeping Refugees Occupied, 1945–1948

Armin G. did not like Americans very much. He also had little love for his erstwhile German protectors or their local government. Armin and his family arrived in Brückenau from Yugoslavia in 1945, ethnic Germans who found themselves on the wrong side of the postwar order in the Balkans. Armin was a consummate troublemaker and a political chameleon, capable of adjusting his entire persona when the need arose. Along with his large family, he lived in temporary quarters in one of Brückenau's resort casinos, from which he occasionally emerged in traditional Bavarian dress carrying an axe and intimidating refugees and townspeople alike.

Problems began in 1946, when Armin told authorities a bizarre story that American soldiers held his family at gunpoint and demanded liquor. When his interlocutors pressed him for specifics, he withdrew his complaint. After the manager of the resort went to speak with Armin, the two fought and both later went to the Americans to complain about the other. "The Germans," wrote one Military Government official to another after hearing both sides, "should be encouraged to 'clean their own house.'" When the Americans visited Armin, along with his seven children and various other relatives, they found him resolutely uncooperative, unwilling to move to new quarters, and enthusiastically displaying Communist symbols and a banner reading "Workers of the World, Unite."

The Americans and their German interlocutors in Brückenau struggled to find a solution to the problem. This included efforts to ship G. to the French Zone under the tenuous pretext that someone with a similar name was wanted there for violent crimes during the war. Armin knew how to operate in the fluid world of postwar Germany. To the Americans, he claimed to be an ethnic German expellee from Yugoslavia. To the Germans, he just as emphatically claimed to be a citizen of Yugoslavia and therefore eligible for DP status. Armin, in his various guises as a German, Yugoslav, nationalist, Communist, or victim of war, outmaneuvered American and German refugee officials with equal stubbornness and skill. In a postwar Germany overrun with the uprooted and occupied by an army with little experience in refugee affairs, individuals like Armin could and did carve out a space for themselves to operate between bureaucracies just learning to deal with the problems of administering a displaced population.

This chapter examines the experience of Wildflecken under American occupation. The face of the Military Government was Company A, 3rd Military Government Regiment.[1] This small unit was joined by various tactical units responsible for providing security, maintaining law and order, and protecting and disposing of vast amount of munitions found at the Muna. The American occupiers eagerly sought local partners, who gradually re-formed the institutions of local government.

This chapter also presents the story of the large mass of German refugees, most of them expellees from points to the east, who shared space with the Americans, local Germans, and the DPs in postwar Franconia. These intertwined stories also connect in many ways to the events taking place in and around the DP camp, presenting a mosaic of life in a district profoundly challenged by the refugee crisis.

Refugee management and refugee affairs were central in the reconstruction of local political, economic, and social life in the district around Wildflecken. American and German officials, themselves bound by orders from superior authorities, had to manage a large and diverse population of expellees, while at the same time contending with the presence of the DP camp just up the hill from town. The solution was to innovate. Local elites, who advocated rural development before the war, now saw an opportunity to do the same in the postwar crisis period. Using locally available resources, occupiers and occupied sought to mitigate the worst of the refugee crisis by seeking long-term solutions rather than quick fixes. While much of this planning later came to naught, there was unquestionably a renewed optimism in the region not long after the end of the war. The push for innovation emerged from the terrible demographic crisis of the postwar years. Expellees made up about fifteen percent of Lower Franconia's population, but at one point more than thirty percent of the population of Landkreis Brückenau.[2] In districts near the border, more refugees from the East arrived every day, further burdening the fragile support system. The presence of the DP camp had three critical effects on the lives of the residents, both long-time and new, in the surrounding district under American occupation.

First, the Polish camp continued to serve as the nexus point for a vast regional underground economy. The creation and establishment of illegal and quasi-legal commerce sat at the center of everyday life in occupied rural Bavaria. Because of its pervasiveness and the changing social and legal context of such commerce, engaging in it was also an implicitly political act that challenged authority while creating a space to air grievances toward occupation and German bureaucracies that many regarded as inefficient or unfeeling.[3] This was particularly true for expellees. Illegal trade linked DPs, expellees, locals, and Americans in a web of complicity and potential conflict. For Germans living on the degraded domestic economy, the black market offered not only a means of acquiring sustenance, but a hedge against currency inflation. Expellees, living in refugee camps or private housing, had widely varied access to food through legal means. Even in an agrarian district, expellees experienced higher rates of food insecurity than locals.[4] The black market in Landkreis Brückenau changed with demographic, legal, and economic conditions, but the centrality and persistence of illegal commerce in the area highlight the pervasive sense of deprivation, want, and urgency felt by many locals and strangers in the postwar period.

Secondly, the Americans, Polish DPs, and ethnic German expellees in the district each claimed a stake in the real property of the base facility itself. DPs, along with the international organizations that worked with them, laid claim to the center of the Wehrmacht base. Expellees began to settle on its unused periphery, built homes for themselves, and began to claim a novel form of local identity. The Americans began to see the utility of maintaining at least a near-term presence in the region and identified the Wildflecken site as well suited to their needs. After 1948, this tripartite conflict over the future of the base emerged as a major stumbling block in relations between local Germans, expellees, DPs, and the American occupying power.

Finally, the presence of the Poles and, to a lesser extent, the Americans helped to create conditions under which expellees could and did begin to integrate into existing communities. Expellees now settled into their own towns on the grounds of the base and began to benefit from American efforts to ensure social peace and economic recovery in the countryside. Local officials quickly described these communities as a new Heimat for those who had lost their old homes after the war. The physical and emotional creation of this new homeland took place in the shadow of the DP camp, which expellees and locals agreed could not be allowed to persist. The process through which expellees integrated into a "second Heimat" took years and was fraught with conflict. While the DP camp and the American occupiers sometimes exacerbated these tensions, the presence of DPs and foreign troops also forced expellees and locals to make common cause with each other.

The American presence in Wildflecken at the end of the war was minimal, so the Americans worked diligently to pass off as much responsibility as possible to locals. From the beginning, the Americans sought to build and support credible German partners who had the cultural and linguistic competency to deal with their countrymen and the administrative experience to manage the everyday complexities of a rural district under occupation. In partnership with the Americans, an effective local government emerged closely linked with the newly re-formed Bavarian state government in Munich. The partnership between local elites and the American occupiers emerged from a shared set of priorities. Broadly speaking, these were the maintenance of law and order, the rebuilding of local institutions, and the establishment of a functioning and legitimate local economy integrated into larger regional redevelopment. While there was disagreement between locals and occupiers over the particulars, there was broad consensus on the more general problems. The creation of this partnership proved deeply and at times painfully difficult. The Americans had a hard time identifying qualified individuals, who in turn sometimes faced popular antipathy and questions about their pasts. The conditions under which local government re-emerged after the war reflected the unstable reality of a rural region overrun by several distinct groups of refugee populations.

During the first spring after the end of the war, an American woman named Ann Warren Griffith came to Wildflecken for two weeks. She worked for the Red Cross and was sent to Wildflecken to fill in for two women who ran a canteen for American troops above the town. In 1950, she recalled her experience in a short piece in the *New Yorker*. "The effects of [Wildflecken's] remoteness was apparent," she wrote. "By that time city Germans had smartened up and learned the life came not from the sun but from the American Occupation Forces, and even rural Germans were catching on. But Wildfleckenites were downright hostile."

Griffith, who achieved some later fame as a writer of science fiction stories, castigated the townspeople for their mean-spirited provincialism and the "Red Cross Girls" for their dangerous naiveté. The Americans she encountered passed the time guarding the Muna and playing cards in the canteen. If Griffith was aware of the massive DP camp one hill over or the German camps scattered through the countryside, neither appeared in her recollections a few years later. Much like Hulme's recollections of life in the camp, Griffith gave a vivid but selective picture of the place inconsistent with the very real everyday challenges faced by the tiny cohort of American personnel assigned to the district.[5]

The American occupation in Landkreis Brückenau was strikingly small. It had two principal components: a Military Government detachment in Brückenau and tactical troops initially tasked with protecting the Muna and keeping order. Military Government Detachment I-331 (later Liaison and Security Office A-331), occupied a tiny office in Brückenau. While the district faced a number of compelling and potentially dangerous problems, so did many other parts of the shattered country. Landkreis Brückenau only rated the smallest possible Military Government detachment.[6] The nerve center of the American occupation consisted of between five and ten American personnel, initially commanded by Captain (later Major) Harry Clark. The commander was a journalist in civilian life who joined Civil Affairs in 1943, serving in France and the invasion of Germany. He was the first MG commander in Weimar before that city became part of the Soviet zone. Of the four officers assigned to the district, only one was a career serviceman. In addition to Clark, the others were an engineer and an oil company sales manager.[7] The detachment commander appears to have gotten along well with local civilians and with the rest of his team, but his reports and communications with his own chain of command show the frustrations felt by many in the occupation over the seemingly insurmountable list of tasks.

The American team in Brückenau suffered from many of the shortcomings common to Military Government offices across occupied Germany. They had little to no German-language skills, no sense of the social or political landscape, no contacts among local elites, and an extraordinarily hazy mission to create from the postwar chaos a functioning locally dominated government. At the same time, they had to abide by regulations insisting on denazification and what the teams perceived as undue haste to stand up German institutions. "We are still sorely lacking qualified and capable personnel to handle the work....," Clark wrote in November 1945. "Assistance has been requested but is evidently unavailable."[8]

The tactical element in the Landkreis for much of 1946 consisted of elements of the 15th Infantry Regiment, 3rd Infantry Division. The regiment had overall responsibility for Lower Franconia, meaning that a single battalion had to cover the northern counties as well as the border with the Soviet Zone. Between border patrol, guarding munitions facilities, internal security, and supervision of 31,000 DPs and almost 5,000 civilian prisoners, the regiment's resources were stretched very thin. At any given time, fifty-two soldiers manned eleven positions around the highly porous Muna at Wildflecken. When the regiment arrived at Wildflecken in early 1946, the only security they provided for the DP camp itself was a single guard post at the main entrance with eight soldiers. When the scope of the task became clearer, a foot patrol and a motorized detachment deployed around the camp perimeter and in the town itself.

The arrival of the 15th also marked the first time that anyone discussed the use of the Wildflecken facility as an American base. In April, 1946, B Company, 1st Battalion arrived in Wildflecken "with the view of installing the 15th Infantry after an evacuation of approximately 12,000 Polish Displaced Persons." Two months later, this plan was "cancelled by higher authorities."[9] While there is no indication of where this plan originated or why it was cancelled, the idea presaged much later debates about the future of the Wildflecken facility and the headaches that it caused. The Wildflecken base complex was large, intact, and modern, enormously useful to the occupying army. It was also home to thousands of DPs who needed to be housed elsewhere if they were moved. The Americans never fully lost interest in building an installation at Wildflecken, but they also could not figure out a way to do so without creating even more problems for themselves.

In large part because of the relative size of the occupation authority, locals appear to have regarded the Americans as a tolerable nuisance in the early days. There were a number of zones of conflict, chiefly over property and fraternization. Locals consistently demanded that the Americans do more to protect them from the DPs on the hill and often expressed annoyance with what they considered the slow pace of postwar economic recovery. That said, there were few instances on violence and little indication of ill will. "Most of the population seem [sic] to appreciate that they live in the American zone which they consider the best of all occupation zones."[10]

The exception to this generally amicable relationship was the German reaction to the arrival of African-American troops in Wildflecken. African-American soldiers cycled through Wildflecken regularly, chiefly as part of labor units who performed construction work and helped with the clearance of the munitions plant. Local officials and some townspeople reacted very strongly and negatively toward black soldiers. American officers made sure to distinguish when a black soldier committed a crime of breach of discipline, suggesting that they shared German ambivalence about African-Americans in their midst. Often complaints had to do with property. On the southern edge of the base, American troops occupied former Wehrmacht barracks, coveted by local authorities as a potential home for evacuees. A number of units passed through the barracks, which suffered considerable damage. After the buildings were handed over in mid-1946, the mayor attempted to get the Military Government to pay for the stoves, bathtubs, windowpanes, and other items that vanished during the troops' residence. The German request and the American response indicated that both sides placed responsibility for the property damage squarely on black troops.[11]

As Heide Fehrenbach has pointed out, the most explicit discussions of race in postwar Germany concerned interracial sex.[12] Here the record in Wildflecken is particularly clear and dismal. After the departure of one of the first black transport units to serve in the area, anonymous letters began to appear through the mail slots of young women believed to have associated with black GIs. Some featured crude drawings of Africans. Another, written in a shaky, child-like handwriting, said only, "Good luck! Slut." Military Government officials were concerned with attitudes like this, which they linked to persistent anti-Semitism and the durability of conservative German social mores.[13] The local MG detachment was still very concerned about a possible resurgence of Nazism and the threat of guerilla warfare in the months after the end of the war, so it saw Nazi holdouts behind every suggestion of local discontent. In all likelihood, the campaign of night letters was probably a result of the sort of conservative, Catholic desire to restore the class and gender boundaries of the prewar, pre-Nazi period. For the postwar right, as Maria Höhn notes in her work on the Rhineland, German women were supposed to return to their traditional roles and to respect gender, class, and racial boundaries.[14] Americans, much less African-Americans, were not a part of that vision of postwar reconstruction.

Another of the concerns common to locals and the Military Government detachment was the continued arrival of German refugees. The continuous flow of expellees during the first eighteen months of the occupation created logistical logjams. While the Americans had no direct responsibility for their welfare, expellees threatened to destabilize the region and make the Americans' task all the more difficult. Clark, acutely conscious that he could not appear to be directly interfering in expellee affairs, always phrased his reports carefully to highlight that concerns about expellee arrivals came from the Germans. "Refugees continue to arrive in Kreis Bruckenau [sic] from the countries now expelling Germans. The opinion has been expressed by the local Refugee authorities that Germany has about reached the end of the line in caring for her own refugees and help must be given from outside the country."[15]

In Brückenau, the problems of managing local German and expellee affairs were compounded by the presence of a large numbers of Polish DPs in the district. The detachment had, at most, two Polish-speakers at any time, which meant that most information about the Polish camp came from UNRRA. As we have seen, the UNRRA team had its own problems with regard to language competency. The detachment's 1946 annual report estimated that DPs were responsible for eighty percent of crimes committed across the district. "During this year, the Wildflecken DP camp was the center of Blackmarket and petty crimes, especially during the first half of the year with as many as 16,000 Displaced Persons."[16]

For the Americans, the connection between the refugee crises was abundantly clear. "A problem of primary importance for the occupation forces [is] the handling of population movement during and after the cessation of hostilities," noted a report from the Army's European Headquarters Public Relations Division in fall 1946. "We now deal with three distinct groups of persons: United Nations Displaced Persons, German expellees, and German refugees – all persons displaced from their homes." The report noted that agricultural production sufficed to feed only half of a population swollen by refugees of various types. At the same time, public opinion polls taken during the first two years of the occupation suggested growing pessimism among expellees and locals, along with deep and widespread resentment toward DPs. One study suggested that only fifteen percent of Germans, expellee and local, believed that Germany bore any responsibility toward the DPs.[17]

The Americans knew that Germans considered the DPs to be a menace and a drain on local resources. Widespread fear led to rumors like the one that circulated in Wildflecken (and apparently in other locations around the American Zone) that Polish DPs would be allowed to loot German homes on November 9, 1945, a date symbolic in Bavaria as the anniversary of the 1918 collapse of the monarchy, the Beer Hall Putsch, and the Kristallnacht riots. It is not difficult to imagine that the memories of the 1938 pogroms were very powerful in the small rural communities of the Sinn Valley. Towns that forced Jewish residents out in a night of violence now feared that Jews might return to reclaim their possessions or that the Americans might allow DP raids to avenge Jewish losses from seven years before. One American intelligence officer remarked at the ubiquity of this belief among rural residents. "Rumor so strong persons who usually pay no attention to rumor began to believe it."[18] Americans also quickly came to understand that locals began to resent the presence of ethnic German refugees and expellees. "Germans who have," wrote Major Clark in February 1946, "should be forced to do their duty and share with the Germans from the East who through no fault of their own were evicted from their homes and lost all."[19]

As far as the Americans were concerned, the key to fixing these intractable and intertwined problems lay in the development of meaningful German leadership in the district. In the absence of German law enforcement, American tactical troops and Constabulary forces could then be used to keep the fragile peace in the district. The presence of the uprooted in the Landkreis, as in so many places across Germany, only made these challenges more difficult.

As happened across occupied Germany, the Americans confronted the critical problem of identifying and promoting local leadership. Military Government officials, faced with limited language skills and the collapse of local institutions, tried their best to find talented, or at least competent, administrators.[20] Denazification in the district happened relatively quickly. During the first two months of the occupation, five district officials lost their jobs, as did most local mayors. The Americans made a number of arrests based on "black lists," both for party or SS activity and for anti-Jewish violence during the Third Reich. In Brückenau itself, the Nazi mayor resigned and was replaced by Otto Kenner, who also ran the local volunteer police. Kenner emerged as the leader of the local Communist Party, a group that had been invisible for twelve years. His rise, which did not last long, was a reminder of the past organizing power of the KPD in the county. Kenner proved to be little but trouble for the Americans, who jailed him a few months later when he organized an unauthorized parade of KPD members in the town. The Landrat, Karl von Freyberg, held on to his position longest, in large part because his administrative skills proved essential for the success of the American occupation. Facing dismissal for his Nazi past, he retired in August.[21]

Having cleared out almost all senior leadership positions in the district, the occupiers now faced the unenviable task of replacing them. In Brückenau, the Americans quickly identified a potentially ideal candidate for the position of Landrat, not from the local population, but from among the expellees. Heinrich Oswald was born in 1901 in the Silesian city of Ratibor (today Polish Racibórz). The child of a railway official, Oswald and his family moved around the eastern edge of the German empire. Oswald studied law in Freiburg and Berlin, then took up a series of administrative positions in Breslau, where he stayed from 1926 until nearly the end of the war. Like so many mid-level bureaucrats in the wake of the war, Oswald's past and his present circumstances intersected in the eyes of the Americans. He was an experienced and able administrator and could provide evidence that he had been persecuted for his political views during the war. During the conflict's final months, he faced dismissal and prosecution for "defeatism." The front moved faster than the justice system and Oswald escaped, fleeing after a long journey to Brückenau. There he quickly emerged as an advisor to the Americans, who then appointed him Landrat.

In addition to his documented brush with Nazi law, Oswald appears to have maintained remarkably cordial relations with Breslau's Jewish community. His sister married a Jewish man, who later wrote that Oswald warned local Jews to get out in 1937, before special protections afforded to Silesian Jews under the 1922 Geneva Convention expired.[22] Another Jewish refugee, living in London, stressed that he "lost his whole family to the gas chambers and have no reason to guarantee the political reliability of any German." Still, he recalled living with the Oswalds for several days before departing and praised Oswald for sending city workers to clean Jewish graves.

There remained, however, a catch. To serve in a responsible position under American occupation, Oswald had to assert that he had never been a member of the Nazi Party. In light of his administrative career, particularly in Lower Silesia, a district in which the Nazis had early and resounding electoral success, this seemed unlikely at best.[23] Brückenau lay a long way from Breslau and records now sat behind Soviet lines. Oswald maintained that he was promoted solely on the basis of competence, and the Americans at least pretended to be convinced. For Military Government officials like Major Clark, Oswald was too good to risk losing. Oswald performed ably in "an extremely trying job because of thorough de-Nazification policies of this and his own headquarters. He is conscientious and able and has been thoroughly screened by CIC and Special Branch of this detachment."[24]

Heinrich Oswald's promotion later caused a great deal of problems for both Germans and Americans. As Clark's letter makes clear, even in the earliest days of the occupation American officials found themselves torn between the need to find experienced administrators and the clear mandate to exclude former party members. There were too few MG officials on the ground with the kind of linguistic and cultural competencies needed to successfully manage the reconstruction effort. As a result, the rebuilding of political life in the region proceeded through a series of compromises that eventually threatened the whole project.

Denazification serves as a cautionary tale about the limits of American ability and willingness to conduct a thorough reckoning with Germany's recent past. As it was across much of the American zone, the effort to denazify local society was, at least initially, energetic and well intentioned, though burdened by enormous administrative responsibilities and increasingly mistrusted by the population. An early MG report on denazification in the district described the process as "snafu." This was not far from the truth. The next March, the Americans turned the process over to local German tribunals (*Spruchkammern*). The *Spruchkammer* that met in Brückenau tried to conduct a serious vetting of the local adult population, along with expellees like Oswald who took up residence there. This proved to be an enormous task and took nearly three years to sort out.

By mid-1946, more than 13,000 district residents submitted questionnaires (*Meldebogen*), with the district Spruchkammer able to clear about fifteen cases per week. The tribunal did not even have its own offices. Despite promises from Oswald, delays hindered the renovation of office space until mid-1948, by which time the tribunal nearly cleared its backlog. Adding to the challenge, the tribunal's chair was a well-respected local lawyer who belonged to the KPD. While not unheard of, it was relatively rare for Communists to serve as Spruchkammer chairmen (*Vorsitzende*).[25] Despite the efforts of both Military Government and local civilian leaders, the chair was forced to temporarily step down during the fall of 1946 following accusations made against him with the Appeals Board in Würzburg that he used the Spruchkammer as a tool of Communist policy. While he resumed his chairmanship, such battles limited the speed and efficiency of the tribunal.

The Spruchkammer in Landkreis Brückenau more than lived up to the tribunals' reputation as "Fellow-Traveler Factories" (*Mitläufer-*

fabriken). In early-1948, for example, as it wrapped up its work, the tribunal heard an astonishing number of cases, and cleared most of them so quickly that there could have been little attention to detail. In three months, the tribunal disposed of 2,977 cases. Of these, they found two in category 1 ("major responsibility") and forty in categories 2 and 3 ("implicated" or "mildly implicated"). The vast majority, ninety-four percent of those found to bear some culpability, ended up in category 4 ("fellow traveler") and likely paid a small fine for their troubles. This percentage was roughly in line with the average across Bavaria.[26] In some cases, no decision proved to be needed. The local tavern owner Volker M. returned in 1947 from captivity in the French Zone. A party member since 1935, the thirty-nine-year-old M. served as a neighborhood organizer (*Blockhelfer*) in Wildflecken and later as a non-commissioned officer in the Wehrmacht. While he clearly rose in the local party hierarchy before the war, his suffered no penalty for his participation, benefitting from one of several amnesties declared in 1947. M. later became a vocal opponent of the American military presence in the district.[27]

Alongside the reconstruction of local administration came the reinstantiation of formal political life. This included the supervised and heavily scrutinized creation of political parties with an eye toward future elections. While technically allowed in the U.S. Zone after August 27, 1945, it took several months before serious organizational work began. Perhaps unsurprisingly, many in American-occupied Bavaria had little interest in party politics so soon after the end of the war.[28] From the beginning, authorities feared that expellee populations would be susceptible to radical politics from the left and right.[29] In particular, there were fears that these new voters would support either the KPD or the WAV (*Wirtschaftliche Aufbau-Vereinigung* or Economic Reconstruction Union), a right-wing populist party that based its appeal on expellee rights and opposition to denazification.

In Landkreis Brückenau, potentially radical parties ran into a variety of hindrances. First, the local KPD suffered from internal divisions, an opaque leadership structure, and frequent brushes with the Military Government like the one that landed its putative leader Otto Kenner in jail.[30] Nonetheless, Communists exercised a great deal of less formal power through institutions like the Spruchkammer. They appear to have had a number of well-placed supporters in local government and were at least rumored to control key local offices. The WAV, despite its best efforts, never managed to gain a foothold in the district and never appeared on the lists of potentially dangerous elements on the electoral landscape.

Residents voted in three more elections during 1946, choosing delegates for the district council (*Kreistag*), the Bavarian constitutional convention, and the Bavarian parliament (*Landtag*). Perhaps the most remarkable aspect of the postwar elections was the speed with which the old political order reasserted itself. The Christian Social Union (CSU), a center-right party descended in part from the prewar Catholic political parties, quickly established dominance in the area with more than seventy percent of all votes cast. Even in the heyday of Weimar democracy, the center-right had never been able to win tallies like this in the Rhön. But the right was not the only part of the political spectrum to re-emerge after the war in strength. Once again, the Social Democrats polled just over twenty percent in Landkreis Brückenau. However, the SPD's tally was slightly lower than average for the region, owing largely to the persistent success of the Communists. While the KPD only counted between 4.5–6 percent of voters in the county, this was the highest total for any area in Lower Franconia outside of the urban areas. This total was roughly consistent with the KPD's performance in the county during the late 1920s.[31]

Several things are clear from the results of these elections. First, expellee voters did not rush to the political margins. It is difficult to establish with certainty how expellee voters responded at the polls, but the results suggest that the newly arrived population was just as likely, if not more so, to vote for the center-right. At the same time, the strain of rural leftist support that had been a key feature of political life in the prewar Rhön persisted after twelve years underground. Even without effective leadership or organization, the Communists continued to exert real influence in the area.

The other notable feature of these elections was low voter turnout. Participation dipped to near fifty percent, markedly lower than in the rest of Lower Franconia. For the Military Government, this could be explained as part of German cynicism and indifference toward democracy. "The population is of the opinion that the last guidance is always the responsibility of the occupying forces and that they actually will guide and determine who will say and what he will say." Landrat Oswald, somewhat more analytically, suggested that one of the reasons for the low turnout was the lack of real options for expellee voters. Unlike many in the Bavarian government who feared Communist subversion among expellees, Oswald recognized that for many expellees the KPD "look like representatives of the Russian system, which they reject based on their experience in their former homelands."[32] The Landrat, himself an expellee, recognized the essential problem among his fellow refugees. The political left carried the stigma of association with the regimes that made them homeless, while the right conjured visions of the sort of narrow nationalism that rendered them expellees. Besides, their concerns were, somewhat naturally in the immediate postwar period, much more pragmatic than political.

Wilhelm Henties won election as the new mayor of Wildflecken. Henties, who survived assault in the camp the previous May, came originally from near Berlin. Nearly forty when elected, he had previously worked as a traveling salesman. Henties moved to the area from nearby Fulda to work in the HVA before joining the police in Brückenau during the war. After his election, he received a quick Spruchkammer review, for which friends testified that he often listened to foreign radio and joined the party only for professional advancement. A local priest testified, perhaps with some degree of exaggeration, that "no one recognized the senselessness and injustice of Nazism more than Herr Henties. No one wished more for the victorious arrival of the Allies and the end of the Nazi plague (*Nazipest*)."[33] The panel placed him in category IV, allowing him to take office. Henties remained an influential citizen of the town for the rest of his life.

During the first two years of the occupation, the primary concerns facing local authorities were space and food. Both of these had everything to do with the presence of large numbers of the uprooted in the rural communities of Landkreis Brückenau. Space remained the most critical problem for expellees. The irony of their situation was that the very aspect of Landkreis Brückenau that made it so attractive to refugee officials, its relative isolation and freedom from the worst of the bombing damage, made it all the more difficult to find housing and steady employment for the thousands of expellees resident in the district.

The physical space of the Wildflecken area became an early site of contention between occupiers and occupied. The Americans guaranteed the security of the DP camp, twenty-two hectares of "fine military barracks, stables, and warehouses plus modern up-to-date officers quarters." At the same time, the Muna also had a number of intact buildings occupied by the Americans in order to remove industrial equipment and ammunition. Shortly after the war, the Landrat requested that ammunition storage facilities, bunkers, and many of the buildings on the Muna remain intact for eventual use by the local population. In the meantime, most abandoned buildings on the training grounds slowly vanished as enterprising German and expellee scavengers made off with building and roofing material.[34]

No aspect of the American occupation period had more durable effects than the considerably more mundane issue of property management. Much of Wildflecken's economy and a considerable amount of the land near the town belonged to the now defunct Wehrmacht. The problem of what to do with all of the land, materiel, and equipment no longer needed by the German war machine proved vexing, but often not in ways that seemed consequential at the time. The biggest problem in the early days of the occupation concerned the vast amounts of ammunition at the Muna. Once that danger passed, questions about the future of the base facility arose.

The issue of German military property has received surprisingly little attention from historians studying the occupation. Vast quantities of now surplus equipment, uniforms, and munitions now passed into the hands of the occupier. The task of locating, cataloging, and decommissioning all of this property required a large bureaucracy, close collaboration with the Germans, and oversight to prevent graft and corruption. On each of these scores, the American record was not particularly good. In the wake of the American arrival in the area, there was looting on a significant scale on the part of local Germans. A year after the end of the war, a Constabulary raid found three truckloads of rifles, ammunition, and various other pieces of military equipment taken from the Muna in a basement near Langleiten. The Constabulary reports from the district are fragmentary, but it is clear from the documentation available that such a haul was not particularly surprising.[35]

The first effort to solve the property problem emerged from SHAEF's Supply Branch in the summer of 1945. Initial plans stressed the need for German cooperation, which in turn required local trustees (*Treuhänder*) to manage Wehrmacht real estate. Supply Branch tried to supply DP camps from surplus military stocks, which explains in part why so many DPs found themselves wearing partial German uniforms, as well as finding ways to disperse military property into the civilian economy. As an internally produced summary of the effort candidly noted, early efforts to organize property ran headlong into "backyard politics, thus permitting uninventoried stocks to evaporate into the local economy without accountability."[36]

In the fall, a more formal structure emerged for property management, eventually called the *Staatliche Erfassungs-Gesellschaft für öffentliches Gut* (Government Corporation for the Utilization of Public Goods) or STEG. This new body set to work cataloging the contents of military facilities across the American zone. It had six offices in Lower Franconia alone, supervising thirty-five dumps. STEG's primary mission was to oversee the conversion of military equipment to peacetime use. Among the items intended for conversion were thirty caliber cartridges (which could be made into rakes), parachutes (underwear), and tanks (farm equipment). The last of these gave the program its motto, "Tanks into Plowshares."[37] At the same time, STEG also attempted to identify and neutralize thousands of tons of surplus ammunition. Remaining munitions, except toxic and chemical weapons, passed into the control of STEG technicians "for the purpose of recovering component parts, all essential to the support of the approved level of German minimum economy." At its height, almost 5,000 STEG employees worked full time on ammunition recovery and disposal.[38]

In the Sinn Valley, STEG had its hands full with its two-headed mission. While DPs needed equipment and supplies, a major ammunition dump remained just up the valley. Removal of this lethal material posed yet another pressing challenge to the American occupiers. This point became all the more clear in July 1945 when Oberriedenberg exploded.

As evening descended on July 27, a train carrying sixty-three cars of ammunition from the Muna sat on a siding at the station in the small community. Guards from Company I, 395th Infantry guarded the train, though one suspects that they were mostly wandering around bored. In the wake of the explosion, one soldier claimed that he saw some Germans, whom he assumed were farmers, standing near the train. "I saw one of them throw an object, that might have been a hand grenade, into a car and run away. I fired a full clip from my rifle at him but he ran away." It was, after all, just a few months after the end of hostilities and fear of attacks by die-hard *Werewolf* guerrillas remained. However, it appears that no such thing happened in Oberriedenberg. Several local women reported that they saw Americans throwing ammunition into a fire, as they often did. "We talked about it, and often wondered if this would happen."[39]

The resulting fire and explosion destroyed the train, train station, nine houses, twelve barns, three hundred yards of track, and a variety of other vehicles. While it seems fairly clear that the whole affair began with bored soldiers testing the effect of fire on captured munitions, Major Clark charitably concluded that the cause was "undetermined."[40] The Oberriedenberg explosion reinforced the tangible sense of fear in the Sinn Valley over the problem of ordnance at the Muna. In Bavaria alone forty people died and more than ninety suffered injuries from unexpended and unexploded ammunition during the second half of 1946. At Wildflecken, the Americans had to guard and eventually dispose of more than 7,000 tons of munitions, part of more than 300,000 tons scattered around Bavaria. The local Military Government office clearly recognized the perils of having so much ordnance so close to a refugee camp. It reported an "unsatisfactory" security situation in late 1946, owing to "insufficient personnel" and "the presence of 14,000 Poles in DP Camp bordering [the] ammunition dump."[41] By October, all that remained were "toxic gas shells and large caliber artillery ammunition, [which] do not invite pilferage."[42]

STEG, and the American occupation effort more broadly, struggled to manage the staggering amount of property that passed through its hands after the war. STEG officials proved corruptible, particularly those who spoke German well enough to conduct back-channel negotiations with native contractors.[43] While the disposition of portable goods like ammunition and military equipment proved challenging, larger problems loomed in the management of real estate. Trustees chosen for their political reliability sometimes proved corrupt, inept, or both. They also developed their own plans for what was to be done with the land that did not always coincide with the wishes of the occupiers or with the best interests of local communities.

In rural Franconia, the lack of construction material after the war posed yet another challenge to the critical task of reconstruction. Regional archives are full of letters like the one sent by a local bureaucrat to various officials on behalf of a Schondra farmer who was trying to build a house on his property to house expellees. The project came to nothing because he could not purchase 320 square feet of concrete anywhere in the district. After years of neglect and frequent use by German and then American armored vehicles, the roads were in terrible condition. While the local government had access to vehicles, there were no buses for public transportation, spare parts, or, crucially, tires. Those farmers who had tractors could not keep them running, further hindering economic recovery. Wildflecken's mayor gave up and simply walked between the scattered villages under his jurisdiction.[44]

The bulk of the region had previously been owned by the Wehrmacht, meaning that it was now the property of the occupation authority. While the property management apparatus of the occupation took some time to develop, the need for land in rural Franconia grew faster than the mechanisms for distributing it. While the Americans attempted land reform in occupied Bavaria, rural Lower Franconia was not a promising site. There were few large estates to divide. In fact, the same tradition of small farms that Otto Hellmuth tried to reverse in the 1930s now hindered efforts to set up expellee farmers with new farmland.[45] In August 1945, Military Government Law Number 54 transferred control of Wehrmacht and other former state property to the government of the Land in which it was located. In the case of Wildflecken, this opportunity was complicated by the continued presence of American troops and Polish DPs on the base, particularly in the administrative buildings and the Muna industrial plant.[46]

The woods, particularly on the grounds of the base, were full of unexploded ordnance from the Wehrmacht training area and had not been regularly hunted in more than a decade. Particularly during the first year after the war, boar and red deer took a terrible toll on corn and potato crops. The local Food Office estimated that between fifteen and twenty-five percent of potatoes never reached harvest because of animal depredation and estimated total animal damage of 175,000 RM. Initially, Germans were forbidden to own weapons, so they could do little. Both locals and expellees complained that they were deprived of both a food source and a means of protecting their crops.[47]

They also resented the special legal status of the DPs when it came to hunting. German farmers continually petitioned for permission to hunt, both for food and to minimize the crop damage caused by wild boars. The Americans granted permission only grudgingly and under strict conditions. Hunters had to register and could only use weapons supplied by the Americans that had to be returned at the end of the day. Meanwhile, the hills regularly echoed with shots from DP hunters off in the woods. While DPs hunted, much to the chagrin of the local population, UNRRA officials could not regulate this practice since the DPs were not supposed to have guns in the first place. Fishing was a different matter altogether. With local wildlife officials operating again, DPs complained of being stopped and asked to pay sixty-five marks for a license. Evidently, this happened enough that DP camp administrators put out a press release emphatically stating that DPs did not have to pay for a permit.[48] For farmers, used to supplementing their income and setting their tables with the bountiful wild game of the Rhön, American restrictions on hunting appeared capricious, counter-productive, and a threat to both their pride and their way of life.

Making matters more complicated, American tactical units now regularly used the disused Wehrmacht grounds for their own training exercises. Despite the best efforts of civilian and military authorities, farmers and hunters routinely crossed onto the base grounds unaware of shooting exercises. German officials regularly communicated their displeasure to the Americans, particularly during harvest season when crops sat in the field and boars wandered around unmolested. When a tank broke down on a country road near Speicherz, a local farmer apoplectically complained that his neighbors had to pull their carts through his field around the disabled vehicle. While these complaints were relatively small, they highlighted the administrative difficulties during the occupation. Complaints originating with small farmers wound their way from town officials to the Landrat, who then passed them on to the Americans. They, in turn, had little interest in accommodating German complaints and gave absurd replies like Harry Clark's suggestion that farmers work in their fields between 5:00 and 9:00 PM to lessen the risk of shooting accidents.[49]

While land use questions divided Germans and Americans, they paled in comparison to the problem of requisitioning. Of all the American policies at the beginning of the occupation, nothing caused more consternation among locals than the requisitioning of housing for occupation troops. Despite efforts by theater commanders to limit the impact of requisitions, much of the authority rested with local commanders. During the summer of 1945, American troops occupied more than 30,000 individual properties across Germany.[50] In Brückenau, residents, evacuees, and expellees grew frustrated with requisitions, which negatively influenced the ability of local authorities to house the uprooted. Evelyn H. complained that her apartment in town was requisitioned, despite the fact that she had served six months in prison for violations of wartime labor laws. She politely suggested that the Americans claim the homes and property of several former Nazi party members living in town. Major Clark phlegmatically replied that "troops were not in a position to distinguish between Nazis and non-Nazis when in need of housing and are not responsible for any injustices in this respect." If Evelyn needed redress, town authorities could help her by seizing the property of others provided "any such action [was] entirely within German law."[51]

For locals, the most galling of the requisitions was the loss of hotel space in Brückenau itself. The hotels, used by both expellees and American troops, were the economic heart of Brückenau and recovery seemed impossible without them. In 1946, the Landrat petitioned the Military Government to stop the requisitioning of homes and to allow the return of hotel space to civilian use. "I would like to point out," he wrote, "that the population is absolutely aware of the fact that the lost war must bring burdens to the inhabitants.... Besides other burdens caused by the war, the confiscation of Bad Brückenau and the presence of 15,000–20,000

DPs have caused enormous economical difficulties."⁵² The campaign to wrest the resort hotels from requisition, which began in earnest in the fall of 1946, demonstrated the resolve and flexibility of Oswald and his staff. When appeals on economic grounds failed, Oswald began pressing the reputed health benefits of the Brückenau springs, "the most powerful kidney, cyst, and heart problem curative in Germany. The use of such a spring is just as important as medicine for the afflicted." Since the Americans made it a policy not to requisition hospitals, it stood to reason that healing springs should be treated the same way. More important, Oswald pledged to use the reopened springs to treat the ill among the DPs, the local population, and the expellees equally. Here he enlisted the aid of George Masset, whose word presumably counted for more with the Americans than did Oswald's. While the American reaction to the proffered health claims does not survive, they did allow the springs to reopen in March 1947. Oswald continued to press for the handover of remaining hotels, pointing to the success of the reopened resort and urging the resumption of tourism "as one of the ways in which employment can be realized, of natives as well as other people living in the Kreis."⁵³

These "other people" were for the most part expellees. The end of the war brought no respite from the westbound convoys carrying ethnic Germans. More than 900,000 expellees arrived in Bavaria during 1946, the majority from Czechoslovakia and Silesia. With no standing urban centers ready to receive them, expellees came to rural districts in disproportionate numbers. At the beginning of 1946, Lower Franconia housed about 40,000 expellees. During the next year, this number increased by 105,000, the highest percentage increase of any district in Bavaria.⁵⁴ The most comprehensive survey of the uprooted in the Landkreis gave a total figure of 7,597. Of these, about 5,000 were classified at the time or later as expellees. More than 3,300 of these came either from the Sudetenland or Silesia, followed by Hungarians and those fleeing from the Soviet Zone. Among evacuees, the majority came from elsewhere in the American zone, with about 1,000 more from the British and French Zones. Many of those who arrived did so with few personal possessions. As the report pointed out, almost 5,000 of these uprooted were women, children, or those considered too old to work. In a district where farming and timbering dominated the economy, those unable to perform manual labor found it difficult or impossible to find work.[55]

Reaction to the arrival of so many dispossessed was, as can be imagined, complicated. Expellees entered a universe of flight in which theirs was just another experience of homelessness and hopelessness. The region's most important newspaper, the *Main-Post*, clearly wrestled with the question of just how to describe these exiles from the East. In the winter of 1946, the editors wrote with anguished pride, irony, and shock at the enormity of the catastrophe that befell Germany:

> The propaganda device "A People Without Space," which inspired Hitler's dreams of conquest, is today bitterly realized. After a six-year crusade through Europe, from the Atlantic to the Volga, at the North Pole and on the Nile, one finds the German people, Hitler's soldiers and widows, in deepest crisis. Not only poor in lives, property and illusions, but also in "living space." Blood and soil were supposed to be the foundations of a new German dominion. Instead, we lost them both: blood and soil.[56]

For the expellees who made their way to places like the Sinn Valley, the question of identity remained open and the boundaries between insiders and outsiders fluid. The relative confessional similarity helped, but no amount of fellow feeling could overcome the most basic obstacle to successful short-term integration: expellees looked, sounded, and behaved as foreigners in existing German communities already facing occupation, urban refugees, and, in places like Wildflecken, large numbers of foreign DPs. Communities already in crisis confronted yet another group turned into victims by the recent conflict. Expellees who thought of themselves as having a clear claim to sympathy chafed at the ambivalent welcome they received at the end of often harrowing treks. "They are the driftwood of war (*das Strandgut des Krieges*)," wrote the *Main-Post*, "but they are German like us and so it is our duty to help them build a new future for themselves."[57]

Despite this ambivalence, there is little evidence of the sort of open hostility found in other districts, particularly those in which religious affiliation among natives and expellees did not coincide. Local officials and the Refugee Office cooperated well together, meeting when needed to smooth out potential conflicts like those that emerged over pay for work done by expellees on local farms.⁵⁸ While it is difficult to prove, it seems likely that one of the most important positive influences on local-expellee relations actually stemmed from the presence of the DP camp. In many rural districts, Silesians and other Eastern European expellees found themselves derided as "*Polacken*," a slur directed at their accents and their proximity to non-German ethnics in their homeland. In Wildflecken and places like it, non-German Eastern Europeans did not need to be imagined. They were very real and, as we have seen, both proximate and ever present in the daily lives of both locals and expellees. In a hierarchy of foreignness, the expellees at least appeared closer to the locals than the DPs ever could. From the beginning of the expellee-local encounter, the presence of other foreigners in the district catalyzed the acceptance, and later the integration, of expellees into local society.

Expellees and locals broadly agreed that the DPs were the single greatest threat to improved social relations. Refugee Administration reports are full of examples of DP criminality, while local officials in the districts around Wildflecken regularly complained about the camp as a "black market center." For locals, the connection between the DP and expellee problems was clear and explicit. As one Refugee Administration official wrote in late 1947:

> The people do not understand how the occupation authority gives more rights to the DPs than to locals. They are of the opinion that the greater part of these "Displaced" (*Verschleppte*) are criminals, asocials, or SS volunteers who are not interested in repatriating. . . . It is about time that these "Displaced" are moved out of the DP camp and those private homes that they occupy to make room for refugees, expellees, and the bomb-damaged.⁵⁹

It is hard not to sense here that the nameless author of this report provided his own opinion as much as that of the rural population he surveyed. The continued presence of DPs on the hill above Wildflecken and the apparent power that DPs had as recipients of direct American assistance angered locals and expellees alike. Whatever their differences, here at least they had a common cause.

This should not paint an overly sentimental portrait of expellee-local relations. While relations between locals and expellees generally functioned at a level above disastrous, there is also plenty of evidence of the sort of petty squabbles and impoliteness that accompanied forced social relations and shared housing between strangers. The stories in Wildflecken mirrored tales told in myriad places across occupied Germany. One local farmer employed a teenage expellee as a laborer, then refused to pay him, arguing that since the boy's family lived in a camp at public expense, such labor should be free. Another farmer refused to sell vegetables to expellees, arguing in the face of all available evidence that he sold all of his produce to local authorities for legal distribution.[60] One early attempt to set up a separate school for Sudeten expellee children ended when local officials refused to recognize the teaching credentials of the sole instructor.[61] These small humiliations, even in the context of broadly stable and non-contentious relations, kept tensions between local and expellees at a steady simmer. "I'd like to see relations between old and new residents improve," said an anonymous expellee when asked about his hopes for the future. "Of course, what I'd really like to do is go home."[62]

The divide between locals and expellees literally factored into every conversation, as the Franconian dialect of the locals jarred with the Sudeten, Silesian, and other accents of the expellees. One solution to this problem was to converse in a language other than German. The Kreis English-Speaking Club, founded in the summer of 1946, "attempt[ed] to improve relations between Bavarians and non-Bavarians."[63] While it is not clear how many people participated, developments like this and the construction of a small *Amerika-Haus* in Brückenau suggested that many in the district sought to integrate themselves into the new order of American-occupied Germany even if they had little interest in its formal politics.

For many expellees their first home was a camp. These structures varied widely, from vast Nissen-hut complexes to simple do-it-yourself shantytowns. In rural areas that suffered little bomb damage, they generally occupied old, abandoned, or easily divided buildings. It is difficult to get a reliable count of camps, since they shifted fairly regularly. On the whole, Bavaria housed more than four hundred camps, or one camp facility for every 100,000 inhabitants. This was the third highest density of camps among states in the West behind Schleswig-Holstein and Lower

Saxony.[64] These camps were often built hastily in the wake of the war and were intended to be temporary. In the postwar emergency, however, many of them acquired an uneasy permanence.

In Landkreis Brückenau, the Bavarian Refugee Administration built six camps in fall of 1945, later expanding to eight. The camps were small and located in abandoned buildings and schools across the district. Capacity varied between six and eight hundred, a small fraction of the problem. For ninety percent of the uprooted, private housing was the only option. While the percentage of camp inhabitants in Landkreis Bruckenau was about half the Bavarian average, it was still roughly consistent with the general trend of expellee housing.[65] The vast majority of the uprooted lived in private homes partially confiscated by the state under Allied Control Council legislation promulgated early in 1946.[66]

Short biographies of those living in the camps reveal the multiplicity of experiences, hopes, and fear among the uprooted. Peter M. came from Mönchengladbach and had been bombed out of both his home and the apartment in Würzburg where he moved his family. He hoped to get work as an accountant. Heinz D. had been a cabinet-maker in the Sudetenland and ran a small hotel in Marienbad. Emil L. from East Prussia spent time in British POW camp, then made it to Wildflecken where he met and married a local girl. Johann T. came from a solidly middle-class family in Łódź but spent the 1930s running a factory in Yugoslavia for his father. Erich M., a carpenter from Berlin, served in the Wehrmacht for the entirety of the war. After time in a POW camp, he came to the Landkreis, settled down with a woman from Oberweissenbrunn, and was "trying to build a new home for myself."[67]

Camp life reflected the confusion inherent in the multiethnic milieu of Eastern Europe. Language remained a critical problem in the camps. "Germans" from a whole host of places found themselves unable to effectively communicate with each other. As a result, the Refugee Office looked for camp leaders who had both administrative experience and knowledge of different languages. The first *Lagerleiter* of the Reussendorf camp, for example, was a fifty-year-old former engineer from Saxony whose career was every bit as varied as his new charges. He fought in the Austrian Army during World War I, worked in Pressburg (Bratislava) between the wars, then served as a translator for the *Luftwaffe*. In addition to German, he spoke Italian, Czech, Polish, Serbo-Croatian, Slovak, and some Hungarian.[68] The fact that his multilingual abilities served as his primary qualification for leadership reminds us of how flexible the boundaries of "German" ethnicity really were at the end of the war.

Finding leadership for the refugee camps proved just as fraught with problems as the process of identifying German political leadership, and for many of the same reasons. The expellees were, by definition, difficult to vet because they tended to come from places uninterested in providing any information about them. Another camp official later became a fugitive from justice after being accused of child abuse. When apprehended in Kaiserslautern in 1949, it turned out that his carefully ordered personal narrative was mostly fiction. While he had spent time in prison during the war, it was not, as he claimed, for political reasons. He joined the SS in 1933 in his native Königsberg (Kaliningrad), but got in trouble constantly for fighting, disorderly conduct, and eventually desertion.[69]

Camp life could be dull, pedestrian, and seemingly pointless for expellees. Some locals, like the farmer who refused to pay his teenage charge, regarded camp dwellers as free-loaders. In the polyglot environment of the camp, factions formed and clashed with each other and with camp officials. Armin G.'s menacing performance in the Brückenau casinos was more than matched by the inhabitants of the Hermannsheim camp. Divided between Sudeten Germans and expellees from the Baltic, the camp became known for wild rumors and outbreaks of violence.[70]

Despite the fact that the Americans officially played a very limited role in expellee affairs in the region, there is abundant evidence of close contact. On the night of August 26, 1946, a group of expellees reported the theft of two cows. On this occasion, American MPs managed to retrieve the animals from a group of DPs who were caught trying to get the animals back into the camp.[71] American constabulary also assisted with the occasional forcible transfer from expellee camps. The Americans were at least partly responsible for one of the few bright spots in an otherwise grim living situation. An MP unit stationed in the district sponsored an annual Christmas party for children. In 1946, they held sixteen such parties for more than 1,400 children, including events held in the expellee camps. Soldiers donated oranges, candy, nuts, and other treats for children who might otherwise go without.[72]

More importantly, the Americans could provide direct support for expellees in the form of employment. After the lifting of the non-fraternization order in late 1945, expellees could technically work for the occupation forces, provided that the army gave preference to DPs. The anti-tank company guarding the Muna, for instance, could easily employ Poles from the camp as civilian laborers but chose to hire almost entirely from the ranks of other refugees. In 1946, twelve of twenty civilian workers came from either the Soviet zone or from Poland/Silesia. Only three came from the Rhön region.[73] This signaled the beginning of a much wider trend in relations between the army and the German population. A series of agreements set the framework through which civilian employment by the army became a driver of economic stabilization and, for refugees, a measure of integration. The U.S. Army became the largest single employer of German civilians in regions where it built bases.[74] Since both Americans and local authorities assumed that the DPs were going to move on, employing expellees made sense as emphasis shifted toward creating stable institutions in the occupied zone.

This deepening contact between Americans and expellees could have far less salutary outcomes. Camp inhabitants were internally divided, with many actively seeking opportunities to work with the Americans and others bitterly opposed to the practice. While much of this divide is hidden in the available records, there is plenty of grim evidence of its consequences. In July 1946, the Constabulary responded to reports that residents of the camp at Neustadt badly beat a teenage expellee after he bragged about working for the Americans. When the Americans arrived, they also found a young woman who had been beaten and had her head shaved after she had a romantic relationship with an American. Fifteen expellees were arrested.[75] These violent acts of collective discipline stemmed from a host of frustrations percolating in the camps. Expellees were poor and bored. Those who worked for or socialized with the Americans had access to goods and cash. Perhaps the young expellee who worked for the Americans talked too much about the fun he was having outside of the camp. There was no doubt a generational divide as well, with some of the younger expellees far more willing and able to leave the camps and interact socially with the Americans. Finally, the story of the beating and humiliation of a young expellee woman provides a reminder of the powerful gender norms that the end of the war and the experience of defeat and expulsion challenged. The camps were temporary places of refuge. If they became communities, they did so only as long as residents had few other options. For the expellees of Landkreis Brückenau, the base facility offered the possibility of creating something far more tangible, a new home outside of the camps.

The most dramatic development in the story of Wildflecken's expellees began a year after the occupation when a small and diverse band of expellees and locals joined to form new towns on the grounds of the former Wehrmacht base. Such "refugee settlements" became a common feature on the landscape of western Germany during the following years, but the Wildflecken experiment was a very early one. Towns like Espelkamp, Waldkraiburg, and Neugablonz attempted to re-create communities in the East now lost while leveraging the skills and professional backgrounds of the expellees to resume productive lives in the West. In the cases of Waldkraiburg and Espelkamp, the new towns were built on top of Muna very similar to the one found at Wildflecken.[76]

In the early summer of 1946, in an effort to consolidate the DP population and cut down on law-breaking, the Americans moved one of the largest concentrations of Poles outside the boundaries of the DP camp back into the facility. The town of Werberg now stood empty for the second time since 1936. Under Law 54, this meant that the town could be settled under Bavarian jurisdiction. For expellees living in the camps, this was a great opportunity. The houses in Werberg were generally in poor condition, but inhabitable. A short walk from Werberg, a few locals still hung on in Reussendorf, which also had a number of uninhabited dwellings last lived in by Eastern European laborers. On August 26, 1946, a small group of expellees from a nearby camp crossed the maneuver area boundary and resettled the town of Werberg.[77] While they undoubtedly had the tacit approval of local refugee officials, they took this initial action on their own initiative. No help other than moral support came from local or state authorities until nearly a year after the first settlers arrived. In May 1947, the Bavarian government, along with a coalition of banks, founded the *Bayerische Landessiedlung* GmbH. This new public-private partnership, charged with financing rural development across the state, had a particular interest in assisting expellee farmers in ventures like the one taking place near Wildflecken. As credit began to flow, more than 15,000 expellee farmers were able to build on and utilize about 42,000 hectares of land across the state.[78] By the time help came, two new communities had emerged from the empty shells of Werberg and Reussendorf.

While the initial decision to resettle the two towns came from the expellees themselves, it was not long before local officials arrived to try to craft their own order out of the chaos. Landrat Oswald and the local refugee agency administrator Anton Beck visited Werberg in its early days, finding thirty-five homes and a number of outbuildings in various states of disrepair. Despite a paucity of construction material, resources flowed into the community through the Refugee Administration. By fall, construction began in earnest on the remaining buildings.

Within a few months, Werberg's population stood at nearly 450, with a steady stream of families moving in and construction projects nearing completion.[79] Farmers, some of whom managed to either bring along or acquire a few animals, could now work plots of land, which they rented from the government, of between five and twenty hectares in size. A 1947 report listed forty-five properties (*Anwesen*) in the community, of which thirty-two were occupied by expellees, two by bombed-out Germans, seven by locals, and six buildings reserved for the future development of industry.[80] A number of local elites began to see Werberg and Reussendorf as the center of a new industrial reinvention of the previously rural Rhön. "There is really no suggestion that the Rhön should be a large agricultural settlement, but it is hoped that industrial planning can begin soon on the grounds of the Wildflecken Manuever Area where thousands of expellees can find work and a home."[81] That struggle later defined the history of these towns.

The *Main-Post* painted an affectionate portrait of Werberg in May 1947. Three men "who have not yet found wives" opened a carpentry business. A Silesian family started a small grocery store, while a former resident returned to reopen the town's tavern. Some local men formed an all-important brass band and had recently played the town's first communal dance. The town's church was also open again. There were terrible stories about the place during the war, rumors that forced laborers had been executed there. Now the bell was back in its tower, the altar restored, and Franciscan monks from a nearby monastery held mass for the townspeople. Residents hoped that they could find an expellee priest in the near future.

Perhaps most important for the future of the town, there were children. Forty kids shared a single classroom and a Silesian nun. There was little furniture and no textbooks, but at least the children had "American noodle soup, cocoa, and chocolate" sent by Catholic charities.[82]

The inhabitants of the rebuilt towns defied easy categorization. Most were expellees, but this categorization covered a range of experiences. Some fled at the end of the war, others ended the war in military service and feared going home, while another group arrived after the compulsory flight of ethnic Germans in the wake of the war began. Georg S., who became one of the leaders of the new community of Werberg, was forty-five years old when he came to Wildflecken. An American POW when the war ended, he frantically sought information about his family, which lived on the eastern edge of the Ueckermünde Heide in Pommerania. This territory stretched across the postwar border between Poland and occupied Germany and many of its ethnic Germans faced forced relocation after the war. Georg's wife and two children arrived in Wildflecken in early November 1945, after a harrowing train journey with a few salvaged possessions. Georg joined them in early 1946 and later got work for the Landessiedlung rebuilding Werberg. Local refugee officials considered him "capable, industrious, and a man of character."[83] Later, when he became one of the most vocal interlocutors between the expellee communities and various German and American authorities, he proved himself to be articulate and forceful. He was, in short, a model Werberger, the sort of man envisioned by refugee officials as a foundation stone for a community born out of the experience of disaster.

Georg's story is well documented because of his later activism. Less well known are the life experiences of others who made the short journey from the camps to Werberg and Reussendorf. A Silesian who left his home with two horses, his wife, mother-in-law, and two daughters, now rented twenty hectares. A family from Romania now farmed fourteen hectares of marginal land, but reported some initial success in breeding

The Hüfner family, resettled in Werberg, probably 1949. *Photo courtesy of Sonja Hüfner.*

cattle. When fodder ran short, other area farmers banded together and contributed to the Werbergers supply to keep cattle alive through the winter.[84]

The resettled towns did not just house expellees. Some of those who moved back were precisely those who gave up their homes in 1937 when the Wehrmacht base opened. The Hüfner family, which left Werberg for Offenbach after the requisition, now came back with four young daughters. Josef, recently returned from a POW camp, and Emma soon added a son named Reinhard, born in 1948.[85] Anna M. and her husband took the cash settlement in 1937 and left their farm in Altglasshütten, moving down the valley to Wildflecken. The end of the war meant a double disaster for Anna, who by then had two children. Her husband was "murdered by Poles" in 1946 and the investments that they made with the settlement money vanished in the collapse of the German economy. After her husband's death, she and her children took the opportunity to move back onto the base grounds, settling on 2.3 hectares with a house and an outbuilding.[86]

These settlers now rented property from the Bavarian government. In some cases, like that of the Hüfners, they were renters in homes that they once owned. It took some time to normalize rental agreements, particularly in a materially poor region where few had access even to devalued old currency. Rents remained artificially low, almost non-existent in some cases, as a way to encourage farmers to stay on the land. Generally, expellee and local farmers were able to rent property on the base for about one fifth of the expected rent for the district.[87] There was good reason for state officials to keep costs low for the settlers of these revived communities. Not only would their success relieve the pressure on refugee camps, but something more fundamental was at stake. Communities like Reussendorf and Werberg represented a new beginning after years of upheaval and war. These were not simply new homes, they were the kernel of a new homeland.

The press and Bavarian officials touted the "Refugee Town on the Rhön" as an early success story in their struggle to integrate newcomers. "For expellees, the chance to have a place of their own is not common," wrote the *Main-Post*. "But here, thanks to their energy and drive a large number of refugees have found a new Heimat on the grounds of the former base at Wildflecken." Anton Beck expressed his confidence in the project. "Despite the fact that Werberg has taken up nearly all of my time in the past few months . . . it brings me great joy to see the first loaf of bread baked, the first calf of the season, or a father's pride when he shows off a newborn resident before the town."[88] Plots were small and animals few, but Werberg seemed to prove that pluck and industry could overcome the long odds facing refugees in a new Germany under construction.

The new settlers of Werberg and Reussendorf faced considerable difficulties as they tried to restart their lives in the Rhön. "It is not easy," the *Main-Post* remarked, "to bring the differing perspectives of Rumanian Germans, East Prussians, Silesians, Sudeten Germans, and Rhön farmers together for a common purpose (*auf einen Nenner zu bringen*)." An American report on the overall land reform effort noted that some of the farmers settled on former Wehrmacht property "received land on lease in excess of their managerial ability."[89] The region's naturally poor soil and the small size of the plots worked against them, as did the absence of capital, construction material, and a cash economy. Security remained a critical problem, as Werberg's settlers discovered on their first night in town when a DP raiding party made off with two cows.[90] More important, perhaps, was the sense of disappointment felt by many farmers that they left behind land that they had once owned and now found themselves tenants. It was another reminder that their new home did not welcome them with open arms. This feeling intensified when one of their own faced a precipitous fall from grace.

The new political system in Landkreis Brückenau faced its first test in late February 1947 when, much to the surprise of the Military Government in Brückenau, a court in Schweinfurt issued an arrest warrant for Landrat Heinrich Oswald. His repeated claim to have not been a member of the NSDAP contradicted records found in Berlin that indicated that he joined the party in the late 1930s. While he posted bond and returned to Brückenau, the situation embarrassed his friends in the Military Government and enraged many of his German constituents. An outpouring of wrath aimed squarely at Oswald emerged in early March.

His most prominent critics came from the KPD rank-and-file. Apparently defying the party's Kreis leadership, about six hundred Communists took to the streets of Brückenau on March 3 to protest against Oswald. The marchers accused the Landrat of personally enriching himself at their expense. "Why is he not still in prison?" asked one speaker. "How is it that he came up with 10,000 RM and walked out a free man? How did Oswald, an expellee, come into possession of this much money?" They also accused him of favoring his fellow expellees over the native population (*"Bist du von Osten, bekommst du hier ein Posten!"*). "We demand of the Kreis government that they petition the Military Government to imprison Oswald for his evidence tampering. Otherwise, it can be said that the little guy gets punished and the big fish walk away."[91]

The demonstration on March 3 evidently surprised all the political leaders in the Landkreis. A few days later, the heads of the three biggest parties in the district (CSU, SPD, and KPD) wrote a remarkably frank joint letter to the Kreistag on the Oswald affair. They stated the obvious; that few believed that Oswald rose through the ranks of the civil service in Breslau without ever joining the NSDAP. At the same time, they agreed that his record in office had been otherwise quite good, particularly his skillful management of the relationship with the Americans. "It should not go unnoticed that since the beginning of Oswald's service in the Landkreis, he has maintained the best possible relations with the Military Government and the Occupation Forces. This has been in the best interest of the Landkreis and its inhabitants." This attitude on the part of the MG detachment mirrored a growing ambivalence on their part toward the denazification process and its impact on local political leadership. Shortly before Oswald's arrest, an MG report complained of the burdens imposed by a policy that "due to their party affiliation excludes many qualified people who actually were only nominal members of Nazi organizations. This excludes a group whose knowledge and abilities could well be utilized in building a new democratic form of government."[92]

Remarkably, Oswald won acquittal at a military court in Schweinfurt. His attorney argued successfully that the records used against him might have been compromised. Other cases across the Western Zones fell apart for similar reasons, though Oswald had the additional benefit of glowing testimonials from former neighbors and the Brückenau Military Government.[93] Despite his acquittal, Oswald's credibility never recovered from the disaster of his arrest. He agreed to step down as soon as local elections could be held. The local Military Government added an interesting twist to the affair in its annual report for 1947, suggesting that the Oswald case hastened the "development of democracy" in the district by encouraging people to "make known their requirements on the elected officials as well as the criticisms of their stewardship, thus causing some officials to change their ways or submit to replacement."[94] Oswald's term ended with the elections of June 1948. The new Landrat, Josef Baus, previously served as a bureaucrat in the local finance office. After the tumult of the Oswald administration, Baus represented a steady hand and the sort of technocratic experience needed to manage the considerable challenges facing the district.

One of the most daunting of these challenges remained the establishment of law and order. It was here that the growing entanglement between Americans, locals, DPs, and expellees was most clearly articulated. In the three years after the end of the war, the right to keep order was keenly contested between Americans and German authorities. At the same time, the persistence of illegal or quasi-legal commerce highlighted the continued material deprivation in the area. Particularly in the first days and months of the occupation, the Americans' law enforcement role was the public face of occupation policies. Efforts to enforce occupation law, more than any other aspect of the military regime, brought home the enormous power imbalance in defeated Germany. Law enforcement, generally referred to as "public safety" by the occupiers, caused enormous frustration for all parties concerned. For the Americans, efforts to police the district ran into conflicting jurisdictions, public apathy, and the problems inherent in doing a difficult job made harder by a lack of language skills or cultural competence. For locals and expellees, occupation law enforcement was both too harsh and not harsh enough. Germans saw themselves as trying to survive, even if it meant working around market regulations. Besides, many reasoned, the real threats to public safety lived up the hill in the DP camp and the Americans seemed willing to allow Poles free run of the countryside. As we have seen, many DPs considered themselves entitled to a certain amount of leeway and deeply resented periodic raids. American troops, living in close proximity to German civilians, increasingly came to agree with many of their complaints. DPs, once regarded as victims of the war, increasingly came to be seen as part of the problem in postwar Germany.

American efforts to enforce the law in rural Germany faced immediate and serious problems of manpower. In the first days after the war, German police were un-uniformed and disarmed, resulting in disasters like the Kleinhenz murders. German police in Brückenau did not receive weapons until the next summer, and then only grudgingly and in response to continued problems with the DP camp. Technically, responsibility for public safety fell upon the Military Government as opposed to tactical troops. In practice, given that the Military Government Detachment in Brückenau consisted of about ten men, most of the heavy lifting would have to be done by operational forces. The formation of the U.S. Constabulary in the summer of 1945 clarified matters somewhat, but these units took time to organize and train. In Landkreis Brückenau, the constabulary was represented by Troop C of the 22nd Constabulary Squadron. The history of this unit tells us something about the hurried reorientation of American combat forces in the wake of the end of the war. The squadron began the war as the 22nd Armored Field Artillery Battalion, landed at Utah Beach on June 13, 1944, and fought its way across France, Germany, and Czechoslovakia. Two years after arriving in Europe, with many of its veterans ready to go home, it was re-designated and sent for quick training in the practicalities of law enforcement in rural Franconia.

Each constabulary squadron had to complete a "practice" raid at the end of its training, a practice recognized and hated by local Germans.[95] While the Military Government detachment generally praised the conduct of the constabulary forces, they also made it clear that such raids netted very little and made it more difficult to administer the district. "It is realized that [possession of American articles] is illegal from the standpoint of Post Exchange regulations but the fact remains that almost every soldier in the ETO at some time gives or barters small amounts of PX supplies to civilians."[96] Raids and arrests threatened the informal but crucial social and commercial relationships that allowed a small MG detachment to administer a large rural district.

On the other hand, the MG detachment had little sympathy for the Poles living above Wildflecken. When the 15th Infantry began its withdrawal from the area shortly after the constabulary arrived, there was an uptick in minor property crimes. The local constabulary began sending regular patrols through the camp "more as a reminder to the people that the area was not completely empty of military forces."[97] Even if the troublemakers comprised a small portion of the camp residents, they caused no end of headaches. The detachment complained of persistent rumors that the Poles were going to be relocated. The result, inevitably, was that "when the Poles learn they are moving they will have one last fling at looting the Kreis for several days." Law enforcement among the

Wildflecken Poles posed its own challenges, chiefly that it was far more difficult to prove black market activity since DPs had the right to possess goods forbidden to Germans. The Americans chose to concentrate their limited resources on finding illegal weapons in an effort to stem the tide of armed banditry. Thus, three Poles were arrested in March for knife fighting and armed robbery; the MG detachment interrogated them with an eye toward identifying armed camp residents. When the arrested men proved willing to talk, CIC investigators from Bad Neustadt and a company of the 15th Infantry stationed at the Muna raided the camp. The raid netted five arrests, including the chief of the camp police, on charges related to illegal weapons and organizing bandit bands that staged attacks in the countryside. "Some elements exist in the population of this camp," the report concluded, "which seem to be constantly engaged in various criminal activities."[98]

On December 18, 1946, 1,600 constabulary troops launched Operation DUCK against the Wildflecken camp, largely because of reports of anti-American (and presumably anti-repatriation) propaganda. The operation was both large and complex, with police in riot gear waiting outside the camp and mobile hospital facilities set up to care for the wounded. Search teams carried with them instructions in Polish to be given to building leaders in the barracks, while officers checked DP identifications against master lists of those wanted for questioning. The operation went off relatively smoothly, with no physical altercations. Results, however, were lacking. The constabulary seized a few weapons, some illegal food, contraband livestock, and U.S. Army property, and the requisite *samogon* still. As an army historian summarized the raid, "Whether the black marketers were just too clever or were not as widespread as believed will never be known, but the US Constabulary showed the Germans and DPs that there would be law and order."[99] What it likely showed, in light of the simultaneous experience of non-DPs in the same area, was that the Army tended to apply overwhelming force in pursuit of impossible objectives in a way that seemed arbitrary and capricious.

For DPs and those arrested for occupation-related crimes, a Military Government court in Brückenau functioned as the highest regional arbiter of justice. The American court started hearing cases in July 1945. Less than a month later, occupation authorities ordered German courts reopened to prevent a backlog of cases from developing. Germans arrested by German police now faced courts very similar to the prewar German justice system.[100] The military court records of Landkreis Brückenau are relatively well preserved. While the records of courts under German jurisdiction have not survived, American courts tried those Germans accused of violating occupation ordinances. These records provide a fascinating snapshot of the problems of law and order in an occupied rural district. Unfortunately, while Poles are identified as such, birthplaces are not provided in surviving records, making it difficult to distinguish between expellees and locals. Between July 1945 and July 1947 the court heard 443 cases. Generally, an American officer served as presiding magistrate, often a captain or the major commanding the MG detachment. Most defendants faced the court without attorneys, though later in the period a few local lawyers, either alone or collaborating with Polish lawyers who were themselves DPs, defended clients. Piotr L., the anti-repatriation leader, played an important role in defending his fellow DPs, no doubt enjoying the opportunity to meet the Americans on equal terms in the courtroom.

Court records rarely describe the nature of an offense beyond an indication of the formal charge. However, it is abundantly clear that the vast majority of cases involved violations of paragraphs 31 and 43, both of which concerned property. For Germans, charges of theft might involve items "from civilian sources," while Poles generally faced accusations of animal theft, weapons possession, or efforts to sell food or U.S. military goods to those not entitled to them. Sentences were generally light, with fines or brief spells of detention common and frequent acknowledgement of factors like age and family status. Poles often found themselves remanded to the care of UNRRA. Anyone convicted of a serious offense likely faced transfer to larger facilities elsewhere in Bavaria.[101]

While awaiting trial or after sentencing, the accused likely found themselves spending time in the small prison (*Amtsgerichtsgefängnis*) in Brückenau. The prison served as yet another example of the hybrid nature of legal authority under the occupation. It held prisoners detained under German law and those subject to American occupation statutes arrested by tactical or constabulary troops. The jail held twenty-one prisoners and was at or near capacity for most of the period. Those given longer custodial sentences or held under denazification tribunals served their time at larger facilities elsewhere in Bavaria.

Germans staffed the prison and American inspection reports generally indicated satisfaction with the degree of cleanliness and the degree to which prisoners were put to work, generally cutting timber. Staff drew their pay from the Brückenau city administration and the prison fell under the general auspices of the Bavarian Ministry of Justice. In the muddy jurisdictional waters of postwar Germany, this led to some awkward questions of legal authority. At one point, the MG detachment sent an officer to tell Heinrich Oswald that he needed to stop personally arresting criminals and bringing them directly to the jail. A German judge faced reprimand when a guard told American inspectors that "two or three times a week" the guards had to organize prisoner work details to perform tasks in and around the judge's house.

The guards, at most four men and one woman, regularly found themselves overwhelmed by the task at hand. Americans suspected that some German criminals were allowed to simply go home at night if they promised to stay out of trouble. In addition, there was at least a hint that some staff proved willing to look the other way while prisoners plotted escape. A guard named Paul E. was finally dismissed after being on duty during several successful escapes. After the last of these, E. admitted that he left his keys in plain sight and neglected to close the door to his office. The chief jailer, L., suffered from painful stomach problems that required surgery. "In view of the fact that most of the prisoners at this institution are husky youths, it is strongly recommended that an assistant be sent Mr. L."[102]

The courts faced a deluge of black marketeering cases. Raids made this worse since constabulary troops tended to haul in anyone found with even negligible amounts of contraband. After the May 1946 raid described above, the Military Government detachment in Brückenau pointed to the acquittals and generally light sentences meted out by the courts as both deleterious for American morale and proof that a saner system of law enforcement was needed. "The troops who picked up these people are naturally not very pleased when the Summary MG court finds them innocent or sentences them very lightly."[103] The detachment commander urged his superiors to consider thresholds for items like cigarettes or rations that might limit needless arrests and futile prosecutions.

Perhaps the most important measure of the continued deprivation experienced by German refugees, both evacuees and expellees, in the postwar period was their role in illegal commerce. The local economy badly needed both staples and luxury items and proved more than willing to support manifestly illegal commerce. "All measures taken seem to be without success as long as there is considerable lack of food, clothing, and agricultural equipment." American intelligence-gathering capabilities were extremely limited and local authorities often had little incentive to really pursue small-scale trading. Here, the Americans grudgingly agreed. "To do so," one MG report suggested, "would necessitate arresting the greater portion of the population."[104]

The inefficiencies and jurisdictional problems engendered by this admittedly *ad hoc* system can be seen in events taking place in the Landkreis during mid-1946. The 27th Constabulary Squadron, training in the area, launched a large anti–black market raid across a number of district communities. Operation GRAB-BAG, the largest constabulary raid of the postwar period, involved more than 4,000 American personnel and targeted sites across Germany and Austria. Given the pressures to find illegal goods, constabulary personnel rounded up dozens of locals and expellees, often on the flimsiest of pretexts. Matters reached an absurd nadir when a mechanic, arrested for possession of several packs of American cigarettes, protested that he got the cigarettes from a constabulary officer as payment for work on a jeep. The man was released with a sheepish apology.

The Military Government in Munich regularly asked its detachments to provide price information about illegal commerce. The numbers sent back can be best regarded as highly approximate. They frequently contradicted each other and varied widely. There were two reasons for this divergence. First, the Americans lacked reliable informants. Second, by their own admission price estimates were largely futile because there was practically no cash economy in the Landkreis. As one American field report from 1947 argued, "There is now very little money among the people. Even among black marketers, money is scarce. The prices on the black market are decreasing because nobody can afford to buy cigarettes and coffee at the exorbitant prices."[105]

The Americans estimated that five to ten percent of food produced in the district went into the black market. When rations tightened, black market values rose. Price information was probably better for material produced outside the district, since presumably consumers were more likely to pay cash. Prices jumped in early 1947. Cigarettes, both a consumer good and a means of exchange, doubled in value between the summer of 1946 and 1947, as did coffee. Butter, on the other hand, which was widely available locally, proved far more stable, with prices between 160 and 200 RM per pound. This price information must be treated with caution. When the Americans claimed that meat was unavailable on the black market in 1947, it contradicted reports of an organized abattoir operating in the DP camp.

The Currency Reform in June 1948 altered matters dramatically across the now-fused American and British Zones. The new *deutsche Mark* proved to be boon for businesses, a bane for small savers who saw much of their assets reduced in the conversion, and an effective end to the persistent illegal economy. Credit markets opened up and the end of price controls in the manufacturing sector helped to spur the reconstruction of industry.[106] But even the resumption of a cash economy could not fully rebuild consumer confidence or the availability of goods. The month after the Currency Reform, Landkreis Brückenau had no sugar.[107]

The black market in the area was inseparable from the problems of the uprooted. While many of the products that so bedeviled American control efforts originated on the grounds of the DP camp, the networks that passed these goods on, either for local consumption or to be taken to recovering urban areas, seems to have been dominated by expellees. While some profited from their activities, most appear to have engaged in this trade as a matter of survival. Here the Currency Reform likely made the expellees' situation worse by forcing them into a cash economy. An investigation into a small black market network in this quiet corner of Germany reveals a great deal about the relationship between expellees and the economic transformation of postwar West Germany.

On the first day of 1949, rural police on foot patrol in the countryside near Wildflecken intercepted twenty-seven-year-old Radu H. walking the roads with a suspicious-looking suitcase. In it, they found almost fifty eggs and seventeen pounds of butter. A few years before, such a haul was worth a great deal. In the wake of the Currency Reforms, such goods were far more widely available and the returns on smuggling considerably diminished. As such, this case might have remained a sad side note. Radu, however, was not inclined to accept the blame alone. He promptly named his co-conspirators, at which point the local police launched their own investigation.

Radu lived in Werberg with his extended family. They came originally from Marginea in eastern Romania and arrived in Franconia in 1946. They found themselves very poor and working on a small plot of land in the new refugee town. Radu readily admitted that he transported black market goods, but "only to find some way to earn some money [*durch Schwarzhandel etwas Geld zu verdienen*]. We are expellees and other than this rented property we have no land or income. Our household has been short of money since the Currency Reform."

Radu told police that he gathered produce from local farmers, then carried it to Frankfurt to find customers. The arrangement worked on trust, with farmers consigning their goods to him and splitting the proceeds later. Police interviewed all of the expellee farmers that Radu named. Of the six people interrogated, only one denied engaging in illegal trade. A thirty-seven-year old Sudeten woman swore that she gave Radu butter for personal use and was shocked to find her gift used in an illegal manner. Others proved considerably less reticent to discuss their roles in the affair. Again and again they told police that, as expellees, they had to do whatever was necessary to survive.

"I am aware that this was punishable," said an East Prussian woman, "but you have to understand that we are expellees and have to fight hard for everything." A former resident of the Black Sea port of Constanța told police that "I had to take this butter from the mouths of my family. For two weeks we have used nothing but beechnut oil in our house. . . . I ask that you go easy on me because of my financial situation. Other than that, I have nothing to say to you."

Finally, police talked to the H. family patriarch. Simon H. was actually one of the more successful of the Werberg farmers. He farmed twenty hectares and owned two horses, four cows, two pigs, and a steer.

Still, he had to support a wife and four adult children. Simon painted a grim picture of life in Werberg. His boys could not find work "so they sit around the house and do nothing." Efforts to rent the labor of his sons and horses came to nothing. He heard on the radio that Switzerland needed young men to work in restaurants and told Radu to go to Frankfurt and apply at the Swiss consulate. Failing that, he wanted his boys to go the U.S. or South America. While he admitted giving his son butter, he claimed that he intended the gift to be used in lieu of spending money for his trip. "I never intended for one of my sons to embarrass our family name by getting involved in the black market."[108]

Minor as it was, the investigation of food smuggling in Werberg offers a rare glimpse into the integration and worldview of expellees living in a "refugee town" shortly after the Currency Reform. Admittedly, these expellee voices were recorded in a time of stress and in the face of authority, but the responses were remarkably similar in ways that must have been distressing to local officials. Almost uniformly, expellee farmers identified themselves as victims of the Currency Reform, neglected wards of the postwar government, and as people living on the margins of the law. While they almost all admitted that they broke or bent the law, each justified their actions as the only reasonable course of action for someone in their position.

Radu, tried in Brückenau, received a fine for his activities. In an indication of how bad the situation had become in the refugee towns, the local Refugee Administration office wrote to the court, petitioning it to reduce the penalty. "The living conditions of expellee families [*Neusiedler*] in Werberg are very difficult.... His father is in no position to pay a cash fine."[109] While there is no indication from the extant documentation of the outcome of the case, the fact that those charged with expellee affairs recognized the deteriorating conditions in Werberg and Reussendorf suggests that they abandoned the optimism of a few years before.

In Wildflecken, this incipient conflict set the stage for yet another set of transformations and a bitter political battle over the future of the region. To understand this, we have to turn to the attitudes and actions of those given responsibility for managing the Wildflecken facility after the war and their efforts to bring about economic development in a district facing staggering challenges.

By 1948, most of the immediate crises of the postwar period had passed. The system of accepting and processing new expellees regularized, German political life emerged, and something resembling a domestic economy resumed. Already, there were stirrings of irritation within German civil society about the slow pace of postwar transition. In rural areas like the Sinn Valley with large expellee populations, calls emerged for tangible economic reforms that would allow the incorporation of refugee populations and ameliorate chronic rural poverty. At Wildflecken, where the DPs sat in the middle of the base facility and expellees settled tenuously along its periphery, all of these problems intersected. One could not be solved without the other, creating a vicious cycle of distrust and impatience. New visions of the future emerged, often contradictory but all based on one premise – that the DP camp had to go. Two questions, what was to be done with the former Wehrmacht base and what was to be done with DPs, connected tiny Wildflecken with decisions made far away and which would have momentous consequences in the Sinn Valley.

FOUR

These People, 1947–1949

In May 1948, a high-level meeting took place in Frankfurt between representatives of the International Refugee Organization (IRO), UNRRA's successor organization, and officials of the American Military Government. More than a year after the disastrous DP camp riots, the situation in Germany looked very different. As rebuilding continued apace, IRO officials faced an increasingly difficult task in convincing anyone that they needed more time and supplies for DPs in their care. When an IRO administrator pressed the Americans for more food aid, a clearly frustrated American official named Hatch worried that such a gesture would infuriate expellees who received no such aid. "It might produce an unrest factor with the Sudeten Germans if more food were taken in to these people." Hatch's irritated retort highlighted the dwindling range of options. "The greatest solution to this problem," he suggested, "[is] in getting these people out of the country."[1]

The frustration and anger of an American official provides a small window into the dramatic transformation of refugee affairs in American-occupied Germany. Between 1947 and 1949, the relative positions of refugee groups in the Rhön and in occupied Germany changed considerably. DPs, legally victims of a terrible war and its uncertain aftermath, became simply "these people." Expellees, on the other hand, assumed a new centrality in emerging visions of a rebuilt and western-oriented Germany. This shift took place at the intersection of several trends that profoundly affected Wildflecken and places like it across the region. The deepening Cold War crisis assumed an uneasy permanence that undercut previous hopes for a resolution to the DP problem. At the same time, rural communities in western Germany responded to the challenge of the expellee problem with what Paul Erker characterized as a "growing modification and 'modernization' of norms and values toward a mobilized, dynamic, industrial society." As a German state in the west emerged from under American "enlightened hegemony," the outlines of a liberal, export-driven economy emerged.[2] Wildflecken provides an excellent example of how this complex process worked on the ground.

Four things happened more or less simultaneously, each influencing and influenced by the others. First, IRO tried to speed the process of DP emigration, largely in order to get the DPs out of Germany before they became a permanent nuisance or before aid from the occupiers ran out. Second, local elites began to see disused bases like Wildflecken as potential centers of economic activity if they could be converted to civilian use. In rural western Germany, this had everything to do with the integration of expellees. Third, American policy toward refugees changed, placing greater importance on the successful integration of expellee populations. Finally, West Germany moved toward limited sovereignty, taking major steps like the 1948 Currency Reform that had an enormous impact on the refugee problem. For Wildflecken, the results of these transformations proved decidedly mixed. American policy and Bavarian institutions converged with the interests of local elites to produce a vision for economic development. An uneasy coalition of modernizers at the local and state levels, with support from the Americans, began to articulate a coherent vision of rural economic transformation that promised to fix the intractable problems of the Rhön region and to provide material support for the expellees. These goals proved to be utterly quixotic, but that does not mean that a number of influential people did not believe in them. As a result, local communities, government officials, and expellees made common cause with each other in an effort to push forward with a plan to remake the area around Wildflecken. The DP camp stood in the way.

Administrative responsibility for the DP camp system changed on July 1, 1947. With UNRRA's mandate expiring, the United Nations established a new organization, the IRO, to take charge of the DP camp system. The new agency faced the task of managing the remaining DP population and ensuring their safe passage out of Germany. Crucially, the Soviet

Union and the Eastern European native states of most remaining DPs did not join the IRO. For the new organization, this meant that there was considerably less political pressure from member states to continue to urge repatriation.[3]

UNRRA, though beset from the start by staffing problems, inadequate training, and a lack of clear mission, accomplished a great deal during its few years of existence. Principally, UNRRA staffers helped to manage the mammoth homeward migration during the summer and fall of 1945 and the great rounds of repatriation thereafter. Ultimately, the task of handling postwar rehabilitation proved too great for such an ad hoc administrative entity. The great cartoonist David Low captured this sense of overwhelming responsibility in a brilliant 1946 cartoon depicting two exhausted relief workers handing boxes of supplies from the back of a truck into a sea of outstretched hands. "Phew," remarks one of the men, wiping sweat from his forehead, "it's time someone provided an UNRRA for UNRRAs."[4] Ephraim Chase, the cynical UNRRA official at the Dillingen camp, phrased matters somewhat more bluntly. "Oft in the stillness of night," he wrote, "I shudder and say to myself: 'Almighty God, for whose sins of omission or commission were we thus punished?'"[5]

IRO had a broadly different mandate from UNRRA. While the agency always asserted that it was interested in repatriation "by all possible means," IRO's hopes rested with finding homes for DPs outside of Eastern Europe.[6] Emphasis shifted from caring for the DPs and sending them back to their place of origin toward finding ways to move DPs out of Germany and on to other countries that needed their labor or could readily absorb them. The task facing IRO was no less enormous than the one that ultimately overwhelmed UNRRA. The new organization became responsible for seven hundred camps with 712,675 inhabitants, seventy-five percent of whom resided in western Germany.[7] IRO had the considerable advantage of being a successor organization. First, this gave its planners the benefit of several years of false starts. IRO had a much more compact administrative structure, closer to the ground, and with considerably more control over its own affairs. Second, it benefited from the accumulated experience of now-veteran field personnel. Many UNRRA staffers, including Kathryn Hulme, remained with IRO.

Finally, IRO had a political wind at its back. Countries in and outside Europe now began public discussions of the possibility of bringing in DPs for humanitarian and economic reasons. Two years after the end of the war, countries were at least willing to consider immigration as a solution to the DP problem. The U.S. State Department's 1947 assessment of the DP crisis emphasized the likelihood that the camps might remain open indefinitely without tangible steps to prevent such a development:

> Although other countries are admitting displaced persons and refugees, the rate at which the total DP population is declining, in camps and out, is disheartingly slow. Unless the United States will permit a portion of these people to begin their lives anew in this country, the problem will be with us for a long time. In the meantime, the cost is high. It is high to the American taxpayer. It is high to the displaced persons and refugees who have no hope in the present.[8]

Former UNRRA staffers, now working for IRO, had a clear sense of the challenges facing the new resettlement initiative. Susan Pettiss, an American who worked at a Jewish DP camp in Munich, described the wrenching choices ahead. Every DP, she wrote, was now "a Hamlet, 'to be or not to be' – to go or not to go.... On the one hand, the specter of remaining in the camps with an unknown future, especially in light of UNRRA's closing, was daunting. On the other hand, news sweeping back into the camps from repatriated compatriots was discouraging."[9]

One of IRO's early initiatives involved surveying its charges in the hopes of getting some sense of how best to foster emigration. The DP population was overwhelmingly male (sixty-three percent), in large part because of its origin in the forced labor programs of the war years. Of those DPs who were working age, sixty percent identified themselves as skilled laborers or farmers, while little more than ten percent self-identified as professionals. The reality was probably somewhat different. Within the camps, rumors abounded that countries willing to accept DPs preferred unskilled or skilled workers as opposed to educated professionals. A significant number of educated DPs appear to have passed themselves off as wage workers in the hopes of getting out of the camps and into the emigration process more quickly.[10]

The irrepressible Piotr L., fresh from the triumph of the anti-repatriation movement at Wildflecken, became as enthusiastic a supporter of emigration as he had been a foe of repatriation. In a speech to the inhabitants of the camp, from which notes were taken and passed to UNRRA administrators, L. told his fellow Poles that "for you, life in the DP camps is coming to a close." Despite his enthusiasm for emigration, he sounded a harsh warning to the other Poles about what they might expect:

> In emigration you will not find UNRRA to support you. No more free living quarters, no more free food, no more free cigarettes. Only work, hard work, and struggle to make your future life. Emigration calls for only sane and morally upstanding individuals. If you are weak or want to make your living on the black market, it will be better if you leave Polish life behind, because such people are not wanted anywhere and particularly in emigration.[11]

There was a certain in irony in Piotr's own situation. The champion of emigration was an unlikely candidate for departure from Germany. He and his wife were over-aged and, despite their knowledge of a multitude of languages, had no skills that might interest potential host countries. IRO faced the challenge of finding homes in emigration for thousands of young DPs with or without skills. For older or overeducated DPs, the wait was only beginning.

IRO immediately took up the question of where to send the remaining DPs. Slowly, potential host countries came around on the question of whether to accept large numbers of DP migrants. The four years after the formation of IRO saw mass emigration from the camps. More than 1.4 million DPs left Germany for homes elsewhere.[12] The process, however, could be achingly slow and left many potential migrants stuck in a bureaucratic web in places like Wildflecken. Small-scale schemes to send DPs to other European countries, notably France, existed previously, but 1947 saw the first efforts to send large numbers of DPs abroad for labor. Belgium, which suffered critical manpower shortages in its mining industry, brought 32,000 (mostly male) DPs on contract beginning in mid-1947. The Belgians eventually extended invitations to dependents as well, but the endeavor suffered from mistrust on both sides and the Belgians certainly never intended for the DPs or their families to remain. At the same time, Australia announced its Revised Immigration Policy that eventually brought 180,000 DPs to the continent. Canada provided a series of programs to bring in DP labor. By the end of 1951, more than 157,000 DPs arrived in the country.[13]

The United States came into the picture relatively late with the Displaced Persons Act of 1948. In its campaign to win passage of the Act, the Truman administration stressed the need to clear the DP camps not only on humanitarian grounds, but because of the changing political situation in Germany and growing American weariness with being compelled to care for these refugee populations. President Truman, trying to sell the Act to a Congress and public skeptical about opening the floodgates of immigration, stressed the practical connections between getting DPs out of Germany and the national security needs of the United States. Crucially, he also emphasized the parallel needs of another group of refugees, the expellees:

> It is unthinkable that they should be left indefinitely in camps in Europe. We cannot turn them out in Germany into the very community of the very people who persecuted them. Moreover, the German economy, so devastated by war and so badly overcrowded with the return of people of German origin from neighboring countries, is approaching an economic suffocation which in itself is one of our major problems. Turning these displaced persons into such chaos would be disastrous for them and would seriously aggravate our problems there.[14]

The Act allowed for the immigration of 205,000 DPs (later raised to 341,000) over the next several years. Some DPs had advantages under the new scheme, while other found themselves marginalized. Forty percent of immigrants had to come from territories annexed by a "foreign power," while thirty percent had to be farmers. This privileged, among others, Balts and some Poles, while disadvantaging Poles from farther west. Immigrants were required to have been in Germany as of December 22, 1945. This cut off large numbers of Jewish DPs and those who fled from Eastern Europe in the wake of the war.[15] Potential immigrants needed sponsorship by an American citizen. For those who had relatives living in the U.S., this was somewhat easier to attain. Voluntary agencies and religious groups collected the names of potential sponsors and matched them with specific DPs living in the camps. With the passage of the DP Act, the trickle of refugees leaving Germany dramatically accelerated and became an increasingly global diaspora. The act had many critics, some of whom found it far too restrictive. One of them was Kathryn Hulme, by now the Care and Maintenance Director for a large swath of IRO camps in Germany. On leave, visiting her home city of San Francisco, she criticized the residency requirement in a local newspaper. "I'm just like a DP – I believed every promise that was ever made by America.... It's not the sort of thing we expected from America after all the talk of help for the DPs, all that soft music."[16]

The DP Act, which was subsequently amended several times in the coming years, reflected the changing nature of America's engagement with the European refugee problem. Section 12 of the act allowed for the immigration of a limited number of expellees. A U.S. House of Representatives subcommittee evaluating the program concluded that the expellee issue remained primarily a German concern, but that it was "in the interest of Europe and America to have an immediate resolution of the refugee problem in Germany." Despite outrage in the U.S., particularly among Jewish groups, over what was seen as a concession toward those who had collaborated in Hitler's war effort, 53,448 expellees came to the United States in the four years that followed. In relative terms, this was a miniscule number. However, the symbolic value of this shift in policy followed a much broader shift in American policy toward Germany in the wake of the war. As stability and economic recovery became a greater priority, the Americans grew increasingly flexible on the fundamental question of refugee management. The connection between the DP problem and the expellee became explicit in American policy.[17]

The creation of these mechanisms for emigration had three very significant effects in Wildflecken and helped to set the stage for the next few years of the region's tumultuous postwar history. First, the Americans established a complicated twenty-two-step process for identifying, vetting, and processing potential immigrants. This system, known as "The Pipeline" was intended to "effectuat[e] a mass migration which was superimposed on a law and procedure couched in terms of individual migration."[18] It was an arduous process that included sponsorship matching, security screening, health checks, and interviews. When things went smoothly, it could take a few months. When they did not, prospective migrants could sit in the pipeline far longer. Wildflecken, a large camp with good facilities, played a critical role in keeping the pipeline moving.

Second, Wildflecken's Polish population placed it at the center of the new wave of DP migration. With the active collaboration of Polish-

American groups, a significant proportion of those allowed into the U.S. (130,000) came from within Poland's pre-1939 borders. American Polonia provided material and political support, plus the ever-important sponsorship that sped the process of DP emigration. In one case, an entire thirty-five-member choir from Wildflecken received sponsorship to come to New York after 1949. The Ogiński Choir, which celebrated its sixty-fifth anniversary in 2010, continues to perform regularly.[19] Poles were the largest group of DP émigrés to Canada, comprising twenty-eight percent of the 128,000 DP immigrants. The same was true in Australia. A third of the 180,000 admitted DPs were Polish, more than twice as many as any other national group.[20]

The DP camp system became more outward looking, increasingly focused on preparing DPs for emigration. This meant offering language and vocational training, along with promoting the possibilities of a new life possibly in a distant land. For both staff and camp residents, the changing purpose of the camp system became increasingly evident before the administrative transformation of the camp system began in earnest. Initial efforts to move DPs relied on a mix of private initiative and the acquiescence of foreign governments. Results in the early days of emigration were decidedly mixed as IRO officials tried to protect their charges from exploitation while also encouraging them to embrace possible schemes for their departure and resettlement.

In spring 1947, trains began to leave Wildflecken bearing DPs on a journey not back to Poland, but to far-off places often beyond Europe's borders. The first steps proved tentative and sometimes embarrassing. One semi-private Canadian initiative, led by an entrepreneur and MP named Ludger Dionne, caused a brief stir both in the DP community and in his native country. Dionne owned a shoe factory attached to a convent in St. George, Quebec. The deeply religious industrialist appeared at Wildflecken in April, seeking one hundred young women, who, according to his publicly stated requirements, had to be Catholic and "virtuous." There was confusion over what happened next, but at some point Dionne made it clear that he expected the women to be verifiably virgins. Hulme was horrified, all the more so because IRO widely publicized Dionne's subsequent visit to the camp. A photo in *Life* magazine shows the small, dour-looking factory owner surrounded by happy female DPs, whom he evidently peppered with questions like, "Do you run around nights?"

Even sympathetic accounts of the Dionne incident highlighted how bizarre the whole sequence of events turned out to be. The affair attracted the attention of Canadian labor unions, religious groups, and Parliament, where one critic labeled Dionne's efforts "a fire sale of human misery." The press dubbed it the "Flying Virgins Incident" and briefly directed some international attention toward Wildflecken. The one hundred women who left Wildflecken for Dionne's factory in Quebec were indeed young, most of them no older than twenty-three. A few had been married, though it is difficult to tell if their spouses remained in Germany or if they were previously widowed.[21] When volunteers overwhelmed demand, many frustrated would-be migrants refused to go back to work in the camp "but held themselves like faithful foolish virgins in instant readiness for the second coming of His Honor, who had promised to take them also into his kingdom of sweated labor, just as soon as he could secure permission for a second shipment."[22]

Shortly thereafter, regular transports to Belgium began. Only large transports, either including dependents or with the promise of permission for dependents to follow later could hope to clear the logjam of the DP camp system. Generally, volunteers for resettlement were slightly older on average than the repatriates of previous years. It seems likely that younger DPs were in a greater hurry to get back to their place of origin to start anew. In addition, DPs with young children likely worried that it would be more difficult for them to secure a place in a resettlement scheme. This may have made them more willing to consider repatriation as an option.

The bureaucracy of resettlement grew ever more complicated as national regulations often worked at cross-purposes with IRO wishes. Many families at Wildflecken had complex resettlement stories, which often took years to unwind. The story of Andrew Zdanowicz's family is a good example. Andrew, by now ten years old, was in the camp with his mother Helena, grandmother, aunt, and uncle. Another uncle lived in England, allowing Andrew's grandmother to join him. The uncle applied for and got sponsorship to go to Australia, while his aunt married a man who got a job building a dam on the Ottawa River in Ontario. Andrew and his mother remained, since it was exceedingly difficult for a woman and child to get authorization to go anywhere. Finally, in May 1951, Helena and Andrew received an invitation to come to Canada, where Andrew became an architect.[23]

The DPs were not the only people swept up in the whirl of emigration. For some IRO staffers, working with the DPs gave them a sense of mission and a taste of adventure. A young Dutch nurse, Johanna Howeler, served as a Nutrition Officer at Wildflecken in 1948. Nutrition was a key component of the camp clearance process, since IRO had to ensure that DPs were healthy enough to pass inspection before departure. Howeler, assigned to the camp bakery, soon learned that nothing at Wildflecken worked quite the way it should. "It all seemed so straight-forward. Soon, however, I realized that the bakery produced far less bread than I expected, and that this was because pigs were being fed and fattened for black market purposes." She also remembered posters depicting Australia, "bathed in sunlight and prosperous." Ultimately, the posters convinced the young Dutch woman that she too should consider emigration. Howeler volunteered to serve on a ship carrying DPs to Melbourne in 1950. Upon arrival, she resigned her IRO commission and spent the rest of her life in Australia.[24]

While debates raged over what was to be done with the facility, life in the Wildflecken camp attained a kind of eccentric permanence. Sports teams now regularly traveled to play, matched with other DP and even non-DP teams. School classes took regular, and sometimes extended, trips into the German countryside for education and recreation. In a few cases, particularly toward the end of the camp's life, older children went to school in the village itself alongside their German neighbors. The centrality of the camp to the local economy diminished considerably with the Currency Reform and the re-emergence of a cash economy, but the routines of daily contact remained, both for good and for bad.

Relations between DPs and locals remained tense, but largely without the violence of the first eighteen months. The community of Wildflecken, particularly its civil administration, began to make it increasingly clear that they were fed up with the presence of the camp, its IRO administrators, and the fact that the name of the town was now indelibly associated with a DP camp. Since they could do little about it, this frustration manifested itself in petty acts of defiance. In October 1948, officials with the Red Cross's International Tracing Service in Bad Arolsen, charged with keeping track of the millions of individuals scattered by the war, began receiving death certificates from the camp stamped simply "Rhön." When they asked about it, the Military Government in Würzburg responded that the mayor of Wildflecken did not like using a stamp with "DP Camp Wildflecken" on it. "The German town of Wildflecken is a small part of the real Wildflecken, called Gutsbezirk Wildflecken, covering the big camp of 10,000 Polish DPs. . . . All further death certificates will be stamped with 'Rhön,' at least as long as the present Burgomaster remains on."[25]

While the sense of pervasive conflict between DPs and locals ebbed after 1947, DP criminality became an entrenched aspect of public perception. Locals blamed crimes, particularly those involving property, on DPs or more nebulous "foreigners." Occupation authorities now tired of receiving reports of unverifiable robberies, which they came to believe might be associated with the far more pervasive problem of illegal trade. The Bavarian Military Government in Munich launched an investigation of cattle raiding in 1948, after Bavarian police officials complained that the vast majority of those responsible for livestock thefts were "foreign nationals." The investigation examined twenty-two cases cited by the Bavarians in which solid evidence existed to prove the perpetrators were DPs. When the Americans looked at the evidence, they found that seven of those cases rested on presumptions, assumptions, and "suspicious behavior" by DPs in rural communities. One Bavarian police official told the Americans that "he has reason to assume that many reported cattle thefts actually never took place. Farmers frequently sell cattle in the black market and simply report such cattle as stolen."[26] Farmers could appeal to assumptions about pervasive DP criminality to disguise the equally (if not more) pervasive existence of illegal commerce.

DPs in 1948 were, as they had been in the earliest days of the camp, both part of and separate from the local community. Across American-occupied Germany, almost 220,000 DPs lived outside of camps. Of these, more than a quarter were Poles.[27] In Wildflecken, DP families lived in the town either as willing free-livers or having lost their DP status for some reason. Zygmunt M. and his family moved several times between camps and rural communities, to the immense frustration of IRO and local officials. Neither set of bureaucrats wanted the family on their books, so they sought to shift responsibility whenever possible. When the IRO requested that the local housing office find the family a place to live "in or around the town of Wildflecken," *Flüchtlingskommissar* Beck fought back and insisted that the IRO find the family another camp that would take them in.[28] In this case, the German bureaucrat won. Most of the time, local officials had little choice and little recourse to deal with problem DPs.

Ex-DPs and free-livers often ended up living in the apartment blocks on the edge of town, where they shared space with their German and expellee neighbors and often came into conflict. Widespread distaste for and anxiety about DPs contributed to public fears about their behavior outside of the camp. The L. family quickly distinguished itself by holding loud parties and threatening neighbors in Block 14 when they complained. "It is because of these people that our home has come into disrepute [*in Verruf gekommen*]," complained the other residents of the building to the local housing office. More specifically, residents claimed that others in town began to describe their building as a "bordello and safe-haven for bandits." The bitter lessons of the early postwar period, and particularly the experience of armed banditry, remained after the decline of organized criminal activity and the transformation of the camp.[29]

Both IRO and American officials developed relationships with the local press in order to disseminate information and mitigate potential conflicts. Intelligence reports from the area reveal that local German officials frequently suggested that the Americans distribute newspaper stories debunking rumors about DPs, like the persistent reports that DPs drew American salaries even if they did not work.[30] At the time, American media relations in it occupation zone stressed economic reconstruction and stability, heavily leavened by reminders of Soviet interference and the dangers of Communist subversion.[31] Negative coverage of DPs interfered with that message. The English-language press emphasized the connection between keeping order and economic recovery. As the local command's newspaper, the *Post-Argus*, described efforts to police DPs:

> Like a German citizen, DPs are required to abide by the laws enforced by Military Government and to German laws. However, many DPs perhaps taking advantage of their status, dealt in the black market and violated other MG laws. This could not be tolerated by the occupying powers, for one of their main missions is to restore economic stability in Germany and Europe and dealing in the black market is a step in the opposite direction. These violations [have] to be curtailed.[32]

Local IRO officials worked hard to manage the image of the camp, particularly after the disastrous start of the previous years. In fall 1948, the nearby *Fuldaer Volkszeitung* ran a photo of a building fortified against robbers. The caption read, "This photograph is not from the war. It was taken recently in a village in the Rhön. It shows one of the many precautions that the inhabitants of this region take to protect themselves against robberies by Poles who wander out of DP Camp Wildflecken."[33] An IRO officer at Wildflecken, who worked previously in Fulda and believed the newspaper to be a hotbed of anti-DP sentiment, turned the matter over to the Americans.

The American response to this minor provocation was interesting because of what it showed about the evolution of the military presence in Wildflecken and broader attitudes toward DPs. The officer in charge of the investigation was CIC Special Agent Chester Wolkonowski, himself a first-generation immigrant assigned to Wildflecken because of his knowledge of Polish, Ukrainian, German, and Russian. After the riots of January 1947, the Americans made at least a limited effort to understand what was going on in the camp. Wolkonowski talked to camp leaders, who complained that "after being persecuted by the Nazi regime, the American authorities allow the Germans to continue their persecution of Poles and DPs in general." Wolkonowski enjoyed good relations with DP camp residents and certainly had no sympathies for the editor or the incendiary message. However, he recommended that the case be closed without any action. This was certainly not anti-DP animus on his part, but rather a reflection of growing consensus among American Military Government officials that German institutions should be allowed to function more or less freely, even when doing so potentially undermined stated American interests.[34]

IRO tried its best to pass along the message to local communities that the Wildflecken camp would eventually close. While they could not and would not say this openly, they certainly made every effort to suggest it in the local and regional press. Another 1947 press release emphasized all of the educational work that was going on in the camp, most notably that DPs received training in industrial skills, English, and Spanish. IRO staff wanted to communicate that they intended to help their charges leave the Sinn Valley, and Germany, as quickly as possible.[35]

In fact, many within IRO began to argue that the best thing to do with Wildflecken was simply to close the facility. As the broader DP population thinned, the camp's full-time resident count dipped below 10,000. The camp owed its existence to the exigencies of the postwar period and the presence of an undamaged Wehrmacht facility. It had never been an especially felicitous spot and the perennial problem of keeping the place running during the winter gave IRO supply officers fits and led to calls for closure. Even with a reduced population, the cold and long winter posed considerable logistical challenges. During the winter of 1948 alone, the camp required 2,650,000 lbs. of food, 1,544,000 lbs. of coal, and 3,432 cubic feet of firewood.[36] All of this had to come, by rail and truck, from depots far removed from the Sinn Valley.

IRO officials debated, in fairly heated terms, the continued necessity of the facility. Many advocated closing the camp and moving its inhabitants elsewhere. Even those who pressed for this course of action could not name another facility that could hold as many people, nor did it seem particularly wise to give up such a desirable piece of real estate for fear that it would be snapped up for use by the army or someone else. The answer, it seemed, was to transform the facility from a residential camp to a Staging Center. There, DPs who had already secured a visa could be held while transportation and other administrative details were worked out at the debarkation port, which was typically Bremerhaven. This had a number of advantages, allowing the consolidation of groups traveling together, opportunities to teach targeted orientation classes, and minimizing the risk of back-ups at ports of exit.

Two problems made this decision difficult, both of which had to do with the U.S. Army. First, nobody knew what the Army wanted to do with the Wildflecken facility. The army still had control over the space as a condition of occupation and could conceivably supersede IRO with little to no notice. A. C. Dunn wrote to Meyer Cohen in February that "it has been intimated to us that it is quite probable that the military plans may not include use of the Wildflecken installation." Intimation, particularly by unknown sources, is not the same as assurance. It took until May before U.S. European Command (EUCOM) officially acceded to the idea of a staging area. "Although present planning does not contemplate need of these facilities for a military purpose in the immediate future," EUCOM replied, "it is possible that they may be required at some future date."[37]

While operational troops might not immediately require the Wildflecken facility, others at EUCOM did not like the idea at all. For the Civil Affairs Division, a transit camp at Wildflecken looked like the worst possible outcome. DPs became a football between the zones, with the French largely unwilling to take significant numbers and the Americans and British struggling with the numbers they had. Civil Affairs wanted to get the DPs out of the American Zone, while a transit camp meant that DPs from any of the western zones could end up in Wildflecken for an indeterminate period of time. IRO's Chief of Operations in Bad Kissingen wrote to EUCOM Civil Affairs, pressing the need for such a camp and trying to allay concerns about its impact on the American Zone:

> This headquarters is fully appreciative of the restrictions of space in the US Zone and has no desire to complicate this most serious problem. However, in the larger aspect of the Emigration movement from Europe it is considered most desirable that some inter-zonal arrangements might be agreed through your office by OMGUS whereby emigrants from other Zones might also be accumulated at the Wildflecken Staging Center for the comparatively short period while waiting shipment.... The use of a Staging Center, centralizing the accumulation of fully-processed emigrants, would inevitably hasten camp closures, concentration of the DP population, and determination of what the final residue or hard core might be, which information is greatly desired by interested Governments.[38]

Wildflecken now sat at the center of the bi-zonal effort to clear DPs as quickly as possible. As matters evolved, the Americans and the British developed a division of labor for managing DP movement. DPs bound for Australia passed through the British system, transiting from Aurich and Delmenhorst in Lower Saxony to Bremerhaven or south to Bagnoli near Naples. Since the British lacked camps of sufficient size to accommodate backflow, Wildflecken functioned as a reserve holding area. It also served as the primary transit point for migrants bound for North or South America.[39]

The change in the camp's status in late spring represented the biggest transformation of the camp since its inception. Within days of the announcement, almost 2,000 Poles received notification to transfer to other Polish camps in the IRO system with seven to fourteen days' notice. Camp transfer logs show dramatic increases in the number of incoming and outgoing movements. The camp lost its exclusively Polish character as a few Balts and even occasional Jews arrived, though by this time the bulk of the remaining DPs in the pipeline were Polish.

The re-introduction of ethnic diversity to the camp caused its own range of problems. Jews, who had lived for several years in their own camps, now found themselves sharing living space with their former neighbors in Eastern Europe. Moshe (Morris) Gordon, a teenage survivor of the Vilna ghetto who arrived in 1949, recalled, "We were thrown together with other nationalities, and some of them were Ukrainians, you know. I couldn't say for certain, but I know that some of them were those murderers who murdered us during the Nazi times." Gordon recalled brutal violence in the barracks, including a robbery that left him hiding behind a door with an axe, convinced that a pogrom had begun.[40]

Aside from the logistics of setting up a transit camp, the change afforded lots of opportunities for camp residents to get jobs with IRO, setting up plenty of chances for politicking. Not inconveniently, troublemakers could be sent away, as happened when a group of Poles with histories of black market dealing received orders to transfer to Gablingen. The camp's Accomodation Officer wearily noted that "there is no doubt that we will be called upon to provide an explanation of this matter." Indeed, the group facing transfer wrote an angry letter to the camp's administration, accusing it of orchestrating the move to prevent them from getting jobs in the new facility.

> Some years ago each of us was either a victim of German KZ Lager or a prisoner of war in Stalag or a labourer in a forced labour camp and we know what it means to be put in a penal transportation.... We don't know the reason for such an unjust treatment by the IRO officers because it was not given to us and we can only suppose this removal is prompted by the desire to deprive us of the possibility to get a job in the newly opened US Zone Staging Center. This job is given now to the strange people and even to non-DP persons.[41]

This document was more complicated than it appeared. By now, the camp had been in existence for five years. For some DPs, it had become a home and they had ties to the place that went beyond economic necessity. One of the signatories was Wicenty M., whose marriage a local woman in 1945 was mentioned in chapter 2. While M., his wife, and their daughter lived on the grounds of the DP camp, they had opportunities to easily move back and forth into the broader German community. Even as the camp transformed into a transit facility, opportunities continued to abound within its borders sufficient to entice residents to remain.

In its new role, Wildflecken briefly played host to one of the strangest refugee odysseys of the postwar period: the Shanghai DPs. While precise statistics are hard to come by, around 17,000 European refugees sought shelter in Shanghai after the Nazi seizure of power. After the war, 15,511 registered as DPs, eighty-seven percent of whom were Jewish. As the Chinese Civil War worsened, the Shanghai DPs became increasingly assertive in their demands to leave China, with an overwhelming majority seeking to go the U.S. or Israel.[42] In 1950, one of the last IRO-chartered vessels carried more than 1,100 Shanghai DPs across the Pacific, through the Panama Canal, and to Naples, where the group split. Half the passengers went on to Israel, while the rest moved into the DP pipeline. By the time a group of 283, all but forty-three of them Jewish, arrived at Wildflecken, the strain of nearly a year of close proximity began to show. Tensions between Jews and non-Jews worsened as their odyssey dragged on, with some complaining that everyone was having "a difficult and hard time."[43] The voyage of the Shanghai DPs did not end with their arrival in Germany. For most, the journey ended with a return trip across the Atlantic to settle in the United States.[44]

As a transit camp, Wildflecken mirrored the larger IRO effort to encourage and facilitate emigration. When emigration slowed, as it did to Australia in late 1949, the backlog manifested itself in Wildflecken. Timing proved critical and any change in the timetable potentially threw everything out of sync. Pregnant women, for instance, could not depart in later stages of pregnancy. Since virtually no pregnant women without a spouse would have been allowed to enter emigration at this point, the inability of an expectant mother to board a ship likely meant either holding the woman's spouse and other children or splitting up a family.

Any trace of infectious disease in a camp, almost inevitable in such circumstances, could quarantine large number of migrants and hold up the process at other camps for lack of transit facilities. For those transiting through the camp, the prospect of being labeled as too ill to travel gave the whole facility an aura of dread. Basha Drang, a twenty-year-old Polish Jewish woman, found herself in Wildflecken in July 1949 after moving between smaller DP camps. Still grieving following the recent loss of her mother, Drang lost a dramatic amount of weight and remembers doctors telling her that she would not likely be allowed to emigrate until she recovered. "It really is what [the name Wildflecken] says –," she recalled from her eventual home in Jerusalem, "the most horrible place." She spent her time in Wildflecken going through endless medical examinations, until eventually she received clearance to emigrate and set out for Bremerhaven.[45]

A 1949 report strongly criticized the endless series of delays. "Wildflecken, although an ideal transit camp with excellent facilities and administration, is fast obtaining an unjustified unsavory reputation. . . . The statement of unrest at the camp is an understatement. The Displaced Persons are finding their life unbearable. They are beginning to complain about most everything. Problems are exaggerated out of all proportion." Fights grew increasingly common, privacy increasingly uncommon, and boredom became a fact of life as DPs whiled away days and weeks in the camp. Measles broke out, likely worsening the delays. DPs who had already repeatedly refused repatriation felt uneasy about being a few miles from the Red Army. "Transits with little to do have too much time to think about it and have become panicky."[46]

For those who left, the outward journey could be long and arduous but generally welcome. Howeler describes the train journey to Ancona as a joyous holiday for DPs previously limited to camp life. "Obviously, the migrants were elated to close off what had been a very difficult period in their lives."[47] Hulme describes one convoy's departure as a celebration of the end of an ordeal:

> The last truck was blessed, the band struck up, the motors roared and there at last our convoy moved out bumper to bumper under the flag-draped arch of the camp's gate. It was just fifteen Army trucks carrying only a handful of the no-longer displaced out that gate for the very last time, but to me it looked like a great green dragon in the dawn with one hundred and eighty brave men riding astride it, beating it with their wildly waving arms until it smoked to speed and disappeared, a streak of green down the deserted highway.[48]

The mood in the camp, and in the DP system more broadly, combined optimism and fatalism in the same breath. IRO made real progress in its migration plans, but the vast size of the problem continued to loom over everyone's head. During its first four years, IRO oversaw a substantial exodus from Germany. A total of 719,536 IRO DPs left western Germany for resettlement, of whom 450,163 came from the U.S. Zone. However, this stream of refugees by no means solved the DP problem in Germany. A "hard core" remained, nearly 175,000 in mid-1949, who for various reasons could not be resettled or repatriated. The largest cohort of these were those with health problems, while most of the rest could not resettle due to some combination of age, skill set, family situation, or background. This fell disproportionately on women, particularly older women or those with children and no partner.[49]

The DP Act stood little chance of further extension after 1950, effectively cutting off immigration into the United States. Camp administrators recognized the need to move quickly, but the urgency of the past two years faded on Washington's end. Kathryn Hulme recalled the frustration of IRO field workers laboring to get remaining DPs cleared for resettlement before the law expired. The process, she wrote, "was like watching an enormous merry-go-round without music, on which all the DPs you have ever known seemed to be permanently stuck. And, if you managed to unseat one . . . you very often saw him back again on the merry-go-round, perhaps transfixed on a different technicality this time."[50]

While thousands moved through the transit facility, this frenetic pace also meant that those DPs who were unable to proceed got stuck in Wildflecken with no obvious way out. By January 1949, the population of the camp was down to 5,500. Wildflecken was one of the last and most important DP sites left in the country.⁵¹ The Wildflecken DP camp, only recently considered for closure, now looked as if it might persist indefinitely, lacking any sort of practical solution to move its residents out of the Sinn Valley. For camp administrators and American occupation forces alike, this impasse was enormously frustrating. Here, they found themselves in broad agreement with a coalition of local businessmen, government officials, and legislators who launched a series of ambitious initiatives intended to radically transform the Rhön. Drawing upon previous efforts at rural economic reform, these elites tried to draw support from Bavaria and from the emerging West German state to support their plans. Where Gauleiter Hellmuth pointed to the rural poverty of the area as a tactic to draw national attention to his plan in the 1930s, the next generation of reformers could add another factor: the disproportionate number of expellees living in the Rhön. Their efforts ultimately largely failed, not least because of overly ambitious plans and some amount of greed and corruption. However, they also faced a singular problem in their quest to bring industry to the Sinn Valley – all of their plans hinged on the conversion of the IRO facility to civilian use. Until that happened, all talk of planned economic transformation was just that.

Advocates of transformative reform agreed that the unused space on the former base represented an extraordinary opportunity to realize their plans, but fundamentally disagreed about how best to proceed. The first group of reformers, who never really managed to organize themselves into a lobby, pushed for agrarian reform not unlike what Hellmuth advocated a decade earlier. Much of the push for land reform came from within the settler communities on the base, where, as a 1948 report noted, "the hunger for land is great."⁵² Farmers in the refugee towns hoped to see the army free up even more land for their use, allowing them to become landowners. Land reform advocates pointed to the same problems that the previous Nazi administration tried to resolve, namely small farms and the fragmenting of land through partible inheritance. Access to land and an end to traditional farming practices that excluded expellee farmers offered one set of solutions to the economic crisis in the Rhön.

The second group of reformers also drew on Hellmuth's legacy to advocate a very different industrial future for the region. For local politicians, the end of the war represented an unprecedented opportunity to leverage Wildflecken's 1930s transformation into a base town. With the Wehrmacht no longer in need of such facilities, it seemed reasonable that they might be converted for economically productive use. Soon after the end of the war, local business and political leaders began to discuss the future of the Wildflecken site. As early as July 1946, the Regierungspräsident of Lower Franconia wrote to Bavarian Prime Minister Hoegner, reminding him of the region's status as a Notstandsgebiet and asking for help to "build healthy social relationships" in a district now overrun by expellees. He mentioned the possibility of locating a textile industry in the area, but one that "avoided the problems associated with home-based work.... Such plans could help solve the expellee problem."[53]

In Bavaria, solving the expellee problem became an increasingly high priority for the American occupation government. By the end of 1947, OMGUS realized that expellees presented a significant challenge to the broader American mission in Germany. Without real economic recovery, Germany would not be stable or secure. The expellee problem was a vicious cycle. Expellees needed to be better integrated economically for recovery to occur, but without real development there was little chance for integration to begin.[54] Since the Americans technically had no responsibility for expellees, they were largely content to pressure the Bavarian government, civil society, and charitable organizations to do something about the crisis. Occupation authorities pressed Bavarian and local governments to employ more expellees, but to little avail. Few expellees found work in the middle or upper levels of the civil service. One of the few parts of the bureaucracy that employed significant numbers of expellees was the Flüchtlingsverwaltung. Of 656 employees in Lower Franconia, 474 were expellees themselves.[55] The veteran New Deal administrator Pierce Williams, one of the "population experts" upon whom the Military Government relied for advice on dealing with expellees, wrote an alarming report in late 1947 that warned against this tendency to "put this particular task in the category of 'German problems.' Without sympathetic collaboration on the part of Military Government and German officials the immigrants will remain an undigested element in German society and instead of being an asset to the community, could become a danger."[56]

Taking up Williams's suggestion, Bavarian Land Director Murray Wagoner played a prominent role in organizing meetings to address "one of the most pressing issues in contemporary life." Along with Jaenicke, Wagoner stressed that the expellees could be put to work "for the enrichment of the Bavarian economy, particularly in the export sector." Wagoner's administration meanwhile prepared a series of reports that stressed the importance of rebuilding industry and moving expellee workers from "non-productive rural areas" into industrial districts. However, German cities remained badly damaged and in need of massive reconstruction before any such movement could take place. If expellees could not be brought to industrial centers, then perhaps industrial centers could be brought to the expellees.[57]

A loose coalition of interested parties converged on identifying opportunities to productively exploit the 18,000-acre site at Wildflecken. In January 1947, the head of the *Siedlungs- und Heimwerkstätten-Gesellschaft*, a quasi-state agency dedicated to resettling expellees, wrote to Jaenicke to suggest that his organization might be interested in helping to develop the Wildflecken facility for industrial use and the employment of Sudeten expellees. While nothing came of this idea, the organization was not the only actor interested in the possibility of developing the site.[58] Two months later, a delegation from the Bavarian Ministry of Economics visited the area, later circulating reports suggesting that the district might be suitable for the construction or expansion of settlements. Critically, initial surveys commented on the number of undamaged and standing houses, including the expellee communities of Reussendorf and Werberg.[59] A Military Government report from early 1947 suggested that these ideas had already reached the ears of the Americans:

> All in all the Wildflecken area contributed much to the income of the Kreis during the Nazi control period and made many jobs for the people of this Kreis and it is the desire of a number of business people plus the local Kreis to again make this area productive and they feel that the Muna area can [start] with the idea in mind of moving eventually to the Lager area ... for the manufacturing

of textiles, leather goods, and other similar articles. By doing this they feel that jobs can be created for the native as well as many of the refugee and expellee population.[60]

The most prominent of the voices belonged to Wilhelm Lüttgen, the owner of a textile plant in Kissingen. Lüttgen saw the base as an untapped resource, primed for development as an industrial facility. Industry across defeated Germany was a shadow of its former self. In the American Zone, industrial production in 1946 stood at twenty-seven percent of its 1936 level. While damage to production facilities proved to be less dire than initially thought, shortages of raw material and labor seriously hampered industrial recovery. A country with enormous coal reserves found it increasingly difficult to mine enough anthracite to restart production, with production levels about half of 1936 capacity.[61]

In early 1947, Lüttgen began to circulate a plan among his friends in local government that laid out an astonishingly optimistic vision for the Rhön and for Wildflecken. He proposed to build a large wool and linen manufacturing center in the hills above Wildflecken, initially in the Muna and the HVA but with an eye toward eventually expanding into the camp area itself. As he pointed out, the bulk of Bavaria's textiles came from areas now occupied by the Soviets. "Because of this, the people of Bavaria and the US Zone face catastrophic shortages. *The solution to the textile and clothing problem is, next to the provision of foodstuffs, the most urgent responsibility of the political leadership.*"[62]

Lüttgen dreamed big. His plan, which attracted a great deal of attention in the weeks after its distribution, promised a 100,000 qm (about 120,000 square yards) of "the most modern industrial facilities in Central Europe," which would employ 4,000 workers. Importantly, these facilities would address not only industrial and technical needs, but "be in accordance with the development of social questions." Crucially, the Lüttgen Plan promised to draw most of its employees from the Sudeten expellee population. Most grandiosely, Lüttgen suggested that his plan, if fully realized, might directly support more than 15,000 people.[63] For a district with a permanent population of little more than 20,000 the planned industrial facility offered a profound transformation that would affect both the local and expellee populations. By Lüttgen's own admission, his planned facility would be enormously costly. The total cost of the factory would probably run to around twenty-five million marks, with start-up costs for other businesses that would gravitate to the area between 800,000 and 1.2 million marks. Lüttgen, a consummate visionary, wanted credit for an idea that he claimed "may well be unique in Europe."[64]

The Lüttgen Plan represented the apotheosis of a generation of modernization schemes in and around the Sinn Valley. The Hellmuth Plan promised to transform the local economy through large-scale agriculture. When the Wehrmacht base arrived, it brought jobs to the region and the promise of turning Wildflecken into a base town with all of the associated services and amenities. The former stalled in the bureaucratic miasma of Nazi agrarian policy. The latter failed because of the war. Now, in the shadow of catastrophic defeat and the arrival of thousands of unwanted refugees, a new hope arose that the upper Rhön might prosper. That optimism was shared by the expellees who set up the restored communities of Werberg and Reussendorf in 1946. Their decision to set aside buildings in the towns for future industrial development demonstrated the appeal of such visions to those most committed to rebuilding the region. Now, in Lüttgen, they found a ready champion.

Lüttgen's vision for rural renewal developed political traction very quickly. It had considerable advantages in the eyes of the Bavarian government. Previous governments classified the Rhön as an economic crisis zone, making it easier to direct development aid toward the area. Lüttgen and his putative partners also brought with them considerable private capital, potentially limiting the need for the Bavarian state to supply start-up costs. Finally, Lüttgen's stated focus on providing jobs for expellees carried two benefits. First, it addressed a broadly recognized challenge to economic recovery. Second, it meant that the powerful and largely unaccountable Flüchtlingsverwaltung got involved.

For Lüttgen and his backers, building a textile plant represented an intermediate step in an enormous reconstruction project designed to transform the Rhön and its inhabitants. "The development of a better transportation networks is vital if the expellees settled in this district are to have access to work places," claimed a report commissioned by Lüttgen. The report proposed construction of a train line from Bischofsheim to the Muna, servicing the planned textile mill. In addition, a new road would connect Wildflecken with Gersfeld in nearby Hessen, with the hope of a train line to follow later. Such a plan would put up to 800 workers to work for up to two years.[65] Lüttgen also promised to resolve the region's coal shortage while providing jobs for nearby miners. Coal mined near Bischofsheim would fuel the plants at Wildflecken, which would finally provide employment for both the poor farmers of the Sinn Valley and the expellees now in their midst.

While the plan's initial drafts did not contain much in the way of specifics, Lüttgen claimed to have big plans for the community of Werberg. He planned to make the small refugee town a center of textile production. If granted use of some of the buildings in the town, he suggested that he would build a plant there that could provide full employment for the expellee farmers and turn the town into a bustling population center of its own. The new transportation network would make Werberg a hub, literally placing the tiny settlement on the map. "By supporting the industry plan in Wildflecken," a Military Government official wrote after reading the proposal, "the refugee problem could be solved to a great extent if the necessary help is offered."[66]

These were extraordinarily ambitious plans. Some of those in government who read the plans closely worried that no amount of hurry could avoid the central problem facing any such project – the continued existence of the DP camp at the heart of the base. Such a development, warned a Munich official, was "to be hoped for. A conversion for the establishment of settlements is at the moment not very achievable."[67] Even those closely associated with Lüttgen and his plan had doubts. Landrat Heinrich Oswald, speaking privately with Flüchtlingsverwaltung officials, worried that the proposal called for too much too fast. Oswald feared that the hoped-for clearing of the DP Camp "upon which the whole plan depends, is right now not particularly close at hand." The official suggested Oswald focus on tangible goals, particularly the development of the Muna and HVA, then worry about the rest of the base later.[68] This sort of thinking was all too typical in the heady days of spring 1947. It later came back to haunt participants and supporters of the plan.

Despite such well-placed concerns, things moved fast after the plan's initial distribution. Little more than a month after he drafted his idea, Lüttgen and a number of local government officials found themselves in Munich at the invitation of the Economics Ministry. The meeting brought together several ministries and Kreis governments. Ministerial officials peppered Lüttgen with questions, but he mollified their concerns by promising capital, equipment, and his not-inconsiderable energy. Before the meeting adjourned, those assembled committed to establishing a para-statal corporation, combining public and private capital, committed to economic development in the Rhön. They scheduled a founding meeting for the corporation in three weeks.[69] The *Rhön-Planung Gesellschaft*, GmbH (RPG), founded in May 1947, represented both the optimism and the desperation of the early postwar period. In its founding document, the RPG committed itself to work with the government to achieve "the economic development of the entire Rhön region." While the DP camp remained closed to the RPG, the land on which the camp sat stayed at the core of its goals. "[We are] particularly interested in the reconstruction and productive organization of the facilities on the former Wildflecken maneuver grounds in preparation for their industrial use and the peopling of its territory in connection with expellee settlement programs."[70]

Funding for the RPG came from several sources. The Bavarian state provided the bulk of its initial capital, 60,000 RM. The regional government of Lower Franconia gave 20,000, while a further 20,000 came from the district governments of Brückenau, Mellrichstadt, Bad Kissingen, and Bad Neustadt. Three months later, the Bavarian state further indicated its confidence in the RPG, granting it effective trusteeship over the territory of the former maneuver grounds. The Americans strongly objected to this, pointing to the close linkages between Lüttgen's private firm and the RPG. As a result, the trusteeship issue remained legally opaque, adding another layer of complexity to the already contentious problem of just who exercised effective control over the property.[71] Given the continued occupation of a considerable part of the grounds by IRO, this gesture was partly symbolic. It did have some practical implications, however. Wilhelm Lüttgen and his allies now had more or less complete responsibility for implementing the vast and ambitious plan that he set forth.

In addition to Lüttgen, several other prominent members of local society sat on the corporation's board of directors. None were more prominent than Heinrich Oswald, then a sitting Landrat. Oswald's role in the RPG put him in a curious position. He represented both the Landkreis and the RPG. Clearly, he could trade on his good relations with the Americans. But it was not always apparent in whose name he acted. He understood as well as anyone the tenuous position of German authorities under the Military Government and frequently appealed to the Americans to act on the RPG's behalf when he could not achieve the desired result in his capacity as Landrat. In June 1947, he appealed to the Military Government in Brückenau to help resolve a dispute over logging with Kreis Neustadt, whom he accused of "not yet realiz[ing] the importance of the [RPG]." In the end, the Americans controlled the facilities at Wildflecken and could nudge recalcitrant local politicians if they believed it to be in their interest. "Without the help of the occupying power we cannot make headway, energetic help is therefore requested, all the more because of the effects these planings [sic] will have are very note-worthy in economical and therefore in political respect for the Western-Zone."[72] His arrest and subsequent departure from the position of Landrat cleared up his status somewhat, but as a trusted ally of the Americans he continued to exercise outsized influence in the German-American relationship.

The RPG received immediate and far-ranging publicity. It showcased everything that the Bavarian government hoped to impress upon its own people, the Americans, and the rest of Germany. Here was the Land government, local authorities, and private industry, working together for economic development. Most important, the partnership would benefit both local communities and expellees. The *Main-Post* wrote in glowing terms about the project. It accepted Lüttgen's most optimistic projections and added its own expectations that such a project would lead to the expansion of the region's train and waterway systems. "The whole plan," it wrote, using an increasingly common local term for the DP camp, "hinges on the clearing of the *Polenstadt*." The plan's framers promised prosperity "not just for the future settlers of the Polenstadt, but also the poor inhabitants of the Rhön villages surrounding it." Much like Lüttgen, the *Main-Post* stressed the importance of the industrial settlement for the overall development of the district and the region, particularly its expellee population. "Hand in hand with this project goes the economic and infrastructural development of the Rhön."[73] Lüttgen met personally with the Bavarian minister president, who pressed the businessman to "move as soon as possible toward implementing the practical aspects of the maneuver ground project."[74]

The story of the RPG makes an important point about the German-American encounter during the occupation. Occupation was big business. Vast amounts of property sat in Allied hands or in legal limbo. The disposition of this wealth, largely through para-statal operations like STEG, offered unprecedented opportunities for commercial ventures with very little of the sort of oversight that might exist in functioning peacetime society. People like Lüttgen now moved freely between commerce and government, empowered to make decisions in which they had vested financial interests. The Americans lacked either the ability or the desire to tightly regulate such transactions and much preferred to allow local elites to handle these affairs for them. Lüttgen headed a corporation, funded with public money, which offered to make him personally very wealthy. Faced with poverty and a refugee crisis, the German and American authorities in Landkreis Brückenau needed quick fixes in 1947. As a report on the affair later noted, local officials "had to and still must work in the interest of settling expellees [*Neubürger*] and drawing industry into the area, such that the unemployed do not fall into the care of public authorities."[75]

Lüttgen promised this and more. But since he did not have to provide operating capital or start-up funds of his own, he had considerable reason to put forth utopian visions and little incentive to move quickly. Lüttgen also had a talent for making enemies, a problem which hindered the RPG from the beginning. A month after the formation of the RPG, Flüchtlingsverwaltung officials wrote the first of what would be many concerned letters, informing Lüttgen that there were "attacks" against him coming from unnamed sources.[76] While it is not clear what those attacks were, the focus was clear – perhaps he had promised more than he could possibly deliver. When Heinrich Oswald, then still Landrat, joined the Board of Directors, he had high hopes for the endeavor. As his own career stumbled and he faced legal challenges related to denazification, he came to regret his affiliation with the RPG.

Initially, RPG had some success attracting businesses to the district. Several small manufacturers, including a cable company and a chemical manufacturer, moved into some of the more than thirty warehouse buildings on the grounds of the former Muna. After a slow start, the Bavarian government extended credit to businesses hoping to start or expand, particularly those that employed expellees. Shortly after the foundation of the RPG, the Bavarian state pledged twenty-five million DM to support expellee industries. While the turmoil of the Currency Reform made this process more difficult, more than 5,000 businesses applied for credit under this scheme during the next two years.[77] The flow of easy credit, combined with the availability of readily convertible production facilities, made the Wildflecken property relatively desirable. However, the factories that came tended to be small, relatively low wage, and often not particularly financially stable. Significant structural impediments hindered the success of the project.

There were four reasons why businesses, and particularly industry, proved reticent to relocate to the Sinn Valley in 1947 and 1948. First, some of this hesitation came from circumstances far beyond the control of the RPG and its leadership. Currency explained part of the reason for the slow development of the Rhön project. In the months before the enormous currency conversion in June 1948, businesses with cash on hand were hesitant to spend it. They preferred to hold Reichsmarks with the near assurance that, in the very near future, a new and far more readily convertible currency would be introduced. In nearby Hessen, for example, a government study found that firms routinely held up to twelve months' worth of raw materials, pending the imminent creation of a cash economy.[78] From a business perspective, the timing of the RPG's efforts could not have been much worse.

Second, any plant owner considering building in the Sinn Valley had to wonder about the intentions of the Americans. The occupying power still had the right to requisition some or all former Wehrmacht property, more or less at will. The RPG had limited rights of trusteeship but the Americans technically still held title to captured property. Beginning in September 1947, the Americans began to systematically identify former Wehrmacht facilities in use for the housing of occupation troops, DPs, or Germans in need. The more than 4,000 identified structures, which included the administrative center of Wildflecken, could not be demolished until the need for housing past.[79] For many established and would-be entrepreneurs, this was simply too great a risk.

Third, the RPG also faced the problem of overpromising in an uncertain market. A few refugee towns and expellee camps did not constitute the vast pool of labor promised by the RPG's leadership. Workers were not likely to arrive before plants began operation and factory owners hesitated to commit before the workers arrived. This caused a great deal of tension within the RPG and in its tenuous relationship with its erstwhile investors in the Bavarian government. A meeting of the Board of Directors devolved into heated words and finger-pointing when Dr. Schober from RPG told government representatives that they could only bring firms to the region "to the extent that living space for workers gets built." The bureaucrats from the Ministry of Finance responded that firms would not come unless they could be assured that risks could be minimized.[80] This circular argument boded badly for the future of the Sinn Valley.

Fourth, the challenges of economic reconstruction and the problem of what do with the remaining DPs loomed large in the minds of the RPG's leadership. The Board of Directors regularly petitioned the government in Munich to use its leverage to speed the process of base clearing. In response, the Ministry of the Interior replied simply that it lacked any authority to do so.

> To our knowledge there is no prospect that the so-called "Caserne City" on the Wildflecken maneuver grounds will be cleared of Displaced Persons in the foreseeable future. As long as access to the Caserne City is forbidden, it will not be possible for you to take possession of any of the extant structures. At the same time, there is also no available capital for the furtherance of non-critical plans. This issue will therefore be deferred for the time being.[81]

The growing frustration on the part of the RPG leadership and its allies was not isolated. Increasingly, voices within the nascent German government on all levels made clear their displeasure at the continued presence of DPs, particularly when the DP camps interfered with the integration of expellees. One of the most important emerging voices on expellee issues, and thus on the DP problem, lived not far from Wildflecken in Hammelburg.

Dr. Maria Probst was one of the most formidable and influential politicians of the early postwar period. Born in Munich in 1902, she spent much of her childhood in Metz. In 1933, she completed a doctorate in his-

Dr. Maria Probst talking with constituents near Wildflecken, 1949.
Photo courtesy of Bundesarchiv, N 1219 Bild-537-090.

tory, writing a dissertation on the Bavarian ruling family in the late eighteenth century.[82] Widowed during the last days of the war, Probst found herself teaching school in Hammelburg. She emerged after the war as an active participant in the reconstruction of political life in American-occupied Germany, both as a journalist for the *Bayerische Rundschau* and as an early member of the CSU. In 1946, she won election to the Landtag and three years later to the Bundestag.[83] Wildly popular in her Franconian district, Probst became a vocal champion of the rights of expellees. She was known for her interest in social issues and in the alleviation of poverty; her deeply Catholic constituents called her by the nicknames "Maria Hilf" and "Maria Heimsuchung" (The Feast of the Visitation). She also had good political reasons for her interest in the expellee problem. Her district included the large and very important expellee camp at Hammelburg. A wartime POW camp, Hammelburg held German civilian internees after the war until its transfer to the Refugee Administration in 1947. During the next two years, 56,000 expellees passed through

Hammelburg before being settled elsewhere.[84] For Probst's constituents, expellee affairs were a problem very close to home.

Probst's personal papers suggest that she read voraciously on the subject. She found foreign opinion particularly useful as disillusion set in across the western democracies over the failure of "orderly" population transfer.[85] One 1948 report clearly influenced Probst because she liberally drew from its statistics and recommendations. "The Expellee Problem in Bavaria" argued against the notion that the expellees were a German problem. "The problem, the origin and cause of which come from international agreement, can only be resolved internationally. The expellee question is one with enormous foreign policy implications and without its resolution the pacification of Europe and the world is not possible."

The report's most important conclusions concerned the United Nations. As the author argued, the international community worked together to help those dispossessed in the Greco-Turkish population transfers of 1923.[86] The UN now needed to help Germany and the expellees in the same manner. The best way to do so was to speed up the emigration or repatriation of DPs and to turn over DP facilities to German authorities for the use of expellees.[87]

The solutions laid out in the report might have been appropriate for circulating manuscripts but was probably not politically expedient for an ambitious Landtag delegate to articulate publicly. Still, the influence of the report can be seen in a Bavarian Landtag session in July 1948. Probst complained that OMGUS ignored the plight of expellees, while allowing DPs to move in and out of camps at will. She particularly criticized the IRO for tacitly allowing the return of DPs who previously left to find work in France or Belgium, eliciting cries of "They don't want to [work]!" from her colleagues. Interior Minister Willi Ankermüller, who grew up near Wildflecken, followed Probst's speech by reading a proclamation to be delivered to the Military Government. The text argued that many of the 242 IRO facilities in Bavaria were filled to less than fifty percent capacity. As a result, space could not be made for expellees. The government urged "the dramatic consolidation of persons in IRO care to make space for expellees, the transfer of under-used or empty casernes, and the long-awaited opening of the French Zone to the entry of expellees."[88]

For Probst, Ankermüller, and their fellow conservatives in the Bavarian parliament, the problems of DPs and expellees were inextricably linked. The key to resolving these challenges lay in asserting the limited sovereignty of Bavaria within the American occupation regime. Only the Americans had the political leverage to influence either IRO or the recalcitrant French. As Bavarian state institutions developed and became more self-confident, frustration grew among its political leadership over the limits of their sovereignty. The expellee issue embodied these boundaries. Munich had ultimate responsibility for the fate of the expellees, but lacked the sovereignty to take what some believed to be the steps necessary to effectively care for them.

Meanwhile, back in the Rhön, matters did not progress as smoothly or efficiently as any of the RPG's investors or signatories hoped. The apparent lack of any plan to close the DP camp hurt the scheme, but it also became increasingly clear that the RPG's leadership had no intention of moving quickly on anything but a scaled-down version of its grandiose plans. Local Flüchtlingsverwaltung officials worried that too much of the scheme rested in the uncertain hands of the RPG. "This cannot and should not be solely the task of the [RPG]. Other points of view will be needed here in any case," wrote a concerned inter-ministerial committee.[89] Notes of disquiet began to creep into correspondence between the RPG and its backers. These concerns reached the highest levels of the Bavarian government. Employment Minister Krehl wrote to the Bavarian Minister President in late 1947, complaining about the RPG. He grew particularly concerned that its leadership remained in Munich, where it might logically relocate to Brückenau or at the very least Würzburg. Krehl reminded the Minister President that the RPG's trusteeship could be rescinded if need be.[90] It is not difficult to read between the lines of such a communication. Nearly a year after its inception, RPG had yet to accomplish anything. While it was likely far too optimistic to expect progress in such a short period, the RPG's founders promised change and they promised it quickly. Now they had to pay for their own rash pledges. Shortly thereafter, the RPG moved its headquarters to Würzburg, but a pattern of distrust emerged that marked the rest of the group's existence.

The bifurcated nature of political power in occupied Germany contributed to the RPG's troubles. In June 1948, an official with the Office for Reparations Affairs (*Amt für Reparations-Angelegenheiten*) visited Wildflecken to inspect the disused Wehrmacht production facilities. He reported back to his office in Munich that the district possessed unused train tracks that might offer a solution to a recently discovered problem facing reparations officials in Munich. A section of track near Ebenhausen (in Upper Bavaria), had been identified as suitable for dismantling and transfer to Yugoslavia. Ebenhausen housed almost 14,000 expellees, nearly twice as many as Brückenau, and had a considerably more advanced industrial base than rural Franconia.[91] Located not far from the recovering urban center of Ingolstadt, Ebenhausen seemed considerably more important than Wildflecken. Reparations Affairs officials announced the imminent seizure and dismantling of twenty-four kilometers of track in the Wildflecken area.

RPG officials and local political leaders were incensed. Such a move "would not only be the death knell of the entire Wildflecken project," wrote the Board of Directors, it would likely force the closure of those businesses that had just begun to operate on the grounds of the Muna who would lose their access to raw material. For once, the RPG's patrons in Munich came through in support of its efforts. After sharp exchanges with the Bavarian Ministry of Economics, the Reparations Office drastically reduced its requisition to four kilometers, with the further understanding that all of the dismantled track would come from siding or spur lines.[92] While the RPG essentially won the battle over the railroad line, it was a pyrrhic victory. Efforts to save the railroad tracks to preserve the industrial development of Wildflecken only highlighted just how little progress had been made. Already the urban clusters of Upper Bavaria began to emerge as industrial centers, leaving rural areas like northern Lower Franconia behind.[93] Once the subject of grand dreams, Wildflecken now fell further and further behind.

By summer and into fall, even those who supported RPG had to acknowledge that the idea was all but moribund. Baus, the new Landrat, appeared before the Board of Directors, which included his predecessor, and "reprimanded them for their to-date non-fulfillment and particularly the lack of small and mid-sized industrial concerns."[94] In July, two members of the RPG board, including Oswald, wrote to Munich that "we greatly regret that, practically speaking, there is hardly any possibility of bringing reliable firms to Werberg."⁹⁵ At the moment in which the German economy began to turn around for the better, disaster loomed for the Wildflecken project.

The Currency Reform represented the real breaking point for the RPG. With credit markets now operating and a wage economy underway, RPG's inactivity over the previous year threatened to leave the region in the lurch as private investment went elsewhere with little prospect of replacement. Many expellees actually lost ground economically after the Currency Reform, since the conversion to wages in the new stable currency led to layoffs. Because expellees were significantly overrepresented in the agriculture sector and consequently suffered sharper job cuts after the reform, places like Landkreis Brückenau suffered disproportionately in the new economy. In his study of expellees in Celle, Rainer Schulze argued that the Currency Reforms, despite their negative impact on the economic situation of expellees, actually helped to convince locals that something had to be done to relieve inequalities.⁹⁶ This certainly seems to have been the case in Landkreis Brückenau as well.

Those who expected the RPG to produce results were also those most infuriated by its failure to do so. During the summer of 1948, these resentments spilled into the streets of Brückenau. As local organizations, in which expellees were strongly represented, lined up to criticize the RPG for its inaction, support for the organization among political leadership in Würzburg and Munich evaporated. "We had high hopes at the founding of the RPG," wrote an expellee assembly in Brückenau in July. "Today, after more than a year, we expellees are facing the fact that the Society has in no way fulfilled our hopes and expectations, which include work places, the founding of firms, and other possibilities on which to base our lives [*Existenzmöglichkeiten*]." The only solution, the expellees wrote, was to dissolve the RPG and use its operating budget to subsidize the lives of their fellow refugees.⁹⁷

Days later, the local chapter of the CSU-affiliated Expellees' Union (*Union der Ausgewiesenen*) joined in the attack. The Union membership expressed particular anger over the situation in Werberg, where a number of its members lived. The RPG's promises to turn several abandoned buildings on the site into factories remained unfulfilled, a visible reminder of the RPG's broader failure to accomplish much of anything.

They railed against the actions of Refugee Administration official Anton Beck, who spoke for the RPG when he promised them more than sixty new jobs to come along with the Lüttgen textile plant in Werberg. "All the support from the expellees for the Lüttgen factory has been pointless and our hopes for wage labor in this plant have over a long period remained unfulfilled." Unlike the earlier expellee manifesto, the Union proclamation did not even ask for additional funds. "We ask that this resolution be passed on to the responsible Ministries, so that something positive might finally happen in Werberg.... We want to earn our bread, not just to be aid recipients."[98]

Behind the not-inconsiderable anger and frustration of the resolution, there was another, equally important development. The Union issued its statement in the interests of "those expellees and locals brought together in Werberg." This statement is, on the surface, surprising. The Union was, after all, dedicated to protecting the interests of expellees. Since the most important threat to the livelihood of expellees was often conflict with locals, the two groups seldom found themselves on the same side. In rural Bavaria, however, where so many expellees found themselves after the war, this apparently endemic conflict changed by 1948. Efforts to find rural development solutions, like the misbegotten RPG, gave expellees and locals a common cause. Even if that cause proved illusory, it set a precedent that the two groups could work together if confronted by a common problem. At Werberg and sites like it, expellees and locals worked shoulder to shoulder, if not always harmoniously. This sense of cooperation, however grudging, became far more important later when Werberg came under threat again.

Even its close ties to local political elites could not save the RPG. When Hans Wutzelhofer, the former Landrat of Marktheidenfeld, visited in August, he was stunned by the juxtaposition between the RPG's promises and their near complete lack of delivery. "Is it acceptable to commit additional [public funds] to an organization whose plans in the Wildflecken area are of a size and magnitude worthy of Adolf Hitler?"[99] The Kreistag in Brückenau took up the matter shortly after the protests. The body "in the interest of the peace and security of the Landkreis order[ed] the immediate dissolution of the RPG, which despite its more than yearlong existence has not fulfilled any of its designated tasks, particularly the creation of jobs."[100] Abandoned by its patrons, the RPG folded with barely a whimper. It left behind a legacy of hard feelings, misspent public funds, and essentially no tangible progress toward its once lofty goals. In the end, the RPG collapsed in a failure of planning, organization, and timing, worsened in turn by a good measure of hubris and likely some portion of greed. In September, authorities began an investigation of the RPG's leadership for accounting irregularities, fraud, and theft.[101] The investigation went nowhere. By this time, many in the community simply wanted to put the whole matter behind them.

The RPG experiment was a disaster in the end, both for its participants and for the people of the Sinn Valley. For Probst and her colleagues in Munich and Bonn, the exercise failed because of poor leadership and the by now obvious conclusion that Lüttgen had no business making the sorts of promises that he made a year before. However, the RPG affair had some important consequences for the region. Chiefly, the mess caused by the administrative failure of the Lüttgen Plan drew considerable attention to Wildflecken and to the unresolved problem of the DP camp. Even as IRO planners debated what to do with the facility, Lüttgen's half-hearted attempt to develop the local economy without the structures at the heart of the old base highlighted the need to press for a quick resolution to the camp's continued existence. Since the question of regional economic development in rural northern Bavaria was intimately linked to the broader problem of expellees, the debate over what to do with the DP camp pitted those Germans, local and expellee, in a coalition against the DPs and their IRO protectors. As German government institutions moved toward fuller sovereignty, the interests of the American occupiers increasingly lined up alongside the Germans. Everyone, it seemed, could agree that the DP camp had to go. The problem remained that no one apparently knew what do with the residents who remained.

The question of what to do with Wildflecken was no closer to resolution at the end of 1948 than it had been eighteen months before. The Economic Committee of the Landtag took up the issue of Wildflecken again in October. After the RPG disaster, the government was back to its starting point. Maria Probst led off the proceedings, reporting on the inefficiency of the RPG and the perilous state of expellees in the district.

A civil servant from the Economics Ministry summed up the accumulated frustrations of the previous year:

> Wildflecken is a problem child [*Sorgenkind*] for virtually all government agencies, but it is only a small slice of the entire Rhön problem – a problem that has been with us for generations and for which no effective relief has yet been found. The camp center is still occupied by displaced Poles [*verschleppten Polen*]. The HVA is in good condition and can be put to industrial use. The Munitionsanstalt is partly destroyed.... The situation is more complicated than anyone could have foreseen.[102]

For those who hoped to turn the maneuver area into an economic and industrial center, 1948 was a singular catastrophe. After the Currency Reform, their hopes looked even more illusory than ever. The RPG fiasco took the wind out of the sails of development advocates. Their task was always not a little bit quixotic. Even if the DP camp closed, the Americans never gave any indication that they might consent to turning the entire base over for industrial development. They delivered this point directly to Hans Körner when he once again approached the Military Government about the DP camp in 1949. The Military Government in Munich assured Körner that "under no circumstances would the current DP facility be turned over for German use."[103]

The stories of the Wildflecken DP camp after 1947 and of the Germans who optimistically hoped to use it to transform their region need to be understood in parallel. The DP camp system entered a period of punctuated stasis after 1947. Thousands of DPs left Germany, but thousands more stayed. The network of camps remained in place, even as the need for it dwindled. As a result, observers and participants inside and outside the DP system grew increasingly frustrated with what seemed like an insoluble problem. Wildflecken sat squarely in the center of this intractable and multi-sided debate. The question of what to do with the facility was, in miniature, the question of what to do in Germany. The Americans scaled back their commitment to Central Europe and expected to continue doing so. German institutions at the local and state levels grew in confidence and responsibility, fully expecting that they would acquire the sovereignty to match their new assertiveness. The expellee issue remained at the core of this appeal for sovereign authority. The remaining DP camps served not only as a blockage to what some hoped would be alternative ways to support the expellee population, but also as visible reminders of the limits of that sovereignty. The IRO, charged with running the camps, badly wanted to consolidate its operations and to find homes for its wards outside the camps.

To all of these groups, Wildflecken came to represent both the possibilities and the limits of postwar reconstruction. While the failure of the RPG, however utopian its visions might have been, likely sealed the fate of any serious effort at rural industrial development in the Rhön, the battle over the facility was far from over.

FIVE

A VICTORY FOR DEMOCRACY, 1949–1952

For the second time in fifteen years, the hill above Wildflecken swarmed with workers and construction crews. In the snows of January 1951, a tent city grew in the Franconian uplands. Where a shrinking but sizable DP population still hung on in the IRO camp, they were joined by U.S. Army Corps of Engineers, specialists, and German contractors. There was a lot of work to be done, repairing buildings, paving roads, and installing the necessary accoutrements of a military installation. Years later, Brigadier General Carl McIntosh recalled his arrival at Wildflecken with the 4th Infantry Division. "The best I can remember of Wildflecken was there had been displaced persons housed there . . . they had burnt down about half of the post and cut down all the trees around there just trying to stay warm . . . they nearly froze to death up there because there wasn't any heat, and nothing was supplied to them. So, we were building a road, setting up rock crushers and building ammunition pads . . . for the future needs of a post, camp or station there." With more than six hundred German workers on the site, living space ran short. Many lived in tents until summer, no doubt a miserable existence in the cold of the Rhön. There was also fun to be had, with contractors building canteens "staffed by husky, friendly German girls" who worked to keep laborers fed. As a Corps of Engineers inspector later wrote, "Naturally wherever troops were stationed near construction work these canteens became a favorite of the troops and caused both Commanding Officers and the Construction Engineers considerable headaches."[1]

For residents of the towns, particularly Reussendorf and Werberg on the grounds of the old base, the construction project must have looked ominous. What would happen next and what would that mean for a region already in flux? Between 1950 and 1953, Wildflecken took on an important role in the evolving Cold War order in Central Europe. In doing so, residents once more found themselves playing an unintended but critical part in debates going on far from its borders.

There was a tremendous disjuncture between the weight given to the refugee problem by the Americans and the West Germans. For the Americans, refugees were a peripheral issue, largely because they were by 1950 almost completely the responsibility of the West German state. For the Germans, refugees were a central plank of negotiations over the future of the American military presence in the country. The status and future of expellees and DPs merged with questions of sovereignty, national security, and the future of the Bonn Republic. For the expellee population and their native neighbors, the ensuing debates had a profound effect on the process of integration, giving these sometimes polarized groups common cause and forcing them to confront a new challenge as uneasy partners.

The stories of the end of the DP camp system, the creation of the American military presence, and the expellee problem in postwar Germany were functionally and symbolically intertwined. These linkages appeared most clearly in questions of space allocation. In Wildflecken and places like it across West Germany, the American presence shifted toward a long-term commitment after the outbreak of war in Korea. This policy shift added a decisive element to the zero-sum game over land. Previously, the contest was between DPs, locals, and expellees. One contender, the DPs, exerted influence far greater than their numbers because of the protection, albeit progressively more disinterested, of the United States. Now the United States entered the disputes over the Wildflecken facility as an active participant. In doing so, the Americans reminded locals and expellees of their enormous power in postwar Germany, a gesture many felt as deeply humiliating as West Germany assumed limited sovereignty in 1949. For many locals and expellees, the experiencing of resisting, however futilely, encroachment by "foreign" DPs and Americans enhanced and catalyzed the integration of expellee populations. If the expellee inhabitants of Reussendorf and Werberg did not become "German," expellees in the Rhön became "Werberger" and "Reussendorfer" just as those towns faced extinction.

The second crucial point here is that the Americans and the West Germans saw the debates over the building of a permanent American military presence in starkly different terms. The Americans were willing and able to negotiate exclusively through the federal government in Bonn. The West German government, on the other hand, was subject to a variety of pressures from its own constituent parts. Particularly in Bavaria, where regional particularism ran very high and doubts remained about the post-1949 political settlement, the government was able to skillfully deflect popular anger over American demands toward Bonn instead of the Bavarian government in Munich. Wildflecken, or the debate over space in which Wildflecken played a critical role, was one node in a much larger and more complex nexus of local, regional, national, and international interests. At the center of all of this sat thousands of refugees left to wonder what the future held for them.

The roots of Wildflecken's rebirth as an American base community lay in the halting steps taken and not taken by all of the concerned parties in the four years after the end of the war. The failure of the Lüttgen Plan and the gradual clearing of the IRO camp left Wildflecken in a state of suspended animation, stuck between stasis and transformation. As the upheavals of the Currency Reforms and the resumption of sovereignty subsided, many in the community held out hope that development, albeit slower and more incremental than the feverish dreams of the RPG, might still come to the Sinn Valley. The refugee problem remained critical. Whether in camps or clinging to tenuous existences in the towns, expellees remained apart even as more came across the border from Czechoslovakia and Soviet-dominated East Germany. As the 1940s came to a close, a new stability seemed to return to the Rhön and the Sinn Valley.

There were some considerable reasons for optimism in the hilly country of northern Franconia. After years of bitter disappointments, 1950 brought some relief in Wildflecken. The industrial credit plan of the Flüchtlingsverwaltung began to bring forth fruit for the first time. Industry across Bavaria, particularly firms that received expellee credits, made steady gains. In 1950, for the first time since the war, industrial production in Bavaria surpassed 1936 levels. During the next year, growth among expellee industrial concerns outpaced the broader industrial economy.[2] As the Landrat later recalled, "German authorities put tremendous effort into the task of making industry interested in our area."[3] In 1949, new industrial enterprises in and around Wildflecken employed more than five hundred workers. Most of these jobs were created in the former Muna, where hopes remained high that a modest industrial center might develop. Ten "expellee enterprises" (*Flüchtlingsbetriebe*) did business on former Wehrmacht property. The most successful of these, the Neustadt-based paper product manufacturer Paul & Co., remains in business as of 2011. The local press, with characteristic enthusiasm, boasted that "on the grounds of the former Wildflecken Muna, springs a new industrial city, Wildflecken on Kreuzberg. . . . here, there are no problems of unemployment."[4]

There were other hopeful signs as well. The area reorganized politically. Wildflecken retained its own mayor and public administration. Much of the surrounding countryside, including many of the expellees in the refugee towns and the Muna above received their own rights of self-government as Neuwildflecken. The new community now had its own mayor and its own municipal services. Importantly, this meant that the expellees living in the reorganized community had a much more distinct political voice than they did previously. This became increasingly evident in the events that followed as expellees emerged as leaders of the political resistance to threats from outside the district. Despite considerable logistical challenges, particularly for the widely spread and resource poor Neuwildflecken, the community could celebrate finally breaking from the legal status imposed on it by the building of the Wehrmacht base in the 1930s.[5] Expellee camp populations declined in the early 1950s, allowing the consolidation of expellees into three small facilities. The overall expellee population declined in relative and absolute terms, comprising about twenty-four percent of the overall Landkreis population.[6] National and international press came to Werberg in November 1950 to witness the presentation of a gift of twenty-six heifers to local farmers by the charity Heifer Project. While small farming continued to dominate the economy and transportation facilities did not improve, the postwar crisis in "Notstandsgebiet Rhön" appeared to be diminishing. As one local newspaper summed up matters at the end of 1951, there was "a lot going on in Wildflecken," much of it positive.[7]

Significant challenges remained. The demographics of the expellee population, which slanted significantly toward the elderly and those too young to work, continued to influence economic development. The case of Magdalene B. was an example of this. Magdalene, an expellee, arrived on a trainload of expellees in 1945 with her two children. Unable to secure employment in the wake of the war, she and her family lived in a camp under the care of the Bavarian state. By 1951, her children moved to Würzburg where the son was in school and the daughter in long-term medical care. By now, Magdalene was too old for factory work or training, so she appealed through the local Flüchtlingsamt for aid moving to Würzburg, where she pledged "not to be a burden to the public welfare."[8] Structural problems also inhibited development. Rental prices for industrial space in Wildflecken were about twice as high as those in nearby Hammelburg, probably owing to the relative paucity of credit in the poorer Landkreis Brückenau. Several firms, which moved in with great haste in the wake of the RPG fiasco, found the going too tough and backed out just as fast. The foremost challenge remained the Army and STEG's continued interest in the Wildflecken facility. STEG still controlled a number of properties on the Muna that might be exploited by local industry. Locals and the Munich government remained most concerned about the continued presence of the DP camp above the town. They badly wanted access to the buildings and grounds of the base, which seemed to offer answers to many of the most pressing infrastructure and economic problems of the area. In Munich, officials from the Economics Ministry and the Expellee Affairs Ministry openly discussed their frustration with the process:

> The Polenstadt is still occupied. The inventory and survey of the buildings like the one you propose cannot happen as long as access to the base is forbidden to us. After previous efforts, it seems certain that any industrial development of the Rhön that requires the occupation and habitation of the Polenstadt will not be economically viable. The enormous textile plan, which had this as a goal, was unable to accomplish it.[9]

The tenuous successes of the Wildflecken project mirrored larger trends within West German society in the year after the assumption of sovereignty. Camps for expellees closed or consolidated, although some remained open until the early 1960s. Despite widespread expellee unemployment (more than thirty-four percent in 1950) and continued housing problems, expellees began to integrate more successfully into the domestic economy at a time when it was primed for takeoff later in the decade. Rainer Schulze, in his study of Celle in Lower Saxony, argues that the early 1950s marked the period when "the native population came to regard the refugees, who had arrived as 'guests,' more and more as 'permanent residents.'"[10]

Both the West German government and the Americans made significant investments in resolving the expellee problem. The federal Housing Construction Law of 1950 (*Wohnungsbaugesetz*) pledged enormous public support for the construction aimed primarily at expellees. The Americans, working through the Economic Cooperation Administration (ECA), launched a series of programs to support expellee housing construction. Both of these initiatives stressed not only the need to build homes for expellees, but the pressing problem of expellees concentrated in rural areas where they were difficult to support, unevenly distributed between Länder, and far from jobs in urban centers where industry was beginning to re-emerge. Over the course of the next half-decade, the percentage of expellees living in refugee camps and as subtenants in apartments plunged by about fifty percent.[11] Increasingly, expellees became visible components of existing communities and proud inhabitants of their own towns.

New settlements inhabited by expellees were one of the most visible and publicized measures of integration. More than twenty such projects were underway at the end of 1950. The "refugee towns," like Werberg and Reussendorf, played an important role in that reimagining of the refugee population. These were projects that West Germans could be proud of, indications that the country could literally and figuratively be rebuilt from the moral and physical damage of the war. The *Main-Post*, assessing the growing phenomenon across Bavaria and West Germany, treated these communities as indicative of a heroic and dynamic spirit in the new Germany. "The towns and cities of the expellees, which now arise out of the rubble with their many productive and industrial facilities, stand to improve and enrich not only Bavaria, but to be a part of an export-driven economy for all of West Germany."[12] The inhabitants of the refugee towns in the Rhön were keenly aware that their fates and the question of what the Americans planned to do with the former Wehrmacht base were inseparable. As Anton Beck told Wildflecken's mayor and a delegation of expellee residents, "the self-sufficiency of Werberg and the entirety of the maneuver area remains up in air and this property belongs not to Germany but to the American army."[13]

The problem was that the future of the Wildflecken facility was just as up in the air for the Americans as it was for the Germans. Throughout this period, the Americans changed their minds about the future of Wildflecken on several occasions. As early as 1948, the Military Government informed local officials that they had approval from Washington to build a training facility on the grounds of the former Wehrmacht base above Wildflecken. However, these plans took pains to take into account the continued presence of DPs and the growing refugee towns. The initial plans came with severe restrictions, notably that both the DP camp and local settlements could not be disturbed. Since even the reduced DP camp monopolized most military buildings on the site, and since the communities like Werberg and Reussendorf sat squarely in the middle of the proposed maneuver grounds, these restrictions were simply untenable. A revised requisition order six months later dropped the provisions about the camp and refugee towns, but otherwise contained very little that suggested how the Americans would demarcate a future base.[14] Beginning in 1949, small numbers of American troops came to Wildflecken and began small-scale training exercises. This was not all that different from the kind of training that the Americans conducted informally during the early years of the occupation and did not arouse too much concern among locals. Since some of these exercises involved raids on the DP camp, many locals and the expellees in Reussendorf and Werberg welcomed the law and order that the Americans brought with them.

Since the American military presence in Germany was shrinking at the time, it seemed quite likely that the proposed base would never be needed, but the threat remained. The resulting status quo did not resolve any of the outstanding questions, but effectively postponed any sort of decision. The *Main-Post*, observing the flurry of activity, wondered about the future of the facility, since there was "as yet no indication" of what was to be done with it or those DPs who remained.¹⁵ The construction crews that went to work in the administrative heart of the old base occupied only a tiny percentage of the total land area. The fate of the surrounding communities hung on what the Americans eventually decided to do with the rest of it.

The local government viewed any formal American presence in the Rhön with some alarm. As early as the end of 1948, the district government registered its concerns with authorities in Munich. In a strongly worded letter, the Landrat urged Munich to resist further American encroachment. His reasoning had everything to do with the expellee problem. First, he claimed that any American base would displace 2,355 Germans living inside the old perimeter. Second, land requisitioned to build the Wehrmacht base rightfully belonged to farmers and was now being farmed again. In closing, the Landrat voiced the same threat so often made by local officials in the years between the war and the creation of a Cold War border state – the potential for such a move to radicalize the population and particularly the expellees:

> The population density here is dangerous. The absorption of those who might eventually be evacuated in the case of a[n] [American] confiscation is simply impossible. The very existence of this Landkreis would be threatened. The Landkreis sits very near to the boundary of the Eastern Zone of occupation. The mood among the population would be seriously influenced in the event of a land confiscation, or worse, the evacuation of the villages. And the terribly poor people here might through such actions become a growth medium for politically radical thoughts.¹⁶

Events half a world away during the summer of 1950 changed the situation dramatically. On June 6, North Korean troops poured across the border to the south. The American Resident Officer in nearby Hammelburg saw these fears reflected in a weekly report, assembled for him by the Landrat, on political opinion in the district. Even taking into account the biases of the conservative bureaucrat collating these reports, what emerges is a profoundly uneasy community uncomfortably close to the probable main line of attack. "The concern that the Korea model could have an impact on West Germany continues to be strong. The captions 'the Electrifying Victories of the North Koreans' reminds the Germans of similar headlines from a bygone age."¹⁷ Germans in 1950 were just five years removed from a devastating war and the experience of defeat and ruin.

Developments in Korea strongly influenced public opinion in West Germany, a fact starkly highlighted in surveys commissioned by the Office of the High Commissioner. In fall 1948, during the Berlin blockade, twenty-four percent of respondents indicated that they feared an internal or external military threat from Communism. Such anxieties decreased markedly with the end of the blockade and the march toward limited sovereignty. By June 1949, this number slipped to sixteen percent. In the wake of war in Korea, many in West Germany became convinced that war would return to Central Europe. A survey in December 1950 found thirty-four percent of West Germans believed that World War III was imminent. Of those surveyed, sixty-seven percent thought there was a "great" or "fairly great" chance that the Korean conflict would be repeated in West Germany.[18] This opinion shift proved critical in the events that followed. German civilians were not the only ones worried about the possibility of war in the region. The governments of the newly formed NATO alliance faced a series of difficult strategic choices to counter a real or potential Soviet threat. West Germany became a front-line state in the emerging Cold War order, a fact not lost on the population. Opponents of the continued Allied presence in that country had to be tempered in order to appear credible to a population that earnestly believed itself to be under threat. Nowhere was this truer than in the border area where the brunt of an assault would fall.

In light of the perceived threat of a Soviet invasion, the military situation of the United States in Germany looked exceedingly precarious. The American combat presence totaled little more than a single division, spread out across the country with a supply line running from Bremen/Bremerhaven south into the heart of central and southern Germany. A Soviet push could easily cut this line, which ran close to the border with the Soviet Zone. Strategically, it made sense to pull the bulk of the American presence westward into the French Zone, centering it in the Palatinate region while building a network of bases further east and south to slow down a Soviet invasion before it reached the key cities of western Germany. In practical terms, this reorientation involved the deployment of four additional American divisions to West Germany, chiefly to Hesse and Bavaria and bringing to total number of American personnel in the country from 120,000 to more than 300,000 by the end of 1952.[19] Throughout 1951, the increased American presence became far more visible across a wide swath of southern and western West Germany. The seven installations, including Wildflecken, that made up the Würzburg Military Post more than doubled in size from the beginning of 1950 until the end of 1951. These facilities housed 35,093 American soldiers and civilians, creating an enormous need for living space and training facilities.[20]

The war in Korea, and the possibility of hostilities in Europe, inspired West Germany's chancellor, Konrad Adenauer, to work toward increasing the country's voice in its own defense affairs while continuing his policy of binding it tightly within the Western alliance. American interest in West Germany extended beyond the military buildup. Now the Truman administration prepared to lift many of the remaining restrictions on German industry in order to support the rearmament of Western Europe and to begin serious consideration of West German rearmament as part of the NATO alliance. All of this meant considerably enhanced sovereignty for the Adenauer government.[21] In October, he created a special agency within the federal government headed by and named for his close ally Theodor Blank. The *Dienststelle Blank* (or *Amt Blank*) supervised West German cooperation with the western allies and served as a shadow Ministry of Defense. While far better known as the precursor to West German rearmament, Dienststelle Blank served a vital role in helping to negotiate the precise geography of West Germany's Cold War remilitarization.

The Allied occupation of Germany, followed by the transition to sovereignty, was shaped by negotiations over how to bear the space demands and the financial costs for the presence of foreign troops. As a West German state took form, it began to push back against some of these requirements. This resistance was in large part a function of domestic politics. German states, particularly those most materially affected by the occupation, complained that the Bonn Republic would not protect them. In Bavaria, this conflict became endemic and a serious challenge for the Adenauer government. Since the beginning of the occupation period, Germany was responsible for paying most of the costs of the Allied occupation. To the frustration of the Federal Republic's government and the individual states, this practice continued after 1949 with the proviso that such expenditures were now a contribution for mutual defense instead of an imposition on a defeated foe. Regardless, occupation and stationing costs took up an incredible thirty-five percent of the zonal and West German budgets. In 1950, this totaled about six hundred million DM per month, of which the United States received forty-six percent as the country with the largest military presence. From that sum, more than ninety-eight percent went to pay shared or American military costs.

As a result of this arrangement, and because there was little will in Washington to compel the American taxpayer to provide for the defense of West Germany, the bulk of the cost would be borne by West Germany. The United States, and particularly the Army Corps of Engineers, supervised construction, but most of the work and the financing came from German sources. In the emergency of 1950, a complicated system developed through which American officials found German contractors, supposedly through an open bidding process, then paid them in vouchers that could be redeemed through the German federal government for marks. This created a number of potential pitfalls. Lacking any real incentive to keep costs low, American military officials did not need to conduct truly fair bidding processes. Allegations of corruption dogged many projects. Even well-intentioned American and German managers ran into problems with language barriers and staff officers inexperienced in managing huge projects.

In addition to the possibility for misuse or incompetence, the process caused a budgeting nightmare for the West German state. The voucher system required that the federal government budget the entire cost of a project from its inception, even when the project would take years to complete and the costs accordingly spread over time. During the building boom, this meant huge sums budgeted but unspent each year. The opposition seized upon these unused pools of money as proof that Adenauer aimed to please the West more than he wanted to facilitate German recovery.[22] Just as important, for the Americans, was the question of how to time construction projects. After the resumption of semi-sovereignty in 1949, it seemed reasonable to assume that the occupation statutes would end or be radically altered at some point in the near future. Since such a change likely meant the end of West German payments for construction, EUCOM tended to spend German money generously while they still had access to it. Projects tended to commence even before any of the parties knew their final disposition.

Given the cost structure and the political implications of these limitations on West German sovereignty, the Adenauer government had to at least appear to push back on some issues, even if the results were a foregone conclusion. This became even trickier when basing questions involved Bavaria, a large state with a long tradition of independence and which often expressed suspicions of outside power. Despite a firm commitment to federalism in the 1949 Basic Law (*Grundgesetz*) of the Federal Republic, the Bavarian Landtag split badly over ratification. After a furious eighteen-hour debate, the body rejected the law 101–63. Finally, the main parties in parliament reached a compromise whereby Bavaria would recognize the Grundgesetz after two thirds of the other states did so.[23] The famous Bavarian "*Jein*" (yes/no) sent a clear message to Bonn that Bavaria would defend its sovereignty. Governed by a coalition of parties across the political spectrum, Bavaria could afford to resist against Bonn and Adenauer. Few issues brought these conflicts into clearer relief than that of the continued presence of American troops on Bavarian soil. If Adenauer hoped to use those troops to bind the new state into the western alliance, he risked the ire of Bavaria.

Debates about the presence of American facilities in Bavaria were not new, but the conditions under which they took place changed rapidly as the American strategic presence in the country and the issue of West German sovereignty transformed between 1947 and 1950. In 1947, the Americans opened the first training area at Grafenwöhr/Vilseck in the Upper Palatinate. This relatively small facility, originally a training area for the Royal Bavarian army, opened to help alleviate concerns about declining combat readiness among American troops on occupation duty.[24] However, its limited size meant that only small units could operate there. There was another problem. More than 1,000 civilians, both local and expellee, lived on the post. At the time, the local housing situation remained dire, so the Americans decided not to remove the refugee population but to temporarily house them in a small corner of the facility.[25]

Aerial view of the Wildflecken facility, 1950.
Courtesy National Archives, photo no. 345621/729.

A large permanent armored American force in West Germany required far more room to train. While EUCOM drew up plans as early as 1948 to utilize the Wildflecken facility, but little had come of it. Now, with quick progress a top priority, the Army revisited its plans for pre-existing Reichswehr and Wehrmacht facilities. Speed took clear priority over planning. EUCOM anticipated that it would need 113 facilities by the end of 1951. Between summer and the end of 1950, it requisitioned fifty-seven casernes across western Germany, among them the base at Wildflecken and parts of the surrounding industrial facilities. In January, construction units broke ground on a rehabilitation project there, chiefly intended to repair and winterize roads and buildings on the facility. By April, costs for the project ran to 5.46 million DM.[26] This is all the more remarkable because at the time, neither EUCOM nor the German government had any real idea what was to be done with the site.

The local press reacted to developments on the hill with uncertainty. Construction meant business and jobs, two things notably lacking in the recent history of the Rhön. The *Main-Post* reported that "a few buildings" on the site were to be converted for housing American troops and that "part of the former maneuver ground will be used for training." The wording here appears carefully chosen to avoid alarming locals, particularly those living on the grounds of the base. In any event, big construction firms from Würzburg and Bad Kissingen now worked on the hill and hired local workers for good wages. Moreover, nothing the Americans said answered perhaps the fundamental question on the minds of local observers: "There is no indication of what is to be done with the 8,000 DPs who currently reside there."[27] In a way that could never have been intended, the DPs acted as a sort of talisman. As long as they were there, locals reasoned, there was little reason to fear that the Americans might take possession of the whole facility.

At the same time that Germans and Americans confronted the question of what the future American military commitment in Germany might look like, the international community also confronted the issue of the remaining DPs. During the summer of 1950, the IRO began to wrap up its operations in Europe. About 150,000 DPs remained in the Federal Republic, approximately a third of them still in camps. Responsibility for their care and maintenance now fell to the federal government. Among other problems in this new arrangement, most of the remaining DPs stayed behind for reasons of age or health. They had few employment prospects and often could not afford to leave camps on the fixed stipend of thirty to forty DM per month.[28] Facing the closure of a number of IRO facilities and a persistent DP population, the Bundestag passed legislation a month later guaranteeing civil rights to those former DPs who had been in West Germany prior to mid-1950. This new category of *Heimatlose Ausländer* (stateless foreigner, hereafter HA) theoretically enjoyed protection from discrimination and the same rights as German citizens.[29] Across Bavaria, 117,538 people qualified, more than half of whom lived in or moved to rapidly industrializing Upper Bavaria. Lower Franconia was relatively lucky in this regard, with almost 4,000 HA and almost of quarter of them concentrated in Würzburg.[30] In Landkreis Brückenau, 688 people met the criteria to be HAs. The vast majority were Polish, but included Latvians, Hungarians, several holders of interwar Nansen passports, and a family of Spaniards. The IRO representative who met with the local government made it clear that, while his organization would continue to help the ex-DPs, they were now effectively the responsibility of German authorities.[31] Those authorities now had to give out IDs and register the HAs with the local employment office. For a district already facing chronic unemployment, this was not welcome news. The DPs of Wildflecken, who for years presented the single greatest stumbling block to the plans of their German neighbors, once again faced an uncertain future.

For the former DPs themselves, the impending closure of the camp meant an expedited process of finding new homes. Most of the remaining inhabitants had some reason why they had not already left. The Warsaw-born accountant Kazimierz G., his wife Juliana, and their adult son were good examples. They applied for emigration earlier, but were turned down. "Head looks sickly," wrote the inspector on their forms, "Makes poor impression. Head and wife overaged for mass schemes." In November 1950, they were moved to a Resettlement Camp for ex-DPs near Augsburg, where they were "transferred to the German economy." The lawyer and anti-repatriation firebrand Piotr L. and his wife also remained in the camp in fall 1950. They left the facility in September. Evidently determined to remain in the area, they sought housing first in Wildflecken, then in Brückenau.[32]

After all of the strife and confusion over the place, the end of the IRO camp at Wildflecken came very quickly. On December 28, 1950, American High Commission John McCloy contacted IRO and requested that the facility be turned over completely by mid-January, a deadline that the IRO pointedly noted they could not meet. A few days later, the first American troops arrived on the base, pitching tents and taking over a few unused buildings. DPs now shared the facility with American troops, who made it clear that they expected the camp to be cleared as soon as possible. The camp's population, now no more than a few hundred HAs, prepared to move out of the camp by the end of February. In the meantime, news of the camp's impending closure briefly fostered optimism among Bavarian refugee officials who still pushed to transfer IRO property into their care. The local expellee office hoped to transfer the population of the urban camp at Schweinfurt to Wildflecken and requested that the Ministry in Munich ask the Americans for "all, or at least part, of the Wildflecken camp to the custody of the Lower Franconian Refugee

Administration. The transfer of just a few buildings will help us to close one of the worst camps in Lower Franconia."[33]

At almost the same time, Kathryn Hulme and her partner Marie Louise Habets left Germany as well. They went to Arizona, where "after six winters in the *Götterdämmerung* fogs of Germany, we needed at least a year of sunshine to burn the mold out of our bodies."[34] Hulme sponsored Habets's application for residency in the U.S. Hulme resumed writing and, two years later, published *The Wild Place*. It won a $5,000 Atlantic Prize for nonfiction in 1952. Despite positive reviews, however, sales were middling. Eventually, the couple found a measure of financial security after the publication of *The Nun's Story* and the success of the film, which earned Audrey Hepburn an Academy Award nomination. They settled on Kauai where they lived the rest of their lives together. Hulme died in 1981 and Habets five years later. *The Wild Place* remained an extraordinary testament to a Polish town that no longer existed and a community now spread throughout the world.

For many of the remaining DPs, transfer to the care of German authorities meant trading one camp for another. By 1952, the Bavarian government ran twenty-four such facilities with 15,044 residents.[35] The remaining population of the Wildflecken DP camp transferred to the custody of the Bavarian government, which met them off the train in Munich on March 19 to take them to a temporary camp at Karlsfeld. Four days earlier, custody of the camp formally transferred from the IRO to the Army Corps of Engineers. Despite some indications that the Bavarians were not quite prepared to receive several hundred ex-DPs, the IRO officer in charge bade them farewell, concluding that "the group of people arriving from Wildflecken gave an impression of being a fine, well behaved and well disciplined group. I took quite some time explaining to the representatives of the group the circumstances under which the transfer had taken place and the temporary nature of their stay in this camp."[36]

Wildflecken's nearly six-year history as a DP camp came to end. By no means did this resolve the question of what it was to become. Nor did the closing of the DP camp settle the question of how to cope with the remaining DPs. At this point, federal and state governments began to negotiate the terms under which financing could be arranged for ex-

DP housing, an issue that swiftly got caught up in the larger problem of finding housing for expellees. When the West German government negotiated the terms of American base construction in the country, the problems of building homes and temporary quarters for locals, ex-DPs, and expellees who were to be made homeless in the process remained at the heart of discussions. In April, the Federal Housing Ministry announced the infusion of thirty million DM in Marshall Plan funds that would be used to build three hundred additional housing units, of which sixty-five percent were designated for expellees and thirty-five percent for former DPs.[37] A Bavarian government commission exploring expellee issues expressed concern that "the continuing influx of expellees and refugees together with the increasing number of kaserne evacuees [former DPs and expellees] is again boosting the housing shortage figure considerably."[38]

The Army announced plans to develop the former uniform and military equipment plant (HVA). The most prominent casualty of this move was the Siemens-Schuckert cable works, which employed 120 people. On behalf of the "poor people of Landkreis Brückenau," the Kreis government wrote to the Americans that the one-month warning received was "short and hard, the psychological impact on the population and the other firms now in the former Muna is quite large. *A binding declaration by the occupying power that the Muna will be closed to such requisitions is hereby requested.*"[39] The town government in Wildflecken was even more annoyed at the loss of the plant. Their protest again directly linked the DP and expellee issues, pointing out that the plant had been located on the HVA because more suitable buildings had been taken up by the DP camp.

> The community of Wildflecken, with 57 percent of its population expellees is one of the poorest in Lower Franconia if not in Bavaria. The people of Reussendorf and Werberg live off their limited agricultural income while those in the former military area of Muna are dependent on industrialization and industrial firms for their livelihood. The German government has worked hard for three years to provide these people with work and bread. This hard work succeeded when Siemens & Schuckert established an important plant here.... It is disastrous that we should lose these works through the actions of the occupying power.[40]

The American construction project at Wildflecken did far more than simply displace some of the new factories in the area. It continued and catalyzed the process of expellee integration that previously depended on the DPs as a motivating factor. The expanding American presence posed an existential threat to the survival of the refugee towns and many feared, with good cause, that a continued building program might force them off their small farms and out of their newly established communities. This threatened both expellees and locals alike and they responded accordingly. In earlier crises, like the leadership vacuum that developed after Oswald's arrest, expellees spoke out with their own voice through their own organizations. While locals often expressed solidarity with expellees, the newcomers remained politically distinct.

Now, facing a new threat, the farming communities of the upper Rhön sought to present a unified front. Any sign of American interest in the Wildflecken facility boded poorly for the farmers whose livelihoods depended on free access to the fields of the old maneuver area. In early 1950, a 120-person group calling itself the "Old, New, and Neighboring Settlers of Reussendorf" gathered to protest against continued American construction. Angry with crop damage and the loss of actual and potential industrial jobs, the group demanded that "no institution other than the Landessiedlung be given control over agriculturally productive Wehrmacht property" and that all such land be handed over to the Bavarian government for distribution.[41] Meetings like this, which became even more common as debates over American basing heated up, continued the process begun two years before during the political battles over the future of the DP camps. While integration still had many hurdles to clear, it grew increasingly obvious that, in places like Wildflecken, the problems of the expellees became the problems of all Germans, particularly when arrayed against an external actor like the U.S. military.

Perhaps unsurprisingly, no one expected Wildflecken to become a battleground in the contest over the American military presence in West Germany. The meeting above aroused some interest in Munich, although officials in the state Settlement Office concluded that "it would not be advantageous for the Prime Minister to intervene directly in this matter."[42] There was little immediate cause for alarm. The West German government clearly anticipated that the Americans would not hold on to Wildflecken, despite the construction efforts going on at the heart of the facility. In March 1951, the Border Control Agency (*Bundesgrenzschutz*) approached EUCOM about taking over the base. A report prepared for senior Border Control officials argued that Wildflecken would not be suitable for the Americans because it was too close to the border, too small to allow for the kinds of maneuvers the Americans wanted, and because "the weather is just too rough (*rauh*) for the Americans."[43]

In early 1951, the concerns of Wildflecken and its surrounding communities were still fairly local in scope. The Americans had a presence in the Rhön and the last DPs were clearly on their way out, even if the terms under which they might leave remained unclear. By mid-summer, the situation changed completely. Wildflecken became a *cause célèbre* both in Bavaria and more broadly, because it was embroiled in a multisided debate over the future of American basing in West Germany. The terms of this debate drew from the tumult of the few previous years. DPs, expellees, locals, and the bureaucracies that represented them once again confronted each other. This time they also faced an American military presence very much in transition as the Cold War moved into a new phase. Wildflecken entered this story as an afterthought and a compromise between competing interests. By the end, this tiny town and its even smaller neighbors became central to the story of the Cold War transformation of rural West Germany.

As the Americans moved quickly to identify, requisition, and clear space for bases after 1950, they ran headlong into the complex reality that many of the former Wehrmacht facilities that survived the war in any reasonable state of repair already housed sometimes large numbers of expellees. Bavarian expellee affairs officials sharply criticized American plans to requisition military facilities that housed expellees. They pointed to the experience of Nürnberg-Schweinau, where expellees threatened hunger strikes and resistance "with the last means at [their] disposal" in the face of American demands.[44] In the Lower Franconian capital of Würzburg, where more than forty-five percent of the 1950 population of 74,000 were born elsewhere, the Americans took an interest in the former airbase on the Galgenberg hill. When the war in Korea broke out, about 1,200 expellees, mostly Sudeten, lived in crowded barracks on the ridge.[45] In August 1950, American authorities ordered the base cleared to allow its conversion for use by U.S. forces. The conversion took a year, with most residents shipped to other camps in the area.[46] The

Galgenberg property was relatively small, the city was rapidly rebuilding and could absorb new workers, the last DPs (in this case Latvians) left several months before, and camps seemed to be at best a temporary expedient anyway. The logistical problems in places like Würzburg paled in comparison to those involving large rural bases now needed by the growing American presence.

To make matters worse, the enormous construction program begun by the West German state the year before to deal with the expellee problem ran into problems of its own. During its first year, more than 370,000 apartments were completed using a mixture of private and public capital, an astonishing figure that represented a sixty-four percent increase in yearly construction. While this success seemed to validate the program's approach, the outbreak of war in Korea caused a brief retrenchment of private investment, threatening the program's future.[47] At precisely the same time that the West German state faced a very real crisis in its ability to finance the construction of housing, the new NATO posture in West Germany threatened to make the entire problem worse by suddenly dispossessing substantial numbers of those whom the program intended to help. Subsequent negotiations over the scope of base building in West Germany must be understood in this light.

In mid-1950, EUCOM approached the Bonn government about identifying sites suitable for a new training area to complement the Grafenwöhr facility. The Adenauer government insisted that any such location be minimally disruptive to industry or existing populations. Bonn declared that the Americans' first choice, near Heilbronn on the Neckar River, would disrupt too many settled communities and was therefore unacceptable. In its place, Dienststelle Blank suggested either a spot in the Eiffel mountains or Wildflecken. EUCOM rejected both of these. The Eiffel was too mountainous and would in any case require delicate negotiations with the French who had already absorbed much of the new defensive posture into their occupation zone. Wildflecken was also unsuitable, at least according to Dienststelle Blank's account of the EUCOM negotiations, because it was "too close to the border with the Soviet Zone and posed a danger of an overshooting incident." The Americans countered with Hammelburg, not far from Wildflecken in Lower Franconia. It seems at least possible that EUCOM simply did not understand the consequences of such requisitions on German communities. The official history of the program, written just a few years later, refers to concerns about relocating "two or three entire villages" in each of the proposed locations. However, the Americans appeared only minimally aware that many of those living in the disputed areas were in fact expellees who only recently fled their homes in the East.[48]

Hammelburg was home to a large and growing community of expellees and one of the most important camps for those still coming across the border. American plans called for an expansion of the existing facility, imperiling the expellee settlements. Hammelburg's Landrat Kaiser argued that any American facility would imperil the newly developed industrial facilities near the town, displace more than 1,800 expellees, and threaten more than 3,000 jobs created in the area under expellee credit schemes. Apparently without consulting the Bavarian government, Dienststelle Blank responded affirmatively to the American request. When the news reached Munich on May 31, senior officials met immediately and decided to protest aggressively against the Hammelburg plan.[49] Almost immediately, Bavarian delegates in the Bundestag in Bonn charged that the Adenauer government was treating their state unfairly, recklessly allowing American base expansion there and undervaluing Bavarian land. One delegate anonymously told a Würzburg newspaper that it was "unimaginable that Bavaria should be asked to carry the entire burden of the growing American military presence in West Germany."[50]

The Americans announced their request for Hammelburg in a press release a few days later. This new "part of the Western Defense System" would, EUCOM argued, be minimally invasive for the German population:

> The proposed area was accepted after assurance by Bonn officials that its use would have a minimum impact upon the German population living there. According to the Minister of Agriculture for the Western Federal Republic the land is not considered good farmland. Germans living in the area will be resettled by the German government.[51]

Whatever assurances EUCOM had from Dienststelle Blank, the announcement did not go over well in Lower Franconia or Bavaria more broadly. It had political repercussions far beyond what EUCOM intended. The announced deal set off a multisided conflict between Bonn, Washington, Munich, and a cluster of small towns in northern Bavaria. It brought the issue of expellees and DPs briefly to fore in the German-American relationship and once again placed tiny Wildflecken at the center of events utterly beyond its control. Most important, this incident tested the limits of semi-sovereign West Germany in the face of the demands of its ally and occupier.

The fight over the Hammelburg facility, which burned most brightly during the summer of 1951, was an enormously complicated affair that had far more to do with sovereignty and national and Bavarian pride than it did with tangible issues of development and economic rationality. It pitted small farming communities and their political champions against each other and against their perceived antagonists in distant capitals. For those opposed to American base construction, the expellees made an ideal symbol for the injustices and humiliation of occupation. When the American Land Commissioner for Bavaria, George Shuster, gave a press conference about Hammelburg in early June, he did his cause few favors by blithely suggesting that the Bavarian government could apply for funds to help house anyone displaced by base construction. The *Münchner Merkur* titled its article about Shuster's statement, "Bonn Controls Bavarian Territory."[52]

The ferocity of the debate makes little sense outside of this context. Base construction, or the expansion of existing Wehrmacht facilities, meant jobs and the type of rural development that an earlier generation of regional leadership actively sought under the Nazi regime. The Wildflecken post, for example, employed 847 German civilians in various capacities.[53] Neither Hammelburg nor Wildflecken had particularly dense populations, and displacement involved at most a few hundred farmers and villagers. However, the symbolic importance of displacement, particularly for those already displaced once by the war, placed the question of American base acquisition at the center of much broader anxieties about the influence of "foreign" elements in the Franconian countryside. In practical and symbolic terms, complaints about DPs and the plight of German expellees now merged into a new debate about the anticipated presence of the U.S. Army in the area.

The Bavarian government moved quickly to try to head off the Hammelburg plan after they became aware of it. In a memorandum to the

Americans on June 4, the government reiterated the arguments that various Bavarian politicians made in the debates over the future of the IRO several years before. Bavaria suffered because it had "the highest number of former Wehrmacht facilities, which are now occupied by DPs and expellees, to clear." The DP issue and the expellee issue were identical, since both required massive investment in housing and infrastructure. "In addition to those DPs who must be moved out of casernes, many German refugees must be removed from them as well. Aside from the massive building costs, this will mean higher rents for expellees; in other words, social deterioration (*Schlechterstellung*)." Finally, the memorandum reminded American authorities of the "structural economic crisis in northern Franconia, which has been worsened by the arrival of expellees" and could best be managed through the development of meaningful industry in the region. These arguments, familiar from 1948, this time led to the conclusion that Hammelburg should be protected. On the other hand, Wildflecken might be a suitable substitute.[54] Hammelburg's Landrat Kaiser made a similar argument to the Dienststelle Blank, claiming that an American base at Wildflecken would relocate few if any expellees.[55] While it is unclear if he was being willfully obtuse or deceptive, he was certainly wrong. Regardless, for any number of influential Bavarian officials, Wildflecken became a palatable alternative to take the place of Hammelburg.

A few days later, the Bavarian State Secretary for Expellee Affairs Theodor Oberländer traveled to Bonn to meet with the Americans. Oberländer presented one of the most distasteful examples of continuity between pre- and postwar German nationalism. An enthusiastic Nazi who took part in Hitler's 1923 Beer Hall Putsch, Oberländer later became an influential "Eastern Researcher" (*Ostforscher*) who gave academic imprimatur to Nazi visions of a German East. During the war, army units that he advised took part in atrocities in the Soviet Union and he spent much of his long life defending his wartime actions.[56] By 1951, Oberländer already played an important part in organizing expellee political groups.

Oberländer presented the Bavarian government's position that Hammelburg contained too many expellees to countenance a base, with or without expansion. In its place, he suggested Wildflecken. "The clearing of the Wildflecken facility should result in the resettlement of only about 400 people out of the coffers of the Bavarian state. If the Americans ignore this appeal, I can see no other way to stop the confiscation of Hammelburg," Oberländer told the *Süddeutsche Zeitung*.[57] The *Münchner Merkur* applauded the move. The *Merkur*'s coverage was notable both for its extraordinary invective and for the renewed and explicit connection it made between the DP problem and the expellee issue in Bavaria. It suggested that a base at Wildflecken would be minimally invasive, could take advantage of all the amenities built by the Wehrmacht during the construction program of the 1930s, and would displace far fewer people:

> There is only one problem – it is still occupied by DPs. And that tips the scales for the six [American] generals who make the decision. Apparently it is easier today, six years after the war, to add 20,000 expellees to the millions who have lost their homes than it is to solve the DP question. Evacuating 10,000 DPs from Wildflecken was the task of the occupation authorities. Kicking 21,000 Germans out their homes – that task falls to the Bavarian government. The American generals happily take the path of least resistance.
>
> For years Wildflecken has been one of the most important centers for smuggling cigarettes and coffee. The day Wildflecken, which the Poles call "Durzyn," becomes an American maneuver area, three groups will be helped: the Hammelburger who will not be made homeless, the displaced, who won't have to keep living a hopeless existence in camps, and the public good, which will be saved from this smuggling center.[58]

The government in Brückenau reacted furiously to the letter. In their response, Kreis officials pointed to the continuing material deprivation in the Wildflecken area and that a requisition of the base would displace ten villages whose population was more than half expellee. This was something of an exaggeration, but highlights how central expellees were in the claims of local communities. But Landrat Baus reserved his greatest indignation for the suggestion that Wildflecken was the center of a smuggling enterprise. "Coffee and cigarettes will no longer be smuggled by DPs from Wildflecken, since they all left four months ago. A 'smuggling center' is no longer there to be dissolved."[59]

The fight over the construction of an American base pitted practical considerations against political realities and the genuine plight of the expellee population. Since it would be impossible for the Americans to find a site in Franconia that was free of expellees, the debate came to center on the brutal calculus of numbers. Here the defenders of Hammelburg had facts on their side. While Wildflecken managed to attract a few factories like Paul & Co., the disastrous failure of the RPG now had serious consequences for the town. Just as important, the farmers of Hammelburg found a champion who would protect them against American encroachment, a woman they now took to calling "Mother" – Maria Probst.[60]

Probst now stepped back into the fight over expellee rights from which she emerged a few years earlier. At a meeting with McCloy in June, she castigated the Americans and the West German government for focusing their attention on Bavaria. Since a small part of the Wildflecken base lay inside the neighboring state of Hesse, at least Wildflecken reflected something more of a compromise. Bavaria, she told McCloy, took in 777,000 more expellees than other state in West Germany, and yet the bulk of those properties to be requisitioned under the new American scheme lay in the state. "Bavaria is, from any perspective, the most directly affected [of the Bundesländer]."[61]

Probst and other Franconian conservatives assailed the Hammelburg idea as an affront to the rights of West Germany's citizens and as an unlawful extension of the American occupation. At a meeting with Ludwig Erhard, Oberländer, and various federal ministries in Bonn, Probst declared that "it must be made clear to the Americans what the repercussions of these requisitions will be. The Americans must choose their maneuver areas in such a way as to spare German territory." To another newspaper, she spoke somewhat more bluntly. "No German consent to Project Hammelburg!"

The Bavarian government hurried to express its opposition to the plan in order to blunt or redirect public anger. The question of the American base at Hammelburg quickly became the debates on the floor of the Bavarian parliament. Wilhelm Hoegner, the once (and future) prime minister, then serving as deputy prime minister and interior minister, took the floor on July 11 to attack both the Americans and the government in Bonn. Hoegner told the deputies that the government knew about American plans for building a maneuver area, but they had not been consulted about Hammelburg before the announcement a few days prior. "It is clear," Hoegner declared, "that without the understanding of the Bavarian government or Bavarian civil authorities, Bavarian territory has been negotiated over and the matter will soon be settled." Amid cries of "unbelievable!" from the delegates, he concluded his remarks by telling his listeners that "as far as this government is concerned, it is clear that any construction of a maneuver area will create victims. It is and has been [our] goal to limit the victimization of the Bavarian people to an absolute minimum."[62] The Landtag Constitutional Committee unanimously approved a motion put forward by the nationalist *Bayernpartei* that "competent local authorities be soon enough informed of the intended requisition of real estate and buildings for the occupation power."[63]

The political consequences of the Hammelburg/Wildflecken debate expanded considerably with the involvement of Bavarian legislators like Probst. CSU delegates from the region began making ominous noises about pulling out of the governing coalition in Bavaria. Since they were unlikely to move toward the Social Democrats or other parties of the left, there was a very real possibility that parties further to the right might benefit from the disintegration of intra-party consensus.[64] Matters reached the point that Ludwig Erhard, Adenauer's powerful finance minister, met personally with McCloy to see if anything could be done.

The Hammelburg affair quickly became an embarrassment for the American High Commission. A transcript of a senior staff conference at HICOG headquarters suggests how unprepared the Americans were for Bavarian reactions and how uncertain they were about how to work with the West German government. Bavarian Land Commissioner George Schuster called the debate "the most important matter of government in Bavaria" at the time. He conceded that Bonn had simply informed Munich about American plans for Hammelburg. McCloy's deputy, General George Hayes, told the other attendees that he tried to warn Theodor Blank that there would be "trouble" in Bavaria, but Blank rebuffed him. Schuster expressed incredulity that "Nobody talked to [Ehard]? It was delivered on his doorstep?" Hayes replied only that "I told him we have got to have the area."[65]

The invective coming from Munich over the Hammelburg plan echoed an equally vocal opposition in the countryside. The language of Probst and her allies found avid listeners in rural Franconia. For many living in region, both expellee and local, the greatest problem with the plan was its suddenness and the sense that they lacked any input into the future of their land. As a local newspaper reported, "The news from ... Theo Blank, that Hammelburg is to be used as a training area for a new US Division came like a bolt from the blue [*Wie ein Blitz aus heiterem Himmel*]. Since then there have been protests and resolutions. There have been speeches and negotiations. Yet still the spectre of the now-awaited confiscation is not averted."[66] Probst's ally, Bishop Julius of Würzburg, hinted rather darkly that "in these villages one now finds agitation against the state and the government." Or, in the words of the *Münchner Merkur*, "a feeling like the Peasants' Wars reigns in Lower Franconia."[67]

The expellees living in Hammelburg, speaking both as a community and through their political champions, expressed what they saw as a direct linkage between their previous experience of dispossession and the present threat. In early June, large protest rallies began in and around Hammelburg. A meeting in Gauaschach, attended by more than 3,000 farmers, appealed to Bonn in the name of the new Basic Law. "We expellees, who have already been forced from house and farm, must remind you that there is a Right to a Homeland [*Recht auf Heimat*] upon which the Bavarian and Federal constitutions are anchored."[68] The next day, a meeting in Wülfershausen produced a similar document:

> We feel it is our duty to make it clear that our moral strength to make a new life under circumstances that we did not understand ... is at an end. We call therefore on all those politicians and the relevant offices of the American occupation authority responsible for this terrible fate – the loss of home and farm in a newly won *Heimat* – to relieve the afflicted population and seek another solution.[69]

The press readily picked up on this rhetoric, highlighting what they considered the double victimization of expellees. "Expellee settlers will be forced to leave their homes for the second time in their lives," reported the *Süddeutsche Zeitung* in August.[70]

The Hammelburg debate also drew on pre-existing fears of political radicalization among expellees and local residents alike. HICOG Political Advisor Helmut Penzel lamented that the KPD "is making the best of this situation."[71] When two KPD "agitators" were arrested in a rural area near Hammelburg, the local press emphasized that they were not locals but came from Munich and the Rhineland. Fearing that association with Communism might dampen public support for their cause, farmers made sure to explicitly distance themselves from the KPD. At a large rally in Hammelburg's Market Square, a rural priest reiterated the fiery rhetoric of the farmers. "We want no other land and soil, whether in Franconia or not. We will stay in our *Heimat,* from which none of us will move." All around him, farmers carried banners proclaiming "We Won't Let Bonn Sell Us." But at the center of the demonstration, larger than the others, was a sign proclaiming "Communists Not Wanted."[72] This sentiment was not just reflected in the streets. The deepening Cold War and the crisis in Korea effectively demolished the KPD's traditional support in the Rhön region. In Landtag elections a few months earlier, the party polled a miserable 0.8 percent in Hammelburg and Brückenau.[73] Not only did expellees reject the KPD's program, but even those who had resumed their support for the party after the war now turned away from it.

If the protesters fought hard to avoid the Communist label, they did not tone down their radical language. It played well in the German press, which found a great story in the narrative of plucky farmers and determined expellees facing down the American military and the Bonn government. A story in the *Süddeutsche Zeitung,* titled "Hammelburg Bravely Defends its Soil" reported ominous talk of sabotage and resistance. The mayor of Wasserlosen told the reporter that "no cannon will fire and no tanks will tear up our fields as long as we hunker down in our farmyards. They can only force us [off] with violence, and they won't shoot at us."[74] The Americans were concerned enough about the Hammelburg affair that McCloy himself wrote to the mayor of Gauaschach, urging him to consider the wider implications of the basing dispute. "While I regret that I have the necessity to move some people against their will, people must bear some inconveniences [*Unannehmlichkeiten*] not only for Germany, but for the whole free world."[75]

By the last week of July, the Hammelburg plan was moribund. At the weekly staff conference on July 24, HICOG leadership talked about what had gone wrong. Schuster told his colleagues that negotiations with Bavarian lawmakers left the Bavarians feeling that their voices had at least been heard. Or, as Schuster phrased it, that "turkey had been talked without any dressing or skin on it.... I think it did a lot of good to talk to them." High Commissioner McCloy told his staff that he met with Maria Probst, to which Schuster replied sardonically that "what bothers Madam Probst is that Hammburg [sic] Refugee Settlement. She thinks that [the American base] could be put somewhere else. At least from Madam Probst's point of view, the world would not be as gloomy a place as it is now."⁷⁶ The Americans had learned a valuable lesson: the Bavarians, and particularly the formidable Dr. Probst, could make a great deal of trouble if they felt excluded from negotiations.

At the beginning of August, the Americans announced a retreat from the Hammelburg plan. EUCOM's headquarters in Heidelberg announced that it "accepted the opposition of the Federal Government and the Bavarian state government and waived its rights in the matter." Instead, the Americans announced the construction of a division-sized training facility at Hohenfels just north of Regensburg and not far from the Czechoslovak border.⁷⁷ Like Wildflecken and Hammelburg, the Hohenfels facility took advantage of an existing German base built in the 1930s. The Bavarian government estimated that the displacement affected about 450 families, most of whom could be relocated to emerging Bavarian industrial centers like Nürnberg or Ingolstadt or to the new state of North Rhine-Westphalia where expellees might hope to find work in urban areas. This number turned out to be somewhat exaggerated. In the end, only about 270 farms needed to be relocated. Despite some protests in the area, the move proceeded swiftly. By October, American troops moved onto the facility, displacing a number of German and expellee farmers. The facility expanded from 28,000 to 40,000 acres and a four-year construction program began to provide permanent facilities for training.⁷⁸ For the moment, the issue of American training areas in Bavaria appeared to be resolved.

Probst celebrated what she called "a victory of democracy over the administration." She blasted the Dienststelle Blank and, by extension, the Adenauer government for its unwillingness to include Bavarian and local officials in the initial negotiations. Repeatedly, the Bavarian government made the case that they were helpless in the matter of American requisitioning. Minister President Ehard claimed that Bavaria "had no choice in the matter." HICOG's Public Affairs Division concluded that Bavarian politicians successfully convinced the press to hold "the Bonn government rather than the US Army at fault."⁷⁹ Probst and Ehard managed the impossible. They convinced their constituents that they supported the defense of West Germany but not the violation of Bavarian sovereignty at the hands of Bonn.

Probst was not the only national politician to openly rejoice at the end of the Hammelburg expansion. The newly formed Block of Expellees and Dispossessed (*Block der Heimatvertriebenen und Entrechteten*, BHE), keenly interested in mobilizing rural expellees in Bavaria, took an interest in the matter. Its controversial founder, Waldemar Kraft wrote to McCloy, criticizing the plan and praising its abandonment. Kraft, a former SS officer linked to war crimes in Eastern Europe, was at the height of his influence following the recent electoral successes of his party in state elections. A fierce critic of the Adenauer government, Kraft and the BHE represented the apparent danger of right-wing radicalization among expellees. For those who claimed to speak for expellees, the base issue was a perfect wedge that could join expellee concerns with broader national debates over West Germany's Cold War future.[80]

Politically, the rush to build bases drove a widening rift between German authorities and their respective constituencies. Of course, the farmers in the Hohenfels area were none too pleased with the outcome. A group of farmers from Hohenfels demonstrated in front of the Bavarian parliament in Munich, led by a representative of the nationalist Bayernpartei. He asked the crowd if "the argument that the confiscation of Hohenfels as opposed to Hammelburg is the lesser evil begs the question of whether Hohenfelser are lesser people than Hammelburger?" A group of the assembled farmers, some of whom claimed to be returned POWs shouted that they had been "forced to stay in Russia" and now felt that they had the right to demand that they remain on their land.[81]

For many in the Wildflecken area, the Hammelburg debate highlighted how exposed the community might be if the Americans decided to build nearby. A farmer whose land lay in the middle of the training area wrote to the Federal Ministry for Expellees, summing up the fears of many: "I have been informed that the territory around Hammelburg will not be seized, but rather the area near Hohenfels. Where does this leave Hammelburg, and where does it leave the Truppenübungsplatz Wildflecken, where I have my farm?"[82]

In mid-1951, the first stage of construction at Wildflecken was complete. While the Wildflecken facility played a role in the Hammelburg dispute, its clear limitations as a training area prevented it from really being a viable option for American planners. Hohenfels could service an entire division, while Wildflecken was suitable for regiment-level training. The newly commenced construction project at Hohenfels anticipated space for 17,000 soldiers, a railway line, and thirty-two firing ranges. Wildflecken could hold at most 5,000 men and ran the very real risk of stray rounds coming close to the border. Nonetheless, in November 1951, EUCOM announced that it was seeking to requisition the entire Wildflecken facility. In fact, the Americans made it clear that they would seek to expand the base to make it more suitable for training. Even to the Army's official historians, the reasoning for the renewed interest in Wildflecken seems to have been obscure. In a study of base construction published just two years later, the authors phlegmatically noted that, in the wake of the Hohenfels decision, "the old Wehrmacht training area at Wildflecken, which had been disapproved for use ... could be used after all, so it too was requisitioned."[83] McCloy wrote personally to Theodor Blank, noting that EUCOM had been "willing to make [a] last minute change" in the negotiations over Hammelburg and now expected prompt cooperation. "EUCOM fe[els] that the German government should be willing to assist them in clearing up another training area."[84]

Despite protests against the previous Wildflecken proposal and base construction in general, most observers had to acknowledge that such projects could bring considerable benefit to nearby communities. After the disappointments of the past year, local political leaders realized that the base also provided opportunities to accomplish some of the goals on which they had nearly given up; construction projects around the base generated at least eight hundred jobs, ranging from manual labor to positions for skilled craftsmen and highly-valued workers with English-language backgrounds.[85] When the commander of the new Sub-Post, Lt. Colonel Gus Schlitzkus, informed the mayor in July 1951 that the growing need for civilian labor at the base "will require an estimated two hundred additional apartments in the vicinity," this provided a chance to petition for federal help to the meet the needs of the occupiers. At the same time, building apartments for base workers could also solve some of the pressing housing shortages in the area. Just two days after Schlitzkus's memo, the president of Lower Franconia wrote to the Bavarian Ministry of the Economy, lamenting the lack of clear direction as to the fate of local expellees but suggesting that at least some of them could find employment with the Americans.[86]

Living space was at a premium, with funding for additional construction limited and tied up in another project directly linked to the issue of American base expansion; the DPs. With the impending closure of remaining IRO facilities, Land governments had to scramble to build homes for refugees unable or unwilling to go elsewhere. In Bavaria, an initial budget of thirty million DM proved insufficient. In July, with debates about Wildflecken's future very much in process, the state added fifteen million DM to the projected expense of a project whose costs now threatened to spiral out of control. For the Bavarian government, once again the questions of how to deal with DPs and expellees merged. But this time, there was a common solution. Money was still available through funds from the Marshall Plan begun in 1948. Initially intended to help fund construction for homes intended for former-DPs, such funds, the Americans now made clear, could also be used to build apartments for those threatened with displacement by American base construction. By summer 1951, Bavaria treated the two programs as essentially one, estimating that it needed temporary and later permanent accommodation for 5,300 DPs and expellees directly affected by the base clearance program. While most of these would need temporary housing, 67,000,000 DM would be needed to build more than thirty apartment complexes across the state to eventually house the displaced.[87]

New housing and jobs associated with it were not the only benefits anticipated in the expansion of the Wildflecken base. Despite the pride and defiance of area farmers, many realized that lives spent working the thin soil of the Rhön would not likely lead to prosperity or even security. Georg S., the Pommeranian civic leader in Werberg, met with Beck, Oberländer, and several other senior officials in Würzburg during the Wildflecken negotiations. Georg bluntly told those assembled that he and many other local farmers had no problem leaving their farms, provided that they received adequate compensation and assistance relocating to places where they could find industrial jobs.[88]

For Georg, other expellees, and locals, the question of where the boundary lines of the new American base might fall remained foremost in their minds. Significantly, Georg was an expellee who spoke on behalf of the whole community, not just in Werberg but in nearby Reussendorf as well. Writing on behalf of the Settler's Committee of Werberg, Georg reminded the state secretary that "the expellee settlers believed themselves to have found a durable existence here now find that they, despite their hard work and deprivation and the useless intervention of public authorities, now stand on brink of the abyss." At the same time, the citizens of Reussendorf also deputized him to speak on their behalf. "The matter of Reussendorf concerns both expellees and locals [Heimatvertriebene und Einheimische]. The original farmers were compensated for the confiscation of their land for the Maneuver Area in 1938 by German authorities. After the collapse of 1945 and the departure of the Wehrmacht and its civilian workers, the locals rebuilt Reussendorf and worked with all of their strength to carve out a new existence."[89]

For the residents of the Wildflecken area, particularly the farmers of Reussendorf and Werberg, the coming months brought a series of agonizing waits punctuated by either relief or disappointment. Successive maps in the archives highlight the wrangling over property. Reussendorf, deep inside the old Wehrmacht grounds, could not survive American use of the area. Werberg, close to the edge, had a somewhat greater chance. As the perimeter of the requisitioned zone pushed to the south and east, the refugee towns seemed very much imperiled. In December, Bavarian Prime Minister Hans Ehard wrote to the American land commissioner, the historian Oron Hale, to urge the Americans to clarify their position on the Wildflecken facility's boundaries as soon as possible.

> The Wildflecken Maneuver Area is a source of great concern to the Bavarian government. Conversations between local German officials and representatives of the Würzburg Military Post have repeatedly suggested that an expansion of the territory in use is necessarily imminent.... The Bavarian government does not argue with the necessity of securing troop training space for the US Army. In the case of Wildflecken, this situation is creating considerable uncertainty among people in the surrounding communities who fear that the territory lost will grow. This fear is hindering the development of critical industry and above all the development of ... the industrial and residential areas [in the] former Muna.[90]

As they did two years before when they feared that confiscation might take place, the people of Reussendorf met to protest against what they saw as ill treatment by their own government. This time they couched their appeal not by directly identifying themselves as expellees, but by making it very clear that they were now suffering expulsion for a second time in less than a decade. "We the inhabitants of Reussendorf are watching the impending unsettling of our village with dread. While we do not want to deny the need to meet the military needs of the Occupying Power, free people can suffer no worse fate than to be expelled from their homeland [als von seiner Heimat vertrieben zu werden]."[91] The word choice here was very important. *Vertreibung* referred explicitly to the postwar experience of ethnic Germans in Eastern Europe. The message being sent was quite clear: American plans for base construction and the German authorities who abetted such plans were no better than the Communist regimes that supposedly threw Germans out of their homelands a few years before.

The peripatetic Maria Probst now appeared again, this time in defense of the expellee and local farmers of Werberg and Reussendorf. In April, she organized a meeting at the tavern owned by former POW Volker M. in Wildflecken. Buses brought villagers in from the surrounding communities and various local notables spoke against the American plan. A number of newspapers sent reporters, one of whom described the mood as "tense, not remarkable given the uncertainty and suspense that hangs over the inhabitants here." While Probst's remarks do not survive, Mayor Lambert of Neuwildflecken expressed anger over the lack of answers or impending solutions: "General Futch says that no one will be turned out in the street, yet winter has come and gone and we still have no houses. What will happen to the people of Reussendorf or the HVA? Already there are American barriers across the Werberg farmers' fields and they are no longer viable."[92]

Two months later, Probst met with American High Commissioner John McCloy in Bad Godesburg to continue pressing the case for abandoning the proposed expansion of Wildflecken. Along with representatives of the Bavarian government, the U.S. Army, and the High Commission, the delegates released a statement to the press asserting that the question of a new maneuver area for the Americans "had been fully analyzed. This proposal has been negotiated over by the Dienststelle Blank in conjunction with the Bavarian government." The meeting protocols suggest a far more interesting discussion. McCloy acknowledged that, as was widely known, Wildflecken was never the first choice of the

Americans. The East German border was too close, the climate too bad, and the level of infrastructure too limited. Probst continued along a line of argument she had used for three years. Bavaria had "770,000 expellees too many" in comparison with other states. Just as she argued that the closing of IRO facilities unfairly punished Bavaria, she now made the case that "of 54 soon-to-be-requisitioned casernes, 28 are in Bavaria. Any way you look at it, Bavaria is the worst affected." In place of Wildflecken, she suggested Bad Orb, on the northern slope of the Spessart hills and safely across the border in Hesse. Before the meeting concluded, McCloy personally assured Probst of his great admiration for her work in the Hammelburg debate. She won the respect of many in the American high command with her brusk and businesslike demeanor and, echoing her own words, McCloy parted by telling Probst that "doubtless the decision in the Hammelburg matter really was a victory for democracy."[93]

Negotiations over the base proved long and tedious, though certainly not for the inhabitants of the threatened settlements. While successive American proposals shifted the southwest boundary of the maneuver area little by little, local farmers protested that any expansion of the base would cut them off from their fields. A series of public meetings in Wildflecken saw locals pour out their anger and frustration as Probst and Landrat Baus tried to convince them that they were doing everything they could "to reach a solution acceptable to everyone."[94] Clearly, no such solution existed. Someone had to lose in the contest of maps. The Americans finally released their map of the new Maneuver Area during the first week of May 1952.[95] Reussendorf fell entirely within the new base area. Its sixty-seven families had to move as soon as possible. Several other smaller communities faced the same fate. Werberg avoided total confiscation, but only just. Of its thirty-five working farms, twenty lost all or much of their acreage.[96] The farmers and would-be industrial workers who resettled the community five years before could remain, but lose a considerable amount of farmland. Furthermore, they now lived right on the edge of an active military facility in which armor and artillery would be in regular use. For many in Wildflecken, the long-feared disaster had now come to pass.

Now local government and the Bavarian state faced the task of moving significant communities of farmers off the land and finding them adequate housing either in the surrounding community or elsewhere in

West Germany. Once again, the DP crisis and the problems of the expellees intersected. The great construction program that had been going on for several years offered the best possible solution. As soon as the American plans were formally announced, regional government officials began to survey the population of the soon-to-be-displaced villages in an effort to ascertain where people hoped to go. The first of these, which talked to 115 heads of household, found that a surprising number wanted to stay in the Wildflecken area. Fifty hoped to move into the grounds of the former Muna, while many of the others expressed a desire to move elsewhere in the Federal Republic. Of those who named a specific place, most wanted to move to the Frankfurt area in the hope of finding work. One enterprising respondent simply asked to be put in a hotel room somewhere in Germany to live out his days. One early estimate suggested that the base clearance required the construction of at least 190 living quarters for those about to be displaced.[97]

In late spring and early summer, letters bounced back and forth between Brückenau, Munich, and Bonn trying to arrange for housing for those about to lose their homes. By August, the Bavarian Ministry of Finance and the Federal ministry agreed to finance the construction of eighty-seven housing units, the majority of which were to be built in Wildflecken or Neuwildflecken. In addition, eighteen would be built in nearby Schweinfurt and a further eight across the border in Hesse.[98] At the same time, bureaucrats in all three places tried to estimate how much the relocation effort would cost. Estimates turned out to be no more than guesses as moving costs skyrocketed and disputes began over what constituted moveable property and how much villagers could claim for improvements and crops. Furthermore, it was clear to all that the new living quarters would not be ready for the evacuation scheduled for later that summer. In desperation, the *Oberfinanzdirektion* in Nürnberg suggested housing the villagers in camps and temporary structures built for former DPs.[99]

During the summer, preparations for evacuation began in earnest. In total, 957 people faced removal from the grounds of the Wildflecken base. Nearly half were expellees, the rest roughly divided equally between locals and former DPs.[100] Cost estimates for the project varied widely, in large part because no one knew how complex an operation the removal would entail. Church property had to be removed, as did movable items and equipment. Farmers were to receive money for crops left un-harvested in the field as well as reimbursement for capital improvements made since the war. Georg S. requested 4,318 DM in compensation for his harvest. Before moving to Hainhausen with her family, the Reussendorf widow Anna M., who previously lost her farm in Altglasshütten, petitioned for 3,200 DM for improvements and the forced sale of her animals and agricultural equipment.[101] Erich M., the proprietor of the "Schmelzhof" farm, filed a series of requests to be allowed to keep his fodder and construction material on the farm, with the hope of picking it up later and using it to build a new home in the nearby village of Kothen. After a year of delay, his request was denied without explanation.[102] Michael P. was somewhat more fortunate. An expellee from Romania, Michael, his wife, and their young daughter lived on the American base where he worked as a laborer. He hoped to find work in Frankfurt and sought compensation for his furniture, three chickens, and a motorbike.[103] By March, the cost of moving all of the families off the base grounds exceeded 400,000 DM.[104]

German authorities continually protested that they were simply not going to be ready to deal with evacuees from the region. HICOG and the Dienststelle Blank sent a series of frustrated notes back and forth. In June, a clearly irritated HICOG official wrote to Theodor Blank that "EUCOM cannot accept entirely the reasoning that construction has only recently started in the Muna and Neuwildflecken areas."[105] Despite German protestations, the project would go forward. In August 1952, the second evacuation of Maneuver Area Wildflecken began. In small groups, families relocated from the town to transit camps or into Neuwildflecken. The *Main-Post* on this occasion lamented that

> these expellees [*Neubürger*] will be resettled across the Main region. It is a difficult exit from this place, that became a *Heimat* after their expulsion and from the people who stood by their side in the first hard months. There can be few towns in the Federal Republic that have as remarkable history – so full of change, sorrow and upheaval, as Reussendorf on the grounds of Truppenübungsplatz Wildflecken.[106]

Many of Reussendorf's residents had cause to agree with that assessment. Most ended up in transit camps, ostensibly temporarily but with no immediate end in sight. In September, a committee of Reussendorfers wrote to the Federal Ministry for Refugees to complain about being housed in the Forchheim camp north of Nürnberg. Their grievances included being forced into an "uncertain future" and being lied to by the state about provisions made for their care:

> Because we have had to leave our homes and work under higher order, we demand a one-time payment for our loss of Heimat. That is, if we are ruled by law or what passes for it ... We demand an indication if this will happen, since we have already vegetated here for eight long weeks.[107]

Yet again, those displaced by the Wildflecken project found their champion in Maria Probst. The Bundestag delegate attacked Finance Ministry *Staatssekretär* Alfred Hartmann for what she believed to be the government's neglect of those resettled not just from Wildflecken, but also from areas around Schweinfurt, Ansbach, Landshut, and Augsburg. "Is the government not clearly aware," she pointedly asked, "that because of these delays settlers have been affected, made to remain in uncomfortable temporary quarters for another year while their agricultural assets lose value?" The Staatssekretär protested that the Bavarian state itself bore considerable financial responsibility for resettlement cost and should not pin blame solely on Bonn. Probst, however, made her point. For her constituents in rural Franconia, responsibility for the trauma of displacement in the face of American power rested firmly outside of Bavaria's borders. Wildflecken played an outsized role in the national political debate over West Germany's relationship with the American military. While this came to an end with the final resolution of the base construction issue in late 1952, Bavarian politicians like Probst successfully managed to insert the story of Wildflecken's residents and doubly dispossessed expellees into the broader problem of creating a workable federal state in postwar West Germany.[108]

Meanwhile, construction in Neuwildflecken moved with agonizing slowness. Despite help from the Americans, the arrival of fall and winter delayed construction badly. Cold temperatures and blowing snow brought efforts to a complete halt, and it became clear that the planned-for completion of the new apartment blocks in Neuwildflecken would not happen by the December deadline. However, by October 1952, just as the cold rains of another Central European autumn arrived, the new town was passably ready. Despite the lack of a school or town hall, sixty new homes had been completed in Neuwildflecken, cause for a public celebration.[109] Such festivities were increasingly common events in a country going through the early stages of an astounding economic transformation. For the citizens of Neuwildflecken, this was a transformative event, creating a new community in the shadow of an occupying army. Neuwildflecken's new inhabitants did not intend to let anyone forget that they had come a long way to reach the Rhön, or that they saw themselves as victims of not one but two expulsions. Almost one hundred Neuwildfleckener staged a photo exhibition to accompany the celebration. Titled "Our Never-Forgotten Silesian Homeland," the event highlighted the still very real differences between expellees and locals in the early 1950s. The mayors of both Wildflecken and Neuwildflecken made a point of visiting the exhibition and "expressing their solidarity" with the expellees. After all, the refugees of yesterday were now constituents in the local politics of the Rhön. In losing their homes in Reussendorf, they completed a process begun years before. Regardless of how tightly they clung to their dreams of going back to Silesia, they were now locals in a new locale.[110]

Over the next few months, the dispossessed of Reussendorf, Werberg, and the other villages on the Wildflecken base had other causes to celebrate. In November, the promised eighteen units opened on Franz-Schubert-Strasse in Schweinfurt. This came as welcome news to expellee Peter W., living with his family in a camp in Bonnland. He wrote to authorities urging them to get his family out of the camp. "I base my appeal on the grounds that I have found work in the [Schweinfurt] area and have a great interest in getting out of temporary housing as soon as possible." The following spring, workers completed the eightieth and last new housing unit in Neuwildflecken, to the immense relief of local government.[111]

However they came to Wildflecken, the vast majority of those who did so moved on. Journeys that began in Poland, Romania, Czechoslovakia, or any number of other places continued as the sojourners faced difficult choices in the postwar period. As with so many other parts of this story of refugees, a few examples will have to stand for the whole. Pablo D., the DP whose claim to Spanish citizenship caused so much trouble for UNRRA officials in the aftermath of the war, emigrated to the U.S. under the DP Act. His wife and children followed after the closure of the camp in 1951. The H. family, the Romanian expellees who became notorious for their role in the local black market, split up in the early 1950s. Some of them emigrated, settling in Buffalo, New York, before their trail vanished. Other members of the family stayed behind and now own several businesses in the Wildflecken area. Piotr L. successfully made the transition to life as a local resident. Along with his family, he moved to Brückenau, where the family is today well established. By now, expellees sought emigration opportunities in considerable numbers. Between 1949 and the middle of 1951, 320 expellees living in Landkreis Brückenau left for the United States.[112]

For the villagers who remained, the future remained uncertain. Werberg existed in the shadow of the American base. One of the remaining H. brothers wrote to Maria Probst in 1949, asking her for help petitioning the Americans to do something about the shells that kept landing in his field. A 1954 article in the *Main-Post* presented the remaining Werberger in very similar terms to the glowing coverage given them seven years before when the expellee settlements were new. The Americans were now a direct threat to this "new Heimat" in the Rhön. "American shells directly threaten the boundaries of the village and venturing into fields adjacent to the shooting ranges is not exactly free of danger. Columns of tanks and troops can be seen moving through the village. This is Werberg." The Hüfner family, which lost its home in Werberg in 1938 only to return in 1946, now left again for good. With few prospects in the isolated community, they relocated to a town near Haßfurt.[113]

Werberg's precarious existence ended in 1966 when the base expanded again. This tiny town, once the proud symbol of expellee dynamism and resilience in the postwar period, had only 219 inhabitants when the orders came to evacuate the area. Three years later, at a ceremony commemorating the loss of the village, Landrat Richard Haenlein praised the enterprise as a sign of what had been possible in the postwar period. "The integration of expellees and the settlement efforts of Werberg can be called a success." By that time, West Germany was a very different place, far more prosperous, comfortable, and secure than when the debates over the future of the base took place in the early 1950s. Still, for the people of Werberg, memories of their recently abandoned home and the lingering trauma of their flight from distant homes at the end of the war remained inextricably twined. Haenlein also recalled meeting an elderly woman at the same event who lamented her "second expulsion from her home village." She told Haenlein, "I cannot get over this." She died shortly thereafter.[114]

Out of the multiplicity of Wildflecken stories in the wake of the Second World War, there is still precious little coherence. Strangers came to Wildflecken for decades. They fought, scratched out meager livings, rallied in their own defense, and watched as forces far beyond that narrow valley intervened again and again to fundamentally alter the nature of the place. If one Wildflecken story stands out to represent the rest, perhaps it is best that the story is obscure and exists in the flimsiest of archival contexts. The Z. family came together, as so many others did, as an accident of history. Stanislaw, a DP from Poland, married Maria, a Silesian expellee. They had three children, and tried to make ends meet in their new homeland in the Rhön. Despite the presence of the American base, good jobs were hard to find. So Stanislaw left his family in a home just down the hill from the old Muna and went to Mülheim near Frankfurt, where he got work in a dyeing plant. In 1961, the family petitioned local authorities for help moving to be closer to Stanislaw. The 310 DM that they received helped bring their time in Wildflecken to an end.[115] Just as it was for so many others, the Z. family's journey brought them to Wildflecken before pushing them on. They arrived in 1945 to find a refugee town. When they left, it was a base town for a Cold War army.

The shift from refugee town to base community brought with it a number of entirely unintended, or at least unexpected, consequences. In the wake of the Americans came young women, sometimes derided as "camp followers," who worked as prostitutes in the surrounding area. As Maria Höhn has shown, this problem was particularly acute in areas around training centers like Wildflecken, Hohenfels, and Grafenwöhr, which witnessed a rapid and steady turnover of American troops. Prostitution was particularly galling because the years of postwar deprivation were over. Women who prostituted themselves, many Germans believed, were doing so to earn a quick living doing something other than supporting the economic reconstruction of West Germany.[116]

Just as the local community and its expellee population came together to oppose the coming of the Americans and the dispossession of expellees to make way for the base, now this new German hybrid community came together to condemn prostitution and the women who practiced it. Maria Probst returned to Wildflecken in 1952 to help with the Kreistag's campaign against prostitution. "The situation," she wrote in a letter to Dienststelle Blank, "is serious and grave." The Kreistag issued a resolution urging German and American authorities to do something about the "thousands of prostitutes migrating from across the Republic in the wake of the American soldiers. These shameless acts represent a nuisance to upstanding citizens, a threat to our developing youth, a burden on the already delicate housing situation and an undue and excessive load on public welfare. Furthermore, it is clear that the prostitutes are mostly from the criminal element and take every opportunity to engage in smuggling and the black market."[117]

The anti-prostitution protests highlighted the remarkable solidarity that emerged in rural Landkreis Brückenau in the face of repeated transformation from outside in the wake of the Second World War. Complaints about prostitutes echoed the language of those who spent years demanding the closure of the DP camp, which critics accused of harboring smugglers, black marketers, and people of low moral character. A cycle that began with the creation of "refugee towns" in the wake of the war now came full circle, with expellees who had been marginal to or outside of the local community now sharing a common narrative of victimization at the hands of other outsiders. In Wildflecken, like in towns across the rebuilt German landscape, the limits of community were re-established in the wake of the war. The boundaries of these new communities shifted markedly as West Germany grew into a Cold War frontier state. Americans, Polish DPs, expellees, and other Germans came to the Rhön after the war, forcing a sometimes painful negotiation over the boundaries of the local. What emerged, in the end, was a new sense of community that acted as a prism through which inhabitants of this small valley and many other places could interpret their new identity as West Germans.

Conclusion

"The deserted village of Reussendorf is starting to disappear," wrote the Commanding Officer of the Wildflecken Detachment in 1953. Civilian trucks doing business on the post left loaded with hidden building material destined for resale on the outside. In the future, gate guards were to search trucks for "any parts resembling a building" and report offenders to headquarters.[1] For the second time in twenty years, the grasses of the Rhön began to reclaim the streets of the small farming village. Once again, Reussendorfer abandoned their homes in the face of confiscation by an army. This time, the experience of dispossession was all the more bitter because all of the inhabitants, whether expellees or former inhabitants who returned in the late 1940s, had already lost their homes at least once before. The expellee settlements, which held so much promise in the dark days of the postwar period, now vanished once again as unscrupulous or opportunistic truckers supplemented their income with free construction material. Today there is virtually nothing left of Reussendorf, Werberg, or any of the tiny towns that once dotted the grounds of the maneuver area. The base, once again the property of the German military, is littered with the remnants of seventy years of military use.

For forty years, the American presence in Wildflecken transformed the land and wiped away many of the traces of what came before. The smallest training area in West Germany, Wildflecken nonetheless hosted more than 300,000 American and NATO troops each year. By 1958, 320 American families lived in post housing. Lieutenant Colonel Wayne Moe, commander of the 3rd Armored Rifle Battalion, 20th Infantry, ordered the old DP barracks painted green, blue, and yellow. As he told

Stars and Stripes, "It's amazing what a few coats of bright paint can do." Eventually, the post proudly included a ski lift and one of the first Burger King restaurants in Europe. Just a few years before the end of the Cold War, the Americans built new apartments for troops and their families in the north of the town. As many locals delight in pointing out, Elvis Presley spent part of his time in Germany stationed at Wildflecken. The future NBA star Shaquille O'Neal lived at Wildflecken as a young teenager. He tried working at the base McDonalds, but was clearly destined for other things. "It snowed a lot and it was cold," he wrote in his autobiography. "This is when I made a really dramatic change in my life because there was nothing to do but play basketball."[2]

Much like the Germans who came before, the weather was perhaps the dominant memory of the place for its American visitors. "At Wildflecken it's 50–50 whether you will see any sun," an American military magazine wrote in 1988. "You can start your day at main post in cold, gray fog and later, sweat your way through a squad assault course on the other side of the mountains under blazing sun and blinding blue skies. After sweltering through the day at the range, you might find yourself shivering through a snow squall on your way back to a cold tent."[3]

Just like those who came before them, the Americans found it necessary to rename the space in rural Franconia where they found themselves. Twenty years before, the Wehrmacht called the place "Hohe Rhön." Polish DPs emphasized that they had a right to live in a Polish town, which they called "Durzyń." The Americans would develop several nicknames for the new base. In honor of its vertiginous landscape, they called it "Top of the Rock." The town below, whose name was difficult for Anglophones to render, was renamed the far more prosaic "Wild Chicken."

There can be little question that the American base benefitted the local community in a way that none of the other competing visions of Wildflecken ever had. In the mid-1980s, the post employed more than six hundred Germans and ran a training program that prepared local youth for administrative jobs. The small town boasted a range of bars, restaurants, car dealerships, and small shops to cater to soldiers, dependents and townspeople. As one American noted, the town and it surroundings had been shaped by the American presence. "Housing construction by German firms, local teams digging cable trenches, road repairs and upgrading by civilian contractors, soldiers using the public German telephone, a clerk making hotel reservations for a group of inspectors, an architect-engineer presenting a construction design."[4]

Life along the inter-German border changed dramatically once more when that militarized frontier collapsed after 1989. Locals tell stories of that extraordinary night in November when many learned about events taking place in Berlin as a few Trabants hesitantly pushed their way down Sonnenstrasse. For the town, the end of the Cold War order was a pyrrhic victory at best. It marked the beginning of the end for the American base and the closely integrated local economy. A year after the Americans departed in 1994, unemployment stood at twenty-two percent.[5] A few years later, Bavarian Minister President Edmund Stoiber lamented the collapse of the town's "military monoculture."[6] Today the *Bundeswehr* houses a simulation command and urban warfare training at Wildflecken, but the lively and lucrative days of the American and NATO facility are long gone.

Ironically, the close of this chapter of Wildflecken's history coincided with the arrival of yet more strangers to the Franconian Rhön. With the end of the Cold War, ethnic Germans from Eastern Europe began to relocate to Germany in search of better opportunities. These "resettlers" (*Aussiedler* or *Spätaussiedler*) were notionally allowed and welcomed under German law. The Basic Law of 1949 promised residency and a path to citizenship for those "members of the German people" still living outside the shrunken boundaries of what was then West Germany. A legal framework established to integrate expellees and to look toward eventual unification with the East now resulted in a wave of new migrants from Russia, Ukraine, Romania, Kazakhstan, and other sites where pockets of German identity remained.[7] For many of these "Germans," the connection to Germany was tenuous. Since many ethnic German communities broke up or were destroyed in the wake of the war, relatively few migrants spoke German well. Many left desperate poverty in their place of origin to come to a society driven by a technologically intensive economy that was itself coping with the economic burden of reunification.

Their arrival was sudden and dramatic. Just like the expellees, their presence had a profound influence on the often small communities in which they found themselves. In 1986, the Soviet Union liberalized its emigration laws. During the three years that followed, about 300,000 ethnic Germans arrived from the collapsing Soviet Union. At the peak of migration in 1994, more than 200,000 resettlers came to Germany before improving economic conditions in the former Soviet Union slowed the pace of migration.[8] The resulting housing crunch necessitated the construction of yet another network of temporary camps. In 1988, the Lower Franconian government built a camp in Oberwildflecken for new arrivals.

For the second time in a half-century, Wildflecken found itself housing large numbers of refugees. Like the expellees at the end of the war, these new arrivals based their claim to legitimacy on being German, while locals expressed wariness about what this development meant for their community. The departure of the Americans opened apartments on the edge of town, which were quickly settled by migrants whose arrival coincided with the collapse of the local economy that followed the transfer of the base. By the end of 1996, almost thirty percent of the populations of Wildflecken and nearby Bad Brückenau were migrants from Eastern Europe.[9] A region confronting economic deprivation now found itself with the burden of immigrants, many of whom lacked job skills. A county shaped by the experience of migration and deprivation after the war treated these new arrivals with the same ambivalence as an earlier generation. Young resettlers quickly acquired a reputation for drunkenness, drug use, and chronic unemployment. Local governments tried to integrate migrants into local communities using sports like boxing that were popular both in the former Soviet Union and Germany. A young resettler from Russia told the *Süddeutsche Zeitung* in 1999: "We don't have a problem. We are the problem. Nobody wants us here."[10] Today Landkreis Bad Kissingen (into which Landkreis Brückenau merged in 1972) is home to about six hundred migrants from Poland and the former Soviet Union.[11] If you walk the streets of Wildflecken today, the impact of these migrants is clear. Despite efforts by the local, state, and federal governments, many Aussiedler remain badly assimilated and economically marginal. Until these migrants move on to a place with more opportunity or the local economy improves, it seems likely that these problems will remain.

Once a year, the Bundeswehr opens the facility for a weekend of hiking. Between 2,000 and 3,000 enthusiastic walkers converge on the site for a very German *Volkswandertag*.[12] In 2010, I joined a band of hikers visiting from Bonn for the weekend and set off from the pretty village of Dalherda. Amidst music, food, and no shortage of drink, we headed into the woods along a tank trail. Our group cut across the hills and plunged down into deep forests that have not seen the logger's axe for more than half a century. In the fields are the remains of armored vehicles used for target practice, now rusting away in the summer sun. I asked our leader, who had a Bundeswehr map of the site, to help me locate the remains of Reussendorf. On a ridge line, in front of a sign warning of unexploded ordnance, we looked down at what once had been the home of Rhön farmers, forced laborers, and expellees. All that was left were a few low mounds where foundations once stood. Without a good map, we would have walked right by it.

Many of those with an adult memory of the towns are gone now, but the surrounding communities are full of the children and grandchildren of those who came to Wildflecken against their will at the end of the war. Today a local group of former Werberg residents is led by Sonja Hüfner, whose father's family was forced out of the village in 1938 and left again in 1955. "If the Bundeswehr gave up Werberg today," the elder Hüfner told a local journalist, "I'd build a house up here."[13] Today in the Wildflecken town park, there stands a simple column surrounded by eight raised stones that display the names of the towns that vanished during the construction of the base. There is no distinction between those displaced by the German construction in the 1930s and the American building project of the 1950s and 60s. Similarly, there is no acknowledgment that many, indeed most, of those displaced during the second round of evacuation were not locals, but expellees. This is all-too appropriate, since it was in fact this experience of double displacement that helped to meld expellees into local communities, both physically and psychologically. Expellees had to become Werberger and Reussendorfer, then to face the loss of their homes once more, before they could become locals themselves. The present generation in the Sinn Valley grew up in the shadow of this experience. As in any community in Germany, the experience of expulsion changed as generations shifted. Accents faded away, regional costumes came out of storage chests less and less often, and the Lutheran church in Wildflecken became a normal part of the community rather than an alien presence that arrived with the expellees.

A short walk away, at the edge of the forest, is the entrance to another monument. The *Kreuzweg der Nationen* (literally "Crossroads of the Nations," but also "Stations of the Cross") cuts 1,000 meters up a hill through the forest. Along the way, there are ten standing stones commemorating the dead of the twentieth century's wars. At the end of the path stands the fence marking the outer boundary of the base. Near the head of the trail, in a glen tucked between the fence and the woods, is a cemetery. The *Polenfriedhof* (Polish Cemetery) is the final resting place of almost 550 Poles who died in the camp during the DP years. The cemetery is stark and still, crowned by a primitivist metal cross over the dates "1939–1945." There is a small chapel on the grounds, adorned with a simple mural of an angel bearing the souls of departed children toward heaven. The guest book records the visits of Polish tourists who come here as a reminder of their country's tortured path through the twentieth century.

Just past the fence, which did not exist in 1945, sit the buildings at the heart of the DP camp. The local historian who took me on a tour of the base showed me a sign, painted on the side of the wall of a stable. In English and Polish, it warned that vandals would be prosecuted. This faded warning is effectively the last visible reminder of the DP camp experience within the base grounds. Sixty years since the last DPs left the property, and with even those who were children in the camp now reaching advanced age, the memory of what was one of the largest refugee camps in Europe is vanishing with each passing season.

Wildflecken has come full circle since 1937. When the Wehrmacht came, the region was rural and impoverished. For seventy years, the town and surrounding countryside existed adjacent to a large military base. Today with the relatively small Bundeswehr presence at Wildflecken, the local economy has shrunk considerably. Many of the town's young people have left for better opportunities elsewhere. Shortly after German unification, UNESCO designated much of the Rhön as a biosphere reservation, spread over three German states, that celebrates and preserves "an open cultural landscape shaped by human use since many centuries."[14] The reserve, along with a natural history museum in nearby Oberbach, has brought a few tourists to the region. Sadly there is little to mark the dramatic story of Wildflecken's extraordinary path through the twentieth century. A dedicated group of local historians are working to change that, but at the moment only a small museum on the grounds of the base commemorates the town's past.

The story of Wildflecken after 1945 deserves to be told not just on its own merits, but because of what it reveals about the workings of rural society in occupied and semi-sovereign West Germany. The postwar period saw intense daily contact between local Germans, American occupiers, displaced persons, and ethnic German expellees. Without seeing the interactions between these groups, which had very different hopes, expectations, and fears for the future, we cannot understand the processes that underlay the construction of a workable society in postwar West Germany.

This book has told three stories which might well be presented separately. The expansion and contraction of the system of DP camps, the arrival and troubled integration of expellees into West German society, and the construction of a network of American garrisons along the Cold War frontier were critical components of the emergence of a democratic West Germany out of the ruins of Hitler's empire. Yet, as the story of a small town in the Franconian uplands tells us, these disparate developments cannot be understood in isolation from each other. In Wildflecken, and in places large and small across Germany, DPs, expellees, soldiers, and locals interacted with each other and with the institutions established to manage the postwar transition. The experience of uprooting, of dispossession, and of foreignness, was ubiquitous in the turmoil of Europe after 1945. These groups came from different places and for different reasons, but the strangers who arrived in Germany and the locals who they found there created a new order.

The fundamentally rural character of the refugee crisis ensured that, at least initially, ethnic German expellees found themselves in places that, while capable of providing a modicum of sustenance and support, were structurally least able to absorb them in the medium or long term. DPs, on the other hand, initially benefitted from favorable treatment by the occupiers, and their privileged economic position placed them in the center of consumer society in which most consumption took place on the gray or black market. As some measure of stability resumed in the Rhön, the relative position of the DPs deteriorated. At the same time, it became apparent that the initial assumption under which the Allies established the DP camp system, that most DPs wanted to go home quickly, was badly misplaced. It became inescapably clear that the camp at Wildflecken was going to remain for an undetermined period of time.

The presence of the Americans and the transformation of the U.S. Army from conqueror to occupier played a vital role in each of these processes. While American policy initially explicitly favored DPs, relations on the ground were far more ambivalent and many officers and Military Government officials strongly preferred to work with locals or expellees. The latter were particularly attractive in the early days of the occupation, since they came from outside pre-existing political structures and could be called upon without openly calling into question their Nazi past. In places like Landkreis Brückenau, the tiny American footprint in the region meant that occupation administrators had to rely on Germans to act as intermediaries both to accomplish day-to-day management tasks and to re-establish local government. The presence of so many expellees made the problems of administration all the more acute. The answer was to find a reliable German partner from within the ranks of the expellees, a decision that the Americans later came to regret.

Expellees in the area sought to create conditions under which they could leave makeshift camps and find some durable solution to their own serious problems of housing and employment. For hundreds of expellees, the solution appeared to be resettling towns abandoned after the construction of the German base in the 1930s. The "refugee towns" faced significant challenges but they instantiated the expellees into local society. The presence of Americans and DPs helped to speed, or at least to catalyze, the social integration of expellees in rural communities. While the expellees were certainly outsiders, they were not as "outside" as the other two groups. For locals, the integration of expellees became and remained a top priority, since integration would relieve the very tangible burdens of providing care. At first, some locals saw the expellees themselves as the biggest stumbling block on the road to recovery. When locals began to see the DPs, and with them the Americans, as the greatest impediment to integration, expellees became *de facto* insiders and found common cause with locals.

Uneasy and unintended coalitions of interest developed between locals, expellees, and the Americans over the eventual fate of the DP camp. As the IRO struggled to close the camps, the Wildflecken facility became, if anything, more entrenched and intractable. At the same time, local and regional elites pursued an ambitious and ultimately ill-fated strategy for promoting rural development. The framers of this project sold the endeavor as a way to promote the economic integration of expellees by creating an industrial complex in the region. This plan required the closure of the DP camp. Its persistence was one of the many reasons that rural development ultimately failed in the Rhön. These dashed hopes and the deeply felt anger among many area residents further pushed expellees and locals together.

The frustration and resentment over the failures of the past few years then deepened with the sudden transformation of the American strategic presence in West Germany after 1950. While the Americans did not prioritize the needs of DPs or expellees in their decision making on issues of base construction, the refugee problem was perhaps the most important consideration for local and state governments in West Germany. As a result, the federal government found itself under pressure from domestic constituencies to fight back against American base requisitions in some areas. Wildflecken was drawn into one such dispute. The need for base facilities clashed with claims of sovereignty and the rights of expellees to live in their "second Heimat."

The story of Wildflecken after 1945 matters, both on its own terms and because it was part of a vast set of processes that have to be seen locally in order to understand just how important they were. Refugees of all types were ubiquitous in Germany after the Second World War. Without keeping them and the organizations tasked with alleviating their plight in the foreground, we cannot fully grasp the postwar transformation of West Germany. In Wildflecken, and in towns and cities across western Germany, the dynamic interaction of groups, individuals, policies, and practice shaped the transition from a defeated and destroyed Reich to a Cold War border state.

Notes

INTRODUCTION

1. Paul Steege, *Black Market, Cold War: Everyday Life in Berlin, 1946–49* (Cambridge: Cambridge University Press, 2007), 15.

2. There are many of these, beginning with William Sheridan Allen's *The Nazi Seizure of Power: The Experience of a Single German Town, 1922–1945* (New York: F. Watts, 1984). Recent examples include Andrew Stuart Bergerson, *Ordinary Germans in Extraordinary Times: The Nazi Revolution in Hildesheim* (Bloomington: Indiana University Press, 2004); Sean Dobson, *Authority and Upheaval in Leipzig, 1910–1920: The Story of a Relationship* (New York: Columbia University Press, 2001); Martin Geyer, *Verkehrte Welt: Revolution, Inflation und Moderne, München 1914–1924* (Gottingen: Vandenhoeck & Ruprecht, c1998); Neil Gregor, *Haunted City: Nuremberg and the Nazi Past* (New Haven: Yale University, 2008); Panikos Panayi, *Life and Death in a German Town: Osnabrück from the Weimar Republic to World War II and Beyond* (London: Tauris, 2007); Til van Rahden, *Jews and other Germans: Civil Society, Religious Diversity, and Urban Politics in Breslau, 1860–1925* (Madison: Wisconsin University Press, 2008); Walter Rinderle and Bernard Norling, *The Nazi Impact on a German Village* (Lexington: University Press of Kentucky, 1993); Helmut Walser Smith, *The Butcher's Tale: Murder and Anti-Semitism in a German Town* (New York: Norton, 2002); and Helena Waddy, *Oberammergau in the Nazi Era* (New York: Oxford University Press, 2010).

3. Atina Grossmann, *Jews, Germans, and Allies: Close Encounters in Occupied Germany* (Princeton: Princeton University Press, 2007), 9.

4. Saul Friedländer, *The Years of Extermination: Nazi Germany and the Jews, 1939–1945* (New York: Harper Collins, 2007), xv.

5. Gerwin Kellerman, *475 Jahre Wildflecken, 1524–1999* (Wildflecken: Marktgemeinde Wildflecken, 1999); Paul Burkhardt, *The Major Training Areas: Grafenwoehr/Vilseck, Hohenfels, Wildflecken* (Weiden: Der neue Tag, 1984).

6. Among others, see Richard Bessel, *Germany, 1945: From War to Peace* (New York: Harper Collins, 2009); William I. Hitchcock, *The Bitter Road to Freedom: A New History of the Liberation of Europe* (New York: Free Press, 2008); Rolf-Dieter Müller and Gerd R. Ueberschär, *Kriegsende 1945. Die Zerstörung des Deutschen Reiches* (Frankfurt: Fischer, 1994); and Friedrich Prinz, *Trümmerzeit in München: Kultur und Gesellschaft einer deutschen Großstadt im Aufbruch, 1945–1949* (Munich: Beck, 1984).

7. "Die Belegung der staatlichen

Flüchtlingslager in Bayern am 1. Oktober, 1959," prepared by Bayer. Staatsministerium für Arbeit und Soziale Fürsorge. StaaWü 460/1.

8. Grossmann, *Jews, Germans, and Allies;* Maria Höhn, *GIs and Fräuleins: The German-American Encounter in 1950s West Germany* (Chapel Hill: University of North Carolina Press, 2002); Sylvia Schraut, *Flüchtlingsaufnahme in Württemberg-Baden 1945–1949. Amerikanische Besatzungsziele und demokratischer Wiederaufbau im Konflikt* (Munich: Oldenbourg, 1995); and Hans Woller, *Gesellschaft und Politik in der amerikanischen Besatzungszone: Die Region Ansbach und Fürth* (Munich: Oldenbourg, 1986).

9. Harold Zink's classic *The United States in Germany, 1945–1955* (Princeton: Nostrand, 1957) has precisely one reference to the refugee issue. Jeffry Diefendorfer, Axel Frohn, and Hermann-Josepf Rupieper, eds., *American Policy and the Reconstruction of West Germany, 1945–55* (Cambridge: Cambridge University Press, 1993) has little more. Earl Ziemke's *The U.S. Army in the Occupation of Germany* (Washington: GPO, 1975) describes the DP camps as a "kind of Army-sponsored underworld" (357). See also Kendall Gott, *Mobility, Vigilance, and Justice: The U.S. Army Constabulary in Germany, 1946–1953* (Ft. Leavenworth, KS: Combat Studies Institute Press, 2005).

10. John Gimbel, *A German Community under American Occupation: Marburg 1945–52* (Stanford: Stanford University Press, 1961), 127–128; Anni Baker, *Wiesbaden and the Americans, 1945–2003* (Wiesbaden: Stadtarchiv Wiesbaden, 2004); see also Adam R. Seipp, "To Come as Conquerors: American Bases and the European Theater, 1941–45," in *Franklin Roosevelt and the Azores During the Two World Wars,* ed. Luís N. Rodrigues (Lisbon: Fundação Luso-Americana, 2008), 323–336.

11. Sylvia Schraut, "'Make the Germans Do It': The Refugee Problem in the American Zone of Post-War Germany," in *Forced Migration in Central and Eastern Europe,* ed. Alfred J. Rieber (London: Frank Cass, 2000), 125.

12. A new wave of DP scholarship has emerged in past decade. See, among others Daniel Cohen, "Remembering Post-War Displaced Persons: From Omission to Resurrection," in *Enlarging European Memory: Migration Movements in Historical Perspective,* eds. Mareike König and Rainer Ohliger (Stuttgart: Thorbecke Verlag, 2006), 87–97; Grossmann, *Jews, Germans, and Allies;* Laura Hilton, "Prisoners of Peace: Rebuilding Community, Identity, and Nationality in Displaced Persons Camps in Germany, 1945–1952" (PhD diss., Ohio State University, 2001); Anna Holian, "Between National Socialism and Soviet Communism: The Politics of Self-Representation Among Displaced Persons in Munich, 1945–51" (PhD diss., University of Chicago, 2005); Henriette von Holleuffer, *Zwischen Fremde und Fremde: Displaced Persons in Australien, den USA, und Kanada, 1946–1952* (Osnabrück: Rasch, 2001); Wolfgang Jacobmeyer, *Vom Zwangsarbeiter zum Heimatlosen Ausländer: Die Displaced Persons in Westdeutschland, 1945–1951* (Göttingen: Vandenhoeck & Ruprecht, 1985); Michael Pegel, *Fremdarbeiter, Displaced Persons, Heimatlose Ausländer: Konstanten eines Randgruppenshicksals in Deutschland nach 1945* (Münster: Lit, 1997); Kim Salomon, *Refugees in the Cold War: Towards a New International History of the International Refugee Regime in the Early Postwar Era* (Lund: Lund University Press, 1991); Patrick Wagner, *Displaced Persons in Hamburg. Stationen einer halbherzigen Integration, 1945 bis 1958* (Hamburg: Dölling und Galitz, 1997); and Mark Wyman, *DPs: Europe's Displaced Persons, 1945–1951* (Philadelphia: Associated University Press, 1998).

13. See, among others, Grossmann,

Jews, Germans, and Allies; Frank Stern, "The Historic Triangle: Occupiers, Germans, and Jews in Postwar Germany," in *West Germany under Construction: Politics, Society, and Culture in the Adenauer Era,* ed. Robert Moeller (Ann Arbor: University of Michigan Press, 1997), 199–229; and Zeev Mankowitz, *Life Between Memory and Hope: The Survivors of the Holocaust in Occupied Germany* (Cambridge: Cambridge University Press, 2002).

14. Daniel Cohen, "Remembering Post-War Displaced Persons," 95.

15. Among others, see Ian Connor, *Refugees and Expellees in Post-War Germany* (Manchester: Manchester University Press, 2007); Katja Klee, *Im Luftschutzkeller des Reiches: Evakuierte in Bayern, 1939–1953* (Munich: Oldenbourg, 1998); Andreas Kossert, *Kalte Heimat: Die Geschichte der deutschen Vertriebenen nach 1945* (Munich: Siedler, 2008); Marion Frantzioch, *Die Vertriebene: Hemmnisse, Antriebskräfte und Wege ihrer Integration in der Bundesrepublik Deutschland* (Berlin: Dietrich Reimer, 1987); Michael Krause, *Flucht vor dem Bombenkrieg: 'Umquartierung' im Zweiten Weltkrieg und die Wiedereingliederung der Evakuierten in Deutschland, 1943–1963* (Duesseldorf: Droste, 1997); and David Rock and Stefan Wolff, eds., *Coming Home to Germany? The Integration of Ethnic Germans from Central and Eastern Europe in the Federal Republic since 1945* (New York: Berghahn, 2002). The case of Bavaria is presented in Franz J. Bauer, *Flüchtlinge und Flüchtlingspolitik in Bayern, 1945–1950* (Stuttgart: Klett-Cotta, 1982).

16. Rainer Schulze's study of Celle: "Growing Discontent: Relations Between Native and Refugee Populations in a Rural District in Western Germany after the Second World War," in Moeller, *West Germany under Construction,* 53–72; Doris von der Brelie-Lewien, *Dann kamen die Flüchtlinge: Der Wandel des Landkreises Fallingbostel vom Rüstungszentrum im 'Dritten Reich' zur Flüchtlingshochburg nach dem Zweiten Weltkrieg* (Hildesheim: Wallstein, 1990); and Schraut, *Flüchtlingsaufnahme in Württemberg-Baden.*

17. Robert Moeller, *War Stories: The Search for a Usable Past in the Federal Republic of Germany* (Berkeley: University of California Press, 2003), 18. See also Norbert Frei, *Vergangenheitspolitik: Die Anfänge der Bundesrepublik und die NS-Vergangenheit* (Munich: Beck, 1996).

18. Elisabeth Pfeil, *Fünf Jahre später: Die Eingliederung der Heimatvertriebenen in Bayern* (Frankfurt: Wolfgang Mentzer, 1951), 8.

19. Malcolm Proudfoot, *European Refugees, 1939–52* (Evanston, IL: Northwestern University Press, 1956), 21.

20. Philipp Ther and Ana Siljak, eds., *Redrawing Nations: Ethnic Cleansing in East-Central Europe, 1944–1948* (Lanham, MD: Rowan and Littlefield, 2001); Richard Bessel and Claudia Haake, eds., *Removing Peoples: Forced Removal in the Modern World* (London: Oxford University Press, 2009).

21. Timothy Snyder, *Bloodlands: Europe Between Hitler and Stalin* (New York: Basic, 2010).

22. Pertti Ahonen, Gustavo Corni, et al., *People on the Move: Forced Population Movements in Europe in the Second World War and its Aftermath* (Oxford: Berg, 2008). Tara Zahra makes a similar argument in her article "Prisoners of the Postwar: Displaced Persons, Expellees, and Jews in Austria After World War II," *Austrian History Yearbook* 41 (2010): 191–215.

23. Jessica Reinisch, "Introduction," in *The Disentanglement of Populations: Migration, Expulsion, and Displacement in Postwar Europe, 1944–9,* eds. Jessica Reinisch and Elizabeth White (New York: Palgrave Macmillan, 2011), xv.

24. Wolfram Wette, "Eine Gesellschaft in Umbruch. 'Entwurzelungserfahrungen'

in Deutschland 1943–48 und sozialer Wandel," in *Flucht und Vertreibung. Zwischen Abrechnung und Verdrängung*, ed. Robert Streibel (Vienna: Picus, 1994), 257–284.

25. Richard Bessel, *Germany 1945: From War to Peace* (New York: Harper Collins, 2009), 262.

26. Christian Habbe, "Der Zweite lange Marsch," in *Die Flucht: Über die Vertreibung der Deutschen aus dem Osten*, eds. Stefan Aust and Stephan Burgdorff (Bonn: BPB, 2005), 249.

27. Paul Erker, "Revolution des Dorfes? Ländliche Bevölkerung zwischen Flüchtlingszustrom und landwirtschaftlichem Strukturwandel," in *Von Stalingrad zur Währungsreform. Zur Sozialgeschichte des Umbruchs in Deutschland*, eds. Martin Broszat, Klaus-Dietmar Henke, and Hans Woller (Munich: Oldenbourg, 1988), 367–425.

28. Report, "Refugees and Displaced Persons in Land Bavaria," undated 1948, NARA RG 319, Box 284; Joachim Braun, *Heimatvertriebene und Flüchtlinge in Unterfranken* (Diplomarbeit: Universität Würzburg, 1984), 27.

29. This makes a particularly interesting comparison with Brelie-Lewien's work on Fallingbostel.

30. Holian, "Between National Socialism and Soviet Communism," 72; George Woodbridge, *UNRRA: The History of the United Nations Relief and Rehabilitation Administration*, 3 vols. (New York: Columbia University Press, 1950), 2:502; "Stenographischer Bericht über die Bayerischen Landtags," July 2, 1948, 1608.

31. Kathryn Hulme, *The Wild Place* (Boston: Atlantic Monthly Press, 1953).

32. Bryce Ryan, review of "The Wild Place," *Phylon* 15, no. 1 (1954): 104.

33. Francesca Wilson, *Aftermath: France, Germany, Austria, Yugoslavia, 1945 and 1946* (Drayton: Penguin, 1947), 101.

34. Hitchcock, *The Bitter Road to Freedom*, 272–280; and Ben Shephard, *The Long Road Home: The Aftermath of the Second World War* (New York: Knopf, 2011), esp. 160–177, 207–211.

35. Gregor, *Haunted City*, 12–13.

36. There are a number of good local studies of expellee-local relations. The exemplar is probably Rainer Schulze's study of Celle.

37. Höhn, *GIs and Fräuleins*, 4. She cites official U.S. government sources for this statistic. Thomas Leuerer gives a much lower estimate of about ten million, but admits that his is largely speculative. Thomas Leuerer, *Die Stationierung amerikanischer Streitkräfte in Deutschland: Militärgemeinden der U.S. Armee seit 1945 als ziviles Element der Stationierungspolitik der Vereinigten Staaten* (Wurzburg: Ergon Verlag, 1997), 332, 339.

1. THE WILD PLACE, 1933–1945

1. Two of the best, and only, sources of local history are Gerwin Kellerman, *475 Jahre Wildflecken, 1524–1999* (Wildflecken: Marktgemeinde Wildflecken, 1999); and Alfred Schrenk, "Die Augesiedlten Dörfer im Truppenübungsplatz Wildflecken" (Zulassungsarbeit für das Lehramt an Volkschulen, Universität Würzburg, 1971). My sincere thanks to both authors for patiently answering my questions in person.

2. Donald Bloxham, *Genocide, the World Wars, and the Unweaving of Europe* (London: Vallentine Mitchell, 2008), 1–2.

3. Tony Judt, *Postwar: A History of Europe Since 1945* (New York: Penguin, 2005), 26.

4. This critique is made explicit in the essays collected in Richard Bessel and Claudia B. Haake, eds. *Removing People: Forced Removal in the Modern World* (Oxford: Oxford University Press, 2009), see esp. 436.

5. Robert Gellately, *The Gestapo and German Society: Enforcing Racial Policy, 1933–1945* (Oxford: Clarendon, 1990), 80.

6. In German, "wild" means both "unauthorized" and "undomesticated."

7. "In Reussendorf heisst es Abschied-

nehmen," *Main-Post,* August 6, 1952. *Heimat* expresses a conception of home that merges local, regional, and national identities. Following scholarly practice, I will leave the term untranslated.

8. Bayer. Statistischen Landesamt, *Statistisches Jahrbuch für Bayern* (Munich: BSL, 1936), 48.

9. Karl Baedeker, *Southern Germany and Austria* (Leipzig: Karl Baedeker, 1883), 68.

10. Peter Spitznagel, *Wähler und Wahlen in Unterfranken, 1919–1969: Versuch einer Analyse der Wählerstruktur eines Regierungsbezirkes auf statistischer Grundlage nach den Erhebungen der Volkzählungen 1925, 1950, 1961 und 1970* (Würzburg: Schöningh, 1979), A1–B8.

11. Walter Ziegler, "Das Selbstverständnis der bayerischen Gauleiter," in *Staat und Gaue in der NS-Zeit: Bayern 1933–1945,* eds. Hermann Rumschöttel and Walter Ziegler (Munich: Beck, 2004), 77–128, 98; Claudia Roth, *Partiekreis und Kreisleiter der NSDAP unter besonderer Berücksichtigung Bayerns* (Munich: Beck, 1997), 33.

12. Gellately, *Gestapo and German Society,* 89.

13. Spitznagel, *Wähler and Wahlen in Unterfranken,* A4.

14. Adam Tooze, *The Wages of Destruction: The Making and Breaking of the Nazi Economy* (New York: Viking, 2006), 182–188.

15. Rolf Memming, "The Bavarian Governmental District Unterfranken and the City Burgstadt, 1922–1939: A Study of the National Socialist Movement and Party-State Affairs" (PhD diss., University of Nebraska, 1974), 23, 26, 32.

16. Elise Schapira, Interview 17391, *Visual History Archive,* USC Shoah Foundation Institute. 2011. Web. May 12, 2011.

17. Cornelia Binder and Michael Mence, *Nachbarn der Vergangenheit: Spuren von Deutschen jüdischen Glaubens im Landkreis Bad Kissingen mit dem Brennpunkt 1800 bis 1945* (Bad Brückenau: self-published, 2004), 49–50. Roland Flade, *Der Novemberpogrom von 1938 in Unterfranken: Vorgeschichte – Verlauf – Augenzeugenberichte* (Würzburg: Schöningh, 1988), 24, 31, 39, 104. Most of the Jewish population dispersed after 1933. Binder and Mence believe that about fifty perished in the Holocaust. See also Baruch Z. Ophir and Falk Wiesemann, *Die jüdische Gemeinden in Bayern 1918–1945* (Munich: Oldenbourg, 1979), 273–274.

18. Gellately, *Gestapo and German Society,* 114, 210.

19. Ian Kershaw, *Popular Opinion and Political Dissent in the Third Reich: Bavaria, 1933–1945* (New York: Oxford University Press, 1983), 27–28.

20. Werner Blessing, "Landwirtschaft in Franken während der Zeit des Nationalsozialismus," in *Zwangsarbeit im ländlichen Franken,* ed. Herbert May (Bad Windsheim: Fränkischen Freilandsmuseum, 2008), 72–84.

21. Memming, "Bavarian Governmental District Unterfranken," 79–83.

22. Ibid., 71–74. Memming pays almost no attention to the industrial component of the plan; Joachim S. Hohmann, *Landvolk unterm Hakenkreuz: Agrar- und Rassenpolitik in der Rhön,* 2 vols. (Frankfurt: Peter Lang, 1992), 2:69. There is an excellent discussion of the Hellmuth Plan in Dan P. Silverman, *Hitler's Economy: Nazi Work Creation Programs, 1933–1936* (Cambridge: Harvard University Press, 1998), 96–120. Silverman and Hohmann disagree on the extent to which adherence to regime ideology affected the outcome of the plan. "Hohmann has failed to grasp the intensity of opposition to Hellmuth's plan from Reich and NSDAP officials in Berlin" (Silverman, 108–109 n. 307). See also Ziegler, "Das Selbstverständnis," 98; "Survey on Industrial Plants, Kreis Brückenau," July 31, 1945, NARA 260/390/41/13/2/648.

23. Ulrich Wirths, *Das "Winterhilfswerke" im Gau Mainfranken: Ein Instru-*

ment des NS-Regimes (Saarbrücken: VDM, 2009), 46–47.

24. Memming, "Bavarian Governmental District Unterfranken," 73.

25. See Robert Citino, *The Path to Blitzkrieg: Doctrine and Training in the German Army, 1920–1939* (Boulder, CO: Lynne Reiner, 1999), 233–234. A very good and accessible discussion of debates within the German army about the feasibility of such an offensive can be found in Wilhelm Deist, et al., eds. *Germany and the Second World War*, vol. 1, *The Build-Up of German Aggression*, trans. P. S. Falla, et al. (Oxford: Clarendon, 1990), 526–537.

26. Paul Burkhardt, *The Major Training Areas: Grafenwoehr/Vilseck, Hohenfels, Wildflecken* (Weiden: Der neue Tag, 1984), 74, 220.

27. Peter M., Akten der Spruchkammer Brückenau, StaaWü, 738.

28. Author communication with Sonja Hüfner.

29. More than seventy years later, the U.S. Army allowed surviving residents and their families to return to visit the ruins of their town. See http://www.army.mil/media/amp/?bctid=808134316001. Thanks to Kathy Nawyn for pointing out this site.

30. Samuel Mitcham, *The German Order of Battle*, vol. 1. (Mechanicsburg, PA: Stackpole, 2007), 138, 157, 283.

31. Quoted in Kershaw, *Popular Opinion and Political Dissent in the Third Reich*, 292.

32. There is not much literature on the Muna system. See Barbara Hillman, et al., *Lw. 2/XI – Muna Lübberstedt. Zwangsarbeit für den Krieg* (Bremen: Edition Temmen, 1996), 12, 31.

33. Tooze, *Wages of Destruction*, 517.

34. Ulrich Herbert, *Hitler's Foreign Workers: Enforced Foreign Labor in Germany under the Third Reich*, trans. William Templer (Cambridge: Cambridge University Press, 1997). In recent years, there have been a number of good local and regional studies of forced labor, both from the perspective of the source and destination of laborers. See, for example, Steffen Becker, "Von der Werbung zum 'Totaleinsatz': Die Politik der Rekrutierung von Arbeitskräften im 'Protektorat Böhmen und Mähren' für die deutsche Kriegswirtschaft und der Aufenthalt tschechischer Zwangsarbeiter und – arbeiterinnen im Dritten Reich 1939–1945" (PhD diss., Humboldt-Universität zu Berlin, 2004).

35. Mark Spoerer and Jochen Fleischhacker, "Forced Laborers in Nazi Germany: Categories, Numbers, and Survivors," *Journal of Interdisciplinary History* 33, no. 2 (Autumn 2002), 187, 189, 196.

36. Alexander von Plato, et al., eds., *Hitler's Slaves: Life Stories of Forced Labourers in Nazi-Occupied Europe* (New York: Berghahn, 2010), 3–5.

37. Much of what follows is taken from Herbert May, ed., *Zwangsarbeit im ländlichen Franken* (Bad Windsheim: Fränkischen Freilandsmuseum, 2008).

38. Herbert May and Rolf Rossmeissl, "Der Ausländereinsatz in Franken: Voraussetzungen-Arbeitsbereiche-Ausmass," in May, *Zwangsarbeit im ländlichen Franken*, 20–36, 30, 35.

39. Leo V. Hahn, "Kriegsgefange und Fremdarbeiter in Würzburg," self-published, 2005, p. 53. Found in general collection, StaatWü.

40. "List of POWs, Labour, and other Units which were stationed or passed through Land and Stadtkreis Brückenau," ITS Archive, Einsatz Fremdvölkischer Arbeitskräfte 43.

41. "Stand der Personen des Heeresgutsbezirk Wildflecken." Gemeindearchiv Wildflecken (GaW), Gemeinde Wildflecken, 6.5.

42. Report, undated. GaW, Gemeinde Wildflecken, 11.3. May, *Zwangsarbeit im ländlichen Franken*, 246; Piotor Filipowski and Katarzyna Madoń, "'You can't say it out loud. And you can't forget': Polish

Experiences of Slave and Forced Labour for the 'Third Reich'," in von Plato et al., *Hitler's Slaves*, 71–85.

43. Gellately, *Gestapo and German Society*, 226, 228.

44. John J. Delaney, "Social Contact and Personal Relations of German Catholic Peasants and Polish Workers (POWs, Civilian, and Forced Laborers) in Bavaria's Rural War Economy, 1939–1945," in *Annali dell'Istituto storico italo-germanico in Trento* 27 (2002): 394–404. Letter from Geheime Staatspolizei Nürnberg-Fürth, June 29, 1944. Staat Wü, Lra Bad Brückenau, 1844.

45. Herbert May and Kristina Patzelt, "'Unerlaubte Beziehungen' Liebe und Sexualität zwischen Deutschen und Zwangsarbeitern," in May, *Zwangsarbeit im ländlichen Franken*, 156–166, 156; Herbert, *Hitler's Foreign Workers*, 131–132; Gellately, *Gestapo and German Society*, 233.

46. May and Patzelt, "'Unerlaubte Beziehungen," 162; May,"Dringend Benötigt – Zwangsarbeiter für die Landwirtschaft," in May, *Zwangsarbeit im ländlichen Franken*, 89.

47. Herbert, *Hitler's Foreign Workers*, 269.

48. Gellately, *Gestapo and German Society*, 216, 247.

49. Ralf Rolfmeissl, "Terror, Schikanen, Mord – Zwangsarbeiter, die als Opfer ihr Grab in Franken fanden," in May, *Zwangsarbeit im ländlichen Franken*, 178–200; GaW, Gemeinde Neuwildflecken, 12.7.

50. May, "Arbeitsweigerung, Arbeitsflucht, Widerstand," in May, *Zwangsarbeit im ländlichen Franken*, 146–154.

51. "Survey of Industrial Plants," op. cit.

52. Report, "Luftangriff im hies. Kreis," November 19, 1943. StaaWü, Lra Bad Brückenau, 1800.

53. Manfred Messerschmidt, "Das Unrecht der NS-Militärjustiz," in *Opfer der NS-Militärjustiz: Zur Notwendigkeit der Rehabilitierung und Entschädigung*, eds. Günter Saathoff, Franz Dillmann, and Manfred Messerschmidt (Cologne: Bundesverband Information und Beratung für NS-Verfolgte, 1994), 11–14.

54. Report of November 28, 1945. StaaWü, Lra Bad Brückenau, 3221. The report lists deaths in Wildflecken for which it is unknown if next-of-kin were notified.

55. Gerwin Kellerman, *475 Jahre Wildflecken, 1524–1999* (Wildflecken: Marktgemeinde Wildflecken, 1999), 80; and Donald Taggert, ed., *History of the Third Infantry Division in World War II* (Washington: Infantry Journal Press, 1947), 348; United States Seventh Army, *Report of Operations: France and Germany, 1944–1945* (Heidelberg: United States Seventh Army, 1946), 768.

56. The literature on Nazi war aims and the importance of ideology is vast. The work of Gerhard Weinberg is central to this historiography. See, among others, his "Germany's War for World Conquest and the Extermination of the Jews," *Holocaust and Genocide Studies* 10, no. 2 (Fall 1996): 121.

57. Peter Padfield, *Himmler* (New York: Henry Holt, 1990), 102; Ian Kershaw, *Hitler*, vol. 2, *1936–1945, Nemesis* (New York: Norton, 2000), 402.

58. See, for instance, Rogers Brubaker, "National Minorities, Nationalizing States, and External National Homelands in the New Europe," *Daedalus* 144, no. 2 (Spring 1995), 111.

59. Paul Robert Magocsi, *Historical Atlas of Central Europe* (Seattle: University of Washington Press, 2002), 104–106. In recent years, there has been a profusion of literature on the history of German ethnic communities in Eastern Europe. See, for example, the work of Andreas Kossert, especially *Ostpreußen: Geschichte und Mythos* (Munich: Siedler, 2005).

60. See James E. Bjork, *Neither German nor Pole: Catholicism and National Indif-*

ference in a Central European Borderland (Ann Arbor: University of Michigan Press, 2008); and Jeremy King, *Budweisers into Czechs and Germans: A Local History of Bohemian Politics, 1848–1948* (Princeton: Princeton University Press, 2002).

61. Carol Fink, *Defending the Rights of Others: The Great Powers, the Jews, and International Minority Protection, 1878–1938* (New York: Cambridge University Press, 2004).

62. Ivan T. Behrend, *Decades of Crisis: Central and Eastern Europe Before World War II* (Berkeley: University of California Press, 2001), 159.

63. One example, of many, was the Romanianization of the Bukovina region awarded to Romania after World War I. See Mariana Hausleitner, *Die Rumänisierung der Bukowina: Die Durchsetzung des nationalstaatlichen Anspruchs Grossrumäniens 1918–1944* (Munich: Oldenbourg, 2001).

64. Valdis O. Lumans, *Himmler's Auxiliaries: The Volksdeutsche Mittelstelle and the German National Minorities of Europe, 1933–45* (Chapel Hill: University of North Carolina Press, 1993); Götz Aly, *Final Solution: Nazi Population Policy and the Murder of the European Jews* (London: Arnold, 1999), 104–133.

65. Martin Dean, "Soviet Ethnic Germans and the Holocaust in the Reich Commissariat Ukraine, 1941–1944," in *The Shoah in Ukraine: History, Testimony, Memorialization*, eds. Ray Brandon and Wendy Lower (Bloomington: Indiana University Press, 2008), 250–254.

66. Doris Bergen, "The Volksdeutsche of Eastern Europe and the Collapse of the Nazi Empire, 1944–45," in *The Impact of Nazism: New Perspectives on the Third Reich and Its Legacy*, eds. Alan E. Steinweis and Daniel E. Rogers (Lincoln: University of Nebraska Press, 2003), 117.

67. Norman M. Naimark, *Fires of Hatred: Ethnic Cleansing in Twentieth-Century Europe* (Cambridge: Harvard University Press, 2001), 110–111; United States Department of State, *Foreign Relations of the United States: The Conference of Berlin (The Potsdam Conference), 1945* (Washington, D.C., 1960), 1495.

68. The indispensible source for eyewitness accounts remains the multivolume *Documentation der Vertreibung der Deutschen aus Ost-Mitteleuropa*, eds. Theodor Schieder, et al. (Bonn: Bundesministerium für Vertriebene, 1954–60).

69. "Ankunft der Elendsgestalten," *Main-Post*, January 25, 2006.

70. Bayerisches Statistisches Landesamt, *Die Flüchtlinge in Bayern* (Munich: BSL, 1948); Heft 142, Beiträge zur Statistik Bayerns, 45.

71. Records of Evakuierten, StaaWü. StaaWü, Lra Bad Brückenau, 3221.

72. Statistics on refugee flows, particularly early ones, are controversial and approximate. See Pertti Ahonen, Gustavo Corni, et al., *People on the Move: Forced Population Movements in Europe in the Second World War and its Aftermath* (Oxford: Berg, 2008), 82–95; Hans Lemberg and K. Erik Franzen, *Die Vertriebenen: Hitlers letzte Opfer* (Berlin: Propylaen, 2001), 272–281. On the Soviet zone, see Phillip Ther, *Deutsche und polnische Vertriebene: Gesellschaft und Vertriebenenpolitik in der SBZ/DDR und in Polen 1945–1956* (Göttingen: Vandenhoeck & Ruprecht, 1998). Many contemporary statistics distinguish between *Reichsdeutsche* (those expelled from inside Germany's prewar borders) and *Volksdeutsche* (those who originated outside those borders). For the sake of simplicity, I will generally not make this distinction.

73. Paul Erker, "Revolution des Dorfes? Ländliche Bevölkerung zwischen Flüchtlingszustrom und landwirtschaftlichem Strukturwandel," in *Von Stalingrad zur Währungsreform. Zur Sozialgeschichte des Umbruchs in Deutschland*, eds. Mar-

tin Broszat, Klaus-Dietmar Henke, and Hans Woller (Munich: Oldenbourg, 1988), 367; Michael Krause, *Flucht vor dem Bombenkrieg: 'Umquartierung' im Zweiten Weltkrieg und die Wiedereingliederung der Evakuierten in Deutschland, 1943–1963* (Duesseldorf: Droste, 1997), 35.

74. George Woodbridge, *UNRRA: The History of the United Nations Relief and Rehabilitation Administration*, 3 vols. (New York: Columbia University Press, 1950), 1:4.

75. Claudena Skran, *Refugees in Inter-War Europe: The Emergence of a Regime* (Oxford: Clarendon, 1995).

76. Tommie Sjöberg, *The Powers and the Persecuted: The Refugee Problem and the Intergovernmental Committee on Refugees (IGCR), 1938–1947* (Lund: Lund University Press, 1991), esp. 153–155; Malcolm J. Proudfoot, *European Refugees, 1939–52* (Evanston, IL: Northwestern University Press, 1956), 115. Organisation Todt was a massive labor organization in the Third Reich that helped to coordinate the activities of compulsory laborers.

77. Woodbridge, *UNRRA*, 2:482–484; Hilton, "Prisoners of Peace," 64; Proudfoot, *European Refugees*, 235.

78. Mark Wyman, *DPs: Europe's Displaced Persons, 1945–1951* (Philadelphia: Associated University Press, 1998), 41, 47.

79. Tadeusz Borowski, *This Way for the Gas, Ladies and Gentlemen*, trans. Barbara Vedder (New York: Penguin, 1976), 164.

80. Francesca Wilson, *Aftermath: France, Germany, Austria, Yugoslavia, 1945 and 1946* (Drayton: Penguin, 1947), 37.

81. Oliver J. Frederiksen, *The American Military Occupation of Germany, 1945–1953* (Heidelberg: U.S. Army Europe, 1953), 74–75.

82. Jan T. Gross, *Revolution from Abroad: The Soviet Conquest of Poland's Western Ukraine and Western Belorussia* (Princeton: Princeton University Press, 2002), 17. Alexander Rossino, *Hitler Strikes Poland: Blitzkrieg, Ideology, and Atrocity* (Lawrence: University of Kansas Press, 2003).

83. Daniel Blatman, "The Encounter Between Jews and Poles in Lublin District after Liberation, 1944–1943," *East European Politics and Societies* 20, no. 4 (2006), 599.

84. Gross, *Revolution from Abroad*, 17.

85. Ulrike Goecken-Haidl, *Der Weg zurück. Die Repatriierung sowjetischer Zwangsarbeiter und Kriegsgefangener während und nach dem Zweiten Weltkrieg* (Essen: Klartext, 2006), 546.

86. "Repatriation Procedure." July 16, 1945, HQ, Seventh Army. Albert Hutler Collection, USHMM.

87. "Repatriation of Polish Nationals." September 1, 1945. Hutler Collection, USHMM.

88. Wolfgang Jacobmeyer, *Von Zwangsarbeiter zum Heimatlosen Ausländer* (Göttingen: Vandenhoeck und Rupprecht, 1985), 83, 85, 122. The French took far fewer DPs (about 33,000) than either of their two allies.

89. Wolfgang Jaenicke, *Vier Jahre Betreuung der Vertriebenen in Bayern, 1945–1949* (Bayer: Staatsministerium des Innern, 1950), 9; Historischen Kommission bei der Bayer, Akademie der Wissenschaft, *Neue Deutsche Biographie*, 10th ed., vol. 10 (Berlin: Dunker & Humblot, 1974), 287. Jaenicke later served as West Germany's ambassador to Pakistan and died in 1968. His original title was the somewhat less formal "Sonderbeauftragten für das Flüchtlingswesen."

90. "Profile: Dr. Josef Winter," *Fränkisches Volksblatt*, April 21, 1955.

91. Report, "Das Flüchtlingsproblem in der amerikanischen Besatzungszone," prepared for General Clay, January 1948. Bundesarchiv Koblenz (hereafter "Ba"), Nachlass Maria Probst (hereafter "Probst"), 627.

92. Ian Connor, *Refugees and Expellees*

in *Post-War Germany* (Manchester: Manchester University Press, 2007), 20. His figures are taken from 1950.

93. Bayerisches Statistisches Landesamt, *Die Flüchtlinge in Bayern* (Munich: BSL, 1948); Heft 142, Beiträge zur Statistik Bayerns, 6–7, 14, 29, 45.

94. Biographical information in KCH 26/625; "Former U.C. Girl and Ex-Ship Yard Worker Wins Book Prize," *Oakland Tribune*, October 25, 1953; Kathryn Hulme, *The Wild Place* (New York: Atlantic Monthly Press, 1953), 7.

95. "History of a Polish Camp," United Nations Archives and Records Management Section S-0425-0006-17. KCH Diary, KCH, August 6, 1945.

2. THE SEIGNEURS OF WILDFLECKEN, 1945–1947

1. The only surviving documentation is Henties's report in GaW, Gemeinde Neuwildflecken, 5.6. He blamed "Russians" for the attack, but Henties's ability to distinguish Russian from Polish is uncertain. My thanks to Walter Koempel, author of a history of Oberbach, for clarifying the identity of the physician.

2. Gray markets been the subject of a vigorous but relatively recent academic debate. A good primer can be found in Seth E. Lipner, *The Legal and Economic Aspects of Gray Market Goods* (Westport, CT: Quorum Books, 1990), 1–11.

3. Morris Krakowsky, Interview by USC Shoah Foundation Institute for Visual History and Education, University of Southern California, North Hills, CA, July 6, 1995, tape 5, 3.00.

4. Jan Dudzinski, Interview by USC Shoah Foundation Institute for Visual History and Education, University of Southern California, Colorado Springs, CO, June 15, 1998, tape 9, 14.30.

5. Interview with Andrew Zdanowicz.

6. "Juden die sich in Wildflecken befinden," August 1945. ITS NKZD, 352.

7. Mark Wyman, *DPs: Europe's Displaced Persons, 1945–1951* (Philadelphia: Associated University Press, 1998), 134–136.

8. This summary does little justice to an extraordinary survival story. Minna Aspler, Interview by USC Shoah Foundation Institute for Visual History and Education, University of Southern California.

9. Report of Ephraim Chase, November 1945. UNARM S-0436-0055-01.

10. "Report on UNRRA Team 302," undated, but late 1945. UNARM S-0436-0008-05. According to Wyman, *DPs* (47), the average size of an UNRRA team was thirteen for a camp population of 3,000.

11. "Report on UNRRA Team 302," undated, but September 1945, in "History of a Polish Camp," hereafter UN ARMS S-0425-0006-17.

12. "Daily Log," September 6, 1945, and proclamation dated September 5, 1945. UNARM 5-0436-0054-04.

13. UNARM S-0425-0006-17, p. 3.

14. September 16, 1945, KCH diary in KCH 5/97. The ellipses are in the original.

15. Report of Ephraim Chase, November 1945. UNARM S-0436-0055-01.

16. Report on Wildflecken DP Center, September 24, 1945. UNARM S-0436-0008-005

17. UNARM S-0425-0006-17.

18. Unless otherwise noted, the accompanying description of the facility is taken from this account; Hilton, "Prisoners of Peace: Rebuilding Community, Identity, and Nationality in Displaced Persons Camps in Germany, 1945–1952" (PhD diss., Ohio State University, 2001), 163–165.

19. October 3, 1945, KCH diary.

20. August 6, 1945, KCH diary; Hulme, *The Wild Place* (Boston: Atlantic Monthly Press, 1953), 132.

21. See, for instance, letter of July 30, 1946. UNRRA Protective Service Office, UNARM-S-0435-0003-0016.

22. Anna D. Jaroszyńska-Kirchmann, *The Exile Mission: The Polish Political Diaspora and Polish Americans, 1939–1956*

(Athens: Ohio University Press, 2004), 82; Anna Holian, "Between National Socialism and Soviet Communism: The Politics of Self-Representation Among Displaced Persons in Munich, 1945–51" (PhD diss., University of Chicago, 2005), 170–173.

23. Files of Piotr L. in ITS 3.2.1.1.

24. Report of February 1, 1947. UNARM S-0436-0008-05.

25. Report by RB Price, January 27, 1947. UNARM S0436-0008-5

26. "Statement of Mr. James McKenzie," January 24, 1947. UNARM S0436-0008-8; Note in KCH 26/264.

27. Oliver J. Fredericksen, *The American Military Occupation of Germany, 1945–1953* (Heidelberg: U.S. Army Europe, 1953), 51–52; Hamadyk interview.

28. Wyman, *DPs*, 112; Report of Ephraim Chase, November 1945. UNARM S-0436-0055-01.

29. KCH diary, September 21, 1945.

30. Request for Labor, MG Brückenau, March 21, 1946. StaaWü, Lra Bad Brückenau, 3267; Akten der Spruchkammer Brückenau, StaaWü, 1232.

31. Kath. Matrikalamt Würzburg, ITS Microfilm 2196; William I. Hitchcock, *The Bitter Road to Freedom: A New History of the Liberation of Europe* (New York: Free Press, 2008), 274.

32. Hulme, *The Wild Place*.

33. Field Supervisor's Monthly Report, July 1946. UNARM S-0436-0041-007; Report from Wildflecken on Scouting, February 3, 1947. UNARM S-0436-0041-07; Letter from J. H. Whiting to Chief of Staff, G-5, 3rd Army, October 2, 1946. UNARM S-43060008-07; Field Supervisor's Monthly Report, June–July 1946. UNARM S-0436-0041-07.

34. Reports of April 13 and 27, 1945. GaW, Gemeinde Wildflecken, 6.5.

35. Interviews with Andrew Zdanowicz and Hamadyk.

36. Hulme, *The Wild Place*, 125.

37. Complaint dated February 16, 1946. StaaWü, Lra Bad Brückenau, 3267.

38. Flyer dated August 23, 1946. StaaWü, Lra Bad Brückenau, 3267.

39. Reports dated February 9, 1946. UNARM S-0436-0008-06.

40. Hulme, *The Wild Place*, 24; KCH diary, October 6, 1945; Letter to AC Dunn, March 2, 1947, both in KCH.

41. Malte Zierenberg, *Stadt der Schieber: Der Berliner Schwarzmarkt 1939–1950* (Göttingen: Vandenhoeck & Ruprecht, 2008).

42. Report of Operations, July 1946. 12th Constabulary Squadron, NARA 338/290/71/32/3/2139.

43. Sample of *Ausländermeldung* files from GaW, Gemeinde Neuwildflecken, 5.8. These files are fragmentary. Data drawn from late 1947.

44. Wyman, *DPs*, 49.

45. Files on M. in ITS Archive, Tracing Files. See report of March 16, 1961 in StaaWü, Lra Bad Brückenau, 3077.

46. Letters from February 2 and 9, 1946, found respectively in GaW, Gemeinde Neuwildflecken, 5.8, and StaaWü, Lra Bad Brückenau, 3246.

47. The correspondence is in StaaWü, Lra Bad Brückenau, 3264.

48. "Memo: Displaced Persons," March 8, 1946. StaaWü, Lra Bad Brückenau, 3267.

49. Report of Operations, July 1946. 22nd Constabulary Squadron, NARA 338/290/71/32/3/2139.

50. Report of Operations, 15th Infantry Regiment, 3rd Infantry Division, Oct. 10, 1945–July 1, 1946, NARA 407/270/54/20/3.

51. See Wolfgang Jacobmeyer, *Vom Zwangsarbeiter zum Heimatlosen Ausländer: Die Displaced Persons in Westdeutschland, 1945–1951* (Göttingen: Vandenhoeck & Ruprecht, 1985), esp. 212–215; Hilton, "Prisoners of Peace," 252.

52. Malcolm J. Proudfoot, *European Refugees, 1939–52* (Evanston, IL: Northwestern University Press, 1956), 175.

53. Francesca Wilson, *Aftermath: France, Germany, Austria, Yugoslavia, 1945 and 1946* (Drayton: Penguin, 1947), 59.

54. Gerwin Kellerman, *475 Jahre Wildflecken, 1524–1999* (Wildflecken: Marktgemeinde Wildflecken, 1999), 83.
55. Earl Ziemke, *The U.S. Army in the Occupation of Germany* (Washington: GPO, 1975), 358.
56. Letter from J. H. Whiting to Chief of Staff, G-5 Section, 3rd Army, October 17, 1946. UNARM S-0436-0008-07.
57. Monthly Historical Report, March 1946. OMG LK Brückenau, NARA RG 260, 390/47/15/4/194.
58. Statements collected in UNARM S-0436-0008-07.
59. Hulme, *The Wild Place*, 94–95.
60. Stimmungsbericht, October 12, 1946. GaW, Gemeinde Wildflecken, 9.13.
61. Report of Operations, July 1946. 22nd Constabulary Squadron, NARA 338/290/71/32/3/2139.
62. Report of July 5, 1946. GaW, Gemeinde Wildflecken, 9.13.
63. "Intelligence: Displaced Persons," July 13, 1946. UNARM S-0436-0008-05.
64. Report, "Raid: Wildflecken," December 26, 1946. UNARM S-0436-0008-07. Emphasis added.
65. Letter from Lra Bad Brückenau to MG Brückenau, January 8, 1947. StaaWü, Lra Bad Brückenau, 3715. Letter from Gemeinde Wildflecken to Landrat, January 24, 1947. GaW, Gemeinde Wildflecken, 9.13.
66. "DPs: Millions of 'Displaced Persons' Stream Across Europe to their Homes," *Life*, July 30, 1945, 13–19.
67. "VE Day Celebration," *The Dragon*, May 17, 1946.
68. Wyman, *DPs*, 19, and UNRRA, 2:498, 515.
69. Report of Ephraim Chase, November 1945. UNARM S-0436-0055-01.
70. Hulme, *The Wild Place*, 47.
71. Yury Boshyk, "Repatriation and resistance: Ukrainian refugees and displaced persons in Occupied Germany and Austria, 1945–48," in *Refugees in the Age of Total War*, ed. Anna C. Bramwell (London: Unwin Hyman, 1988), 198–201; Lynne Taylor, "The Classification of DPs in Post-Second World War Germany," in *Survivors of Nazi Persecution in Europe after the Second World War*, ed. David Cesarani, et al. (London: Vallentine Mitchell, 2010), 44–45.
72. Interviews with Zdanowicz and Hamadyk.
73. Petition of November 6, 1945. NARA RG 260/390/47/18/163.
74. ITS, Pablo D. See also StaaWü, Lra Bad Brückenau, 3092.
75. "General Remarks," undated, but clearly 1946. UNARM 5-0425-0068-14. Underlined in original.
76. Transcript of interview with Stefan Czyzewski, April 8, 1998. United States Holocaust Memorial Museum Archive, RG-50.030*0387.
77. "UNRRA Monthly Team Report, 15/7/46." UNARM 5-0436-0008-05.
78. Proudfoot, *European Refugees*, 221–222.
79. Report on Visit to Wildflecken DP Camp, August 15, 1946. UNARM S-0436-0008-05.
80. "Aschaffenburg," report from Protective Service Office, July 30, 1946. UNARM 5-0435-0003-16.
81. Ibid.
82. G. Masset to A.R.Truelson, September 14, 1945. UNARM 5-0436-0008-05.
83. "Inspection of Camp by Brig. Gen'l Williams" and "The New Military Regime at Wildflecken," both September 17, 1945. UNARM 5-0436-0008-05.
84. Wyman, *DPs*, 71; Letter of March 24, 1947. IRO Archive, AN, AJ/43/897.
85. Memo, "All-Out Repatriation," December 24, 1946. UNARM 5-0436-0008-03.
86. UNRRA, *Displaced Persons Operations: Report of Central Headquarters for Germany* (Washington: UNRRA, 1946), 5, 59.

87. Hulme, *The Wild Place*, 151.
88. Wyman, *DPs*, 70–71.
89. Wyman, *DPs*, 84.
90. "Visit to Wildflecken Polish DP Camp, 9 November 1946." UNARM 5-0436-0008-05.
91. Report of December 6, 1946. NARA RG 319, CIC, IRR Files, Box 34.
92. "Recapitulation of Some Recent Incidents at Wildflecken." UNARM S0436-0008-05.
93. "Visit to Wildflecken Polish DP Camp, 9 November 1946." UNARM 5-0436-0008-05.
94. "Report on Incident at K-7," UNARM S0436-0008-05.
95. Undated. UNARM 5-0436-0008-07.
96. Flyer in UNARM 5-0436-0008-07.
97. Descriptions of the January 22 riot from Hulme, *The Wild Place*, 158–160; also in "Incident at K-7 (22 Jan 1947)," "Statement of Mrs. Nowicka," and "Report on Nationality Screening Incident," by K. Hulme, January 22, 1947. UNARM 5-436-8-5; and "DP's in Camp Riot: Mob 'Soviet' Aides," *New York Times*, February 7, 1947.
98. "Facts Pertaining to the Accidents in the DP Camp Wildflecken." UNARM S-0436-0008-07.
99. Letter to the inhabitants of the DP Assembly Center in Wildflecken, by Major Samuel S. Kale, U.S. Army, January 22, 1947. KCH 26/623.

3. KEEPING REFUGEES OCCUPIED, 1945–1948

1. The functional designation for administrative units changed several times over the course of the occupation. Brückenau was initially designated Team I-12A3 and later A-331. To prevent confusion, this chapter will refer only to unit designation. For an explanation of the changing terminology of the occupation, see Christoph Weisz, ed., *OMGUS-Handbuch: Die amerikanische Militärregierung in Deutschland, 1945–1949* (Munich: Oldenbourg, 1995), esp. 146.
2. Martin Kornrumpf, *In Bayern angekommen: die Eingliederung der Vertriebenen: Zahlen, Daten, Namen* (Munich: Olzog, 1979), 65; Monatsbericht, January 1948. BHStA, LaflüVerw 2331.
3. Excellent recent studies of black markets in postwar Germany are Malte Zierenberg, *Stadt der Schieber: Der Berliner Schwarzmarkt 1939–1950* (Göttingen: Vandenhoeck & Ruprecht, 2008); and Paul Steege, *Black Market, Cold War: Everyday Life in Berlin, 1946–1949* (Cambridge: Cambridge University Press, 2007).
4. Earl Ziemke, *The U.S. Army in the Occupation of Germany* (Washington: GPO, 1975), 351–352; Ian Connor, *Refugees and Expellees in Post-War Germany* (Manchester: Manchester University Press, 2007), 26–27.
5. Anne Warren Griffith, "Babes in the Wildflecken Woods," *New Yorker*, October 28, 1950, 61.
6. Weisz, *OMGUS-Handbuch*, 162.
7. Detachment report, July 17, 1945, NARA 260/390/41/13/2/608.
8. Harold Zink, *The United States in Germany, 1945–1955* (Princeton: Nostrand, 1957), 171–175; Weekly Military Government Report, November 11, 1945. OMGB, Executive Office, NARA 260/390/41/13/2/648.
9. Report of Operations, 15th Infantry Regiment, 3rd Infantry Division, 10 Oct 1945–1 July 1946. NARA 407/270/54/20/3.
10. Quarterly Historical Report, January 14, 1947. NARA 260/390/41/13/2/194.
11. Letter of June 22, 1946. Lra Bad Brückenau 3267, StaaWü.
12. Heide Fehrenbach, *Race After Hitler: Black Occupation Children in Postwar Germany and America* (Princeton: Princeton University Press, 2005), 11.
13. A copy of this postcard, and a description of others, in NARA 260/390/14/2/648.

14. Maria Höhn, *GIs and Fräuleins: The German-American Encounter in 1950s West Germany* (Chapel Hill: University of North Carolina Press, 2002), 130.
15. Monthly Historical Report, May 1946. Intelligence Division, OMGB, NARA 260/390/47/15/4/194.
16. Annual Historical Report, 1947. OMGB, NARA 260/390/47/19/4/194.
17. Report, "Population Movements," October 6, 1946. NARA 319, CIC, Box 34; Report #52, February 12, 1948. NARA FOD, Box 1528.
18. Weekly Intelligence Report, February 9, 1946, in same. In an unpublished paper, Laura Hilton points out that this rumor was common in communities near DP camps across Bavaria. My thanks to her for providing me with a copy.
19. Weekly MG Report, November 11, 1945. NARA 260/390/41/13/2/648.
20. Zink, *The United States in Germany*, 171–173.
21. 3rd MG Regiment War Diary, August 1945. OMGB, NARA 260/390/41/13/2/61 and Monthly Historical Report, May 1946. Intelligence Division, OMGB, NARA 260/390/47/15/4/194.
22. Carole Fink, *Defending the Rights of Others: The Great Powers, the Jews, and International Minority Protection, 1878–1938* (Cambridge: Cambridge University Press, 2004), 279, 334.
23. On Breslau (today Wrocław), see Sebastian Siebel-Aschenbach, *Lower Silesia from Nazi Germany to Communist Poland, 1942–49* (New York: St. Martin's, 1994), 17–21; and Gregor Thum, *Die Fremde Stadt: Breslau 1945* (Berlin: Siedler, 2003), 16–18.
24. Documents on Oswald come from Akten der Spruchkammer Brückenau 1272 and Rg. v. Uf 23481, both in StaaWü.
25. Lutz Niethammer, *Die Mitläuferfabrik: Die Entnazifizierung am Beispiel Bayerns* (Berlin, Dietz: 1982), 526.
26. Niethammer, *Die Mitläuferfabrik*, 618–619; Cornelia Rauh-Kühne, "Life Rewards the Latecomers: Denazification During the Cold War," in *The United States and Germany in the Era of the Cold War, 1945–1990: A Handbook*, ed. Detlef Junker (New York: Cambridge University Press, 2004), 62–72.
27. Akten der Spruchkammer Brückenau, StaaWü 1782.
28. Barbara Fait, "Supervised Democracy: American Occupation and German Politics" in Junker, *The United States and Germany*, 57–64.
29. Ian Connor, "The Bavarian Government and the Refugee Problem, 1945–1950," *European History Quarterly* 16, no. 2 (April 1986), 131–153.
30. The general state of confusion in the KPD can be seen in GaW, Gemeinde Wildflecken, 1.2.
31. Bayer. Statistischen Landesamt, *Statistisches Jahrbuch für Bayern* (Munich: BSL, 1947), 336–343.
32. Weekly Intelligence Report, LK Brückenau, December 7, 1946. NARA 260/350/41/13/2/656; and Stimmunsbericht, December 4, 1946, in same.
33. Akten der Spruchkammer Brückenau, StaaWü 602.
34. Report, "The Wildflecken Area," undated. NARA 260/390/47/19/4/194.
35. 22nd Constabulary Squadron Report of Operations, July 1946. NARA 338/290/71/32/2/2139.
36. "Narrative History of Programs for Transfer of CEM and U.S. Surplus to the German Economy in Bavaria," December 1949. BaK Z 45 F, OMGUS, 17/8149/1. STEG's official history is Dr. Kurt Magnus, *One Million Tons of War Material for Peace: The History of STEG* (Munich: Richard Pflaum, 1954). I will use the acronym STEG because it was in common use at the time. Between August 1945 and the Bizonal fusion in April 1947, it was technically the *Gesellschaft für Erfassung von Rüstungsgut*, or GER.

37. Ibid. Despite the importance of STEG for the rebuilding of West German industry, it has been almost ignored by historians. See Douglas Bell's ongoing doctoral dissertation at Texas A&M University.
38. "Program E, Recovery of Munitions Components," September 4, 1946. OMGB Public Safety Branch, NARA, RG 260/390/42/28/6–7; Magnus, *One Million Tons*, 17.
39. "Report on Fire – Oberriedenberg," July 30, 1945. NARA 260/350/41/13/2/684.
40. Ibid.
41. "Security of Captured Enemy Ammunition Dumps in Bavaria," November 14, 1946. Intelligence Division, NARA RG 260/390/47/18/163; and "Security of Captured Enemy Munitions," December 12, 1949, in same.
42. "Security of Wildflecken Captured Enemy Material Depot," October 4, 1946. NARA 498/290/56/25/7/361.
43. See STEG files in BaK Z 45 F, OMGUS, 17/8149/1, for reports on legal proceedings against Americans and Germans working with and for STEG.
44. Letter from Flüchtlingsamt Brückenau (Beck) to Kreisbaumeister, Brückenau, July 22, 1947. StaaWü, Landesratsamt Bad Brückenau, 3056; Report dated October 16, 1947. Lra Bad Brückenau 3715, StaaWü.
45. Monatsbericht, Rg. v. Uf., January 1948. BHStA, LaFlüVerw 2332.
46. Karl Lowenstein, "Law and the Legislative Process in Occupied Germany," *Yale Law Journal* 57, no. 6 (April 1948), 998.
47. Letters from Dr. Hage to various occupation offices in NARA 260/390/47/19/4/194.
48. Press release, October 28, 1947. AN AJ/43/897.
49. See, for example, letters in Lra Bad Brückenau 3715 and 3267, StaaWü.
50. Oliver J. Fredericksen, *The American Military Occupation of Germany, 1945–1953* (Heidelberg: U.S. Army Europe, 1953), 120; Zink, *The United States in Germany*, 129.
51. Letters of June 22 and February 18, 1946. Lra Bad Brückenau 3267, StaaWü.
52. "Appeal against requisitions of living quarters," November 26, 1946. Lra Bad Brückenau 3715, StaaWü.
53. Correspondence in BHStA, LaflüVerw, 1428; Letter from Oswald on July 16, 1947. NARA 260/390/47/19/4/194.
54. Wolfgang Jaenicke, *Vier Jahre Betreuung der Vertriebenen in Bayern, 1945–1949* (Munich: Bayerisches Staatsministerium des Innern, 1950), 7–8.
55. Statistische Unterlagen zur Vorlage von Notberichten an OMGUS, March 12, 1948. Lra Bad Brückenau 3715, StaaWü.
56. "Am Strom der Flüchtlinge," *Main-Post*, January 30, 1946. "People without Space" (*Volk ohne Raum*), "Living Space" (*Lebensraum*), and "Blood and Soil" (*Blut und Boden*) were all familiar tropes of Nazi racial propaganda.
57. "200,000 Flüchtlinge kommen nach Mainfranken," *Main-Post*, December 29, 1945.
58. See for example the meetings between Beck, the Gemeinderat Wildflecken, and at least one local priest described in Protokollbuch Gemeinderatssitzung Wildflecken, March 3, 1948, in GaW, Wildflecken, Band 2.5. Monatsbericht, October 1947. Rg v. Uf, BHStA, LaflüVerw 2332.
59. Monatsbericht, Rg. v. Uf., December 1947. BHStA, LaflüVerw 2331.
60. These and other similar reports can be found in Lra Bad Brückenau 3056, StaaWü.
61. Memo of January 1, 1949. Lra Bad Brückenau 3163, StaaWü.
62. "Was erwarten sie im neuen Jahr?," *Main-Post*, December 30, 1947.
63. Monthly Historical Report, March 1946. Intelligence Division, OMGB, NARA 260/390/47/15/4/194.
64. Uwe Carstens, *Leben im Flüchtling-*

slager: Ein Kapitel deutscher Nachkriegsgeschichte (Husum: Husum Verlag, 1994), 6.

65. Meryn McLaren, "'Out of the Huts Emerged a Settled People': Community Building in West German Refugee Camps," *German History* 28, no. 1 (2010): 26.

66. Conner, *Refugees and Expellees*, 32–33.

67. Biographies collected in Lra Bad Brückenau 3163, StaaWü.

68. BHStA, LaflüVerw 123.

69. Ibid.

70. "Report of Incidents at the Refugee-Camp Hermannsheim," April 20, 1949. NARA 260, Field Operations Division, Box 1533.

71. Alfred Schrenk, "Die Augesiedlten Dörfer im Truppenübungsplatz Wildflecken," Zulassungsarbeit für das Lehramt an Volksschulen, Universität Würzburg, 1971, 53.

72. Several reports on Christmas parties can be found in NARA 260/390/47/19/4/194.

73. Fragebogen in StaaWü, Lra Bad Brückenau, 3700.

74. Dewey A. Browder, "The GI Dollar and the Wirtschaftswunder," *Journal of European Economic History* 23, no. 3 (Winter 1993), 607. See also Historical Division, U.S. Army Europe, *The Employment of Local Nationals by the U.S. Army in Europe, 1945–1966* (Heidelberg: U.S. Army Europe, 1968), esp. 19–34.

75. 22nd Constabulary Squadron Report of Operations, July 1946. NARA 338/290/71/32/2/2139.

76. Andreas Kossert, *Kalte Heimat: Die Gesichchte der deutschen Vertriebenen nach 1945* (Munich: Siedler, 2008), 110–113; Conner, *Refugees and Expellees*, 31; Brenda Melendy, "Narratives, Festivals, and Reinvention: Defining the Postwar German Homeland in Waldkraiburg," *Journal of Popular Culture* 39, no. 6 (2006), 1049–1076.

77. Alfred Schrenk, "Die Augesiedlten Dörfer," 53.

78. Wolfram Ruhenstroth-Bauer, "Die Bayerische Landessiedlung GmbH als Instrument bayerischer Agrarpolitik unter besonderer Berücksichtigung der Eingliederung heimatvertriebener Landwirte" (PhD diss., TU München, 1976), 13.

79. "Flüchtlinge wieder auf eigener Scholle," *Main-Post*, 15 October 1946.

80. Letter from Bayer. Staatsmin für Ernährung, Landwirtschaft und Forsten (Poehlmann) to Staatsekretär für das Flüchtlingswesen, April 8, 1947. BHStA, LaflüVerw 1664.

81. "Flüchtlinge wieder auf eigener Scholle," *Main-Post*, October 15, 1946.

82. Ibid.

83. Files in StaaWü, Lra Bad Brückenau, 3166.

84. "Flüchtlinge wieder auf eigener Scholle," *Main-Post*, October 15, 1946.

85. Personal correspondence with Sonja Hüfner.

86. This information is drawn from her 1954 request for damages related to the later evacuation of Reussendorf. Hers and others are filed in BHStA, LaFlüVerw, 1215.

87. Report from Bundesministerium der Finanzen. Ausgleich von Ernteausfall und Investitionen für die in Werberg verbliebenen Pächter und Randanlieger. August 3, 1953 BaMa, Amt Blank BW 9/3507.

88. "Flüchtlinge wieder auf eigener Scholle," and "Werberg, das Flüchtlingsdorf in der Rhön," *Main-Post*, June 3, 1950.

89. Undated report, likely 1947. NARA, RG 260, Food, Agriculture and Forest Section, Box 13.

90. Schrenk, "Die Augesiedlten Dörfer," 34.

91. Rg. v. Uf 23481, StaaWü.

92. Ibid.; Weekly Intelligence Report, LK Brückenau, December 7, 1946. NARA 260/350/41/13/2/656.

93. Rg. v. Uf 23481, StaaWü.
94. "Annual Historical Report, 1 July 1946–30 June 1947," NARA RG 260/390/47/19/4/194.
95. Frederikson, *The American Military Occupation of Germany*, 58–68.
96. Monthly Historical Report, May 1946. Intelligence Division, OMGB, NARA 260/390/47/15/4/194.
97. 22nd Constabulary Squadron Report of Operations, July 1946. NARA 338/290/71/32/2/2139.
98. Ibid.
99. Kendall Gott, *Mobility, Vigilance, and Justice: The U.S. Army Constabulary in Germany, 1946–1953* (Ft. Leavenworth, KS: Combat Studies Institute Press, 2005), 21–23.
100. Zink, *The United States in Germany*, 308–310.
101. Register of Military Government Court, Summary Court Brückenau. NARA RG 466, Box 39.
102. Various inspection reports, 1946–49, found in NARA RG 466, Box 39.
103. Monthly Historical Report, May 1946. Intelligence Division, OMGB, NARA 260/390/47/15/4/194.
104. Detachment Annual Report, 1946–47. NARA 260/39047/19/4/194.
105. Weekly Report of Field Team for RB Ober-Mittel- and Unterfranken," October 17, 1947. NARA 260/390/47/18/6.
106. H. J. Braun, *The German Economy in the Twentieth Century: The Third Reich and the Federal Republic* (New York: Routledge, 1990), 154–156.
107. Ibid.; Detachment Annual Report, 1947–1948. NARA 260/39047/19/4/194.
108. Investigation and interrogation records in in Lra Bad Brückenau 3274, StaaWü.
109. Letter from Flüchtlingsamt Brückenau (Beck) to Amtsgericht Brückenau, February 8, 1949. StaaWu, Lra Bad Brückenau, 3056.

4. THESE PEOPLE, 1947–1949

1. Report on conference, May 12, 1948. AN, AJ43/915/55/2.
2. Paul Erker, "Revolution des Dorfes? Ländliche Bevölkerung zwischen Flüchtlingszustrom und landwirtschaftlichem Strukturwandel," in *Von Stalingrad zur Währungsreform. Zur Sozialgeschichte des Umbruchs in Deutschland*, eds. Martin Broszat, Klaus-Dietmar Henke, and Hans Woller (Munich: Oldenbourg, 1988), 367–425; Christoph Buchheim, "From Enlightened Hegemony to Partnership," in *The United States and Germany in the Era of the Cold War, 1945–1990: A Handbook*, ed. Detlef Junker (New York: Cambridge University Press, 2004), 255–270.
3. Laura Hilton, "Prisoners of Peace: Rebuilding Community, Identity, and Nationality in Displaced Persons Camps in Germany, 1945–1952" (PhD diss., Ohio State University, 2001), 196–201.
4. Reprinted in David Low, *Low's Cartoon History, 1945–1953* (New York: Simon and Schuster, 1953), 17.
5. Report of Ephraim Chase, UN-ARM S-0436-0055-01.
6. Quoted in "Foreign Affairs Background Summary: The international Refugee Agency," U.S. Department of State, March 1947.
7. Malcolm J. Proudfoot, *European Refugees, 1939–1952: A Study in Forced Population Movement* (Evanston, IL: Northwestern University Press, 1956), 409.
8. "Foreign Affairs Background Summary: Displaced Persons," U.S. Department of State, January 1948.
9. Susan T. Pettiss with Lynne Taylor, *After the Shooting Stopped* (Crewe: Trafford, 2004), 206–207.
10. Louise Holborn, *The International Refugee Organization: A Specialized Agency of the United Nations, Its History and Work, 1946–1952* (London: Oxford University Press, 1956), 190.

11. Text of speech in UNARM S-0436-008-05. The notes from the speech are translated and contain numerous grammatical and spelling errors. I have made every effort to retain the original text but have modified the text slightly.

12. Hilton, "Prisoners of Peace," 404.

13. Hilton, "Prisoners of Peace," 417–418; Henriette von Holleuffer, *Zwischen Fremde und Fremde: Displaced Persons in Australien, den USA, und Kanada, 1946–1952* (Osnabrück: Rasch, 2001), 113–115; Mark Wyman, *DPs: Europe's Displaced Persons, 1945–1951* (Philadelphia: Associated University Press, 1998), 191.

14. Letter to Congress, July 7, 1947. Document No. 382, 80th Congress, 1st Session.

15. Hilton, "Prisoners of Peace," 426.

16. "DP Aide Discouraged by US Refugee Bill," *San Francisco News*, February 4, 1949.

17. Haim Genizi, *America's Fair Share: The Admission and Resettlement of Displaced Persons, 1945–52* (Detroit: Wayne State University Press, 1993), 99–104; Displaced Persons Commission, *The DP Story: The Final Report of the United States Displaced Persons Commission* (Washington, GPO, 1952), 37, 366.

18. Displaced Persons Commission, *The DP Story*, 76.

19. http://www.facebook.com/pages/Oginski-Mens-Choir/112129182211047.

20. Anna D. Jaroszyńska-Kirchmann, *The Exile Mission: The Polish Political Diaspora and Polish Americans, 1939–1956* (Athens: Ohio University Press, 2004), 112–113, 137; von Holleuffer, *Zwischen Fremde*, 115, 134.

21. Name list in ITS, NKZD 352. I then searched a sampling of names in the Tracing Files.

22. For a description of the incident, see Kathryn Hulme, *The Wild Place* (Boston: Atlantic Monthly Press, 1953), 173–178; "Help Wanted: Female," *Time*, May 19, 1947, *Time* online archive, http://www.time.com/time/magazine/article/0,9171,933654,00.html; "100 Girls and a Dionne," *Life*, June 2, 1947, 45–48.

23. Personal correspondence with Andrew Zdanowicz, ITS Archive Tracing Files.

24. Johanna F. Coy-Howeler, "Some memories of nutrition work forty and more years ago," *Australian Journal of Nutrition and Dietetics* 52, no. 1 (March 1995), 47.

25. Letter from H.P. du Chatelet to ITS, October 19, 1947. ITS Archive, NKZD 352.

26. Report of December 14, 1948. NARA RG 260, Box 19.

27. "Number of Displaced Persons Living Outside of Assembly Centers . . . ," September 20, 1948. NARA RG 319, Box 284.

28. Letters of December 6 and December 10, 1948. StaaWü Lra Bad Brückenau, 3068.

29. Letter of July 24, 1948. StaaWü Lra Bad Brückenau, 3068.

30. Wurzbürg Military Post, Weekly Intelligence Summary, October 17, 1948. NARA RG 338, 37402/810.

31. Larry Hartenian, "The Role of Media in Democratizing Germany: United States Occupation Policy 1945–1949," *Central European History* 20, no. 2 (1987), 180–181.

32. "The Task of Replacing Displaced Persons," *Würzburg Post-Argus*, September 27, 1947.

33. Report: "Anti-DP Propaganda," October 26, 1948. NARA RG 260/390/47/18–19/163.

34. Personal correspondence with Chester Wolkonowski; Report: "Anti-DP Propaganda," October 26, 1948. NARA RG 260/390/47/18–19/163.

35. Undated. NARA RG 260/390/47/18–19/163.

36. Press release, October 23, 1947. AN AJ/43/897.

37. Letters dated February 1 and May 3, 1949. AN AJ/43/825.

38. Letter of March 24, 1949. AN AJ/43/825.

39. The mechanics of resettlement changed regularly throughout the next few years. A helpful schematic can be found in an April 1950 report in the Control Office for Germany and Austria and the Foreign Office: Control Commission for Germany (British Element), Prisoners of War/Displaced Persons Division: Registered Files FO 1052/31, National Archives (Britain), cited in the document database *Post-War Europe: Refugees, Exile, and Resettlement, 1945–1950* (http://www.tlemea.com/postwareurope/index.htm).

40. Morris Gordon, Interview by USC Shoah Foundation Institute for Visual History and Education, University of Southern California, Albany, NY, November 12, 1997, tape 6, 17.30.

41. Petition of March 13, 1950. AN AJ/43/825.

42. The most complete study of Jewish refugees in Shanghai is David Kranzler, *Japanese, Nazis, and Jews: The Jewish Refugee Community of Shanghai, 1938–1945* (New York: Yeshiva University Press, 1976), esp. 580–581.

43. Documents in AN AJ/43/824. Shanghai group files in AN AJ/43/825.

44. Details of the voyage are in Georg Armbrüster, "Das Ende des Exils in Shanghai: Rück- und Weiterwanderung nach 1945," in *Exil Shanghai, 1938–1947: Jüdisches Leben in der Emigration*, eds. Georg Armbrüster, et al. (Teetz: Hentrich und Hentrich, 2000), 183–200.

45. Basha Drang, Interview by USC Shoah Foundation Institute for Visual History and Education, University of Southern California, Jerusalem, April 17 1996, tape 2, c.10.00.

46. Report by C. W. Townsend, undated. AN AJ/43/825.

47. Howeler, "Some memories," 47.

48. Hulme, *The Wild Place*, 186.

49. Holborn, *The International Refugee Organization*, 441; Proudfoot, *European Refugees*, 430.

50. Hulme, *The Wild Place*, 245.

51. Holborn, *The International Refugee Organization*, 442, 482–484; Inspection Report, IRO Archive, AN, AJ/43/820.

52. Monatsbericht, Rg. v. Uf., January 1948. BHStA, LaflüVerw 2332.

53. Letter from Regierungspräsident Stock to Hoegner, July 3, 1946. BHStA, LaflüVerw 790.

54. Sylvia Schraut, "'Make the Germans Do It: The Refugee Problem in the American Zone of Post-War Germany," in *Forced Migration in Central and Eastern Europe*, ed. Alfred J. Rieber (London: Frank Cass, 2000), 123.

55. Statistische Erhebung zur Unterbringung von Flüchtlinge in Unterfranken. Bestand Innenministerium BHStA 80137.

56. "Assimilation of Immigrant Expellees and Evacuees in the US Zone," undated. NARA RG 260, Box 19. Williams served in a variety of capacities during the FDR administration, including work with the Federal Emergency Relief Administration.

57. "Militärregierung und Flüchtlingsfrage," *Main-Post,* January 27, 1948; "Report on Refugees and Displaced Persons in Land Bavaria," undated 1948. NARA RG 319, Box 284.

58. Letter dated January 30, 1947. BHStA, LaflüVerw 1664.

59. Reports in BHStA, LaFlüVerw 1664. See, for example, the survey of February 2, 1947.

60. Report "The Wildflecken Area," NARA RG 260/390/47/19/4/194. *Die Weber* is Gerhart Hauptmann's 1893 drama depicting the plight of piecework weavers in mid-nineteenth century Silesia.

61. Thomas Berger and Karl-Heinz Müller, *Lebenssituationen 1945–1948* (Hannover: Niedersächsichen Landeszentrale für politische Bildung, 1983), 45; Richard

Bessel, *Germany 1945: From War to Peace* (New York: Harper Collins, 2009), 354.

62. "Errichtung einer Woll- und Leinenindustrie in der Rhön," February 7, 1947. BaK, NL Maria Probst, N/1219, 630.

63. Ibid.

64. "Bericht über die Rhönplanungs-gGmbH und die Tätigkeit ihrer Geschäftsführung," BaK, Maria Probst Papers, N/1219, 628.

65. "Ergänzung des Gutachtens ... über die Verkehrsfragen und ein Bahnprojekt in Raume Wildfleckens," prepared by Oberengineur Hans Kiehne, June 1948. BHStA, MWi, 3710.

66. Report of October 16, 1947. Lra Bad Brückenau 3715, StaatWü.

67. Letter from Poehlmann (Staatsmin. für Ernährung, Landwirtschaft und Forsten) to Staatssek, für das Flüchtlingswesen, April 8, 1947. BHStA, LaFlüVerw 1664.

68. Report, March 24, 1947. BHStA, LaFlüVerw 1664.

69. "Vormerkung: Verwertung des ehemaligen Truppenübungsplatzes Wildflecken," March 20, 1948. BHStA, LaFlüVerw 1664.

70. "Vertrag," May 8, 1947. StaaWü Lra Bad Brückenau, 3163.

71. "Bericht über die Rhönplanungs-gGmbH und die Tätigkeit ihrer Geschäftsführung," BaK, Maria Probst Papers, N/1219, 628.

72. "Rhön-Project in Wildflecken" June 21, 1947. NARA RG 260/390/47/19/4/194. It is unclear if Oswald knew English. This letter does not indicate that it was translated.

73. "Grösste Flüchtlings-Industriesiedlung Bayerns in der Rhön," *Main- Post*, March 18, 1948.

74. "Bericht über die Rhönplanungs-gGmbH und die Tätigkeit ihrer Geschäftsführung," BaK, Maria Probst Papers, N/1219, 628.

75. Ibid.

76. Letter dated April 8, 1947. BHStA, LaflüVerw 1664.

77. Wolfgang Jaenicke, *Vier Jahre Betreuung der Vertriebenen in Bayern, 1945–1949* (Munich: Bayer. Staatsministerium des Innern, 1950), 14–17.

78. Christoph Buchheim, "Marshall Plan and Currency Reform," in *American Policy and the Reconstruction of West Germany, 1945–1955*, eds. Jeffry Diefendorf, Axel Frohn, and Hermann-Josef Rupieper (New York: Cambridge University Press, 1993), 72.

79. Oliver J. Frederiksen, *The American Military Occupation of Germany, 1945–1953* (Heidelberg: U.S. Army Europe, 1953), 96–97.

80. Proceedings of a meeting of the Aufsichtsrats der Rhön-Planung GmbH, Bad Kissingen, July 5, 1948. BHStA, LaflüVerw 1664.

81. Letter from Minn to Rhön-Planung, July 18, 1948. BHStA, LaflüVerw 1664.

82. Maria Probst, *Die Familienpolitik des bayerischen Herrscherhauses zu Beginn des 19. Jahrhunderts* (Aalen: Scientia Verlag, 1974).

83. Bayer. Akademie der Wissenschaft. *Neue Deutsche Biographie*, 20th edition (Berlin: Duncker & Humboldt, 2000), 735.

84. "Regierungs-Flüchtlingslager Hammelburg," July 30, 1948. BaK, Maria Probst Papers, N/1219, 628; "Neue Heimat für Acht Tage," *Frank. Volksblatt*, November 16, 1962. Hammelburg was later used as one of the most important transit camps for those fleeing East Germany.

85. See, for instance, Matthew Frank, *Expelling the Germans: British Opinion and Post-1945 Population Transfer in Context* (Oxford: Oxford University Press, 2007).

86. The author may have been referring to the Greek Refugee Settlement Commission, founded by the Council of the League of Nations in 1923 to assist the Greek government in integrating more than one million refugees from Anatolia.

See Claudena M. Skran, *Refugees in Inter-War Europe: The Emergence of a Regime* (Oxford: Clarendon, 1995), 161–165.
87. Manuscript, "Das Flüchtlingsproblem in Bayern," December 1948. BaK, NL Maria Probst, N/1219, 627.
88. "Stenographischer Bericht über die Verhandlung des Bayerischen Landtags, 2 Juli, 1948," BaK, NL Maria Probst, N/1219, 627.
89. Letter of November 11, 1947. BaK, NL Maria Probst, N/1219, 623.
90. Copy of letter, dated November 10, 1947. BaK, NL Maria Probst, N/1219, 623.
91. Aktenvermerk, June 16, 1948. BHStA, MWi, 3710; Martin Kornrumpf, *Bayern-Atlas* (Munich: Leibniz Verlag, 1949), 65.
92. See collection of letters in BHStA, MWi, 3710.
93. Bayer. Statistischen Landesamt, *Statistisches Jahrbuch für Bayern* (Munich: BSL, 1952), 327.
94. "Bericht über die Rhönplanungs-gGmbH und die Tätigkeit ihrer Geschäftsführung," BaK, Maria Probst Papers, N/1219, 628.
95. Letter from Rhön-Planung, July 27, 1948, to Bayer. Bauernsiedlung Inspektion, signed Oswald and Schober. BHStA, LaflüVerw 1664.
96. Rainer Schulze, "Growing Discontent: Relations Between Native and Refugee Populations in a Rural District in Western Germany after the Second World War," in *West Germany under Construction: Politics, Society, and Culture in the Adenauer Era*, ed. Robert Moeller (Ann Arbor: University of Michigan Press, 1997), 69.
97. Resolution, July 31, 1948. BHStA, LaflüVerw 1664.
98. Resolution, August 6, 1948. BHStA, LaflüVerw 1664.
99. Letter to Bavarian Finance Ministry, October 14, 1948. BaK, Maria Probst Papers, N/1219, 630. On Wutzelhofer, see Arani Verlag, *Wer ist Wer?* (Berlin: Arani Verlags, 1948), 260.

100. Kreistag Brückenau, Sitzung von 7, August 1948. BaK, NL Maria Probst, N/1219, 630.
101. Aktenvermerk, September 22, 1948. BHStA, LaflüVerw 1664.
102. Bayer. Landtag Ausschuss für Wirtschaft. Sitzung von 17.10.48. BaK, NL Maria Probst, N/1219, 630.
103. Letter from Körner to Lra Brückenau, March 21, 1949. StaaWü, Lra Bad Brückenau, 4290.

5. A VICTORY FOR DEMOCRACY, 1949–1952

1. "Construction in Germany: US and French Zone," MS by Col. A. M. Eschbach, 1953. United States Army Corps of Engineers Archive (hereafter USACE), Military Files, Box 32. Letter from Commander, Wildflecken Sub-Post, to Military Post Würzburg and Bürgermeister Wildflecken, July 3, 1951. BHStA, MWi, 22419; Brigadier General Carl D. McIntosh Oral History, Interviewed by Lt. Col. James R. Engelage, 1986, SOOHP, Carl D. McIntosh Papers, Box 1, MHI. My thanks to Brian and Dinny Linn for bringing this last reference to my attention.
2. Bayer. Statistisches Landesamt, Statistisches Jahrbuch für Bayern (Munich: BSL, 1952), 176–177.
3. Bericht über die Verhältnisse des ehem. Muna-Geländes Wildflecken. Written by Landrat Baus, August 8, 1953. StaaWü, Lra Bad Brückenau, 4290.
4. Letter of August 1, 1949. BaK, Maria Probst Papers, N/1219, 633; "Ich darf nicht mehr klagen, ich habe wieder Arbeit," *Main-Post*, November 25, 1951.
5. Joachim Braun, "Heimatvertriebene und Flüchtlinge in Unterfranken (Zeitlicher Verlauf, räumliche Verbreitungsmuster, bevölkerungs- und wirtschaftsgeographische Auswirkung)" (Diplomarbeit, Universität Würzburg, 1984), 120–121; Hanns Hubert Hofmann and Hermann Hemmerich, *Unterfranken: Geschichte seiner Verwaltungsstrukturen seit*

dem Ende des Alten Reiches, 1814 bis 1980 (Würzburg: Sturz, 1981), 29.

6. Report, "Über die Prüfung der Geschäftsführung und des Personalstandes des Flüchtlingsamtes Brückenau am 19. February 1952," BHStA, LaflüVerw 123; Letter from MWi (Heilmann) to MInn Flüchtlingswesen, February 3, 1949. BHStA, LaflüVerw 1664.

7. Publicity Report, Field Operations Division, November 15, 1950. NARA 466/250/72/13/3; "In Wildflecken-Gutsbezirk ist viel geschehen," *Brückenauer Anzeiger,* January 3, 1951.

8. Letter from Flüchtlingsamt Brückenau to Flüchtlingsamt Würzburg, January 4, 1951, StaaWü, Lra Bad Brückenau, 3056.

9. Letter from MWi (Heilmann) to MInn Flüchtlingswesen, February 3, 1949. BHStA, LaflüVerw 1664.

10. Report in StaatWu, Regierung von Unterfranken, 16408; Connor, *Refugees and Expellees in Post-War Germany,* 145; Rainer Schulze, "Growing Discontent: Relations between Native and Refugee Populations in a Rural District in Western Germany after the Second World War," in *West Germany Under Construction: Politics, Society, and Culture in the Adenauer Era,* ed. Robert G. Moeller (Ann Arbor: University of Michigan Press, 1997), 69.

11. Memo of September 26, 1951. Office of the Land Commissioner for Bavaria, NARA 466/250/72/3/1; Connor, *Refugees and Expellees in Post-War Germany,* 140–141.

12. "Städte und Dörfer für Vertriebene entstehen," *Main-Post,* Heimat im Osten supplement, January 12, 1951.

13. "Ausserordentliche Gemeinderatssitzung am 3.3.1948," Protokollbuch Gemeinderatssitzung Wildflecken, April 5, 1946. GaW, Gemeine Wildflecken, Band 2.5.

14. Memo from MG Field Operations Division, November 13, 1948; and U.S. Army Real Property Requisition, May 27, 1949. StaaWü, Lra Bad Brückenau, 4286 (III).

15. "Ausbau in Wildflecken," *Main-Post,* December 12, 1950.

16. Memo from Landratsamt, "Beschlagnahme des ehem. Truppenübungsplatzes Wildflecken zwecks Wiederbenützung als Truppenübungsplatz," November 8, 1948. StaaWü, Lra Bad Brückenau, 4286 (III).

17. Wochenbericht, July 28, 1950. StaaWü, Lra Hammelburg, 2399.

18. Anna J. Merritt and Richard J. Merritt, eds., *Public Opinion in Semi-Sovereign Germany* (Urbana: University of Illinois Press, 1980), 111.

19. Thomas Leuerer, *Die Stationierung amerikanischer Streitkräfte in Deutschland: Militärgemeinden der U.S. Armee seit 1945 als ziviles Element der Stationierungspolitik der Vereinigten Staaten* (Wurzburg: Ergon Verlag, 1997), 335; Hans-Jürgen Schraut, "U.S. Forces in Germany, 1945–1955," in *U.S. Military Forces in Europe: The Early Years, 1945–1970,* eds. Simon W. Duke and Wolfgang Krieger (Boulder, CO: Westview, 1993), 172–175; Bryan T. van Sweringen, "Variable Architectures for War and Peace," in *The United States and Germany in the Era of the Cold War, 1945–1990: A Handbook,* ed. Detlef Junker (New York: Cambridge University Press, 2004), 219.

20. Statistical Report, Würzburg Military Post, December 1951. NARA RG 338, 37042, Box 812. The facilities were Aschaffenburg, Bad Kissingen, Giebelstadt, Kitzingen, Schweinfurt, Wildflecken, and Würzburg.

21. Melvin Leffler, *A Preponderance of Power: National Security, the Truman Administration, and the Cold War* (Stanford: Stanford University Press, 1992), 385–387.

22. An excellent description of the system and its contemporary critics can be found in the files of an investigation into corrupt and inefficient practices among Army officers in "Report and

Recommendations of the Judge Advocate General of the Army Submitted Pursuant to the Directive of the Chief of Staff, United States Army, Dated 25 August 1954." USACE, Military Files, Box 32. See also Hubert Zimmermann, "Occupation Costs, Stationing Costs, Offset Payments," in Junker, *The United States and Germany*, 333–340.

23. Heinrich-August Winkler, *Germany: The Long Road West*, vol. 2, 1933–1990, trans. Alexander Sanger (New York: Oxford University Press, 2006), 124–126; Friedrich Prinz, *Die Geschichte Bayerns* (Munich: Piper, 1993), 506–509.

24. Oliver J. Fredericksen, *The American Military Occupation of Germany, 1945–1953* (Heidelberg: U.S. Army Europe, 1953), 172.

25. Paul Burkhardt, *The Major Training Areas: Grafenwoehr/Vilseck, Hohenfels, Wildflecken* (Weiden: Der neue Tag, 1984), 105–106.

26. U.S. Army Europe, *The U.S. Army Construction Program in Germany, 1950–1953* (Heidelberg: U.S. Army Europe, 1953), 68.

27. "Aufbau in Wildflecken," *Main-Post*, December 12, 1950.

28. Malcolm J. Proudfoot, *European Refugees, 1939–52* (Evanston, IL: Northwestern University Press, 1956), 432.

29. Klaus Bade and Jochen Oltmer, *Normalfall Migration* (Berlin: Bundeszentrale für politische Bildung, 2004), 66; Laura Hilton, "Prisoners of Peace: Rebuilding Community, Identity, and Nationality in Displaced Persons Camps in Germany, 1945–1952" (PhD diss., Ohio State University, 2001), 470–471.

30. Report: Die Ausländer in Bayern, Informationsdienst des Bayer. Statistischen Landesamtes, June 3, 1952. StaaWü, Rg. v. Uf, 16303.

31. Aktenvermerk über die Besprechung mit dem Vertreter der IRO, June 12, 1950. StaaWü, Lra Bad Brückenau, 3608.

32. Both in ITS 3.2.1.1.

33. Letter from Rg v. Uf (Bayer) to Minn, Flüchtlingswesen, January 1, 1950. BHStA, LaflüVerw 1664.

34. "'The Nun's Story' Continued," *Honolulu Advertiser*, January 4, 1960.

35. Report: Die Ausländer in Bayern.

36. Telegrams in AN AJ/43/825 and AJ43/915/55/2.

37. See, for example, Vorschläge für die Verhandlung des Bundestagsabgeordneten Blank mit der Allierierten Hohen Kommission, November 24, 1950. Bundesmin. der Finanzen, Ba, B 150, 469.

38. Memo of October 1, 1951, quoted in NARA 278/250/902/48/06.

39. Letter of January 29, 1951. BHStA, MWi 22419.

40. Letter of February 12, 1951. GaW, Gemeinde Neuwildflecken, 25.3.

41. Meeting on March 27, 1950. StaaWü, Regierung von Unterfranken 17363.

42. Report of Oberste Siedlungsbehörde, "Resolution der heimatvertriebenen Bauern und der Siedler auf dem ... Wildflecken." StaaWü, Lra Bad Brückenau, 4286 (II).

43. Report, undated, but March 1951. BaK, B106, 13353.

44. Summaries of January 8, January 10, and April 28, 1951, in "German News Items on Expellees and Refugees." NARA 278/250/902/48/06.

45. Report, *Flüchtlingsnot in Westdeutschland*. Part of a larger report given by Dr. Robert Boehringer of Geneva at the Neuen Helvetischen Gesellschaft on March 30, 1950. StaWü, Flüchtlinge und Vetriebene 2.

46. "Flüchtlingslager Galgenberg wird geräumt," SZ, August 25, 1950.

47. Günther Schulz, *Wiederaufbau in Deutschland: Die Wohnungsbaupolitik in den Westzonen und der Bundesrepublik von 1945 bis 1957* (Düsseldorf: Droste, 1994), 266–267.

48. U.S. Army Europe, *The U.S. Army Construction Program*, 86.
49. Ibid., 86–87; Meeting at Landwirtschaftministerium München, May 30, 1950. Bayer. Hauptstaatsarchiv, LaFlüVerw, 905; Report of July 9, 1951, Bayer. Staatsministerium der Finanzen, BHStA, Bestand Staatskanzlei, 15115. Statistics on jobs from "Städte und Dörfer für Vertriebene entstehen," *Main-Post*, Heimat im Osten supplement, January 12, 1951.
50. "Unterfränkischen Boden leichtfertig preisgegeben?," *Main-Post*, June 1, 1951.
51. Press release, June 11, 1951, BHStA, Bestand Staatskanzlei, 15115. Quoted from the English-language version.
52. "Bonn verfügt über bayerisches Gebiet," *Münchner Merkur*, June 8, 1951.
53. Statistical Report, Würzburg Military Post, December 1951. NARA RG 338, 37042, Box 812.
54. Memorandum, June 4, 1951. BHStA, LaFlüVerw, 905.
55. "Unterfränkischen Boden leichtfertig preisgegeben?," *Main-Post*, June 1, 1951.
56. Michael Körner, ed., *Grosse Bayerische Biographische Enzyklopädie* (Munich: KG Sauer, 2005), 1416.
57. "Wildflecken statt Hammelburg," *Süddeutsche Zeitung*, June 14, 1951.
58. "Bayern weigert sich 21,000 Deutsche zu vertreiben," *Münchner Merkur*, July 9, 1951.
59. Letter from Landrat Baus, July 10, 1951. StaaWü, Lra Bad Brückenau, 4286 (II).
60. "Hammelburg verteidigt tapfer seinen Boden," SZ, July 12, 1951.
61. Auszug dem Protokoll über die Besprechung am 19.6 bei Mr. McCoy in Bad Godesberg. StaaWü, Lra Bad Brückenau, 4286 (II).
62. Debate in Bavarian Landtag, July 11, 1951. BHStA, LaFlüVerw, 905.
63. Letter from Helmut Penzel to J. P. Bradford, August 21, 1951. NARA 466/250/72/11/4/1.
64. "Hammelburg! Prestigeangelegenheit für Dienststelle Blank? Schicksal der bayerischen Koalitionsregierung durch Hammelburg betroffen," *Main-Echo*, July 2, 1951.
65. Transcript, HICOG Staff Conference, June 5, 1951. NARA 466/260/68/16/2.
66. Ibid.
67. "Schicksal der 31 Gemeinden noch ungewiss," *Main-Post*, June 9, 1951; "Schwere Geschütze im Hammelburger Bauernkrieg," *Münchner Merkur*, June 10, 1951. The Peasants' Wars (1525–1526) was a social and religious conflict across large swaths of Central Europe. A local noble and peasant leader, Florian Geyer, remains a folk hero in Franconia.
68. Resolution, June 3, 1951. BHSta Bestand Staatskanzlei 15115.
69. "Die zweite Heimat verlieren?," *Main-Post*, June 4, 1951.
70. Summaries of August 15, 1951, in "German News Items on Expellees and Refugees," NARA 278/250/902/48/06.
71. Letter from Helmut Penzel to J. P. Bradford, September 15, 1951. NARA 466/250/72/11/4/1.
72. "Schicksal der 31 Gemeinden noch ungewiss," *Main-Post*, June 9, 1951; "Wir wollen in unserer Heimat bleiben!," *Main-Post*, July 30, 1951.
73. BSL, *Statistisches Jahrbuch für Bayern* (Munich: BSL, 1952), 444.
74. "Hammelburg verteidigt tapfer seinen Boden," SZ, July 12, 1951.
75. Letter of July 26, 1951, reported in "Regiert man gegen den Volkswillen?," *Ostdeutsche Zeitung*, August 8, 1951.
76. Transcript, HICOG Staff Conference, July 24, 1951. NARA 466/260/68/16/2.
77. "Hammelburg bleibt verschont," SZ, August 8, 1951.
78. Letter from Helmut Penzel to J. P. Bradford, September 15, 1951, in NARA 466/250/72/11/4/1; Burkhardt, *The Major Training Areas*, 230–231.

79. Report for June, 1951. NARA 466/250/72/13/3.
80. "Truppenübungsplatz Hammelburg wird nicht vergrössert," SZ, June 13, 1951.
81. Information über die Demonstration der Hohenfelser Bauern, August 13, 1951. BHStA, Bestand Staatskanzlei, 15116.
82. Letter to Bundesminister für Vertriebene, Sept 16, 1951. BHStA, LaflüVerw, 1203.
83. U.S. Army Europe, *The U.S. Army Construction Program*, 89–90; Robert Grathwol and Donita Moorhus, *Building for Peace: U.S. Army Engineers in Europe, 1945–1991* (Washington: Center for Military History, 2005), 83.
84. Letter from McCloy to Blank, BaMa, Amt Blank, BW 9/3507.
85. Letter from Rg v. Uf, Bezirksplannungstelle, to Bayer. Staatsministerium für Wirtschaft., Betr: Unterbringung der allierterten Streitkräfte. July 5, 1951.
86. Letters in BHStA, MWi, 22419.
87. Inter-Ministerial Committee, Bonn, July 18, 1951. Ba, B 150, 630; "Bonn verfügt über bayerisches Gebiet," *Münchner Merkur*, June 8, 1951; minutes of the Inter-Ministerial Committee, July 9, 1951. BHStA, LaflüVerw 568.
88. March 31, 1952. StaaWü, Lra Bad Brückenau, 3169.
89. Letter from Settler Committee Werberg to Oberländer, March 20, 1952. BHStA, LaflüVerw, 1203.
90. Letter dated December 18, 1951, in BHStA, MWi 22419.
91. Resolution of the inhabitants of Reussendorf, January 15, 1952. StaaWü, Lra Bad Brückenau, 4826 (I).
92. "Wohin mit den Bewohnern des Truppenübungsplatzes?," *Brückenauer Anzeiger*, April 23, 1952. There is an article of the same name, with very similar text, in the same day's *Fränkisches Land*.
93. Auszug dem Protokoll über die Besprechung am 19.6 bei Mr. McCoy [sic] in Bad Godesburg. StaaWü, Lra Bad Brückenau, 4286 (II); see also the related press release in same.
94. "Wildflecken fordert Sofortmassnahmen," *Main-Post*, April 21, 1952.
95. There are a variety of "final" maps in German and American archives. The one here described can be found in StaaWü, Rg v. Uf, 17363.
96. "Umsiedlung so bald wie möglich," *Main-Post*, May 14, 1952.
97. Report of May 12, 1952. StaaWü, Rg. v. Uf, 17363. Report on employment and housing, September 7, 1951. BHStA, MWi 22419.
98. "Report: Verstärkung der Allierten Streitkräfte im Bundesgebiet: hier: Räumung des Truppenübungsplatzes Wildflecken," Bundesministerium der Finanzen (Schäffer), June 28, 1952. StaaWü, Lra Bad Brückenau, 3165.
99. Letter from LaFlüVerw to Oberfinanzdirektion Nürnberg, June 1952. BHStA, LaflüVerw, 1215.
100. Letter from Dr. Kihn, Regierunspräsident, to Bayer. Staatsministerium für Wirtschaft, Feb. 21, 1952, Betr: Unterbringung der allierten Streitkräfte StaaWü, Rg v. Unterfranken, 17079.
101. Anna M. did not file a petition until 1954. BHStA, LaflüVerw, 1215; StaaWü, Lra Bad Brückenau, 3166.
102. "Historical Report, Civil Affairs Section, Wildflecken Detachment," undated, 1953. NARA RG 338, Box 389.
103. Umsiedlungsantrag, September 1952. BHStA, LaflüVerw, 1215.
104. Report of March 21, 1953, in BHStA, LaflüVerw, 1215.
105. Letter from Zinn Garrett to Blank, June 13, 1952. Ba-Ma, Amt Blank BW 9/3507.
106. "In Reussendorf heisst es Abschiednehmen," *Main-Post*, August 6, 1952.
107. Letter sent from Emil Kreller, in the name of Evakierten from Reussen-

dorf, to Bundesminister für Flüchtlinge Lukaschek, September 14, 1952. BHStA, LaflüVerw, 1215.

108. Bundestag protocol, March 25, 1953.

109. From StaaWü, Reg. v. Ufr, 17364.

110. "Richtfest für 60 Wohnungen," *Fränkisches Volksblatt*, October 13, 1952.

111. "Wohnungen für Familien von Übungsplatz Wildflecken," *Main-Post*, November 17, 1952; Letter in StaaWü, Lra Bad Brückenau, 3168; "Bauschwierigkeiten wurden überwunden," *Main-Post*, April 18, 1953.

112. Various records related to emigration, StaaWü, Lra Bad Brückenau, 3092.

113. Letter of March 19, 1954. Ba-Ma, Amt Blank, BW 9/3506; "Im Gestrüpp der 'Kompetenzen,'" *Main-Post*, February 27, 1954. Personal communication with Sonja Hüfner.

114. Alfred Schrenk, "Die Augesiedlten Dörfer im Truppenübungsplatz Wildflecken," (Zulassungsarbeit für das Lehramt an Volksschulen, Universität Würzburg, 1971), 57–58, 202–203.

115. Case in StaaWü, Lra Bad Brückenau, 3077.

116. Maria Höhn, "'You Can't Pin Sergeant's Stripes on an Archangel': Soldiering, Sexuality, and U.S. Army Policies in Germany," in *Over There: Living with the U.S. Military Empire from World War Two to the Present*, eds. Maria Höhn and Seungsook Moon (Durham, NC: Duke University Press, 2010), 126–127.

117. From a file titled "Prostitution auf üb-Plätzen Wildflecken, Grafenwöhr, Hohenfels," Ba-Ma, Amt Blank, BW 9/3504.

CONCLUSION

1. "Gate Guard at Ammunition Supply Point," November 23, 1953, NARA 338/290/71/32/3-4.

2. "Duty Tour at Wildflecken Keeps Yanks in Shape," *Stars and Stripes*, October 1, 1958; Shaquille O'Neal, *Shaq Talks Back* (New York: Macmillan, 2002), 18.

3. "The Rock in the Clouds," *Soldiers*, July 1988, 45. See also the undated installation history from the Installation Collection, U.S. Army Heritage and Education Center.

4. Paul Burkhardt, *The Major Training Areas: Grafenwoehr/Vilseck, Hohenfels, Wildflecken* (Weiden: Der neue Tag, 1984), 256.

5. Gerwin Kellerman, *475 Jahre Wildflecken, 1524–1999* (Wildflecken: Marktgemeinde Wildflecken, 1999), 114.

6. Unpaginated introductory remarks in Kellermann, *475 Jahre Wildflecken*.

7. Marianne Takle, "(Spät)Aussiedler: From Germans to Immigrants," *Nationalism and Ethnic Politics* 17, no. 2 (2011): 162–163.

8. The complexities of this story are well summarized in Andreas Heinrich, "The Integration of Ethnic Germans from the Soviet Union," in *Coming Home to Germany? The Integration of Ethnic Germans from Central and Eastern Europe in the Federal Republic*, eds. David Rock and Stefan Wolff (New York: Berghahn, 2002), 77–86.

9. Statistics courtesy of the KWADRO integration project, sponsored by the German federal government and Landkreis Bad Kissingen. http://www.regierung .unterfranken.bayern.de/ unsere _aufgaben/2/2/17638/index.html.

10. "Wir haben kein Problem, wir sind das Problem," SZ, January 23/4, 1999.

11. Bayerisches Landesamt für Statistik und Datenverarbeitung, *Ausländer in Bayern am 31. Dezember 2009* (Munich: BLSD, 2010), 16–17.

12. "Wandern und Feiern im Truppenübungsplatz," *Main-Post*, July 5, 2008.

13. http://www.rhoenpuls.de/start/ detailansicht-ihrer-auswahl/artikel/ verschwundenes-werberg/.

14. http://www.unesco.org/ mabdb/br/brdir/directory/biores .asp?mode=all&code= GER+09.

BIBLIOGRAPHY

ARCHIVAL MATERIAL

Archives nationales de France (AN)
AJ/43: *Organisation international pour les réfugiés*

Beinecke Rare Book and Manuscript Library, Yale University
Kathryn Hulme Papers, Yale Collection of American Literature, Beinecke Rare Book and Manuscript Library, MSS 22 (KCH)

Bayerisches Hauptstaatsarchiv, Abteilung Würzburg (StaaWü)
Bestand Landratsamt Bad Brückenau (Lra Brückenau)
Bestand Landratsamt Hammelburg (Lra Hammelburg)
Bestand Regierung von Unterfranken (Rg. v. Uf)

Bayerisches Hauptstaatsarchiv, Munich (BHStA)
Bestand Innenministerium (MInn)
Bestand Landesflüchtlingsverwaltung (LaflüVerw)
Bestand Staatskanzlei (StK)
Bestand Wirtschaftsministerium (MWi)

Bundesarchiv Koblenz (Ba)
B 106 *Bundesministerium des Innern*
B 150 *Bundesministerium für Vertriebene, Flüchtlinge und Kriegsgechädigte*
NL *Maria Probst*
Z 45 F OMGUS

Bundesarchiv – Militärarchiv, Freiburg (Ba-Ma)
BW 9 *Dienststelle Blank*

International Tracing Service Archive, Bad Arolsen, (ITS)
Nachkriegszeitdokumente (NKZD)
Tracing Service Files

National Archives and Records Administration, Suitland, Md (NARA)
RG 111: *Office of the Chief Signal Officer*
RG 260: *Records of the United States Occupation Headquarters, World War II*
RG 227: *Records of the Displaced Persons Commission, 1948–1952*
RG 319: *Records of the Army Staff*
RG 338: *Records of U.S. Army Organizational, Tactical, and Support Organizations, WWII and Thereafter*
RG 466: *Records of the U.S. High Commissioner for Germany*
RG 549: *Records of U.S. Army Europe*

Gemeindearchiv
Wildflecken (GaW)
Gemeinde Wildflecken
Gemeinde Neuwildflecken

Shoah Foundation Visual
History Archive
Ernest Abraham
Minna Aspler
Basha Drang
Jan Dudzinski
Joe Friedman
Alex Gelbart
Felix Goldberg
Morris Gordon
David Gurvitz
Morris Krakowsky
Josek Melcer
David Newman
Elise Schapira
David Schuster
Malka Wainzstain

Stadtarchiv Würzburg (SdtWü)
Flüchtlinge und Vertriebene

United Nations Archival Records
Management (UNARM)
UNRRA *Files*

United States Army Corps
of Engineers History
Office (USACE)
History Files

United States Army Heritage
and Education Center
Oral History Collection
Installation Collection

United States Holocaust
Memorial Museum Archive
Albert Hutler Collection
Oral History Collection

NEWSPAPERS AND PERIODICALS
Brückenauer Anzeiger
The Dragon
Fränkisches Volksblatt
Honolulu Advertiser
Kronika
Life
Main-Echo
Main-Post
Münchner Merkur
New Republic
New Yorker
Oakland Tribune
New York Times
Ostdeutsche Zeitung
Phylon
Post-Argus (Würzburg)
Rhoenpuls.de
San Francisco News
Soldiers
Süddeutsche Zeitung (SZ)
Tevzeme
Time
Unterwegs
Wiadonosci Polskie

Published Sources
Ahonen, Pertti, Gustavo Corni, et al., eds. *People on the Move: Forced Population Movements in Europe in the Second World War and its Aftermath.* Oxford: Berg, 2008.
Ahonen, Pertti. *After the Expulsion: West Germany and Eastern Europe.* Oxford: Oxford University Press, 2003.
Allen, William Sheridan. *The Nazi Seizure of Power:* The Experience of a Single German Town, 1922–1945. New York: F. Watts, 1984.
Aly, Götz. *Final Solution: Nazi Population Policy and the Murder of the European Jews.* London: Arnold, 1999.
Arani Verlag. *Wer ist Wer?* Berlin: Arani Verlag, 1948.
Armbrüster, Georg, et al., eds. *Exil Shanghai, 1938–1947: Jüdisches Leben in der*

Emigration. Teetz: Hentrich und Hentrich, 2000.
Aust, Stefan, and Stephan Burgdorff, eds. *Die Flucht: Über die Vertreibung der Deutschen aus dem Osten*. Bonn: BPB, 2005.
Bade, Klaus, and Jochen Oltmer. *Normalfall Migration*. Berlin: Bundeszentrale für politische Bildung, 2004.
Baedeker, Karl. *Southern Germany and Austria*. Leipzig: Karl Baedeker, 1883.
Baker, Anni. *Wiesbaden and the Americans, 1945–2003*. Wiesbaden: Stadtarchiv Wiesbaden, 2004.
Bauer, Franz J. *Flüchtlinge und Flüchtlingspolitik in Bayern 1945–1950*. Stuttgart: Klett-Cotta, 1982.
Bauerkämper, Arnd, Konrad H. Jarausch, and Marcus H. Payk, eds. *Demokratiewunder: Transatlantische Mittler und die kulturelle Öffnung Westdeutschlands*. Göttingen: Vandenhoeck & Ruprecht, 2005.
Bayer. Akademie der Wissenschaft. *Neue Deutsche Biographie*, 20th edition. Berlin: Duncker & Humboldt, 2000.
Bayer. Statistisches Landesamt. *Statistisches Jahrbuch für Bayern*. Munich: BSL, 1936.
———. *Statistisches Jahrbuch für Bayern*. Munich: BSL, 1946.
———. *Statistisches Jahrbuch für Bayern*. Munich: BSL, 1948.
———. *Statistisches Jahrbuch für Bayern*. Munich: BSL, 1949.
———. *Statistisches Jahrbuch für Bayern*. Munich: BSL, 1952.
———. *Die Flüchtlinge in Bayern*. Munich: BSL, 1948.
———. *Dritte Bundestagswahl in Bayern*. Munich: BSL, 1957.
Becker, Steffen. "Von der Werbung zum 'Totaleinsatz': Die Politik der Rekrutierung von Arbeitskräften im 'Protektorat Böhmen und Mähren' für die deutsche Kriegswirtschaft und der Aufenthalt tschechischer Zwangsarbeiter und –arbeiterinnen im Dritten Reich 1939–1945." PhD diss., Humboldt-Universität zu Berlin, 2004.
Behrend, Ivan T. *Decades of Crisis: Central and Eastern Europe Before World War II*. Berkeley: University of California Press, 2001.
Benz, Wolfgang, ed. *Deutschland unter alliierter Besatzung, 1945–1949/55*. Berlin: Akademie Verlag, 1999.
Berger, Thomas, and Karl-Heinz Müller, eds. *Lebenssituationen 1945–1948*. Hannover: Niedersächsichen Landeszentrale für politische Bildung, 1983.
Bergerson, Andrew Stuart. *Ordinary Germans in Extraordinary Times: The Nazi Revolution in Hildesheim*. Bloomington: Indiana University Press, 2004.
Bessel, Richard. *Germany 1945: From War to Peace*. New York: Harper Collins, 2009.
Bessel, Richard, and Claudia Haake, eds. *Removing Peoples: Forced Removal in the Modern World*. London: Oxford University Press, 2009.
Binder, Cornelia, and Michael Mence. *Nachbarn der Vergangenheit: Spuren von Deutschen jüdischen Glaubens im Landkreis Bad Kissingen mit dem Brennpunkt 1800 bis 1945*. Bad Brückenau: self-published, 2004.
Bjork, James E. *Neither German nor Pole: Catholicism and National Indifference in a Central European Borderland*. Ann Arbor: University of Michigan Press, 2008.
Blatman, Daniel. "The Encounter Between Jews and Poles in Lublin District after Liberation, 1944–1943." *East European Politics and Societies* 20, no. 4 (2006): 598–621.
Bloxham, Donald. *Genocide, the World Wars, and the Unweaving of Europe*. London: Vallentine Mitchell, 2008.
Bramwell, Anna C., ed. *Refugees in the Age of Total War*. London: Unwin Hyman, 1988.

Borowski, Tadeusz. *This Way for the Gas, Ladies and Gentlemen,* translated by Barbara Vedder. New York: Penguin, 1976.

Brandon, Ray, and Wendy Lower, eds. *The Shoah in Ukraine: History, Testimony, Memorialization.* Bloomington: Indiana University Press, 2008.

Braun, H. J. *The German Economy in the Twentieth Century: The Third Reich and the Federal Republic.* New York: Routledge, 1990.

von der Brelie-Lewien, Doris. „*Dann kamen die Flüchtlinge*": *Der Wandel des Landkreises Fallingbostel vom Rüstungszentrum im „Dritten Reich" zur Flüchtlingshochburg nach dem Zweiten Weltkrieg.* Hildesheim: Wallstein, 1990.

Browder, Dewey A. "The GI Dollar and the Wirtschaftswunder." *Journal of European Economic History* 22, no. 3 (Winter 1993): 601–612.

Broszat, Martin, Klaus-Dietmar Henke, and Hans Woller, eds. *Von Stalingrad zur Währungsreform. Zur Sozialgeschichte des Umbruchs in Deutschland.* Munich: Oldenbourg, 1988.

Brubaker, Rogers. „National Minorities, Nationalizing States, and External National Homelands in the New Europe." *Daedalus* 144: 2 (Spring 1995): 107–132.

Bundesministerium für Vertriebene. *Vertriebene, Flüchtlinge, Kriegsgefangene, Heimatlöse Ausländer, 1949–1952.* Bonn: Bundesministerium für Vertriebene, 1953.

Burkhardt, Paul. *The Major Training Areas: Grafenwöhr/Vilseck, Hohenfels, Wildflecken.* Weiden: Der neue Tag, 1984.

Carafano, James Jay. "Mobilizing Europe's Stateless: America's Plan for a Cold War Army." *Journal of Cold War Studies* 1, no. 2 (1999): 61–85.

Carstens, Uwe. *Leben im Flüchtlingslager: Ein Kapitel deutscher Nachkriegsgeschichte.* Husum: Husum Verlag, 1994.

Cesarani, David, et al., eds. *Survivors of Nazi Persecution in Europe after the Second World War.* London: Vallentine Mitchell, 2010.

Citino, Robert M. *The Path to Blitzkrieg: Doctrine and Training in the German Army, 1920–1939.* Boulder, CO: Lynne Reiner, 1999.

Cohen, G. Daniel. "Between Relief and Politics: Refugee Humanitarianism in Occupied Germany, 1945–1946." *Journal of Contemporary History* 43, no. 3 (2008): 437–449.

———. "Remembering Post-War Displaced Persons: From Omission to Resurrection." In *Enlarging European Memory: Migration Movements in Historical Perspective,* edited by Mareike König and Rainer Ohliger. Stuttgart: Thorbecke Verlag, 2006.

Connor, Ian. *Refugees and Expellees in Post-War Germany.* Manchester: Manchester University Press, 2007.

———. "The Bavarian Government and the Refugee Problem, 1945–1950." *European History Quarterly* 16, no. 2 (April 1986): 131–153.

Coy-Howeler, Johanna F. "Some memories of nutrition work forty and more years ago." *Australian Journal of Nutrition and Dietetics* 52, no. 1 (March 1995): 46–51.

Deist, Wilhelm, et al., eds. *Germany and the Second World War,* vol. 1. *The Build-Up of German Aggression,* translated by P. S. Falla, et al. Oxford: Clarendon, 1990.

Delaney, John J. "Social Contact and Personal Relations of German Catholic Peasants and Polish Workers (POWs, Civilian, and Forced Laborers) in Bavaria's Rural War Economy, 1939–1945." *Annali dell'Istituto storico italo-germanico in Trento* 27 (2002): 394–404.

Department of State. *The Axis in Defeat.* Washington, Department of State, 1945.

Diefendorfer, Jeffry, Axel Frohn, and Hermann-Josef Rupieper, eds. *American Policy and the Reconstruction of West*

Germany, 1945–55. Cambridge: Cambridge University Press, 1993.
Displaced Persons Commission. *The DP Story: The Final Report of the United States Displaced Persons Commission.* Washington: GPO, 1952.
Dobson, Sean. *Authority and Upheaval in Leipzig, 1910–1920: The Story of a Relationship.* New York: Columbia University Press, 2001.
Duke, Simon W., and Wolfgang Krieger, eds. *U.S. Military Forces in Europe: The Early Years, 1945–1970.* Boulder, CO: Westview, 1993.
Eley, Geoff. "Europe after 1945." *History Workshop Journal* 65 (2008): 195–212.
Elliott, Mark. *Pawns of Yalta: Soviet Refugees and America's Role in their Repatriation.* Urbana: University of Illinois Press, 1982.
Erker, Paul. *Vom Heimatvertriebenen zum Neubürger: Sozialgeschichte der Flüchtlinge in einer agrarischen Region Mittelfrankens 1945–1955.* Wiesbaden: Franz Steiner, 1988.
Fehrenbach, Heide. *Race After Hitler: Black Occupation Children in Postwar Germany and America.* Princeton: Princeton University Press, 2005.
Friedländer, Saul. *The Years of Extermination: Nazi Germany and the Jews, 1939–1945.* New York: Harper Collins, 2007.
Fink, Carol. *Defending the Rights of Others: The Great Powers, the Jews, and International Minority Protection, 1878–1938.* Cambridge: Cambridge University Press, 2004.
Flade, Roland. *Der Novemberpogrom von 1938 in Unterfranken: Vorgeschichte – Verlauf – Augenzeugenberichte.* Würzburg: Schöningh, 1988.
Frank, Matthew. *Expelling the Germans: British Opinion and Post-1945 Population Transfer in Context.* Oxford: Oxford University Press, 2007.
Frantzioch, Marion. *Die Vertriebenen: Hemmnisse, Antriebskräfte und Wege ihrer Integration in der Bundesrepublik Deutschland.* Berlin: Dietrich Reimer, 1987.
Fredericksen, Oliver J. *The American Military Occupation of Germany, 1945–1953.* Heidelberg: U.S. Army Europe, 1953.
Frei, Norbert. *Vergangenheitspolitik: Die Anfänge der Bundesrepublik und die NS-Vergangenheit.* Munich: Beck, 1996.
Fritz, Stephen. "This is the Way Wars End, With a Bang not a Whimper: Middle Franconia in April 1945." *War and Society* 19, no. 1 (2000): 121–153.
Garson, Robert A., ed. *The Roosevelt Years: New Perspectives on American History, 1933–1945.* Edinburgh: Edinburgh University Press, 1999.
Gatrell, Peter. "Introduction: World Wars and Population Displacement in Europe in the Twentieth Century." *Contemporary European History* 16, no. 4 (2007): 415–426.
Gellately, Robert. *The Gestapo and German Society: Enforcing Racial Policy, 1933–1945.* Oxford: Clarendon, 1990.
Genizi, Haim. *America's Fair Share: The Admission and Resettlement of Displaced Persons, 1945–1952.* Detroit: Wayne State University Press, 1993.
Gerwarth, Robert, ed. *Twisted Paths: Europe 1914–1945.* Oxford: Oxford University Press, 2007.
Geyer, Martin. *Verkehrte Welt: Revolution, Inflation und Moderne, München 1914–1924.* Gottingen: Vandenhoeck & Ruprecht, 1998.
Gimbel, John. *The American Occupation of Germany: Politics and the Military, 1945–1949.* Stanford: Stanford University Press, 1968.
———. *A German Community under American Occupation: Marburg 1945–52.* Stanford: Stanford University Press, 1961.
Goecken-Haidl, Ulrike. *Der Weg zurück. Die Repatriierung sowjetischer Zwangsarbeiter und Kriegsgefangener während*

und nach dem Zweiten Weltkrieg. Essen: Klartext, 2006.

Gott, Kendall. *Mobility, Vigilance, and Justice: The U.S. Army Constabulary in Germany, 1946–1953*. Ft. Leavenworth, KS: Combat Studies Institute Press, 2005.

Grathwol, Robert, and Donita Moorhus. *Building for Peace: U.S. Army Engineers in Europe, 1945–1991*. Washington: Center for Military History, 2005.

Gregor, Neil. *Haunted City: Nuremberg and the Nazi Past*. New Haven: Yale University Press, 2008.

Gross, Jan T. *Revolution from Abroad: The Soviet Conquest of Poland's Western Ukraine and Western Belorussia*. Princeton: Princeton University Press, 2002.

Grossmann, Atina. *Jews, Germans, and Allies: Close Encounters in Occupied Germany*. Princeton: Princeton University Press, 2007.

Hahn. Leo V. *Kriegsgefange und Fremdarbeiter in Würzburg*. Self-published, 2005.

Hartenian, Larry. "The Role of Media in Democratizing Germany: United States Occupation Policy 1945–1949." *Central European History* 20, no. 2 (1987): 144–190.

Hausleitner, Mariana. *Die Rumänisierung der Bukowina: Die Durchsetzung des nationalstaatlichen Anspruchs Grossrumäniens 1918–1944*. Munich: Oldenbourg, 2001.

Heidrich, Hermann, et al., eds. *Fremde auf dem Land*. Neustadt: Verlagsdrückerei Schmidt, 2000.

Herbert, Ulrich. *Hitler's Foreign Workers: Enforced Foreign Labor in Germany under the Third Reich*, translated by William Templer. Cambridge: Cambridge University Press, 1997.

Hillman, Barbara, et al. *Lw. 2/XI – Muna Lübberstedt. Zwangsarbeit für den Krieg*. Bremen: Edition Temmen, 1996.

Hilton, Laura. „Prisoners of Peace: Rebuilding Community, Identity, and Nationality in Displaced Persons Camps in Germany, 1945–1952." PhD diss., Ohio State University, 2001.

Hitchcock, William I. *The Bitter Road to Freedom: A New History of the Liberation of Europe*. New York: Free Press, 2008.

Hohmann, Joachim S. *Landvolk unterm Hakenkreuz: Agrar- und Rassenpolitik in der Rhön*. 2 vols. Frankfurt: Peter Lang, 1992.

Holborn, Louise. *The International Refugee Organization: A Specialized Agency of the United Nations, Its History and Work, 1946–1952*. London: Oxford University Press, 1956.

von Holleuffer, Henriette. *Zwischen Fremde und Fremde: Displaced Persons in Australien, den USA, und Kanada, 1946–1952*. Osnabrück: Rasch, 2001.

Holler, Joanne. *The German Expellees: A Problem of Integration*. Washington, D.C.: George Washington University, 1963.

Höhn, Maria. *GIs and Fräuleins: The German-American Encounter in 1950s West Germany*. Chapel Hill: University of North Carolina Press, 2002.

Höhn, Maria, and Seungsook Moon, eds. *Over There: Living with the U.S. Military Empire from World War Two to the Present*. Durham, NC: Duke University Press, 2010.

Holian, Anna. "Between National Socialism and Soviet Communism: The Politics of Self-Representation Among Displaced Persons in Munich, 1945–51." PhD diss., University of Chicago, 2005.

Horwitz, Gordon J. *Ghettostadt: Łódź and the Making of a Nazi City*. Cambridge: Belknap, 2008.

Hulme, Kathryn. *The Wild Place*. Boston: Atlantic Monthly Press, 1953.

Jacobmeyer, Wolfgang. *Vom Zwangsarbeiter zum Heimatlosen Ausländer: Die Displaced Persons in Westdeutschland, 1945–1951*. Göttingen: Vandenhoeck & Ruprecht, 1985.

Jaenicke, Wolfgang. *Vier Jahre Betreuung der Vertriebenen in Bayern, 1945–1949.* Munich: Bayerisches Staatsministerium des Innern, 1950.

Jaroszyńska-Kirchmann, Anna D. *The Exile Mission: The Polish Political Diaspora and Polish Americans, 1939–1956.* Athens: Ohio University Press, 2004.

Judt, Tony. *Postwar: A History of Europe Since 1945.* New York: Penguin, 2005.

Junker, Detlef, ed. *The United States and Germany in the Era of the Cold War, 1945–1990: A Handbook.* New York: Cambridge University Press, 2004.

Kellerman, Gerwin. *475 Jahre Wildflecken, 1524–1999.* Wildflecken: Marktgemeinde Wildflecken, 1999.

Kershaw, Ian. *Popular Opinion and Political Dissent in the Third Reich: Bavaria, 1933–1945.* New York: Oxford University Press, 1983.

King, Jeremy. *Budweisers into Czechs and Germans: A Local History of Bohemian Politics, 1848–1948.* Princeton: Princeton University Press, 2002.

Klee, Katja. *Im Luftschutzkeller des Reiches: Evakuierte in Bayern, 1939–1953.* Munich: Oldenbourg, 1998.

König, Mareike, and Rainer Ohliger, eds. *Enlarging European Memory: Migration Movements in Historical Perspective.* Stuttgart: Thorbecke Verlag, 2006.

Körner, Michael, ed. *Grosse Bayerische Biographische Enzyklopädie.* Munich: KG Sauer, 2005.

Kornrumpf, Martin. *In Bayern angekommen: die Eingliederung der Vertriebenen: Zahlen, Daten, Namen.* Munich: Olzog, 1979.

———. *Bayern-Atlas.* Munich: Leibniz Verlag, 1949.

Kossert, Andreas. *Kalte Heimat: Die Geschichte der deutschen Vertriebenen nach 1945.* Munich: Siedler, 2008.

———. *Ostpreußen: Geschichte und Mythos.* Munich: Siedler, 2005.

———. "Endlösung on the ‚Amber Shore': The Massacre in January 1945 on the Baltic Seashore – A Repressed Chapter of East Prussian History." *Leo Baeck Institute Yearbook* 49 (2004): 3–21.

Kranzler, David. *Japanese, Nazis, and Jews: The Jewish Refugee Community of Shanghai, 1938–1945.* New York: Yeshiva University Press, 1976.

Krause, Michael. *Flucht vor dem Bombenkrieg: „Umquartierung" im Zweiten Weltkrieg und die Wiedereingliederung der Evakuierten in Deutschland, 1943–1963.* Düsseldorf: Droste, 1997.

Leffler, Melvin. *A Preponderance of Power: National Security, the Truman Administration, and the Cold War.* Stanford: Stanford University Press, 1992.

Lemberg, Eugen, and Friedrich Edding, eds. *Die Vertriebenen in Westdeutschland.* 3 vols. Kiel: Ferdinand Hirt, 1959.

Lemberg, Hans, and K. Erik Franzen. *Die Vertriebenen: Hitlers letzte Opfer.* Berlin: Propylaeen, 2001.

Lipner, Seth E. *The Legal and Economic Aspects of Gray Market Goods.* Westport, CT: Quorum Books, 1990.

Low, David. *Low's Cartoon History, 1945–1953.* New York: Simon and Schuster, 1953.

Lowenstein, Karl. "Law and the Legislative Process in Occupied Germany." *Yale Law Journal* 57, no. 6 (April 1948): 994–1022.

Lumans, Valdis O. *Himmler's Auxiliaries: the Volksdeutsche Mittelstelle and the German National Minorities of Europe, 1933–45.* Chapel Hill: University of North Carolina Press, 1993.

Lüttinger, Paul. „Der Mythos der schnellen Integration. Eine imperische Untersuchung zur Integration der Vertriebenen und Flüchtlinge in der Bundesrepublik Deutschland." *Zeitschrift für Soziologie* 1 (1986): 20–36.

Magnus, Dr. Kurt. *One Million Tons of War Material for Peace: The History of STEG.* Munich: Richard Pflaum, 1954.

Magocsi, Paul Robert. *Historical Atlas of Central Europe*. Seattle: University of Washington Press, 2002.

Mankowitz, Zeev. *Life Between Memory and Hope: The Survivors of the Holocaust in Occupied Germany*. Cambridge: Cambridge University Press, 2002.

Martin, Terry. "The Origins of Soviet Ethnic Cleansing." *Journal of Modern History* 70 (December 1998): 813–861.

May, Herbert. *Zwangsarbeit im ländlichen Franken*. Bad Windsheim, Fränkischen Freilandsmuseum, 2008.

McLaren, Meryn. "'Out of the Huts Emerged a Settled People': Community-Building in West German Refugee Camps." *German History* 28, no. 1 (2010): 21–43.

Melendy, Brenda. "Expellees on Strike: Competing Victimization Discourses and the Dachau Refugee Camp Protest Movement, 1949–49." *German Studies Review* 28, no. 1 (2005): 107–125.

———. "Narratives, Festivals, and Reinvention: Defining the Postwar German Homeland in Waldkraiburg." *Journal of Popular Culture* 39, no. 6 (2006).

Memming, Rolf. "The Bavarian Governmental District Unterfranken and the City Burgstadt, 1922–1939: A Study of the National Socialist Movement and Party-State Affairs." PhD diss., University of Nebraska, 1974.

Mitcham, Samuel. *The German Order of Battle*, vol. 1. Mechanicsburg, PA: Stackpole, 2007.

Moeller, Robert. *War Stories: The Search for a Usable Past in the Federal Republic of Germany*. Berkeley: University of California Press, 2003.

Moeller, Robert, ed. *West Germany Under Construction: Politics, Society, and Culture in the Adenauer Era*. Ann Arbor: University of Michigan Press, 1997.

Müller, Rolf-Dieter, and Gerd R. Ueberschär. *Kriegsende 1945. Die Zerstörung des Deutschen Reiches*. Frankfurt: Fischer, 1994.

Murphy, Richard Charles. *Guestworkers in the German Reich: A Polish Community in Wilhelmian Germany*. Boulder, CO: East European Monographs, 1983.

Naimark, Norman M. *Fires of Hatred: Ethnic Cleansing in Twentieth-Century Europe*. Cambridge: Harvard University Press, 2001.

Niethammer, Lutz. *Die Mitläuferfabrik: Die Entnazifizierung am Beispiel Bayerns*. Berlin, Dietz: 1982.

O'Neal, Shaquille. *Shaq Talks Back*. New York: Macmillan, 2002.

Ophir, Baruch Z., and Falk Wiesemann. *Die jüdische Gemeinden in Bayern 1918–1945*. Munich: Oldenbourg, 1979.

Padfield, Peter. *Himmler*. New York: Henry Holt, 1990.

Panayi, Panikos. *Life and Death in a German Town: Osnabrück from the Weimar Republic to World War II and Beyond*. London: Tauris, 2007.

Pegel, Michael. *Fremdarbeiter, Displaced Persons, Heimatlose Ausländer: Konstanten eines Randgruppenshicksals in Deutschland nach 1945*. Münster: Lit, 1997.

Pettiss, Susan T., and Lynne Taylor. *After the Shooting Stopped*. Crewe: Trafford, 2004.

Pfeil, Elisabeth. *Fünf Jahre später: Die Eingliederung der Heimatvertriebenen in Bayern*. Frankfurt: Wolfgang Mentzer, 1951.

Pittaway, Mark. *Eastern Europe, 1939–2000*. London: Arnold, 2004.

von Plato, Alexander, et al., eds. *Hitler's Slaves: Life Stories of Forced Labourers in Nazi-Occupied Europe*. New York: Berghahn, 2010.

Probst, Maria. *Die Familienpolitik des bayerischen Herrscherhauses zu Beginn des 19. Jahrhunderts*. Aalen: Scientia Verlag, 1974.

Prinz, Friedrich. *Die Geschichte Bayerns*. Munich: Piper, 2003.

———. *Trümmerzeit in München: Kultur und Gesellschaft einer deutschen*

Großstadt im Aufbruch, 1945–1949. Munich: Beck, 1984.
Proudfoot, Malcolm J. *European Refugees, 1939–52.* Evanston, IL: Northwestern University Press, 1956.
Radspieler, Tony. *The Ethnic German Refugee Problem in Austria, 1945–1954.* The Hague: Martinus Nijhoff, 1955.
van Rahden, Til. *Jews and other Germans: Civil Society, Religious Diversity, and Urban Politics in Breslau, 1860–1925.* Madison: Wisconsin University Press, 2008.
Reinisch, Jessica. "Introduction: Relief in the Aftermath of War." *Journal of Contemporary History* 43, no. 3 (2008): 372–392.
Reinisch, Jessica, and Elizabeth White, eds. *The Disentanglement of Populations: Migration, Expulsion, and Displacement in Post-war Europe, 1944–9.* New York: Palgrave Macmillan, 2011.
Reuss, Thomas. *Öffentlichkeit und Propaganda: Nationalsozialistische Presse in Unterfranken 1922–1945.* Bad Neustadt: Kolumbus, 1988.
Rieber, Alfred J., ed. *Forced Migration in Central and Eastern Europe.* London: Frank Cass, 2000.
Rinderle, Walter, and Bernard Norling. *The Nazi Impact on a German Village.* Lexington: University Press of Kentucky, 1993.
Rock, David, and Stefan Wolff, eds. *Coming Home to Germany? The Integration of Ethnic Germans from Central and Eastern Europe in the Federal Republic since 1945.* New York: Berghahn, 2002.
Rodrigues, Luís N., ed. *Franklin Roosevelt and the Azores During the Two World Wars.* Lisbon: Fundação Luso-Americana, 2008.
Rossino, Alexander B. *Hitler Strikes Poland: Blitzkrieg, Ideology, and Atrocity.* Lawrence: University of Kansas Press, 2003.
Roth, Claudia. *Parteikreis und Kreisleiter der NSDAP unter besonderer Berücksichtigung Bayerns.* Munich: C. H. Beck, 1997.
Ruhenstroth-Bauer, Wolfram. "Die Bayerische Landessiedlung GmbH als Instrument bayerischer Agrarpolitik unter besonderer Berücksichtigung der Eingliederung heimatvertriebener Landwirte." PhD diss., TU München, 1976.
Rumschöttel, Hermann, and Walter Ziegler, eds. *Staat und Gaue in der NS-Zeit: Bayern 1933–1945.* Munich: Beck, 2004.
Saathoff, Günter, Franz Dillmann, and Manfred Messerschmidt, eds. *Opfer der NS-Militärjustiz: Zur Notwendigkeit der Rehabilitierung und Entschädigung.* Cologne: Bundesverband Information und Beratung für NS-Verfolgte, 1994.
Shephard, Ben. *The Long Road Home: The Aftermath of the Second World War.* New York: Knopf, 2011.
Salomon, Kim. *Refugees in the Cold War: Towards a New International History of the International Refugee Regime in the Early Postwar Era.* Lund: Lund University Press, 1991.
Schieder, Theodor, et al., eds. *Documentation der Vertreibung der Deutschen aus Ost-Mitteleuropa.* Bonn: Bundesministerium für Vertriebene, 1954–60.
Schraut, Sylvia. *Flüchtlingsaufnahme in Württemberg-Baden, 1945–1949. Amerikanische Besatzungsziele und demokratischer Wiederaufbau im Konflikt.* Munich: Oldenbourg, 1995.
Schrenk, Alfred. "Die Augesiedlten Dörfer im Truppenübungsplatz Wildflecken." Zulassungsarbeit für das Lehramt an Volkschulen, Universität Würzburg, 1971.
Schröder, Stefan. *Displaced Persons im Landkreis und in der Stadt Münster, 1945–1951.* Münster: Aschendorff Verlag, 2005.
Schulz, Günther. *Wiederaufbau in Deutschland: Die Wohnungsbaupolitik in den*

Westzonen und der Bundesrepublik von 1945 bis 1957. Düsseldorf: Droste, 1994.
Skran, Claudena. *Refugees in Inter-War Europe: The Emergence of a Regime*. Oxford: Clarendon, 1995.
Siebel-Aschenbach, Sebastian. *Lower Silesia from Nazi Germany to Communist Poland, 1942–49*. New York: St. Martin's, 1994.
Silverman, Dan P. *Hitler's Economy: Nazi Work Creation Programs, 1933–1936*. Cambridge: Harvard University Press, 1998.
Sjöberg, Tommie. *The Powers and the Persecuted: The Refugee Problem and the Intergovernmental Committee on Refugees (IGCR), 1938–1947*. Lund: Lund University Press, 1991.
Smith, Helmut Walser. *The Butcher's Tale: Murder and Anti-Semitism in a German Town*. New York: Norton, 2002.
Snyder, Timothy. *Bloodlands: Europe Between Hitler and Stalin*. New York: Basic Books, 2010.
———. "To Resolve the Ukrainian Problem Once and For All: The Ethnic Cleansing of Ukrainians in Poland, 1943–1947." *Journal of Cold War Studies* 1, no. 2 (1999): 86–120.
Spitznagel, Peter. *Wähler and Wahlen in Unterfranken, 1919–1969: Versuch einer Analyse der Wählerstruktur eines Regierungsbezirkes auf statistischer Grundlagenach den Erhebungen der Volkszählungen 1925, 1950, 1961 und 1970*. Würzburg: Schöningh, 1979.
Spoerer, Mark, and Jochen Fleischhacker. "Forced Laborers in Nazi Germany: Categories, Numbers, and Survivors." *Journal of Interdisciplinary History* 33, no. 2 (Autumn 2002): 169–204.
Steege, Paul. *Black Market, Cold War: Everyday Life in Berlin, 1946–49*. Cambridge: Cambridge University Press, 2007.
Steinweis, Alan E., and Daniel E. Rogers, eds. *The Impact of Nazism: New Perspectives on the Impact of the Third Reich and its Legacy*. Lincoln: University of Nebraska Press, 2003.
Streibel, Robert, ed. *Flucht und Vertreibung. Zwischen Abrechnung und Verdrängung*. Vienna: Picus, 1994.
Takle, Marianne. "(Spät)Aussiedler: From Germans to Immigrants." *Nationalism and Ethnic Politics* 17, no. 2 (2011): 161–181.
Taggert, Donald, ed. *History of the Third Infantry Division in World War II*. Washington: Infantry Journal Press, 1947.
Ther, Phillipp. *Deutsche und polnische Vertriebene: Gesellschaft und Vertriebenenpolitik in der SBZ/DDR und in Polen 1945–1956*. Göttingen: Vandenhoeck & Ruprecht, 1998.
Ther, Philipp, and Ana Siljak, eds. *Redrawing Nations: Ethnic Cleansing in East-Central Europe, 1944–1948*. Lanham, MD: Rowan and Littlefield, 2001.
Thum, Gregor. *Die Fremde Stadt: Breslau 1945*. Berlin: Siedler, 2003.
Tooze, Adam. *The Wages of Destruction: The Making and Breaking of the Nazi Economy*. New York: Viking, 2006.
Turnwald, Wilhelm, ed. *Documents on the Expulsion of the Sudeten Germans*. Munich: University Press Dr. C. Wolf & Sohn, 1953.
Waddy, Helena. *Oberammergau in the Nazi Era*. New York: Oxford University Press, 2010.
Wagner, Patrick. *Displaced Persons in Hamburg. Stationen einer halbherzigen Integration, 1945 bis 1958*. Hamburg: Dölling und Galitz, 1997.
Weinberg, Gerhard. "Germany's War for World Conquest and the Extermination of the Jews." *Holocaust and Genocide Studies* 10, no. 2 (Fall 1996): 119–133.
Weisz, Christoph, ed. *OMGUS-Handbuch: Die amerikanische Militärregierung in Deutschland, 1945–1949*. Munich: Oldenbourg, 1995.

Wenz, Ernst. *Truppenübungsplatz Wildflecken*. Fulda: Parzeller, 1939.
Werner, Hans. *Imagined Homes: Soviet German Immigrants in Two Cities*. Winnipeg: University of Manitoba Press, 2007.
Willoughby, John. *Remaking the Conquering Heroes: The Social and Geopolitical Impact of the Post-war American Occupation of Germany*. New York: Palgrave, 2001.
Wilson, Francesca. *Aftermath: France, Germany, Austria, Yugoslavia, 1945 and 1946*. Drayton: Penguin, 1947.
Winkler, Heinrich-August. *Germany: The Long Road West*, vol. 2, 1933–1990, translated by Alexander Sanger. New York: Oxford University Press, 2006.
Wirths, Ulrich. *Das 'Winterhilfswerke' im Gau Mainfranken: Ein Instrument des NS-Regimes*. Saarbrücken: VDM, 2009.
Woller, Hans. *Gesellschaft und Politik in der amerikanischen Besatzungszone: Die Region Ansbach und Fürth*. Munich: Oldenbourg, 1986.
Woodbridge, George. *UNRRA: The History of the United Nations Relief and Rehabilitation Administration*. 3 vols. New York: Columbia University Press, 1950.
Wyman, Mark. *DPs: Europe's Displaced Persons, 1945–1951*. Philadelphia: Associated University Press, 1989.
Zahra, Tara. "Prisoners of the Postwar: Displaced Persons, Expellees, and Jews in Austria After World War II." *Austrian History Yearbook* 41 (2010): 191–215.
Ziemke, Earl. *The U.S. Army in the Occupation of Germany*. Washington: GPO, 1975.
Zierenberg, Malte. *Stadt der Schieber: Der Berliner Schwarzmarkt 1939–1950*. Göttingen: Vandenhoeck & Ruprecht, 2008.
Zink, Harold. *The United States in Germany, 1944–1955*. Princeton: Nostrand, 1957.

Index

Note: The abbreviation "DP" refers to displaced persons. Page numbers in *italics* indicate photographs.

Adenauer, Konrad, 35, 190–192, 200–201, 206, 209–210
African-American soldier, 103–104
agriculture: and American base debate, 198, 201–202, 213, 215; and economic recovery, 184; and forced labor, 34, 36, 91; and land tenancy, 32–33, 161–162; and manual labor, 118–119; and Rhön region politics, 26
Aime, George, 74–75
air raids, 40
alcohol, 72–73
Allied forces, 47–48, 59
Altglasshütten, 217
American Zone. *See* U.S. Zone
Amerika-Haus, 121
ammunition and ordnance, 112–116
Anders Army, 67, 68, 92–93
animal theft, 135
Ankermüller, Willi, 173
Anna M. (pseudonym), 217
Ansbach, 218
anti-communism, 68, 72, 95, 208, 214
anti-repatriation movement, 15, 72, 84–96, 195
anti-Semitism, 27, 104
archival privacy laws, 19
Armia Krajowa (AK), 67
Armin G. (pseudonym), 97–98, 123

arms market, 78–80
Aschaffenburg, 12, 22, 44, 53, 89
Atlantic Prize, 196
Augsburg, 218
Ausgewiesene (term for refugees), 18
Auslandereinsatz (foreign labor deployment), 33–34
Aussiedler (post–Cold War migrants), 225
Australia, 146, 150–151, 157, 159
Austria, 48, 122, 137

B Company, 1st Battalion, 102
baby boom, 70–71
Bad Arolsen, 35, 152
Bad Brückenau: and American base debate, 204; and American requisitioning problems, 117; and anti-repatriation sentiment, 195; and camp riots, 55; crime and black market activity, 73–74, 123; cultural influence of American occupation, 121; economic crash after Cold War, 226; and economic development, 167–168; elections, 208; ethnic German refugees, 97; and expellee affairs, 104–105; and food supplies in DP camps, 64; and foreign labor, 35; and Henties, 111; and history of the Rhön region, 23, 24; and housing for DPs, 216; and illegal commerce, 140; and jurisdictional issues, 135–136; and *Kristallnacht* riots, 27; and law enforcement, 132–136; and legal status of DPs, 77; and local leadership, 106–108; and militarization of Germany,

32; and Nazi forced labor system, 37; political system of, 130–131; population of, 26–27; and refugee politics, 174–177; and resettlement of refugees, 220, 226; and scope of American occupation, 101–102; and tourism, 117–118. *See also* Landkreis Brückenau
Bad Kissingen, 23, 77, 156, 167, 194
Bad Neustadt, 167
Bad Orb, 215
Baltic states and Balt refugees, 35, 50, 85–86, 123, 147, 157
banditry, 15, 79–83, 134–135, 152–153
banking, 125–126
barracks at Wildflecken, 20
barter economy, 56–57, 73
base complex at Wildflecken, 103
Basic Law (*Grundgesetz*), 192, 207, 225
Baus, Josef, 131–132, 204, 215
Bavaria: and American base debate, 183, 201–202, 205–206; and Cold War politics, 190; and durability of DP camps, 9–10; and economic development, 163, 167, 168, 170, 175; and expellee problems, 45, 52–53, 162; and fear of DP retaliations, 105; and Hammelburg base plans, 202–203; and housing for refugees, 212; and industrial development, 183–184, 186; and jurisdiction over DPs, 196; and Marshall Plan funds, 212; and political reconstruction, 109; and protests against American base construction, 199; and refugee politics, 51–52, 174, 177–178, 215–216; and resettlement of displaced farmers, 218; and rural life, 9; and scope of refugee crisis, 4–5; and sovereignty issues, 192; and stateless foreigners, 194
Bavarian Army, 30
Bavarian Landtag, 173
Bavarian Military Government, 152
Bavarian Ministry of Economics, 163, 175
Bavarian Ministry of Justice, 136
Bavarian Ministry of the Economy, 211–212
Bavarian People's Party, 24
Bavarian Refugee Administration, 19, 122
Bavarian state government, 100
Bayerische Flüchtlingsverwaltung, 19, 125–126
Bayerische Rundschau, 172
Bayernpartei, 206, 210
Beck, Anton: and American base debate, 187, 212; conflicts with the IRO, 153; leadership skills of, 52; and resettlement efforts, 126, 129; and RPG experiment, 177
Beer Hall Putsch, 105, 203
Belgium, 146, 150, 173
Berlin blockade, 189
Bessel, Richard, 9
Bilzingsleben, 59
Bischofsheim, 166
black market: and American base debate, 204; and barter economy, 56–57; and currency reforms, 138–140; and emigration efforts, 146; and ethnic German expellees, 230; and food supplies, 72, 135, 137–138, 140, 151; and free-livers, 76; and law enforcement, 77–78, 83, 132–134, 136–138; and livestock theft, 152; and Polish camp at Wildflecken, 99; and Polish DPs, 105; and ration cars, 87; and UNRRA requisitions of local resources, 63–64; and UNRRA supplies, 72–75
black soldiers, 103–104
Blank, Theodor, 190, 203, 206–207, 211. *See also* Dienststelle Blank (Amt Blank)
Blatman, Daniel, 49
Block of Expellees and Dispossessed (*Block der Heimatvertriebenen und Entrechteten*, BHE), 210
Bloodlands (Snyder), 7–8
Bolsheviks, 94
Bonn Republic: and American base debate, 200, 201–202, 206; and Bavarian sovereignty, 192; and Cold War politics, 190; and housing for DPs, 216; and refugee politics, 182–183
Border Control Agency, 198–199
border patrols, 102
Boy Scouts, 71–72, 92–93
Brelie-Lewien, Doris von der, 6
Britain, 157

INDEX

British Zone, 53
Brubaker, Rogers, 42
Brückenau. *See* Bad Brückenau; Landkreis Brückenau
Bruno S. (pseudonym), 91
Buchenwald, 58
Bundestag, 194
Bundeswehr, 224, 227, 228

Canada, 146, 149–150, 151
canteens, 181
Catholic Church: and culture of Franconia, 23; and Lower Franconian politics, 24; and Nazi forced labor system, 36; and population of Wildflecken camp, 86; and Probst, 172; and Rhön region politics, 25, 26; and social conservatism, 104; and welfare organizations, 67
Celle, 186
Central Europe: and Cold War politics, 182; ethnic background of, 21, 41–42; postwar control of, 44; postwar crisis, 96; and refugee crises, 5, 14; and refugee politics, 179; wartime transformation of, 21
Chase, Ephraim, 60, 63–64, 70, 144
Chetniks, 92
children, 127
Chinese Civil War, 158
Christian Social Union (CSU), 110, 131, 172, 176, 206
Christianity, 59
Churchill, Winston, 44
citizenship issues, 85–86, 93
Civil Affairs Division (of EUCOM), 156
Civil Militia, 94
civil society, 141
civilian labor, 17, 124, 211
Clark, Harry, 101–102, 104, 106–108, 114, 117
climate of Wildflecken area, 224; and American base debate, 199; and base construction, 218–219; and food supplies, 155; and the *Hungerwinter,* 92; McIntosh on, 181; of Rhön region, 23
coal reserves, 164, 166
Cohen, Daniel, 6
Cohen, Meyer, 90, 156

Cold War: and American base debate, 188–189, 208, 210; and American cultural connection to Germany, 17; and anti-repatriation sentiment, 96; and construction of American facilities, 12; end of, 224; impact on DP problem, 142–143; impact on Wildflecken, 22; influence on refugee policy, 5–6; international significance of Wildflecken, 182; and property conflicts, 10; and refugee crises, 1–2; and remilitarization of Germany, 189–190; scholarship on, 6–7; and transformation of West Germany, 199; and U.S. military presence in Germany, 3. *See also* repatriation efforts
collaborators, 79
commerce: and Currency Reform of 1948, 11; economic relations among refugees, 15–16; in Franconia, 22–23; Jewish role in rural economies, 26–27; and legacy of American presence, 17–18; and militarization of the Rhön region, 31–33; and the Rhön Plan, 30; and rise of Nazism, 28–30; underground camp economies, 56–57, 72; of Wildflecken region, 15. *See also* black market; economic development and recovery
Communists and Communism: and American base debate, 207–208; and the Berlin blockade, 189; Communist Party of Germany (KPD), 106, 108–111, 130–131, 207–208; and denazification tribunals, 108–109; ethnic German refugees, 97; and Lower Franconian politics, 24–25; and Oswald's arrest, 130–132; and political reconstruction, 111; and refugee politics, 7; and Rhön region politics, 26
Company A, 3rd Military Government Regiment, 97
Company I, 395th Infantry, 114
conscription of labor, 33–34
Constabulary forces: and camp security, 95, 106, 124; and forced removals from camps, 123; and illegal commerce, 75, 77, 81, 112–113, 136; and law enforcement, 133; and legal status of DPs, 77; and

scholarship on DP camps, 5; and security issues, 112
corruption, 74, 178, 191
credit markets, 138, 170, 185
crime: and anti-repatriation sentiment, 89; associated with DPs, 81, 83, 105, 132–135, 152–154, 157–158, 204; banditry, 15, 79–83, 134–135, 152–153; and black market activity, 99; and ethnic tensions, 157–158; and law enforcement efforts, 132–140; livestock theft, 79–81, 80, 123, 135, 152; murders, 54–55; organized crime, 89, 138–139; sexual violence, 37–38; and social relations in DP camps, 120–121. *See also* black market; corruption
cultural life of DP camps, 71
currency reforms, 11, 137–140, 143, 151, 170, 176, 179, 183
Czechoslovakia, 43–45, 58–59
Czyzewski, Stefan, 88

Dalherda, 23, 227
Dawid L. (pseudonym), 91
death certificates, 152
demographic shifts, 52–53, 75, 99, 185
denazification, 106–108
deutsche Mark, 138–140
Dienststelle Blank (Amt Blank), 190, 200–201, 209, 214, 217. *See also* Blank, Theodor
Dionne, Ludger, 149–150
diseases in DP camps, 159
Displaced Persons (DPs). *See* expellees; *specific ethnicities and nationalities*
Displaced Persons Act, 147–148, 160, 219–220
Displaced Persons Branch, 47
district councils (Kreistag), 110
documentary records, 11
Drang, Basha, 159
Dudzinski, Jan, 58
Dunn, A. C. (pseudonym), 90, 156
durability of DP camps, 9–10

East Germany, 18
Eastern Europe: "bloodlands," 7–8; and emigration efforts, 144; and end of the Cold War, 224; and ethnic cleansing, 44; and expellees, 3, 41–43, 43–44, 53, 214; and Jewish refugees, 147; and Nazi racial ideology, 41; and refugee crises, 6; and repatriation efforts, 56, 85, 92
Eastern Zone, 188
Ebenhausen, 175
Economic Committee, 178
Economic Cooperation Administration (ECA), 186
economic development and recovery: and anti-prostitution campaigns, 221–222; and attitudes toward occupation forces, 103; and civilian labor for the military, 124; and credit markets, 138, 170, 185; and currency reforms, 11, 138–141, 143, 151, 170, 176, 179, 183; and demographic shifts, 185; and disused bases, 143; and end of the Cold War, 224, 226; export economy, 163; and illegal commerce, 137; and industrialization plans, 126–127; and inflation, 138; and local development plans, 143; and the Lüttgen Plan, 165–169; poverty, 9, 15, 28–29, 172, 197; and refugee politics, 173–174; regional economic development, 178; and resettlement of refugees, 161–162; and the Rhön Plan, 30; and rise of Nazism, 29–30; and tourism, 117–118; and unemployment, 29, 169, 184, 186, 195, 225–226; and Werberg, 220. *See also* commerce; industry and industrial development
Economics Ministry, 167, 179, 185
education of refugees, 71, 121, 149
Eisenhower, Dwight, 47
Eisenhower Platz, 64
elections, 91, 110, 111, 131–132, 208
Emil L. (pseudonym), 122
employment of refugees, 124
England, 150–151
enlightened hegemony, 143
entertainment in DP camps, 71
Erbhofen, 28, 30
Erhard, Hans, 213
Erhard, Ludwig, 205, 206, 209–210
Erich M. (pseudonym), 122, 217
Erker, Paul, 9, 143

Espelkamp, 124
estrangement, 6
ethnicity of refugees: and crime among DPs, 157–158; and diversity in DP camps, 57–58, 122–123, 157; and diversity in Wildflecken, 11; ethnic background of Central Europe, 21, 41–42; ethnic cleansing, 7, 44, 49, 65; and local-expellee relations, 120–121; and political parties, 43; and repatriation efforts, 85, 91. *See also specific ethnic groups*
European Headquarters, 105
Evakuierte (term for refugees), 6, 18
Evelyn H. (pseudonym), 117
Expellee Affairs Ministry, 52, 185
"The Expellee Problem in Bavaria" (report), 173
expellees: and American base debate, 188; and anti-repatriation movement, 15; and changing positions of refugee groups, 142; and the Cold War, 5–6; and cultural integration, 231; and designation of refugee groups, 105; and economic reforms, 141; establishing identity of, 119; and forced relocations, 127; and industrial development plans, 184; integration of, 3; jurisdiction over, 8, 12, 14; political clout of, 184; and political reconstruction, 109; and prior scholarship, 4; and Probst, 173; and "refugee towns," 16; rights of, 215; in rural districts, 118; scholarship on, 7; and the underground economy, 139; and U.S. military build-up, 16–17
Expellees' Union (*Union der Ausgewiesenen*), 176–177
export economy, 163

Faulhaber, Michael, 26
Federal Housing Ministry, 196
Federal Ministry for Expellees, 210
Federal Ministry for Refugees, 217–218
Federal Republic of Germany, 11, 191, 192, 207. *See also* West Germany
Fehrenbach, Heide, 103–104
15th Infantry Regiment, 3rd Infantry Division, 102, 133–134

Finance Ministry, 218
fishing, 116
Five Years Later (Pfeil), 7
Florian-Geyer-Strasse, 64
Flüchtlinge (term for refugees), 18
Flüchtlingsverwaltung, 162, 165–166, 169, 174, 183, 185
"Flying Virgins Incident," 150
Föhrenwald, 4
food supplies: and black market activity, 72, 135, 137–138, 140, 151; and failures of American administration, 58; and local administration of DPs, 111; and logistical difficulties, 155; and ration cards, 76, 87; and refugee politics, 142; and UNRRA mission, 64–65. *See also* agriculture
forced labor: and agriculture, 34, 36, 91; and character of Wildflecken, 22, 41; and end of war, 40–41; and prisoners of war, 34–37, 39; and repatriation efforts, 91–92; as source of DP problem, 8, 15, 39
forced repatriations, 50, 84–85, 92, 96
Forchheim camp, 218
forestry, 22, 29. *See also* timber industry
4355 Quartermaster Baking Company, 75
4th Infantry Division, 181
France, 146, 173
Franciscans, 23
Franconia, 5, 22, 121, 204–205. *See also* Lower Franconia
fraud, 178
free-livers, 76
French Zone, 97, 189
Freyberg, Karl von, 106
Friedland, Maria, 59, 60
Friedländer, Saul, 3–4
fugitive foreign workers, 39
Fuldaer Volkszeitung, 154
Futch, General, 214

Galgenberg camp, 12, 199–200
game and wildlife of Wildflecken, 115–116
gasoline, 74, 77–78
Gauaschach, 207
Gavaud, Robert, 40
Geneva Convention, 107

Georg S. (pseudonym), 127–128, 212–213, 217
German League for Defense and Defiance (*Deutschvolkische Schutz und Trutzbund*), 27
Gestapo, 37–38, 39
Goosens, Paul, 61, 74
Gordon, Moshe (Morris), 157
governance of DP camps, 66–69, 122–123
Government Corporation for the Utilization of Public Goods, 113
Grafenwöhr, 200
Grafenwöhr/Vilseck, 12, 30–32, 48, 192
gray market, 15, 56–57. *See also* black market
Gregor, Neil, 3, 14
Griffith, Ann Warren, 101
Grossmann, Atina, 3
guerilla warfare, 104

H. family (pseudonym), 219–220
Habets, Marie Louise, 61, 96, 196
Haenlein, Richard, 220–221
Hale, Oron, 213
Hamadyk, Anna, 69
Hamburg, 47–48
Hammelburg, 35, 171–173, 185, 188, 200–211, 215
Harrison, Earl, 59–60
Hartmann, Alfred, 218
Haßfurt, 220
Hayes, George, 206
Heeresverpflegungsamt (HVA), 33, 35, 166, 179, 197
Heifer Project, 184
Heilbronn, 200
Heimatlose Ausländer (term for refugees), 18–19, 194
Heinz D. (pseudonym), 122
Hellmuth, Otto, 25–26, 28–30, 36, 115, 161–162
Hellmuth Plan, 165
Henlein, Konrad, 43
Henties, Wilhelm, 54, 111
Hepburn, Audrey, 61, 196
Hesse, 190, 215, 216

Heydrich, Reinhard, 37
High Commission for Occupied Germany (HICOG), 189, 195, 206–209, 214, 217
Himmler, Heinrich, 32, 41
Hitler, Adolf, 41, 119
Hoegner, Wilhelm, 162, 205
Hohenfels, 12, 31, 48, 210–211
Höhn, Maria, 104
Holy Roman Empire, 23
Home Army (*Armia Krajowa*), 67
hotels, 27, 61, 117–118
Housing Construction Law, 186
housing facilities, 111–112, 121–122, 170, 196, 226
Howeler, Johanna, 151, 159–160
Hüfner, Sonja, 227
Hüfner family, 127–128, 127, 220
Hulme, Kathryn, 62; and anti-repatriation sentiment, 94–95; background, 12–14, 54; characterization of Wildflecken camp, 72–73; and composition of UNRRA staff, 60; on corruption in camp administration, 69; departure from Germany, 196; on ethnic tensions, 65; and the IRO, 144–145, 147–150; and livestock theft, 80; and official UNRRA history, 61; and postwar baby boom, 70–71; promotion, 96; and repatriation efforts, 91; on resettlement efforts, 160; and UNRRA command over DP camps, 61–63
Hungarians, 194
hunting, 115–116

identity of DPs, 86–87
industry and industrial development: and American base debate, 201; and American "enlightened hegemony," 143; and Cold War rearmament of Germany, 190; and the Flüchtlingsverwaltung, 162, 165–166, 169, 174, 183–185; and forced labor, 34, 36; and militarization of Germany, 29–30; and refugee politics, 161–169, 203; and transportation infrastructure, 175; at war's end, 39; and the Wildflecken Maneuver Area, 126

inflation, 138
inheritance laws, 24, 32–33
integrated history, 3–4
integration of refugees, 119, 182, 198, 225
International Refugee Organization (IRO): and American base debate, 183, 194–195, 196; and base closures, 212; and camp closures, 155–157; and closure of Wildflecken camp, 195; completion of mission, 194; and crime among DPs, 154; and economic development, 161, 167, 178; and emigration efforts, 16, 142–146, 148–151, 153, 155, 158, 160, 180; and emigration of DPs, 142–144; and employment of DPs, 157–158; and Hammelburg base plans, 203; and media relations, 153–154; and Probst, 173; and refugee politics, 173–174, 180, 215; and relocation of refugees, 157, 181; scope of mission, 144; and "stateless foreigner" designation, 194–195
International Tracing Service, 19, 35, 152
interracial sex, 103–104
isolation of refugee populations, 13–14
isolation of Wildflecken, 21, 112
Israel, 158

J. (pseudonym), 68, 89
Jaenicke, Wolfgang, 51–52, 163
Jewish refugees, 3, 6, 26–27, 58–60
Johann T. (pseudonym), 122
Johannes, Benedict, 26
Juliana G. (pseudonym), 195
justice system, 134–135

Kahn, Bettina, 36
Kaiser (Hammelburg Landrat), 201, 203
Kalte Heimat (Kossert), 7
Kazakhstan, 225
Kazimierz G. (pseudonym), 195
Kenner, Otto, 106, 109
Kleinhenz, Bruno, 54, 132
Koch, Erich, 30
Konitz, 3
Korean War, 16, 182, 188–190, 199, 208
Körner, Hans, 179

Kossert, Andreas, 7
Kraft, Waldemar, 210
Krakowsky, Morris, 58
Krehl (Employment Minister), 174
Kreigstag, 177
Kreis English-Speaking Club, 121
Kreis Neustadt, 168
Kreistag, 110
Kreuzberg, 23, 24, 184
Kreuzweg der Nationen monument, 228
Kristallnacht riots, 27, 105
Krzysztof D. (police chief) (pseudonym), 79

L. (jailer) (pseudonym), 136
L. family (pseudonym), 153
labor laws, 117
Lagerleiter position, 122–123
Lambert (Mayor of Neuwildflecken), 214
land tenure issues: and American base debate, 210; and ethnic German refugees, 99; in Lower Franconia, 24; and postwar housing crisis, 10; and property controlled by occupation forces, 169; and rural Franconia, 32–33; and scope of American occupation, 103; support for reforms, 161
Landessiedlung, 127
Landkreis Bad Kissingen, 226
Landkreis Brückenau: and American base debate, 188, 197; and anti-prostitution campaigns, 222; Bavarian Refugee Administration camps, 122; and the black market, 99; and the Commission for Refugee Affairs, 52; and credit shortages, 185; and currency reforms, 138, 176; and denazification tribunals, 108–109; elections, 110–111; and ethnic German refugees, 45, 53, 99; and expellee affairs, 104; and foreign labor, 35; and industrial development, 169; influence of American military in, 230; and jurisdictional issues, 135; and law enforcement, 82–83, 106, 133–135; and Lower Franconian politics, 24–25, 28; and militarization of Germany, 29; and Oswald's arrest, 130–

131; and political reconstruction, 109; and resettlement of refugees, 124–125, 220; and scope of American occupation, 101, 230; and stateless foreigners, 194; and tourism, 24. *See also* Bad Brückenau
Landpolizisten, 82–83
Landsberg, 60
Landshut, 218
Landtag Constitutional Committee, 206
language skills, 122–123, 146, 149, 191
Latvian refugees, 194
law enforcement: and American mission of Germany, 132–133; and black market activities, 77–78, 83, 132–134, 136–140; and illegal commerce, 132; and Oswald's arrest, 130–132, 136; and rebuilding German institutions, 82–83, 100–101, 134–140
leadership of refugee camps, 122–123
League of Nations, 46
legal status of DP camps, 66
Ley, Robert, 32
Life, 83, 149–150
livestock theft, 79–81, 80, 123, 135, 152
local histories, 5, 21–22
logging. *See* timber industry
logistical issues, 104
Low, David, 144
Lower Bavaria, 53, 211–212
Lower Franconia: and American base debate, 200–201; arrival of UNRRA mission, 61; cultural composition of, 22; DP camps in, 63; and economic development, 167; and employment issues, 211–212; expellee population in, 9, 44, 52–53, 99, 118, 162, 194–197, 199, 207, 226; and industrial development, 175; and jurisdiction over DP camps, 63; and land reforms, 115; land tenancy issues, 24; and Nazi forced labor system, 34–35, 38–39; and Nazi race laws, 38; and political reconstruction, 110; political structure of, 24–29; and rise of Nazism, 27–28; scope of American occupation in, 102; and STEG's mission, 113
Lower Franconian Refugee Administration, 195–196

Lower Saxony, 53, 121–122
Lower Silesia, 107
lumber, 64
Lutherans, 86, 228
Lüttgen, Wilhelm (Lüttgen Plan), 164–169, 178, 183

Magdalene B. (pseudonym), 185
Main Valley, 40
Main-Post: on American base construction, 217; on American base debate, 187–188, 193–194; on Eastern-European expellees, 119; on expellee towns, 186; on industrial development, 126, 168; on resettlement of refugees, 129–130
Maliszewski (Major), 93
Maneuver Area–Upper Rhön (Truppenübungsplatz Hohe Rhon), 31
Maneuver Area–Wildflecken (Truppenübungsplatz Wildflecken), 210, 213, 215, 217
manufacturing, 163–170, 164. *See also* industry and industrial development
"March of the Displaced Persons, The" (*Life*), 83
Marja L. (pseudonym), 68
marketplaces, 72
marriages among refugees, 70
Marshall Plan, 196, 212
Masset, George, 61, 74–75, 82, 89, 95–96, 118
May, Herbert, 34
McCloy, John, 194–195, 206, 208–211, 214–215
McIntosh, Carl, 181
measles outbreaks, 159
medical care in DP camps, 71
Mellrichstadt, 167
Michael P. (pseudonym), 217
Middle Franconia, 22, 35
Mikalajczyk, Captain, 94
militarization of Germany, 20, 30–33
military courts, 135
Military Government (MG): and American base debate, 187; and anti-repatriation sentiment, 68; and Bavarian economic development, 163; and closure of

DP camps, 179; cultivation of local leadership, 106–108; and death certificates of DPs, 152; and denazification, 106–108; and economic development, 166, 168; and ethnic conflicts, 65; and ethnic German refugees, 97, 98; and German sovereignty, 154–155; and illegal commerce, 136–137; and the IRO, 142; and law enforcement, 83, 132–133, 134; and legal status of DPs, 77; and Oswald's arrest, 131; and political reconstruction, 110; and racism, 104; and refugee politics, 173; and repatriation efforts, 84–85, 89, 95–96; and scope of American occupation, 101–102; and surplus military equipment, 114; and underground economy, 75

Military Government Law Number 54, 115, 125

military training in Wildflecken, 116

mineral springs at Wildflecken, 118

mining industry, 166

Ministry of the Interior, 51, 171

Moe, Wayne, 223–224

Moeller, Robert, 7

monasteries, 24

monetary policy, 138–140

Mülheim, 221

Muna (munitions plant): and American base debate, 197, 216, 217; as bombing target, 39–40; buildings of, 112; and civilian labor, 124; construction of, 33; and industrial development, 164–166, 175, 184; and Nazi labor programs, 39; security of, 62, 101, 102; surplus military equipment from, 112–113; towns build at site of, 125

Münchner Merkur, 202, 204

Munich, 9–10, 216

Municipal Committee, 92–93

Municipal Council, 66–67, 69, 87–88, 90

Municipal Government, 66, 69

Muracciole, Rene, 61, 70–71

murder, 43–44, 54–55, 132, 157

Naples, Italy, 92

Napoleonic Wars, 26

Narodowe Siły Zbrojne (NSZ), 67

Natalya N. (pseudonym), 76–77

nationalist politics, 67–69, 203, 206

Nationalsozialiste Deutsche Arbeiterpartei (NSDAP), 25–26, 130–131

Nazis and Nazism: and economic development programs, 29–30; and forced labor, 22, 33–36, 37–39; and racial ideology, 36, 38, 41, 104; and Rhön region politics, 25–26

Neubürger (term for refugees), 18

Neugablonz, 124

Neustadt, 29

Neuwildflecken, 184, 216, 217, 218–219

New York Times, 95

New Yorker, 101

news media, 184

nicknames for Wildflecken area, 224

North Atlantic Treaty Organization (NATO), 190, 200

Nowicki (Polish repatriation consultant), 88

Nun's Story, The (1959), 61, 196

Nürnberg, 3, 216

Nürnberg-Schweinau, 199

Oberländer, Theodor, 203–204, 205, 212

Oberriedenberg explosion, 113–114

Oberwildflecken, 226

Office for Reparations Affairs, 175

Office of Military Government (OMGUS), 156, 162, 173

Ogiński Choir, 149

"Old, New, and Neighboring Settlers of Reussendorf," 198

O'Neal, Shaquille, 224

Operation Carrot, 91–92

Operation DUCK, 134

Operation GRAB-BAG, 137

oral histories, 17, 67

ordnance security, 113–114

organized crime, 89, 138–139

Ostarbeiter (Soviet laborers), 35, 36–37

Oswald, Heinrich: arrest of, 130–132, 198; on elections, 111; and industrial development plans, 175–176; and law enforcement, 130, 136; and the Lüttgen Plan,

166–169; and rebuilding of Werberg, 126; and tourism industry, 118
"Our Never-Forgotten Silesian Homeland" (exhibit), 219

Pablo D. (pseudonym), 219
Paisly, Captain, 49
Paul & Co., 184, 215
Paul E. (pseudonym), 136
Penzel, Helmut, 207
"People Without Space, A," 119
Peter M. (pseudonym), 31, 122
Peter W. (pseudonym), 219
Pettiss, Susan, 145
Pfeil, Elisabeth, 7
Piotr L. (pseudonym), 67–68, 89, 94, 135, 145–146, 195
"Pipeline, The," 148, 158
Poland and Polish DPs: and American base facilities, 102, 125; American support for, 149; and anti-repatriation sentiment, 84–96; and camp safety issues, 114–115; cemetery at Wildflecken, 228; cemetery of, 228; and character of Wildflecken camp, 11, 196, 204; and civilian labor, 124; and crime, 132–135, 152–154, 204; cultural influence of, 4, 6, 222, 224, 226, 228; and economic development plans, 179; and emigration efforts, 146–149, 159; establishing identity of, 86–87; ethnic makeup of Poland, 42–43; and ethnic tensions, 65, 120, 129; and forced repatriations, 50–51; and free-livers, 153; and German expellees, 45; and law enforcement, 132, 134; and legal status of DPs, 77; Military Government attitude toward, 65; and Nazi forced labor system, 33–34, 36–38; occupied by Red Army, 49; and postwar control of Central Europe, 44; and postwar refugee movements, 48–52; and property on base facilities, 99–100; and refugee politics, 104–106; religious division of, 11; removal from DP camps, 124; Soviet invasion of Poland, 59; "stateless foreigner" designation, 194; transfer between DP camps, 157; typical experience of, 221; and the UNRRA mission, 54, 57–59, 61–62; and use of pseudonyms, 19; and World War II, 43–45
Polenfriedhof (Polish Cemetery), 228
police forces. *See* Constabulary forces; law enforcement
Polish Committee, 68, 93, 95
Polish Repatriation Mission in Berlin, 92
Polish Union in Germany (*Zjednoczenie Polskie w Neimczech*), 67
political parties, 109, 203–204. *See also specific party names*
political reconstruction, 109–111. *See also* sovereignty issues
politics in refugee camps, 13, 15, 96; and anti-repatriation sentiment, 88, 94–95; and organized crime, 89; and weapons, 79
Post Exchange, 133
Post-Argus, 154
Potsdam Conference, 44
poverty, 9, 15, 28–29, 172, 197, 225
Prague Uprising, 58–59
pregnant DPs, 159
Presley, Elvis, 224
prisoners of war: Hammelburg camp, 172; and Nazi forced labor system, 34–37, 39; and opposition ot American base plans, 210; and resettled German towns, 127–128; and residents of DP camps, 66, 122; Volker M., 214
privacy issues, 19
Probst, Maria, 172; and American base debate, 206–207, 209–210, 214–215, 218, 220; anti-prostitution campaign, 222; and refugee politics, 171–174; and resettlement of displaced farmers, 218; and RPG experiment, 178–179
Propaganda Ministry (Nazi), 29–30
property crimes, 80–81, 152
property management, 112–114, 115–116
property rights, 10, 169. *See also* land tenure issues
prostitution, 221–222
protest and demonstrations: and American base debate, 198, 208, 211; and anti-repatriation sentiment, 94–96; Kitchen

7 riot, 94–96; and Oswald's arrest, 130–131
Protestantism, 25
Proudfoot, Malcolm, 7, 78
Prusso-German Empire, 23–24
pseudonyms, 19
public relations, 105
public safety, 132. See also law enforcement
public/private cooperation, 167

racial ideology, 36, 37, 41, 103–104
radical political parties, 109
Radu H. (pseudonym), 138–140
raids on refugee camps, 133, 134, 136
railroads, 165–166, 175
ration cards, 76, 87
records and record keeping, 4, 34–35, 45, 107, 152
Red and White Civic Militia, 68
Red Army, 2, 41, 44, 49, 88
Red Cross, 101, 152
Refugee Administration, 126, 140, 172–173, 177
Refugee Office, 119–120, 122–123
rehabilitation projects, 193
Reich Security Main Office (RSHA), 37
Reich Security Service (SD), 36
Reichswehr, 30, 193
Reinisch, Jessica, 8
remoteness of Wildflecken, 101
repatriation efforts: anti-repatriation sentiment, 15, 72, 84–96, 195; and expellee politics, 173; forced repatriations, 50, 84–85, 92, 96; and IRO mission, 144; and media coverage, 83–84; and violence in DP camps, 56
requisitioning issues, 117
Resettlement Camp, 195
resettlement of refugees, 16–17, 43, 125–127, 127–130, 127, 230. See also repatriation efforts
Reussendorf: and American base construction, 187, 197–198, 213–215, 217–218; current state of, 227; disappearance of, 223, 227; and DP camp administration, 122; and DP tent city, 181–182; and economic development, 163, 165; and history of the Rhön region, 23; and industrial development, 126; and integration of refugees, 182; and militarization of Germany, 31; and Nazi forced labor system, 38–39; and refugee politics, 140, 219; and refugee settlements, 186; and relocation of expellees, 127–130; resettlement of, 125–126, 129–130; uninhabited dwellings, 125
Revised Immigration Policy, 146
Revolutionary Committee, 39
Rhön Plan, 30
Rhön region: and agrarian reform, 161–162; Allied capture of, 40; and American base debate, 181–185, 183, 187–188, 193, 198–199, 208, 212; biosphere reservation, 228–229; and changing positions of refugee groups, 142; and civilian labor, 124; Cold War's impact on, 208; and criminal activity among DPs, 81, 83, 154; current state of, 223–225, 227–228; and economic development, 126, 161, 164–165, 167–168, 170, 174, 179–180; and expellees, 96; and food supplies, 64–65; and foreign labor, 35; historical background of, 22–26; and hunting, 116; and militarization of Germany, 28–32; and Nazi forced labor system, 38; and Neuwildflecken, 219–222; and political reconstruction, 110–111; and refugee politics, 142–143, 152, 174, 219, 230–231; resettlement of, 129–130
Rhön-Planung Gesellschaft, GmbH (RPG), 167–171, 174–179, 183, 215
Romania, 44, 225
Roosevelt, Franklin D., 44, 46
Rouwens, Gaston, 61
rubble time (*Trümmerzeit*), 4
rural areas: and de-provincialization, 9; and economic development, 115, 125–126, 177–178, 231; importance of studying Wildflecken, 229; and law enforcement issues, 132; and refugee politics, 177; rural character of refugee crisis, 229; rural character of Wildflecken, 9, 26–27, 45
Rusinek, Zygmunt, 66, 88

Russia, 42, 59, 225–226. *See also* Soviet Union
Russian immigrant, 36–37
Ryan, Bryce, 13

samogon, 70, 72, 134
Sauckel, Fritz, 33
Schleswig-Holstein, 53, 121–122
Schlitzkus, Gus, 211
"Schmelzhof" farm, 217
Schober, Dr., 171
schools, 121. *See also* education of refugees
Schraut, Sylvia, 6
Schulze, Rainer, 6, 176, 186
Schuster, George, 206, 208
Schweinfurt: and closure of Wildflecken camp, 195; and ethnic German expellees, 44, 53; and housing for DPs, 216; and Oswald's arrest, 130; population of, 22; and postwar base facilities, 12; and refugee politics, 219; and resettlement of displaced farmers, 218
screening of refugees, 93–94, 111
Serbian refugees, 92
Settlement Office, 198
Settlers Committee of Werberg, 213
sexual violence, 37–38
Shanghai DPs, 158
She'erit Hapletah (surviving remnant), 6
Shuster, George, 202
Siedlungs- und Heimwerkstätten-Gesellschaft, 163
Siemens, 30, 197
Silesia, 52, 107, 118, 120, 219
Simon H. (pseudonym), 139–140
Sinn Valley: and American base debate, 183; and anti-repatriation sentiment, 96; commerce in, 15; and currency reforms, 170; and economic development, 141, 161, 171, 178; and ethnic German expellees, 119; and German militarization, 21, 33; historical background of, 24; and land tenancy in rural Franconia, 33; legacy of American presence in, 17–18; and Nazi militarization, 2; relationship with Wildflecken DP camp, 56; and rise of Nazism, 27–28; social/cultural integration in, 227–228; and surplus military equipment, 113, 114; and tourism, 24; and U.S. military presence, 11–12; and variety of refugee groups, 2
Skyline Barracks, 12
Slovakia, 45
Smith, Helmut Walser, 3
smuggling, 204
Snyder, Timothy, 7–8
Social Democrat Party (SPD), 24–25, 110, 131, 206
social deterioration (*Schlechterstellung*), 203
social engineering programs, 43
sources on Wildflecken, 4, 14, 17
sovereignty issues: and American base debate, 183, 202; and the Berlin blockade, 189; and Cold War remilitarization, 191–192; and economic development plans, 178; and expellee politics, 231; and property rights, 10; and refugee politics, 179–180; West German limited sovereignty, 2–3, 143, 182, 185–186, 202
Soviet POWs, 39
Soviet Union: annexation of Polish territory, 49–50; and Cold War tensions, 189; and ethnic German expellees, 45; invasion of Poland, 59; and the IRO, 143–144; and Nazi forced labor system, 35; and post–Cold War migrants, 225–226; and postwar refugee flows, 43, 44, 50–51; and refugee crises, 6; and repatriation efforts, 88
Soviet Zone, 18, 58, 189
space housing issues, 182
Spätaussiedler (post–Cold War migrants), 225
sponsorship of émigrés, 149
sports, 151, 226
Spruchkammern (denazification tribunals), 108–109, 109–110
Staatliche Erfassungs-Gesellschaft fur offentliches Gut (STEG), 113–115, 169, 185
Stalin, Joseph, 6, 44
Stanislaw Z. (pseudonym), 221
Stars and Stripes, 224
State Commissioner for Refugee Affairs, 51

stateless persons, 47
Stern, Frank, 3
Stoiber, Edmund, 224
Süddeutsche Zeitung, 203–204, 207, 208, 226
Sudeten German Party, 43
Sudetenland and Sudeten refugees, 43, 52, 53, 118, 139, 164
suicides among the Wehrmacht, 40
Supply Branch, 113
Supreme Headquarters, Allied Expeditionary Force (SHAEF), 46–47, 49
surplus military equipment, 112–113

Tak-Tak Schön. *See* Rusinek, Zygmunt
tent cities, 181–182
terminology for refugee groups, 18–19
textile industry, 164, 165–166
3rd Armored Rifle Battalion, 223–224
Third Army HQ, 79
Third Reich, 8, 21
Thuringia, 58, 59
timber industry, 15, 29, 37, 64, 118–119, 136, 168
tobacco, 72–74, 204
tourism, 24, 117–118
trains, 165–166, 175
transit camps, 217–218
transportation infrastructure, 84, 165–166
tribunals (*Spruchkammern*), 108–109
Troop C, 22nd Constabulary Squadron, 133
Truman, Harry, 59–60, 147, 190
Trümmerzeit (rubble time), 4
Truppenubungsplatz Hohe Rhon, 31
Truppenubungsplatz Wildflecken, 210
12th Constabulary Squadron, 75
20th Infantry Division, 223–224
22nd Armored Field Artillery Battalion, 133
27th Constabulary Squadron, 137

Ukraine and Ukrainian refugees: and anti-DP sentiment, 154; and anti-repatriation sentiment, 95; and Basic Law of 1949, 225; and ethnic conflict, 49, 85–86; Nazi violence against, 35, 49; and post–Cold War migrants, 225; and postwar population dynamics, 42–43; and repatriation efforts, 85, 92–93, 95; and resettlement of refugees, 157; and Wildflecken camp population, 57, 59
Umsiedler (term for refugees), 18
unemployment, 29, 169, 184, 186, 195, 225–226
Union der Ausgewiesenen (Expellees' Union), 176–177
Union of Polish Centers in Northern Bavaria, 67
United Nations (UN), 8, 143–144, 173
United Nations Educational, Scientific and Cultural Organization (UNESCO), 228–229
United Nations Relief and Rehabilitation Administration (UNRRA): and anti-repatriation sentiment, 93, 96; assumption of command over DP camps, 61–63; and camp politics, 15; composition of staff, 60–61; and corruption, 74; and crime among DPs, 80, 82; and cultural life of DP camps, 71–72; and definition of displaced persons, 46–47; and DP camp facilities, 64; and emigration efforts, 144; and ethnic tensions, 65–66; and food security, 64–65; formation of, 46; and Hulme's background, 54; and the IRO, 16; and jurisdiction over DPs, 51; and language barriers, 104–105; and local development plans, 143; and repatriation efforts, 68, 84, 90–91; and responsibility for DPs, 48–49; and screening of DPs, 93–94; and social networks among DPs, 21; structures sought by, 10; and underground camp economies, 56–57
United States, 147–148, 158, 160, 182, 191, 219–220
United States Air Force, 12
United States Forces, European Theater (USFET), 49
Upper Bavaria, 175
Upper Franconia, 22, 35, 203
Upper Palatinate (Oberpfalz), 30, 192
U.S. Army: and American base debate, 214; assumption of occupation role,

230; and camp riots, 95; and Central European refugee crises, 14; control of Wildflecken facility, 16; and DP camp closures, 156; and forced repatriations, 50–51; and growth of Wildflecken DP camp, 54; Hulme's frustration with, 63; and industrialization plans, 185; influence on refugee policy, 5; and postwar base facilities, 10, 12; and repatriation efforts, 89

U.S. Army Corps of Engineers, 181, 191, 196
U.S. Congress, 147–148
U.S. Department of State, 145
U.S. European Command (EUCOM), 156, 192–193, 199–201, 211, 217
U.S. House of Representatives, 148
U.S. Seventh Army, 40, 50
U.S. Third Army, 63, 89
U.S. Zone: and economic development, 164; and Jewish DP camps, 60; and political reconstruction, 109; and postwar refugee flows, 51; and refugee politics, 158; and resettlement of refugees, 160

Verschleppte (term for refugees), 18–19
Vertriebene (term for refugees), 18
victimhood stories, 14
Vilseck, 12
violence among refugees, 54–55, 78–80, 124, 157–158
vocational training, 149
Volker M. (pseudonym), 109, 214
Volksdeutsche, 42
Volkswandertag, 227
voluntary organizations, 147

Waffen-SS, 32, 40
Wagoner, Murray, 163
Waldkraiburg, 124
Watson (U.S. General), 89–90
weapons, 135
Wehrmacht: construction of training facilities, 30; former officers of, 109; impact on Wildflecken area, 228; and medical staff, 71; and militarization of the Rhön region, 30–33; and the Rhön region, 224; soldiers executed, 40; surplus facilities and equipment, 113, 115, 130, 141, 162, 170, 187–188, 193, 198, 199, 202–203

Weimar Germany, 24, 27, 110
welfare organizations, 67
Werberg: absorbed by American base, 220; and American base debate, 187, 197, 213, 215; disappearance of, 223, 227; and DP tent city, 181–182; and economic development, 165, 166; history of, 23, 24; and industrial development, 126; and integration of refugees, 182; and refugee politics, 177; and refugee settlements, 186; and relocation of expellees, 127–130, 127; resettlement of, 125–126

Werewolf guerillas, 114
West Germany: and American base debate, 183, 196, 200; archival privacy laws, 19; and Central European refugee crises, 14; and Cold War tensions, 189–190; Cold War transformation of, 199, 222; and cultural impact of refugees, 229; and international significance of Wildflecken, 4–5; and Nazi militarization, 2; and property rights, 10; and scope of refugee problem, 182–183; and sovereignty issues, 2–3, 143, 182, 185–186, 202; terminology for, 19; and U.S. military buildup, 16

Wette, Wolfram, 8
Whiting, J. H., 79
Wicenty M. (pseudonym), 75–76, 158
Wiesbaden, 12
Wild Place, The (Hulme), 12–14, 74–75, 196
Wildflecken: American cultural influence, 224; base facility, *193*; Cold War transformation of, 221; economic crash after Cold War, 226; and ethnic German expellees, 52; forced laborers in, 40–41; historical background, 21–22; and housing for DPs, 216; and militarization of Germany, 20–21, 32–33; monument to, 227; and rise of Nazism, 28; variety of transformations in, 1

Wildflecken Maneuver Area, 126, 213, 215, 217
Wildflecken Staging Area, 156

Williams, Pierce, 162
Wilson, Francesca, 48–49, 78
Winter, Josef, 52
Winter Assistance (*Winterhilfswerk*), 29
Wirtschaftliche Aufbau-Vereinigung (WAV), 109, 110
Wohnungsbaugesetz (Housing Construction Law), 186
Wolfratshausen, 4, 60
Wolkonowski, Chester, 154
World War I, 30, 41, 42, 46
Württemberg-Baden, 6
Würzburg: and American base debate, 12, 194, 199–200; and demographics of Franconia, 22, 185; and expellee populations, 44, 53, 174–175; and Nazi forced labor system, 35
Wutzelhofer, Hans, 177

Yalta Agreement, 49–50
Young Plan, 26
Yugoslavia, 97–98

Z. Family (pseudonym), 221
Zdanowicz, Andrezj (Andrew), 59, 150–151
Zdanowicz, Helena, 151
Zygmunt M. (pseudonym), 153

ADAM R. SEIPP is an Associate Professor of History at Texas A&M University, where he teaches courses in European military and social history. He earned his PhD at the University of North Carolina – Chapel Hill in 2005. He is also the author of *The Ordeal of Peace: Demobilization and the Urban Experience in Britain and Germany, 1917–1921.*

www.ingramcontent.com/pod-product-compliance
Lightning Source LLC
Chambersburg PA
CBHW070401100426
42812CB00005B/1592